ReOrienting the Sasanians
East Iran in Late Antiquity

Khodadad Rezakhani

EDINBURGH
University Press

Edinburgh University Press is one of the leading university presses in the UK. We publish academic books and journals in our selected subject areas across the humanities and social sciences, combining cutting-edge scholarship with high editorial and production values to produce academic works of lasting importance. For more information visit our website: edinburghuniversitypress.com

© Khodadad Rezakhani, 2017

Edinburgh University Press Ltd
The Tun – Holyrood Road
12(2f) Jackson's Entry
Edinburgh EH8 8PJ

Typeset in 11/13pt Sabon by
Servis Filmsetting Ltd, Stockport, Cheshire

A CIP record for this book is available from the British Library

ISBN 978 1 4744 0029 9 (hardback)
ISBN 978 1 4744 0030 5 (webready PDF)
ISBN 978 1 4744 0031 2 (epub)

The right of Khodadad Rezakhani to be identified as the author of this work has been asserted in accordance with the Copyright, Designs and Patents Act 1988, and the Copyright and Related Rights Regulations 2003 (SI No. 2498).

Contents

List of Illustrations	iv
Acknowledgements	vii
Series Editor's Preface	ix
Maps	xi
Preface	1
Introduction	7
1 The Sasanians and the Sistanis	27
2 The Kushans and the Sasanians	46
3 The Kushano-Sasanians in East Iran	72
4 The Iranian Huns and the Kidarites	87
5 The Alkhans in the Southern Hindu Kush	104
6 The Hephthalite 'Empire' and its Successors	125
7 Sogdiana in the Kidarite and Hephthalite Periods	147
8 The Nēzak and Turk Periods	157
9 Tokharistan and Sogdiana in the Late Sasanian Period	176
10 General Conclusions and Postscript	185
11 Epilogue and Excursus on the *Shahnameh*	194
Bibliography	199
Index	235

List of Illustrations

Fig. 1.1	Coin of Indo-Parthian Sanabares (© CNG 252, Lot 213).	28
Fig. 1.2	Ardashir's copper Marw issue, SNS I type IIIa/3a (© CNG 332 Lot 155).	30
Fig. 1.3	Silver tetradrachm of Maues (© CNG 369, Lot 299).	33
Fig. 1.4	Silver tetradrachms of Vonones with (?)Spalahores (© CNG 69 Lot 834).	34
Fig. 1.5	Silver drachm of Gondophares (© CNG 66, Lot 824).	36
Fig. 1.6	Silver drachm of Sanabares with Pahlavi legend on the obverse (© CNG 176, Lot 106).	38
Fig. 1.7	Copper issue of Farn-Sasan (Courtesy of the American Numismatic Society).	42
Fig. 1.8	Reverse of the coin of Vahshir, king of Persis, showing a man looking right paying respect to a fire altar (© Photo courtesy of British Museum, 1894, 0506. 2386).	42
Fig. 1.9	Coin of Ardashir as the Sasanian King of Kings, showing on the reverse a fire altar set on a pedestal (© CNG 997, Lot 337).	43
Fig. 2.1	Early Kushan 'Heraios' with the word ΚΟΙΙΑΝΟΥ (*sic*, 'of Kushan') on the reverse. The 'control mark' ΣΑΝΑΒ is located between the horse's legs (© CNG Triton XVIII, Lot: 265).	55
Fig. 2.2	Coin of *Soter Megas* (© CNG 324, Lot 237).	58
Fig. 2.3	Coin of Vima Takto, with the Kharoshti legend *Maharajaasa Rajadirajasa Devaputrasa Vima Takha* on the reverse (CoinIndia MAC 2896var).	59
Fig. 2.4	Copper tetradrachm of Vima Kadphises, minted in Kapiśa, showing the canonical standing king on the obverse and the god Oēšo/Śiva and the bull Nandi on the reverse (CNG 361, Lot 768).	60

List of Illustrations   v

Fig. 2.5   Gold issue of Vima II Kadphises, showing the Kushan
          tamgha behind the king's head on the obverse and
          the figure of Oēšo/Śiva on the reverse, flanked by
          the *tamgha* and the Buddhist *Tiratana* (© CNG 152,
          Lot 159).   61
Fig. 2.6   Gold reliquary casket of Kanishka, British Museum,
          with figures of the Buddha and of deities (© CC BY-SA
          3.0; public domain; no alterations).   63
Fig. 2.7   Gold issue of Kanishka, showing the goddess Nana on
          the reverse (© CNG 362 Lot 247).   64
Fig. 2.8   Silver tetradrachm of Kanishka, with the Buddha on
          the reverse (© CNG 314 Lot 227).   65
Fig. 2.9   Copper tetradrachm of Huvishka with the god *Oado*
          (Wind) (© CNG 323 Lot 188).   67
Fig. 2.10 Gold coin of Kanishka II, in the style of Vasudeva,
          with Oēšo on the reverse (© CNG 347 Lot 311).   69
Fig. 2.11 Gold issue of Vasudeva II; note the changing facial
          features (© CNG 334 Lot 211).   70
Fig. 3.1   Sasanian relief at Rag-ī Bibi in northern Afghanistan
          (© François Ory).   75
Fig. 3.2   Copper drachm of Ardashir 1, Kushanshah, minted in
          Marw (© CNG 319, Lot 177).   76
Fig. 3.3   Gold dinar of Pērōz 1, with 'the Exalted God' on the
          reverse (© CNG Triton XIX Lot 2148).   81
Fig. 3.4   Gold scyphate dinar of Hormizd 1, Kushan King of
          Kings (© CNG Triton XVIII, Lot 867).   82
Fig. 4.1   Victory relief of Shapur II over Julian the Apostate
          (© Author).   92
Fig. 4.2   Silver drachm in the name of *Kidara, king of the
          Kushans* (© das Antlitz des Fremden).   96
Fig. 4.3   Gold dinar of Kidara-Kushan in Brahmi script (© *das
          Antlitz des Fremden*).   98
Fig. 5.1   Silver drachm, unknown Alkhan authority, showing
          the typical Alkhan bust type on the obverse (© *das
          Antlitz des Fremden*).   107
Fig. 5.2   Silver drachm of Khingila, with Bactrian inscription
          'Khingila, of the Alkhan' (© *das Antlitz des
          Fremden*).   111
Fig. 5.3   Billon drachm issue of the Alkhan–Nēzak 'Crossover'
          series (© *das Antlitz des Fremden*).   113
Fig. 5.4   Silver drachm of Mihirakula with a Brahmi inscription
          (© *das Antlitz des Fremden*).   116

Fig. 5.5	Silver drachms of Zabokho, naming him as 'the King of the East' (© *das Antlitz des Fremden*).	119
Fig. 6.1	Silver drachm, Hephthalite, imitating the coins of Sasanian Pērōz (© *das Antlitz des Fremden*).	130
Fig. 6.2	Hephthalite *tamgha* (© *das Antlitz des Fremden*).	139
Fig. 7.1	Silver obol of anonymous local authority in Samarkand, possibly under Kidarite rule (© CNG 360, Lot 233).	152
Fig. 8.1	Silver drachm, early (late fifth-/early sixth-century) Nēzak, possibly from 'Ghazni'(?), with the Pahlavi inscription *Nēzak Shah* (© *das Antlitz des Fremden*).	161
Fig. 8.2	Billon drachm issue of the Alkhan–Nēzak 'Crossover' series with a pseudo-Pahlavi inscription (© *das Antlitz des Fremden*).	162
Fig. 8.3	Billon drachms of the Turk Shahis of Zawulistan, with the Bactrian inscription 'Sero' (© *das Antlitz des Fremden*).	165
Fig. 8.4	Buddhist stupas from Kefiriat Tepe in the Kabul Valley (© 2011 Alka Patel).	168
Fig. 8.5	Silver drachms of *Tegin, king of Khurasan*, perhaps from Kabul? (© *das Antlitz des Fremden*).	168
Fig. 8.6	Silver drachm of Phrom Kesar, declaring his victory over the Arabs in a Bactrian inscription (© *das Antlitz des Fremden*).	172
Fig. 8.7	Copper drachms of Pangul with Pahlavi and Bactrian inscriptions, from the Rakhvat/Al-Rukkhaj mint in Sistan (© *das Antlitz des Fremden*).	173
Fig. 9.1	Countermarked silver drachm of Sasanian Hormizd IV, year 11 (AD 588–9), minted in *BHL* (Balkh) (© *das Antlitz des Fremden*).	177
Fig. 9.2	Relief showing a fantastic creature; mural from Panjikent at the State Hermitage Museum (© Author).	180
Fig. 11.1	Rostam on his horse; mural from Panjikent at the State Hermitage Museum (© Author).	196
Fig. 11.2	Head of Rostam in the mural from Panjikent at the State Hermitage Museum (© Author).	196
Fig. 11.3	Silver drachms of Lakhana Udayaditya from Gandhara (© *das Antlitz des Fremden*).	196

Acknowledgements

The process of writing a book perhaps owes as much to one's own intellectual interests as it does to the influence and help of others, and this book is no exception to that rule. Consequently, aside from acknowledging the direct help of colleagues and friends, I ought to mention the influence of my mentors in the writing of this monograph. I owe my intellectual development to many, but Chester Dunning, Martin Schwartz, Michael Morony, Patrick Geary, and Claudia Rapp stand above others in helping me find direction in my scholarly pursuit. Among these, Michael Morony has borne the responsibility of my PhD education and mentored me ever since. Although this book is not the result of my doctoral work, I still felt his critical eye watching over me while working on it. Touraj Daryaee, my real-life best friend and longest-running mentor, has patiently acted as a sounding board and guiding light throughout much of my academic life so far. I thank them both profusely.

Michael Alram and Nikolaus Schindel introduced me to numismatics, a field used extensively in this book. They also read the final manuscript of the work and provided critical comments and many corrections, for which I am grateful. All remaining mistakes remain my responsibility alone. Nicholas Sims-Williams, Frantz Grenet, and Judith Lerner, true scholars, responded to my enquiries, answered my questions, and provided me with hard-to-reach material, for which I am in their debt. Judith Lerner was also the source of friendly and enthusiastic support and gave encouragement in times when it was most needed. Klaus Vondrovec kindly gave answers to my enquiries and provided me with articles and pictures. Fatema 'Gougouli' Soudavar has always been a warm and wonderful supporter and friend, and the Soudavar Foundation have also made the research for this book possible through their generous support. I am most grateful for their kindness. I also wish to thank Dr François Ory, Dr Alka Patel and Dr Daniel Schmutz (of *das Anlitz des Fremden* project) for their kindness in providing me with the photographs I needed, as well as the Classical Numismatic Group for their generosity and speed in granting me the rights to their wonderful collection of coins. Many other friends and colleagues, including Giusto Traina, Klaus Geus, Omar Coloru, Michael Shenkar, Frantz Grenet, Robert Hoyland, Kamyar Abdi, Shervin Farridnejad, Adam Benkato, Arash Zeini, Pavel Lurye, Pierfrancesco Callieri, Wouter Henkelman, Matthias Pfisterer, Gershon Lowenthal, Robert Schaaf, and James Howard-Johnston, have taken an interest in all or parts of this work and have contributed to its development through fruitful discussions and thought-provoking questions. My students and friends at various classes, particularly in Berlin, always proved to be sources of great inspiration and pushed me to clarify my arguments and sharpen my points. I am particularly grateful to the inquisitive nature of Arash Azizi, and Yusef Sa'adat and the great insights of Soheil Delshad.

My friends Philip Grant, David Bennett, and Shervin Farridnejad also read all or parts of the manuscript and provided me with many useful comments and corrections. Dr David Bennet also took on the additional pain/pleasure of making the index for the book. Rasmus Elling, Reza Zia Ebrahimi, and David Bennett (the BBMG), great scholars in their own right, are my closest friends and their help has always gone above and beyond just scholarship. My mother, Lara Ghiassi, is my original inspiration and language guru and the one who first inspired me to pursue scholarship. My father, Javanshir Bonyab, inspired me with intellectual curiosity and always supported my academic pursuit. Neither of them ever took me too seriously, for which I am most thankful. Last but not least, my much better half, Sara Mashayekh, has been my closest friend and toughest intellectual sparring partner, who both encouraged me during the process of the writing of this book and challenged me at every stage. This book would not have been possible without her.

Khodadad Rezakhani
Berlin, August 2016

Series Editor's Preface

Edinburgh Studies in Ancient Persia focuses on the world of ancient Persia (pre-Islamic Iran) and its reception. Academic interest with and fascination in ancient Persia have burgeoned in recent decades and research on Persian history and culture is now routinely filtered into studies of the Greek and Roman worlds; biblical scholarship too is now more keenly aware of Persian-period history than ever before; while, most importantly, the study of the history, cultures, languages, and societies of ancient Iran is now a well-established discipline in its own right.

Persia was, after all, at the centre of ancient world civilisations. This series explores that centrality throughout several successive 'Persian empires': the Achaemenid dynasty (founded c. 550 BCE) saw Persia rise to its highest level of political and cultural influence, as the Great Kings of Iran fought for, and maintained, an empire which stretched from India to Libya and from Macedonia to Ethiopia. The art and architecture of the period both reflect the diversity of the empire and proclaim a single centrally constructed theme: a harmonious world-order brought about by a benevolent and beneficent king. Following the conquests of Alexander the Great, the Persian Empire fragmented but maintained some of its infrastructures and ideologies in the new kingdoms established by Alexander's successors, in particular the Seleucid dynasts who occupied the territories of western Iran, Mesopotamia, the Levant, and Asia Minor. But even as Greek influence extended into the former territories of the Achaemenid realm, at the heart of Iran a family of nobles, the Parthian dynasty, rose to threaten the growing imperial power of Rome. Finally, the mighty Sasanian dynasty ruled Iran and much of the Middle East from the second century CE onwards, proving to be a powerful foe to Late Imperial Rome and Byzantium. The rise of Islam, a new religion in Arabia, brought a sudden end to the Sasanian dynasty in the mid-600s CE.

These successive Persian dynasties left their record in the historical, linguistic, and archaeological materials of the ancient world, and Edinburgh Studies in Ancient Persia has been conceived to give scholars working in these fields the opportunity to publish original research and explore new methodologies in interpreting the antique past of Iran. This series will see scholars working with bona fide Persian and other Near Eastern materials, giving access to Iranian self-perceptions and the internal workings of Persian society, placed alongside scholars assessing the perceptions of the Persianate world from the outside (predominantly through Greek and Roman authors and artefacts). The series will also explore the reception of ancient Persia (in historiography, the arts, and politics) in subsequent periods, both within and outwith Iran itself.

Edinburgh Studies in Ancient Persia represents something of a watershed in better appreciation and understanding not only of the rich and complex cultural heritage of Persia, but also of the lasting significance of the Achaemenids, Parthians, and Sasanians and the impact that their remarkable civilisations have had on wider Persian, Middle Eastern, and world history. Written by established and up-and-coming specialists in the field, this series provides an important synergy of the latest scholarly ideas about this formative ancient world civilisation.

Lloyd Llewellyn-Jones

Maps

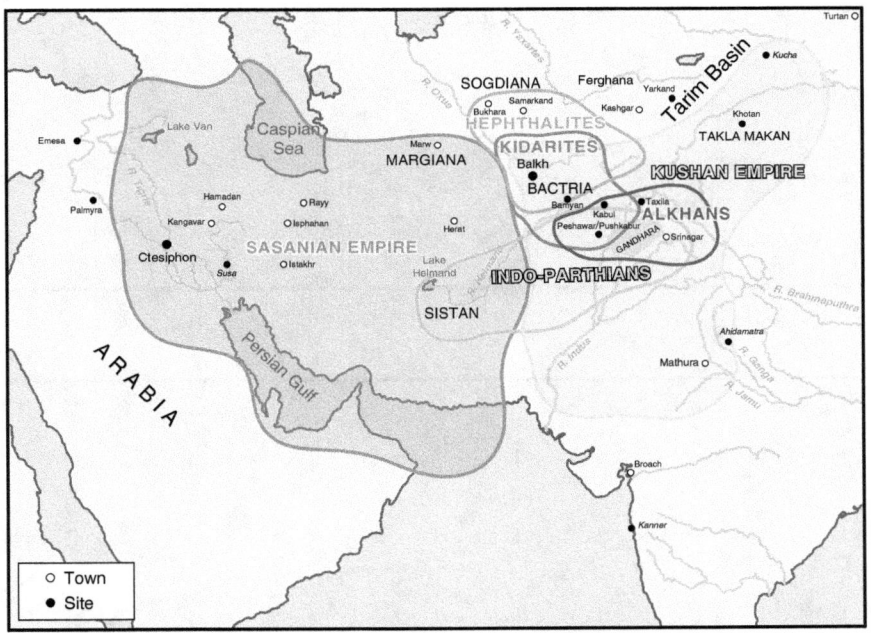

1 General

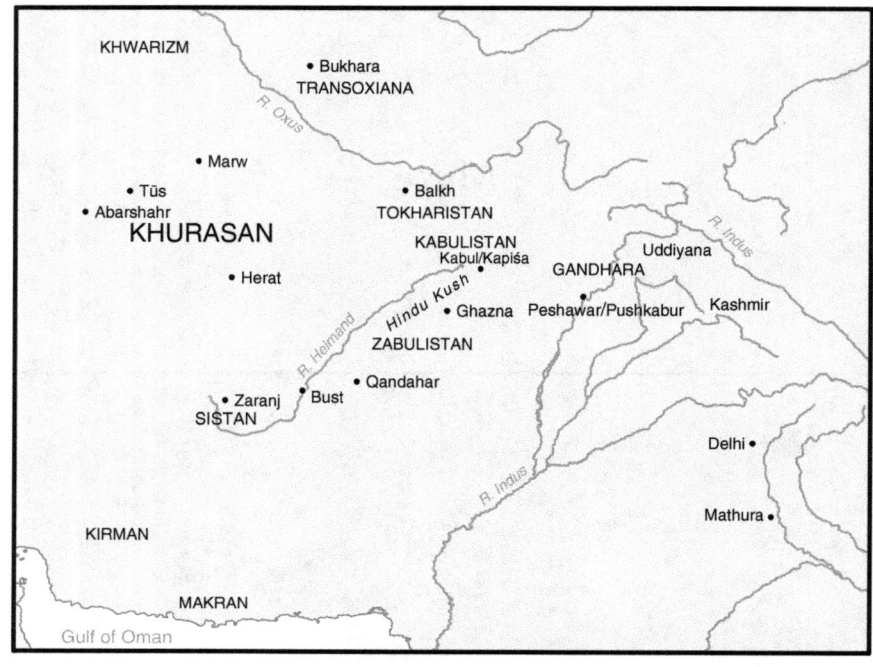

2 General East Iran

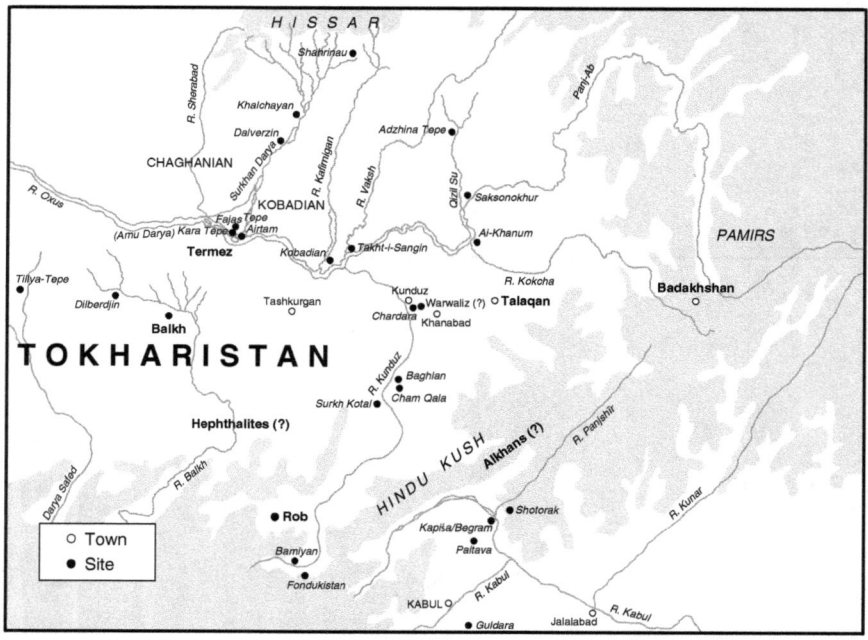

3 Tokharistan

Maps xiii

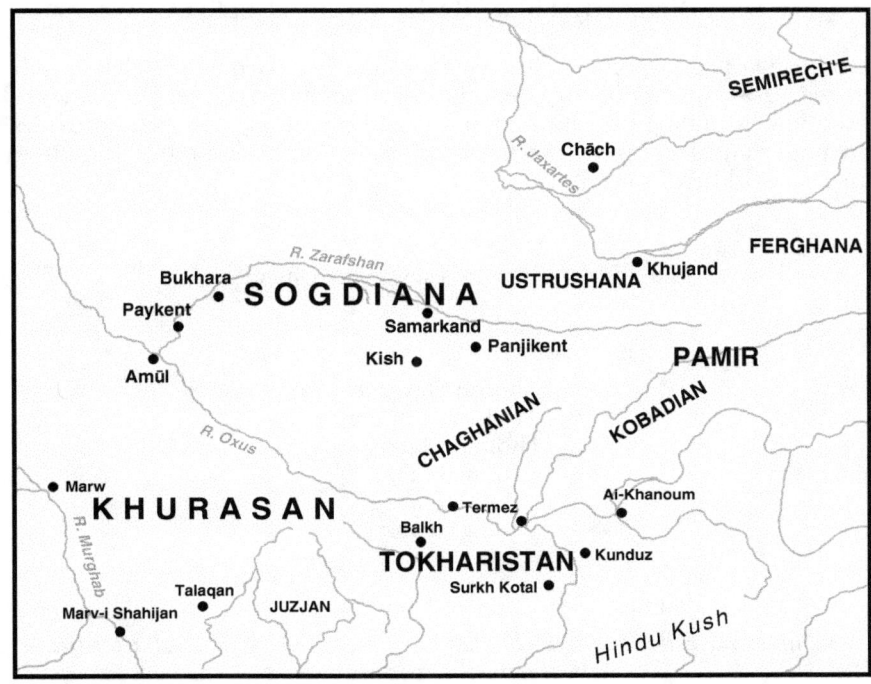

4 Sogdiana

5 Gandhara

EDINBURGH STUDIES IN ANCIENT PERSIA

Dealing with key aspects of the ancient Persian world from the Achaemenids to the Sasanians: its history, reception, art, archaeology, religion, literary tradition (including oral transmissions) and philology, this series provides an important synergy of the latest scholarly ideas about this formative ancient world civilisation.

SERIES EDITOR
Lloyd Llewellyn-Jones, Cardiff University

EDITORIAL ADVISORY BOARD
Touraj Daryaee
Andrew Erskine
Thomas Harrison
Irene Huber
Keith Rutter
Jan Stronk

TITLES AVAILABLE IN THE SERIES
Courts and Elites in the Hellenistic Empires: The Near East after the Achaemenids, c. 330 to 30 BCE
By Rolf Strootman

Greek Perspectives on the Achaemenid Empire: Persia through the Looking Glass
By Janett Morgan

Semiramis' Legacy: The History of Persia According to Diodorus of Sicily
By Jan P. Stronk

ReOrienting the Sasanians: East Iran in Late Antiquity
By Khodadad Rezakhani

FORTHCOMING TITLES
Sasanian Persia: Between Rome and the Steppes of Eurasia
By Eberhard Sauer

The Bactrian Mirage: Iranian and Greek Interaction in Western Central Asia
By Michael Iliakis

Plutarch and the Persica
By Eran Almagor

Visit the Edinburgh Studies in Ancient Persia website at
edinburghuniversitypress.com/series/esap

Preface

Oriental studies in general, and Iranian studies in particular, has been a stronghold of micro-specialists for much of its history. Scholars in the tradition of European 'classics', concentrating on primary sources and trained vigorously in ancient and modern languages and other methods of source analysis, scrutinise sources that are 'recovered' from the east, looking for details of the lives of the distant Orientals. This is much the same way that scholarship has long been conducted for European history itself, going back to what sources were available and trying to reconstruct how things might have been.[1] In this approach, 'history' was something that emerged from the convergence of knowledge created by philologists, archaeologists, scholars of religion, numismatists, and other scholars concerned with 'primary' sources.

However, in the nineteenth and twentieth centuries, 'history' also emerged as an independent field, establishing its own methodology and approach to the past. This 'new history', quite apart from the idea of history as chronography and concern with events, has in a sense become the framework for most other means of producing 'historical knowledge'. The devices used by this new history are varied and borrowed mostly from social sciences rather than 'humanities'[2] – as much as the division is an artificial one mostly valid in the Anglophone world. This is an approach to the past that takes into consideration not only the *evidence* of the past – 'the sources' – but also the idea of the past, the 'narrative' which gives each of these sources a purpose and a place within a larger framework. The conflict between the two types of history, the two approaches, has never made for a very smooth result, but at least in the case of European history, it seems to have been accepted that a

---

[1] The genesis and development of this are laid out in the work of Wolf 2010.
[2] A good survey of this can be found in Wallerstein 2004: 1–22.

(new) historical approach is a valid form of inquiry, and it has in fact become the primary form of historical research in the 'European' context, defined broadly.

In Oriental studies, and Iranian studies more than many other branches of that general field, this conflict is more prominent. Conversely too, the conflict has barely existed, as 'new historians' have rarely approached the field.[3] Iranian studies is still a field dominated by philologists, archaeologists, art historians, numismatists, and scholars of religion (often a combination of two or more of these) who, due to their access to primary sources, determine what little 'narrative' can be related. Those within this field are very familiar with the need for this type of approach, as the variety of languages, the breadth of the area covered, and the sheer length of the time considered under the rubric of something called *Iranian Studies* is well beyond the ability of one person or specialism to grasp. In this sense, Iranian studies is a mirage, a general name used to bring together a wide variety of scholars who work broadly on subjects relating to either the country of Iran or what is perceived as the Iranian, and sometimes Persianate, world. Within this wide field, historians are frequently sidelined, or perhaps never really taken seriously. Those approaching from neighbouring fields are, perhaps rightly, subjected to training in languages and other skills that historians in fields of European studies are usually not exposed to. So, being a good, even a *proper*, Iranist first and foremost means being a philologist, an archaeologist, a numismatist, or a sigillographer. Only then is one allowed to engage in creating a narrative, thus being a historian, and even then this is commonly dismissed as a fanciful and spurious pursuit.

The above picture is made even clearer when one approaches the 'peripheries' of this field, the areas or time periods less explored. As an example, one can bring the case of the pre-Islamic history of Iran, where Achaemenids and Sasanians have had a much better representation than the Arsacids, to whom scholars both ancient and modern have been unkind. While Achaemenids already benefit from a sort of 'narrative' set out for them by ancient Greek historians, and Sasanians are well represented in the Islamic histories, the Arsacids suffer from the fact that no proper narrative of their entire history exists. As such, even when they are considered, it is as an appendix to 'Hellenistic' history of the post-Alexandrine Near East,

---

[3] See Chakrabarty 2009 for a general criticism of this; although relating mostly to the case of India, it can be expanded to Iran as well.

or as an antithesis of perceived Sasanian centralisation and cultural domination.

The main reason for this is that the Achaemenids and Sasanians did profit from the existence of ancient narratives, which allowed them to be known fully as historical entities. This in turn lets modern scholars scrutinise these narratives on the basis of other sources and present new knowledge about them, correcting the established narratives and refining our understanding of them. Indeed, most approaches to the histories of these two periods can be seen as correctives to the existing narratives, from corrections to chronologies of their period to a different understanding of their ideologies. The lack of an ancient narrative for the Arsacids, however, prevents modern historians from scrutinising their history in a similar manner. As a result, the study of Arsacid history is yet in the period of figuring out the order of its kings, or even the names of some of its rulers, with very little known about the social, economic, cultural, or even political history of that time period.

Perhaps even direr is the case that the present monograph aims to approach: the history of the regions in Central Asia and the Hindu Kush, which this book calls 'East Iran'. While something is known about the history of the region after Alexander, and much more is known following the entry of Islam into the area in the eighth century, the period between the fall of the Graeco-Bactrians and the rise of Islam, roughly the turn of the Christian Era to AD 900, can be called 'the Dark Ages'. Scholarship of the Orientalist type, based on the ingenious achievements of philologists, archaeologists, numismatists, and many others, has clarified many details about the course of history in this region. Some characters and peoples of whom we previously only knew the names – Kanishka the Great, Khingila, the Sogdians – have now been exposed to the light of history. New sources, coming to light due to this unprecedented amount of attention, have clarified many problems. Many of these are in details such as the name of the grandfather of Kanishka the Great, only revealed in the mid-1990s via the find of a new inscription. Other sources, like the Bactrian Documents, say less about political history, but provide us with a fascinating window onto the life of people in northern Afghanistan over an impressive period of time. Discovery and systematic analysis of coins now allow us to know much more about the history of people whom we used to lump under the title of 'Hephthalites' (based on scanty notices in Byzantine sources) and who were hidden behind the mysterious names of Kidara, Khingila, or Akhshunwar.

To a historian who is used to approaching history through a narrative, this information is fascinating, but practically useless. Scholarship on 'East Iran' appears to those from the outside to be a collection of disjointed islands inhabited by extremely erudite people. But there are no bridges to be seen, and there is no map with which to understand the position of each island. In a sense, the geographical analogy might be apt. 'East Iran' is so distant to most historians that many, like Strabo or other ancient geographers, could not really tell what lies there and could not navigate their way through its waterways. Entering the field means being exposed to opposing narratives at almost every turn, with things being so uncertain that there is still no consensus on whether Kanishka ruled in the first, second, or third century AD!

As a historian, one trained in global history and concerned with Sasanian history, I have been fascinated by East Iran. As I approach various aspects of Sasanian history, I can see clearly that the narrative that presents them as a 'western'-leaning empire (e.g. the eastern rivals of the Romans etc.) is lopsided at best. It is clear to me, as it is to anyone who looks at the course of Sasanian history, that the whole of their history indeed had a strong eastern aspect as well, one that at points even overshadowed its much better-publicised western one. This realisation has naturally led me to look into the history of the east, to Central Asia and the rest of the lands lying to the east of the Sasanian Empire, trying to understand its course parallel to the Sasanian period. Despite my own training in philology and numismatics, my first approach, of course, was to study the secondary sources, the works of scholars who have produced a wealth of knowledge in each of the fields relating to the study of this region.

However, as one approaches these sources, the image of the disconnected islands, or perhaps dispersed pieces of a gigantic puzzle, becomes overwhelming. The knowledge that is produced does not join in a narrative, something that would allow it to be viewed as a whole and to be scrutinised. Consequently, any attempt at revising, correcting, or adjusting a narrative cannot be proposed, as no narrative really exists in the first place. Each of the theories and approaches is opposed, disputed, and modified within the small fields to which it belongs. The result is that all of this knowledge does not get the opportunity to make it outside the immediate field. Instead, basic misunderstandings still dominate the history of this region and time period, the simplest example of it being that even a reputable modern work on the history of the period still refers to the entire grouping of Iranian Huns as the 'Hephthalites'.[4] Essentially, those who do not directly work on the history of East Iran are often ignorant of even the most basic parameters of it.

For me, this appears to be an unmaintainable state of things. As a Sasanian historian, I felt the need to know the history of East Iran during the Sasanian period well, or at least be familiar with its general framework and its major issues. However, the more I looked for something to organise the information and provide a picture, the more I realised the absence of such. Previous attempts such as the chapters of the *History of Civilizations of Central Asia*, even considering their uneven treatment of the period, were greatly outdated. Monographs on the region are rare, and great achievements such as the history of Sogdian traders are concerned with only part of the region and only a certain segment of its population. Works that present the latest research on the sources relating to the period take narratives as mere means of supplementing the detailed presentation of the material, not as legitimate tools of historical inquiry by themselves. The answer to the questions concerning this missing piece of historical methodology, something that should be natural and obvious, is often that a narrative cannot, and even should not, be written. Perhaps tellingly, this was something that was also said for Sasanian history, and is still being repeated for the Arsacid one.

Nonetheless, I started this book as a collection of notes in order to organise the history of East Iran for myself and to create the narrative that would allow me to compare it to Sasanian history and study their relationship. My approach was to understand the region in its relation to Sasanian Iran, but also to comprehend it in its own terms. For this, as is my habit and training, I was most comfortable in taking the political history as a basic framework. Within the history of each political unit, I read and organised my notes on the basis of the latest research that I could access. I understood that many conflicting ideas exist about almost each part of the history of the region. Like a historian, I often chose what appeared to me to make most sense – or fit best together, to maintain the puzzle analogy – when organising my thoughts and readings. This means that at points, I have smoothed over complications, taken some meagre evidence – often the only evidence available – as 'facts', and provided a narrative that could help me fit in the rest of the scholarship and evidence.

---

[4] Examples abound, and can be brought pretty much by anyone acquainted with the fields of Roman, Iranian, or Islamic history. For one concerned with the history of Sasanian Iran, see Dignas and Winter 2007.

This attempt at understanding the history of East Iran helped me considerably in understanding the history of the Sasanian Empire too. It then occurred to me that others who might want to approach the same region but dared not do so, because the islands are too far apart and the sea too tumultuous, might benefit from my attempt at fashioning a narrative. This is the genesis of this monograph, and this is the audience I have had in mind: someone like myself, or even further away from the history of East Iran, who might have an interest in the region or benefit from knowing the basic framework of it.

From the start, I realised that this approach would leave me open to conflicts with many experts of the region and the period. As I mentioned, a historian's approach – which by necessity requires some simplification and projects a distance – is not yet quite approved or welcomed. A scholar of Iranian studies is still required to be a specialist in a certain region, to employ a particular micro-historical approach, and to be dexterous in a precise skill, which would allow him or her to address individual issues. Macro-history, and worse yet global/world history, is interpreted as the approach of someone who does not have the exactitude of understanding the nuances of one word, a single coin, or a certain mural. Even though my training has been in similar fields, and I consider myself capable of discerning the finer points of the related research, still I know that my approach could be considered that of a generalist and not a work of groundbreaking scholarship.

Be that as it may, I believe that such an approach is necessary and missing in the field. I realise that by not addressing all the conflicting opinions that lie behind each of the statements I make, I leave myself open to charges of being oblivious to them or to misunderstanding my sources. The point of this monograph is not to present my groundbreaking research or my own take on each of the arguments surrounding the details I present, something that is much better done in academic articles. It is, on the contrary, to present a summary of different results, and hopefully through the narrative itself demonstrate the accounts I have preferred and to which I have given precedence. This would automatically also mean that I know, indeed I expect and hope, that much of what I present here will be refuted, corrected, and revised, with any luck some of these by myself. In the end, having a framework for a subject has the benefit that it can be improved, expanded, renovated, and perfected, while having no framework would mean that all the pieces lie around, in perfect shape, without ever making a complete picture. I hope that readers, specialists or general, approach the book in this spirit and take away from it a general knowledge of East Iran in late antiquity.

Introduction

MEDIEVAL EAST IRAN AND ITS LATE ANTIQUE ROOTS

Around AD 1000, when Ferdowsi was composing his famous *Shahnameh* and narrating an idealised history of the kings of Iran, Tūs, his native city in the northeastern territories of Khurasan, seemed a natural place in which to undertake such task. It was in the heart of the Samanid lands, between Neishabur, Balkh, and Bukhara. Samanids, the masters of Transoxiana and much of the adjoining lands, were great patrons of Persian literature and all manners of learning, and presided over a brilliant period of cultural production that was to affect the rest of the history of the greater region. The first great Persian poet, Rudaki, was a retainer at their court, and great scholars of the Islamic world such as Avicenna or al-Biruni spent their early careers at the Samanid court. Bal'ami, a Samanid minister, translated the great history of al-Tabari into Persian, and al-Tabari's famous *Tafsīr* was also translated into Persian at the Samanid court. At that moment in time, the Samanids embodied the concept of Iran, the *Ērānšahr* of the Sasanians, even more than their rivals in the west, the Buyids.[1] Yet, 400 years before, Samanid Khurasan did not exist as a unit. Ferdowsi's native Tūs was a border town of the Sasanian Empire, and Bukhara was a rich merchant city of Sogdiana. Balkh, the ancestral homeland of the Samanids, was the dilapidated former capital of the Kushans and the Hephthalites. In AD 650, Sistan and Zabulistan, the centres of the newly emerging Ghaznavid power

---

[1] For a view of the cultural revival of the Buyids, see Kraemer 1992. On Samanid traditions, see Meisami 2000.

which succeeded the Samanids in the early eleventh century, were border regions ruled by little-known local chiefs whose names could not even be clearly comprehended by Muslim historians.

What had happened that allowed the Samanids and other 'Khurasani' powers that followed them to turn this peripheral region into a centre? What turned the 'cleavage' of Central Asia[2] into the important region of Khurasan, a cradle of the new Persianate civilisation and the cultural world of Eastern Iran? The fact is, not many knew at the time, and not many more have cared to know ever since. The multiple linguistic sources for the history of the region, the disparity of the same evidence, and a lack of narrative sources from which historians – trained in treating texts rather than objects – could write a history has prevented us from knowing this region well. Furthermore, the parallel political powers and the variety of political and cultural systems baffle those trying to present a coherent history of this region. Despite all these difficulties, and with caution regarding the limitations of sources and the possibilities of providing a narrative, this book will try to present a history of the western and southern parts of Central Asia in the period before its rise as a power in the medieval period. This is the period in which, this book will argue, the political and cultural elements of this region merged to create a unit which we should call *East Iran*.

This East Iran, known from the brilliant cultural productions and awesome political powers that emerge from it throughout the medieval period, is born of a world that itself emerged from the vestiges of the great Kushan Empire. The various entities that dominated it – the Sogdian city states, the Oxus principalities, the 'Hunnic' rulers, the Hephthalite 'Empire', the Alkhans, and the West Turkic khaganate – all help form an aspect of medieval East Iran, and this book is concerned with studying this formative period and its actors.

THE EAST AND THE WEST

In accounts of the history of Iran as a modern nation-state or an ancient kingdom, or even a medieval cultural zone, the west traditionally receives a more thorough treatment than the east. Historians know, and others soon come to realise, that 'Iran' is commonly considered to be really the 'west' of the cultural zone, while the east appears as a periphery of a centre that lies in the west. This is perhaps the reason why the western part of this zone,

---

[2] To quote Hodgson 1963. See also Rezakhani 2016.

rather than the east, saw fit to call itself 'Iran', the term reflecting a cultural zone, when they both arrived at the threshold of the period of modern nation-states. The western region, relying for its 'heritage' on the available historical texts, was rewarded more quickly than the east with narrative histories and documents originating in the Mediterranean world, with which the Europeans had first explored the history of the Orient. For this region, the history of the Achaemenids is told using the narratives of Greek historians such as Herodotus and Xenophon, both looking at the entity from the west and imagining the heart of that empire to be in Mesopotamia and its environs, with its 'capitals' in Persepolis, Susa, Babylon, and Ecbatana. The decidedly 'eastern' Arsacids were considered eastern nomads who usurped the power of the west, both the Achaemenid and the Hellenistic ones. They still seem to remain as 'foreigners' and 'intruders' in the history of Iran. Against the interruption caused by the Arsacids, the Sasanians are then considered the restorers of the old order and founders of the 'Second Persian Empire' in AD 223–4. The Sasanian Empire, the great centralising dynasty of Iranian history according to the modern historian's narrative, eventually collapsed when it was attacked from the west by the Muslim armies. It was thrown into calamity when its centre of power in Ctesiphon, located in the west in *Asurestan* or *Dil-i Ērānšahr* in Mesopotamia, fell to the conquerors (Crone 2012: 1–2).

It is, however, in the east that a new *Iranian intermezzo*[3] started to interrupt the concert of history. In the ninth and tenth centuries AD, political forces from Khurasan and Sistan were the ones that first tried to carve out zones of power for themselves. They are also the ones that used cultural elements such as the Persian language in order to promote their claim to independence. This is when it becomes rather difficult to ignore the east, as it becomes more than relevant in the history of Iran and the greater Islamic world, and it remains so for several hundred years, until the rise of the Safavids in 1501. The forces of Khurasan changed the face of the Islamic Caliphate in 750 when Abu-Muslim toppled the Umayyad Caliphs and helped install Al-Saffah as the first Abbasid Caliph.[4] The Khurasanis, remaining the most important military contingent of the Abbasid Caliphate in the next few generations, were

---

[3] As coined by Minorsky 1953: 110.
[4] Shaban's entire book on the subject is essentially devoted to explaining the local Khurasani context of the Abbasid Revolution, and to my knowledge is the only book considering this event from an eastern point of view: Shaban 1979.

even given their own quarter in the newly built city of Baghdad. Harun al-Rashid (786–809) spent his last days in Khurasan and was buried there, and his faithful vizier Ja'far al-Barmaki and his sons hailed from a family of the Buddhist elite from Balkh. Harun's half-Khurasani son al-Ma'mun (AD 813–33) became the embodiment of 'the Golden Age'[5] of the Abbasid Caliphate. He also captured the Caliphal seat from his brother al-Amin with the help of yet another Khurasani army. Among these, the Sogdians, an important if lesser-noticed part of this Khurasani army, came to dominate certain aspects of the greater Islamic world for several generations, before losing their prominence to, and essentially integrating into, the Turkic troops who in fact originated from Sogdiana itself (De la Vaissière 2007)!

Khydar Al-Afshin, the scion of the Afshin rulers of Ustrushana in eastern Sogdiana, was the commander of the armies of 'al-Mu'tasim (833–42) in his subjugation of the rebels Babak and Mazyar. He acted autonomously enough to install his own commander, and fellow Sogdian, Abulsaj Dēvdād b. Dēvband, as the governor of Azerbaijan and allow him to establish his own Sajid dynasty (889–929) there. Another Sogdian, or Sogdianised Turk, a descendant of the Ikhshid rulers of Samarkand called Muhammad al-Ikhshid, founded the Ikhshidid dynasty of Egypt, the first independent dynasty of Egypt in the Islamic period (925–69). Other locals of the region – such as the Mikalids, descendants of the last king of Sogdiana, Dēwaštīch, who died resisting the Muslim conqueror in 728 – became important parts of Muslim society. Finally, it was from this region that the Samanids, the Ghaznavids, the Seljuks, the Mongols, the Timurids, and various other powers rose to control the rest of Iran, and at times the Middle East. Central Asians are seen all over the *Islamicate world* (to use another term coined by Marshall Hodgson). Far from being a periphery, Central Asia of the medieval period was indeed a centre for and by itself, and soon enough, a centre for the whole of the *Lands of the Eastern Caliphate*.

This book is then aiming to look at the roots of this centrality. What causes this 'peripheral' land, this 'cleavage', to occupy such a central role? Even a cursory look at its history reveals that from its own point of view, Central Asia was always a centre for the areas immediately surrounding it. But it is undeniable that in the medieval

---

[5] The concept of 'the Golden Age' is, of course, a later historiographical creation, but one that has taken a firm enough hold over the conceptualisation of Islamic history; see Lombard 1975 for an interesting take on the concept.

period, this centrality is spread to most of the West Asian and even South Asian world. It is, however, within a decidedly 'Iranian' cultural milieu that this centrality occurs, if for nothing other than the fact that the language most used to spread this influence is New Persian. The world in which these changes occurred, however, was moulded into this particular sociocultural shape through centuries of interactions between different cultural, political, and environmental zones. The process that was started by the Kushans was completed by their successors. The Sasanians, commonly thought of as a western power, in fact interacted closely with this region and more often than not were either influenced by it or forced to change their policies because of its realities. The emergence of this region as East Iran was not so much a triumph of the Sasanians as a local creation that was lent to the west. Contrary to what is assumed, the direction of borrowing and influence was not always from the west to the east. The Iranian (or if you wish the medieval *Persianate world*) was as much an original creation of the sociocultural world of East Iran as the result of importation of ideas, mainly the linguistic carrier, from West Iran. This is the process which I call here the shifting of the concept of Central Asia to that of Eastern Iran. But before I go any further, it is fitting to clarify my use of geographical and cultural terms here.

FROM CENTRAL ASIA TO EAST IRAN

In order to clarify and justify my use of the term *East Iran* throughout this book, and to dismiss charges of cultural imperialism – I hope it becomes clear throughout that I in fact stand firmly at the opposite end of the spectrum on the issue – I feel it is necessary to explain how I arrived at the concept itself. The use of the term 'Iran' at present, and due to the misbehaviour of modern politics, stands in disfavour, implying aspirations of cultural and political dominance from the nation-state of Iran. The normal claim is that the territories and states neighbouring the nation-state of Iran were in fact 'parts' of the nation-state itself, torn apart by a combination of local mismanagement and all manner of European (in this case including Russian), imperial designs.[6] As such, citizens of Afghanistan, the Central Asian republics, and even Iraq or the Caucasus see this term as an expression of a desire by Iran to control these territories politically. But any historian of the region knows that it would be impossible to look at the history of the region between the Jaxartes and the

---

[6] See Kashani-Sabet 2014 for an interesting summary, and discussion, of such views.

Euphrates without somehow considering the term 'Iran', which was used, at least in the higher circles of cultural production, to refer to the expanse – in various contexts. Other terms, from the *Persianate world* (which is more concerned with the Islamic period) to *Ērānšahr* (highlighting a late antique focus), are used to compensate for the politically sensitive term *Iran*. To me, this is spurious and even more confusing, since these uses are often quite inaccurate or ignorant of historical and geographic realities. Persian, despite its high cultural status, was by no means the singular language of this expanse, even in the area of belles-lettres and high culture. Nor did Sasanian *Ērānšahr* include the territories of interest in this book: those of Sogdiana, Bactria/Tokharistan, Sistan, and Zabulistan. However, all of these territories, in one way or another, did relate to the term *Iran* in the period of their rise to prominence.

But why 'Eastern' and 'Western Iran', it might be asked? In this, I am taking my inspiration from the educational system. Having taught the history of this region in various settings from a traditional classroom to a podcast, I am often confronted with widespread confusion when reaching the medieval period. The dominant understanding of the history of Iran as the history of the nation-state of Iran implies that the progress of history might be viewed in the context of a central state as well. Consequently, while the 'fall' of the Sasanians to Muslim forces and the rise of the Caliphate is well comprehended, albeit in terms of foreign conquest and dominance, the rise of powers such as the Saffarids, the Buyids, and the Samanids creates much confusion. For the average student, it is incomprehensible why so many 'kings' ruled 'at the same time', and 'in the same territory' too. The question of 'who was ruling where' is constantly raised, with exasperation ensuing upon learning that no one power ruled 'all of Iran' in this period. The same state of affairs plus political realities are also at the root of 'nationalising' histories of Afghanistan, Tajikistan, and Uzbekistan, among other places, where dynasties are made into national political entities, with Samanids as a Tajik kingdom or the Hephthalites as an Afghan one, to just mention two examples.

Faced with this problem, I was forced to think deeply about a way to explain the matter, one that did not necessarily dwell too much on explaining the dominance of the modern nation-state concept and postmodern dismissal of national historical narratives. This is when I realised that it would be easier to talk about two *Irans* in this period: an Eastern and a Western one.

Enumerating a number of reasons for this division might help in convincing the readers as to the merit of the use of such terms.

First of all, as mentioned before, the focus of the historiography of Iran has commonly been on the west. Greek and Roman sources detailing the history of the Achaemenids, Seleucids, Arsacids, and Sasanians gave the view that the epicentre of all events was first in Mesopotamia and then in the Zagros region. Muslim historians such as al-Tabari or Yaqubi, writing in the Islamic tradition of universal history, viewed everything from a centre in Mesopotamia and Syria. Even the translation of the history of al-Tabari by Bal'ami, which took place in the Samanid *East Iran*, still gave precedence to the events in the west. On the other hand, local histories, such as *Tarikh-e Bokhara* or *Tarikh-e Sistan*, despite their focus on regions of the east, ignored the larger narrative of events, and so were deemed useless for the larger focus of modern historians. These historians, often Europeans or European educated, naturally cared more for the history of the western regions, which had consequences for the 'European' civilisations of Greece and Rome. In this context, the history of East Iran was largely left out of narratives or only mentioned when it displayed relevance to the history of the west. While this is considered a loss, as there is no consistent narrative for the history of the east such as exists for that of the west, it also presents a unique opportunity. This is the chance for consideration of the history of East Iran outside the normal historical frameworks into which we are accustomed to fit most of our modern inquiries. East Iran provides a convenient unit in which to study history outside the confines of patterns and themes, allowing us to discover its own themes and dynamics.

A second reason, which serves to justify the use of the geographic and cultural term, is the problem of the inefficiency of the normal terminology. Traditionally, 'Transoxiana' (Arabic *Mawara-un-Nahr*), referring to the territories of historical Khwarazm, Sogdiana, Chach, and the Ferghana and Ustrushana Valleys, is the term used in the Arabo-Persian historical and geographical treatise. It is, aside from its particular myopic connotations, inaccurate and non-inclusive, as it does not cover Tokharistan, Zabulistan, Sistan, or Kabulistan, which show a certain cultural unity with Transoxiana in the medieval period. I find the term *Khurasan* (from Middle Persian (MP) *Khwarāsān* 'the Rising Sun, the East', Arabic *Khurasan*), despite its attraction, to be similarly problematic, as some of the territories further to the east, as well as Sistan and Zabulistan again, were never considered part of that region. The modern scholarly term 'Central Asia', despite its usefulness, ignores a cultural unit with boundaries, as it is an attempt to be unbiased without considering realities. It runs into problems mostly with the Sino-centric term *Inner Asia*, which includes the territories of Eastern Turkistan and the Mongol-Kyrgiz Steppe that are never really integrated into the cultural unit of our concern here, despite mutual influences.

'East Iran', however, is quite useful, as it shows not only a medieval historical reality, but also a historical process. While political control in these territories is often dispersed and largely independent in antiquity, they form a definitive cultural, and sometimes even political, unit in the medieval period. This unit has clear cultural affinities with the territories in 'Cis-Oxania', and the Iranian Plateau even as far as Mesopotamia. As mentioned before, it also becomes the source and centre of production for many of the cultural products that come to define both Western and Eastern Iran. In the period of East Iranian dominance, Neishabur and Marw were united with Bukhara and Balkh in the same political and cultural unit. The medieval world of East Iran certainly had a unique and independent identity, while it was firmly connected to the rest of the Iranian world.

What is of particular interest is the emergence of this East Iranian world in the medieval period. Two issues are presumed here; one is the fact that this world, while existing as independent territorial entities before, takes the shape of a coherent unit in the medieval period. The other is that this formation has its roots in the previous period, that of late antiquity, where certain forces shape it into the above-mentioned unit. The aim of this book is then to study these roots, to understand why and how this unit is formed, and under what circumstances it starts showing affinities with the regions to its west, forging the medieval identity of Khurasan first and then Iran as a whole, while maintaining its own clearly East Iranian identity. Through studying the political and cultural history of its constituting units, as well as their relations with the Sasanians, the following will narrate the emergence of a world region from smaller units during the formative period of late antiquity. The presentation of the narrative, if anything, is the major aim of the book, one on which further research can be based.

EAST IRAN AND THE SASANIANS IN CONTEXT

Sasanians were the dominant political force in the Near East for most of the period of late antiquity.[7] Their historiography, established

---

[7] The concept of late antiquity is a relatively recent addition to the established historical periodisation, particularly in the English-language scholarship. German and French writers

through the efforts of many scholars during the last century or so, is still relatively young and in the process of completion. Their significance in the historiography of Iran might be that, unlike the Achaemenids, the Sasanians were never forgotten in the popular imagination or the traditional historiography of Iran.[8] With the exception of some fantastic narratives regarding Ardashir I (the founder of the dynasty) and the popular tales about Wahram V and Khosrow I Anusheruwan, Sasanian history was rather accurately represented[9] in later works of the Islamic period, even in literary works such as Ferdowsi's *Shahnameh*. It is clear from the narrative of Muslim historians such as al-Tabari or Dīnawarī that the Sasanians' history was well known and that they were credited with the establishment of many of the institutions of the Islamic period. They were also the ancestors of choice for Islamic Iranian dynasties such as the Buyids or the Samanids – even if through indirect or forged links – and it was to their imperial glory that these dynasties aspired (Bosworth 1978).

However, both Islamic and modern historiography present the Sasanians as a political force of Mesopotamia and *West Iran*. For the Muslim historian, the Sasanians were the masters of *al-'Iraq* (the *Sawād* and *Jazeera* of the Islamic sources), the heart of the Abbasid Caliphate – and indeed the designated heart of the Sasanian Empire too.[10] They were the ones who built fabled cities such as Ctesiphon and Jundisabur and were the masters of prosperous Khuzestan, the breadbasket of the Caliphate. They were also the originators of traditions, the royal etiquette, and the good taste that was so much appreciated and revered in the Baghdad of Harun al-Rashid and

---

used the term before English-writing historians also decided to adopt it, most famously under the direction of Peter Brown in his *The World of Late Antiquity: AD 150–750* (1971, which also sought to establish a time frame for the concept. See also Brown et al. 1997 for a discussion of the geographical and temporal extent and application of the term. However, as early as 1957, Franz Altheim had used the term to talk about the Sasanians: Altheim and Stiehl 1957.

[8] See Yarshater 1983 for a discussion of this historiography and its cultural implications.

[9] One could rightly take umbrage at the adjective *accurately* as it is used here. A better expression might be that the structure of our present state of knowledge about the Sasanians is built upon the narratives provided by the historians of the Islamic period, supplemented by what can be found in Roman (Greek and Latin), Syriac, Armenian, Georgian, and Middle Persian sources, as well as archaeology, numismatics, art history, and sigillography. In this sense, 'accurately' is a circular argument, as the accuracy of 'facts' about Sasanian history is commonly measured by their agreement with the basic narratives provided by Arabic and Persian writers of the Islamic period. Challenging this, in a way, is one of the purposes of the present volume.

[10] Sasanians used the term *Dil-ī Ērānšahr* 'the Heart of the Iranian Domains' to refer to Mesopotamia. Alternatively, the region was given the name of *Sūristan*, from *Āsūristan* 'Assyria'. See Mohammadi Malayeri 1379/2000: vols II and III.

al-Ma'mun. They were then, for the Muslim historians, first and foremost a 'Mesopotamian' power.[11]

In the modern, European-origined historiography, the Sasanians are the great enemies of the Romans and their Byzantine successors, their western neighbours. Here, the Sasanians are again a quintessentially western(-orienting) power whose main importance for the study of history is its 'resistance' to Roman expansion. Sasanians were the power that 'blocked' the Roman expansion to the east and was there to rival the Byzantines.[12] This framing of Sasanian history is true for both the western historians and the 'native' historians[13] whose work they have commonly influenced. While the former might look for those episodes of Sasanian history that affected their relationship with Rome and Byzantium, the native historians often scrutinise the same history to see how it came to culminate in the Arab-Muslim invasion of their territories, which again took place from the direction of the west.[14]

This imposes another burden on the study of Sasanian history. While the Sasanian Empire was a pre-modern political entity and certainly not a nation-state, it is most commonly contextualised as part of the history of Iran as defined by its modern boundaries and limits. While this is justifiable in some senses, it should be kept in mind that the Sasanian realm extended beyond the modern nation-state and is as much part of a 'native' history of Iraq or Afghanistan as it is that of Iran. The influence of the Sasanians, furthermore, extended to where even their political power might not have, East Iran in this case being a glaring example. This combination of political and cultural influence resulted in a zone of influence that has recently been

---

[11] Morony 1984 is the most comprehensive study of the effects of the Sasanians on early Islamic Iraq and the administrative, social, and religious heritage of the Sasanians that was transmitted to the Caliphate. For a discussion of the cultural aspects of this Sasanian influence as demonstrated in the Islamic sources, see Mohammadi Malayeri 1379: vol. I.

[12] The volumes of the Roman Eastern Frontier and the Persian Wars (Dodgeon and Lieu 1991; Greatrex and Lieu 2005) are a good demonstration of this approach, which concentrates mostly on the issues of war and confrontation; cf. Howard-Johnston's many contributions, conveniently gathered in Howard-Johnston 2006, with a further study of the Sasanian army, Howard-Johnston 2008. Dignas and Winter 2007, not concentrating on war per se, are also most interested in its absence, though still looming under the heavy shadow of conflict.

[13] I do realise the problematic nature of this term and its particular postmodern connotations (Chakrabarty 2009: ch. 4), but in the absence of a deeper study of the histories of the Sasanians written by historians originating from the former territories of their control, I am taking the shallowest definition of this term into consideration. This would be among the very first sections of the present work that I would change if such studies proved forthcoming.

[14] For example, see Zarrinkoub 1975. For an example of a modern study, see Daryaee 2003, where the precedents, and aftermath, of the Islamic conquests are studied in the local context of Persis.

termed *Ērānšahr*, as a way of contextualising the Sasanian history.¹⁵ This idea sees the area between the Oxus/Amu Darya (perhaps more reasonably the Jaxartes/Syr Darya) and Euphrates as a common historical ancestor of what became the medieval lands of the *Eastern Caliphate*, and eventually the Persianate world.¹⁶

All of the above then highlights what is deemed here to be the most prominent problems of the study of Sasanian history. The western focus of the study of Sasanian history, as well as its containment within the historiography of a modern nation-state, have taken away from what is arguably one of the major characteristics of Sasanian political and socio-economic history. This, specifically, is the presence of cultural, social, and political elements of the Sasanian Empire in East Iran and a reciprocal presence of cultural, social, economic, and political influences of East Iran in Sasanian society, particularly in its political structure, cultural tradition, and royal ideology.

This *East Iran*, as mentioned before, is not a territorial concept aiming to claim the political ascendance of the Sasanians, let alone the modern nation-state of Iran, over any lands. It is rather the simple idea that the region, which formed the famous region of Khurasan in the medieval period, itself possessed, before the full realisation of this end, an internal cohesion. This cohesion, rather than owing its existence to any influence of the Sasanians, or being a reaction to it as a case of secondary state formation, is the continuation of a pattern set by the Kushans. Consequently, the collapse of the Kushans, the fashioners of East Iran, might be taken as the beginning of late antiquity in this region. Kushans were indeed the originators of many of the norms and patterns that became the prominent features of local political, social, and cultural life. These patterns included a path of conquests from the north, often originating in the steppe and flowing over to Bactria, and eventually crossing the Hindu Kush to settle in Kabulistan and Gandhara and further east in north India. The dominance of these patterns, often in the absence of unifying political units, commonly determined the fate of the region as a whole.

---

¹⁵ Daryaee 2010; in Persian, the greatest proponent of the idea seems to be S. Javad Tabatabaee in a sociological context: see Tabatabaee 1388/2009.

¹⁶ Among the many things one has to deal with in writing the history of the region is the terminology used and its potential for being misunderstood. Neither *Iran* nor *Persian/Persianate* is used here as they are sometimes meant in the more extreme nationalist readings. While I have laid down much of what I mean by 'Iran' or *Ērānšahr* above, I should make clear that I am not alleging the 'dominance' of Persian as a language in this region, but rather the role of Persian-speaking Muslims, and Persian itself as the second language of Islam (see Frye 1975) in creating a cultural zone which prevailed for much of the medieval and early modern period. This is further discussed above.

These, adopted by the Sasanians themselves and perfected by the Kidarites and their successors, became the means through which East Iran emerged as a unit. This unit, like all other sociopolitical units, possessed ideologies, institutions, and structures that allowed for its distinct existence, and let it become the prevailing agent in the emergence of the greater unit of Khurasan.

This book, however, cannot pretend to cover all aspects of this process, or claim the presentation of a comprehensive summary of all of these institutions and ideologies. Instead, it aims at filling a particular gap, the important gap of 'narrative' history, the basic tools of a historian. In order to achieve this, it gives precedence to political history, with necessary doses of cultural and social history. Out of necessity. however, and in order to provide a coherent and accessible narrative, it avoids going off at major tangents on other aspects of history and refers to matters on linguistics, art history, or religious history in passing, and mainly as a source of completing the main narrative. Specialised readers, particularly philologists and historians of religion, might find the lack of detailed analysis of the linguistic world of East Iran, and little talk of religion, curious or negligent. In both these cases, the book is intentionally refraining from going into details, since despite the dominance of the study of these subjects in our general knowledge of the history of East Iran, their effect in clarifying the course of events is less than expected.

The fact of the matter is that the study of the history of Central and West Asia has commonly been the forte of philologists, and to a lesser extent, archaeologists. In the case of East Iran in particular, the study has also benefited from the ingenious insights of numismatists, as coins have so far proven to be the most reliable, and readily available, source of knowledge for this. This has deprived *historians*, in the precise sense of the word, of engaging in their most productive practice, namely studying the macro- and micro-structures and challenging given narratives in order to forge more reliable ones. Lack of narrative sources, thus, has rendered the history of East Iran, and greater 'Central Asia' for that matter, before the tenth century a bit of a black hole, a *terra incognita*, for historians. At the same time, archaeologists, philologists, and numismatists, providing the awe-inducing amount of knowledge that they could gain from the material of their chosen fields, have naturally not been as inclined as historians to contextualise their findings. The final result is a lack of a guiding structure against which new discoveries can be placed, and of course the narrative itself can be challenged and altered.

Admirable contributions such as the UNESCO *History of Civilizations of Central Asia* boasted chapters which attempted to provide a sort of narrative that would be useful for understanding the history of greater Central Asia. These, however, were filled with detailed, and often contradictory, studies of primary material, themselves adding to the confusion regarding the actual narrative of history. Important efforts by scholars such as Grenet, Sims-Williams, Cribb, and Errington and Curtis include excellent demonstrations of how 'history' can be deduced from material culture, and how creatively the written sources can be used, even if to complicate matters further. Etienne de la Vaissière's 2007 (originally 2002) history of the Sogdian merchants was a gargantuan and impressive study of one of these Central Asian units. Nonetheless, it paid curiously little attention to actual Sogdiana and its local context and instead concentrated much more on the Sogdian trade network. Other studies of archaeological discoveries from the region often include creative sections connecting material culture with various Roman, Chinese, Indian, Arabic, Persian, and Armenian notices, rendering micro-narratives that are convenient at the time, but don't comprehensively connect to each other. A historian of this area, then, basing their work on textual evidence and often working off of a main narrative, would be lost in this world of multiple languages, coins, seals, and archaeological material. Even worse is the case of a historian not concentrating on the history of the region who simply, due to the sheer variety of sources, would be almost unable to get beyond the first page of any modern study. The students of this region should only be pitied, although not many exist due to the fact that it would be simply cruel to ask an undergraduate student to page through detailed studies of coinage, archaeology, or seals of this region.

Apart from this matter, the problem with older works such as the aforementioned *History of Civilizations of Central Asia* is their datedness. Since the publication of those volumes, several new studies have emerged that have enormously improved our understanding of the history of late antique Central Asia. The most important of these are the discovery, and publication, of the Bactrian Documents. A great collection of primary texts, the Bactrian Documents are the archive of a local king of southern Bactria/Tokharistan, which contain much valuable information, although in a very local setting.[17] The

---

[17] Sims-Williams 2002 for an introduction to the collection; Sims-Williams 2001a and 2007 (hereafter abbreviated as BD I and BD II in this volume) are the published volumes of the collection. Another short introduction can be found in Rezakhani 2010a.

significance of the collection, apart from providing new knowledge about the Bactrian language, the local history of the region of its origin in Southern Bactria, and the Bactrian calendar, has been to engender new interest in the history of Bactria and Central Asia in general. The knowledge that has also emerged as the result of the context created by this collection has been determining in increasing our understanding of the history of the region. Apart from the Bactrian Documents, the other significant set of material has been the publication of the seals related to the documents, which have themselves proven to be invaluable to the history of the region. The long-term project of several institutions and projects in Vienna and Bern, providing a complete update of the 1967 volumes of Robert Göbl on the coinage of this region, has resulted in the emergence of excellent resources providing a solid basis for research in this period: two magnificent volumes in 2013 and 2014, as well as an extremely useful bilingual website project.[18] As such, our knowledge of the numismatics of the region has now increased manifold, in fact for the first time allowing for the creation of a basic narrative of the history of the region and clarifying many problems that previously challenged scholars. The archaeology of the region, however, has not yet been as fruitful as one might hope, mainly due to political troubles, although some archaeological material has emerged that aids us in corroboration of the information gained from other sources.

This volume, then, is based on these significant new publications and material, as well as the few previous attempts at creating a narrative. Placing itself somewhere between those occupied with material culture and primary texts and traditional text-based historians, this monograph's prime motive is to provide a continuous and comprehensive history of East Iran during the Sasanian period. As high as the aim of the monograph might be, it is well aware of its limitations. The fact is that presenting a comprehensive picture of the political, economic, social, religious, and artistic history of East Iran, allowing every historian to pick and choose the subject of his or her liking and further its findings, is impossible in one volume, and certainly for a single author. Instead, the volume concentrates mainly on political history, and sometimes, based on the interests of its author, economic and social history. In order to compensate, it

---

[18] Pfisterer 2013 and Vondrovec 2014. The website *Das Antlitz des Fremden* provides an overview of the whole project, as well as making many excellent sources available online: http://pro.geo.univie.ac.at/projects/khm/.

aims to cover a long period of time: late antiquity – roughly matching the length of Sasanian history. It does not, however, stick to the strict limit of AD 224–651, the period of Sasanian rule. It is meant to be as much a history of the Sasanian world in East Iran as a history of East Iran in the Sasanian world. Consequently, the region deserves its own chronological boundaries, and in fact imposes them on those who want to study it. Therefore, the period that this book covers is roughly from the first century AD to the beginning of the eighth century AD. The starting point is really the discussion of the foundations of the Indo-Parthian and Kushan Empires, while the end approximately matches the conquest of Tokharistan and Sogdiana by the Muslims, while in Kabulistan and Zabulistan it stretches even to the early ninth century. These limits, or arbitrary starting and stopping points, are really enforced by the available documents, as will become clear throughout the volume.

In the temporal sense, a certain level of uncertainty needs to be accounted for. Much of the chronology of the region is known only within its relationship with the neighbouring states, and less often in an absolute sense or verifiable with external calendars. Issues such as the Era of Kanishka are notoriously controversial, rendering us nearly unable to establish the absolute dates of the reigns of individual rulers of the Kushan Empire. This is the reason that the history of the mighty Kushan Empire is treated nearly in its entirety here, despite the fact that its 'golden age' most probably happened before the Sasanians took the throne in their home province of Persis/Fars. Here, I am interpreting the time period of 'late antiquity' a bit more widely than normal, and tend to include the late 'Hellenistic' (or in regional terms, Arsacid/Parthian) period within its study as well. So, within this wider concept of late antiquity, the dates discussed are sometimes speculative, and this should be considered when trying to understand the chain of events.

Structurally, the work is divided into several chapters. The first chapter details the first encounter of the Sasanian founder, Ardashir I (AD 224–41) with the east, in relation to the Indo-Parthians of Sistan. The narrative, out of necessity, will then backtrack to the foundations of the Indo-Parthians in the early first century in order to contextualise the Sasanian conquest of the region. The second chapter aims at the same goal, this time looking at the encounter of the Sasanians with the mighty Kushans in Bactria/Tokharistan. Similarly, it provides a quick, perhaps too quick, summary of the history of the Kushans, and their demise, in order to present the idea of the emergence of East Iran and the importance of Sasanian presence there. The third chapter, concerned with the history of the Sasanian cadet branch of Kushano-Sasanians, is mostly a discussion of the problems associated with the history of this very little-known dynasty and is, out of necessity, quite brief.

Chapter 4 embarks on the narrative of the Hunnic/Chionite invasion of East Iran and the emergence of the Kidarites, the first dynasty who controlled Bactria and moved south to control south of the Hindu Kush as well. The Alkhans, another Chionite dynasty who significantly move to the south of the Hindu Kush to control Kabulistan, Zabulistan, and Gandhara, are the subject of the fifth chapter. Here, the contribution of the chapter is to repeat once again the numismatic suggestion that the Alkhans, contrary to all previous expressions of their history, are not the same as the Hephthalites. By demonstrating this, the chapter hopefully succeeds in providing a history of this important dynasty in its own terms and separates it from their previous presentation as a branch of the Hephthalites. Chapter 6 is concerned with the 'genuine' Hephthalites, those dominating Tokharistan and perhaps Sogdiana, and famously defeating and killing the Sasanian King of Kings Pērōz and acting as kingmakers of the Sasanian realm for a couple of generations.

The seventh chapter is the only one not concerned with a dynasty, rather being geographically oriented in the region of Sogdiana during the Kidarite and Hephthalite periods. The history of the Sogdians is generally better known than that of Tokharistan, and its basic narrative history has already been established in previous works. As a result, what this book aims to achieve by establishing a basic narrative of the history of East Iran has been at least partially achieved for Sogdiana already. Here, issues of connection between Sogdiana and Bactria are given more attention in order to understand the proposed East Iranian setting of both regions. Chapter 8 is concerned with the history of the two dynasties of the Nēzak and the Western Turks, both rising to prominence as the result of a joint Western Turk–Sasanian effort in eradicating the 'Empire' of the Hephthalites in AD 560. Concentrating initially on the area of Kabulistan and Zabulistan, the domains of the Nēzak, the chapter then provides a narrative of the history of Tokharistan and Sogdiana under the control of the Western Turk, and sets the stage for the arrival of Islamic dominance in the region. This chapter thus addresses the main theoretic point of the whole volume, namely the emergence of the concept of Khurasan within the Sasanian world, detailing the juxtaposition of local and imperial institutions that allowed for the creation of such a concept.

The ninth chapter provides some details about the region of Sogdiana, both in its homelands of the Zarafshan River Valley and in its extension beyond the Jaxartes. Sogdiana in general has received less attention in the current monograph due to its marginal status in relation to the political entities that are the focus of this book. However, its gradual integration, alongside Tokharistan, into the concept of Khurasan requires some details about its history in the terminal late antique period. Chapter 10, containing the general conclusion, provides a formulation of the narrative provided in the book and sets the stage for the historical period that follows, looking a little ahead in history. The final chapter, an excursus on the *Shahnameh*, is an attempt to locate the most famous cultural product of the Iranian world in its East Iranian context, both providing an example of the importance of the region and demonstrating the cultural continuities in East Iran.

A BRIEF NOTE ON THE SOURCES

Primary sources on the history of Central Asia, particularly the region of East Iran, are extremely rare. In the cases of their occasional existence, they can seldom be trusted to provide a reliable narrative. Most previous studies have relied heavily on the few cursory notices available in Chinese, Byzantine, and Arabic sources, all of which suffer from the disadvantage of having been written from extreme temporal and geographical margins. As a result, this book, despite using these same sources for general guidance, instead utilises modern studies of archaeology, numismatics, sigillography, and palaeography in order to draw much of its intended picture.

Chinese dynastic histories, as well as universal works, are used for the information they provide on the origins of many of the entities mentioned throughout the book. Among these, the histories of the Han dynasty, both the *Han Shu* and *Hou Han Shu*, are used for the earlier periods, particularly as they relate to Kushan history (Hulsewé and Loewe 1979). The same sources, along with Sima Qian's *Shiji*, are used for the 'Indo-Parthians' (Watson 1961). For both entities, the information is heavily supplemented with numismatic studies of the last few decades, including the updated works and discussions of Michael Alram, Nikolaus Schindel, Joe Cribb, Osmund Bopearachchi, Elizabeth Errington, and Robert Bracey, among many others.

The history of the Iranian Huns, whether the Kidarites or the Alkhans and the Hephthalites, is normally narrated on the basis of a combination of scattered notices in Roman sources, such as

Ammianus Marcellinus, or much later notices in the *Tang Shu* and the reconstructed *Wei Shu* (Enoki 1969). Much has been made of the small passage by Procopius in his *History of the Wars* in forming a picture of the Hephthalites. Despite its importance, this famous notice is much misused, although widely accepted uncritically as a basic description of the Hephthalites. By using alternative research on numismatics, as well as corrective information from archaeological sources, this book provides a more accurate picture of the famous Hephthalites, attempting to distinguish what are called 'genuine Hephthalites' from the rest, including the Alkhans and the Nēzak. Alkhans, much abused in the Indian sources and commonly confused with the Hephthalites, are given a prominent place, again based on numismatics, and are considered within their own context. The context, however, is still quite vague.

Islamic sources, mostly the narratives of conquests preserved in al-Baladhuri's *Futūh ul-Buldan* (1866), Ibn A'tham's *Kitāb al-Futūh* (1392; 1986), and of course al-Tabari's great history, mainly define the terminal Hephthalite, as well as the Western Turk and early Islamic, epochs. All of these are used extensively here, supplemented by the numismatic and archaeological evidence. Additionally, in order to provide better context for the Western Turk period in Kabulistan, Zabulistan, and Sistan, Persian sources such as *Tārīkh-e Sīstān* (Bahar 1387) and *Tārīıkh-e Bukhara* (Al-Narshakhi 1387), commonly ignored by Islamic historians, are mined for their valuable information.

Apart from the narrative sources, special mention has to be made of the great collections of primary material that have emerged as important tools for historians of Central Asia. The Mount Mugh Documents, published in the 1960s, have been a surprisingly neglected set of sources considering their value in understanding the history of Sogdiana in the late antique period.[19] Of course, their application, in both geographical and temporal scope, might seem limited, solely addressing the first two decades of the eighth century directly. However, the eyewitness account that they provide us is invaluable for understanding the political, social, and economic history of Sogdiana for a longer period of time. The fact that they fit snuggly into Islamic narratives of the conquest of the region is another valuable aspect of these sources.

---

[19] These documents were published in three volumes by three different translators: Freiman et al. 1962–3; the revised volume by Livshits is now translated into English along with further documents: Livshits 2015c.

Similarly, the newly discovered Bactrian Documents (Sims-Williams 2001a; 2007), which have become available only in the last twenty years or so, provide an exciting avenue of research. Again, despite their limitation to a small area of southern Bactria/Tokharistan, they are indispensable sources for first-hand accounts of the history of this region in late antiquity. The fact that they span from the fourth to the eighth centuries makes them additionally attractive. Despite their uneven distribution, these documents are unprecedented primary sources showing us aspects of the social and economic history of East Iran during late antiquity.

Of course, as mentioned before, numismatic, sigillographic, epigraphic, and archaeological sources often form the backbone of the narrative provided throughout the volume. The comprehensive study of the numismatics of the region has for long been the volumes by Göbl (1967). Others have challenged many of his ideas throughout the past few decades, although the basic schema still largely holds, as demonstrated by the recent volumes published by the Austrian Academy (Pfisterer 2013; Vondrovec 2014). Valuable information, gained through comparison with the coinage of the Sasanian dynasty, is provided among the pages of the great SNS project, again from the Austrian Academy.[20] Alongside numismatics, seals, and seal impressions from the region, including those accompanying the Bactrian Documents, there has opened a whole new window on the study of the region, with fascinating results (Lerner and Sims-Williams 2011). Epigraphic information, particularly the Kushan royal inscriptions and inscriptions found in various places in Gandhara and northern India, have added significantly to our knowledge, clarifying major information such as the basic genealogy of the Kushan kings.[21] Archaeological and art historical studies of the region, ranging from excellent works by Soviet archaeologists to ongoing projects in Afghanistan and Central Asia, have allowed us to understand the extent of the cultural, political, and economic power of the entities discussed here.[22] All of these are now supplemented by information from 'alternative' sources – Armenian, Chinese, Syriac, and Persian ones – that were less considered in forming the narratives provided so far. Still, it is to be taken for granted that what emerges from all of these, even though relying

---

[20] In this case, particularly the second volume: Alram and Gyselen 2012; and the contribution of Schindel in the same volume; Schindel 2012.
[21] Among many others, see Sims-Williams and Cribb 1996.
[22] Including the many contributions to the volumes of these two conferences: Alram and Klimburg-Salter 1999; Alram et al. 2010.

on the impressive efforts of many scholars, is quite incomplete, and with the increase in sources, and updates in their interpretations, many of what is given here will prove to be obsolete and eventually modified.

1 The Sasanians and the Sistanis

INTRODUCTION

The first encounter of the Sasanians with the east took place in the initial stages of the dynasty's foundations, during Ardashir's eastern campaigns, sometimes after his defeat of Artabanus IV (c. AD 224), the last major Arsacid authority (Daryaee 2009: 3–4; Grabowski 2011: 207–33). Ardashir probably took a northeastern route first (Alram 2007: 227–42), conquering the important town of Marw, which henceforth became the most secure Sasanian base of activities in the northeastern parts of their territories. It was after this success that Ardashir turned his attention further south and headed to the region of *Sistan* (MP *Sīstān*, from Sakistan, *Saka-stan, 'the land of the Sakas').[1] Various members of the so-called Indo-Parthian dynasty (Fröhlich 2004) had ruled Sistan since the time of Gondophares in the first century AD.[2] However, this Indo-Parthian 'empire' was effectively divided, following Gondophares' own demise, into two parts, with different successors ruling either part and occasionally trying to control the whole domain, as indicated by their coinage. Sistan proper, the former satrapi of Drangiana and the neighbouring Arachosia (to emerge as Zabulistan in the later periods)[3] and the most important western possession of the Indo-Parthian

---

[1] Sistan, per se, is used to refer to the province known through the Achaemenid inscriptions and works of Greek geographers as *Drangiana*. For a useful sketch of the region, see Bosworth 1968: 1–3.

[2] On the first-century date of Gondophares, see Senior 2001–6: I.198, where he proposes an accession date of AD 19. Alram, however, suggests the dates of 'AD 20 to post 46': Alram 1999: 23.

[3] For the later history of Zabulistan, see Chapter 8 below.

Fig. 1.1. Coin of Indo-Parthian Sanabares (© CNG 252, Lot 213).

dynasty, eventually fell to a successor, and perhaps a usurper, named Sanabares. It is with the descendants of Sanabares in Sistan that Ardashir first had to compete over control of the eastern flank of his nascent empire.

THE ORIGINS OF THE SASANIANS IN PERSIS

Before describing the encounter between Ardashir and the Indo-Parthians, we must understand the origins of the Sasanians in Persis itself and the importance of the rule of the east in the formation of Ardashir's empire.[4] The most common narratives of the foundation of the Sasanian dynasty provide a semi-legendary background for the Sasanian founder and often highlight certain parts of his career in order to suggest a divine providence for his conquests. This was, in reality, essentially a usurpation of the throne of his father and brother, and ultimately that of the local Persis authorities.[5] Al-Tabari, the most prominent source for the life of Ardashir, provides a rather detailed résumé of his conquests, although this incorporates many legends (al-Tabari, I.813–22). The famous late Middle Persian text, *Kārnāmag ī Ardaxšīr ī Pābagān* ('The *Vita* of Ardashir son of Pābag', henceforth *KAP*), additionally presents a quite legendary tale of his origins, as well as providing a family tree that details Ardashir's complicated relationship to Sasan, after whom the dynasty is called

---

[4] For a discussion of this and the circumstances of Ardashir's rise, see Daryaee 2010: 236–55.
[5] A brief history of the local dynasty of Persis and their fate is provided in Wiesehöfer 1994, and their coins, our major source for their history, are catalogued in Klose and Müseler 2008.

by later historians.⁶ The basic outline of Ardashir's career is stated clearly by the sources, placing his origins in Persis and his youth at the court of the local ruler *Juzihr/Gozihr* (not mentioned in *KAP*, which instead has him at the court of the Arsacid Artabanus IV) and his eventual rebellion against the same local ruler.⁷

Geographically, al-Tabari locates Ardashir's early career in *Darabjird* (MP *Dārābgird*) in eastern Persis. As the local *argbed* (fortress-master, castellan), Ardashir is presented as the main instigator of a rebellion, along with his father Pābag, against Jūzihr (MP *Gozihr).⁸ The thrust of his initial conquests, however, is towards the west, mostly focusing on the conquest of Persis itself, and then Khuzestan, Mešān, Suristan (i.e. *Mesopotamia*), and Media. The only exception to this westward expansion is a brief foray into Kerman to the east of Persis early in his career, where he subdued a local ruler bearing the Parthian name of Balāsh/Walāš (al-Tabari I.817).⁹ However, following his coronation in Ctesiphon and the formation of the district of *Bih Ardashir* (MP *Weh-Ardashir*, '[built] better by Ardashir'), Ardashir headed over to the east (al-Tabari I.819). His conquest of the east started from Istakhr (MP *Staxr*), the capital of Persis, whence he proceeded initially against *Sajistan* (the common Arabic rendering of Sistan, from Sagistan/Sakistan) before conquering Jurjān (Gurgān/Hyrkania), Abarshahr (Neishapur), Marw, Balkh, and Khwarazm, 'as far as the farthest frontiers of Khurāsān' (al-Tabari I.819). In the same passage, al-Tabari relates that Ardashir returned to Marw, which henceforth appears as the capital of the newly conquered districts in question. However, upon his return to *Jūr* (MP *Gūr* or Ardashir-Khurrah; later *Firuzabad*), his headquarters and the site of his greatest palace in Persis (al-Tabari I.817), he received envoys and submission from the kings of 'the Kūshan, of Tūran, and of Makrān' (al-Tabari I.820). Al-Tabari's account of the conquest of the east by Ardashir concludes there.

Al-Tabari's account is obviously highly exaggerated and incorporates much of the later Islamic understanding of the Sasanian control of East Iran, including the use of historically anachronistic *Khurasan*,

---

⁶ Now see Macuch 2014: 80–94 for a very interesting take on this descent based on the available Middle Persian sources.

⁷ Some new Persian sources (e.g. the *Shahnameh* of Ferdowsi) suggest that following the defeat of Dara (Darius III) by Alexander, his descendants, including the eponymous ancestor of the Sasanians, Sasan himself, escaped to India and stayed there for four generations. The eastern origins of the Sasanian royal family have been speculated on by other scholars, most recently Olbrycht 2016. See the further discussion below.

⁸ See al-Tabari 1999, note 13, for a discussion of the etymology of this name.

⁹ See also Alram 2007: 233 for a discussion of the order of Ardashir's conquests.

Fig. 1.2. Ardashir's copper Marw issue, SNS I type IIIa/3a (© CNG 332 Lot 155).

a later Sasanian administrative division.[10] It is unlikely that Ardashir really reached anywhere north of Marw, where he might have issued coins (Alram 2007: 231; Alram and Gyselen, 2003), and it is almost certainly impossible to imagine his complete conquest of the Kushan Empire, as will be discussed in the next chapter.

What is of interest to us here is the prominence of the conquest of Sistan in this narrative, in a way acting as a gateway to the subjugation of East Iran as a whole. In Sistan, Ardashir came face to face with Farn-Sasan, perhaps the last Indo-Parthian ruler of that province and a scion of the ruling dynasty of the region. In a way, Ardashir's victory over Farn-Sasan and his removal from the throne of Sistan is the true confirmation of power for the Sasanian founder. The control of the east was indeed the affirmation of the establishment of his power. Although not mentioned in Al-Tabari and unknown to most latter historians, Farn-Sasan and his Indo-Parthian ancestors were in fact among the most important political entities of much of East Iran in the two centuries prior to the rise of the Sasanians.

INDO-PARTHIANS AND INDO-SAKAS

Indo-Parthians is a name given by modern scholars to a dynasty of rulers with loose kinship connections to each other and ruling over the areas south of the Hindu Kush, as far east as northern India. At the height of their power, the Indo-Parthians, sometimes

---

[10] On this, see Chapters 7 and 8 below. On the Sasanian administrative divisions, see Gyselen 2001.

called the *Pahlavas*[11] (Alram 1986: 244–5), controlled Sistan and Arachosia, and occasionally Gandhara, Sindh, Kashmir, Jammu, as far as Mathura during the first century AD.[12] Their rise is sometimes connected to the episode of the Saka conquest of the eastern regions of the Arsacid Empire (Daffinà 1967) and the establishment of the Indo-Saka (or Indo-Scythian) dynasty; they thus rose to power out of the confrontation between the Arsacids and the invading Saka tribes during the reign of Phraates II and Artabanus I.[13]

In characterising the dynasty as part of a larger Saka presence in Iran, historians have connected the history of the Indo-Parthians to that of Maues and the 'dynasty' of Azes, the great rulers of the Indo-Scythian[14] kingdom of northwest India. The basis of this assumption, despite problems, is mostly the numismatic information, considering the coinage of the Indo-Parthians in the context of the larger Indo-Saka coin series (Alram 1986: 218). This framing has proven useful in many cases, at least for the numismatists, in limiting the expanse of Indo-Parthian chronology. The old dating of the beginning of the Indo-Parthians' rule, around 124–115 BC (Tarn 1951: 223), and their relative chronology relied mainly on the perceived connections between them and the Indo-Scythians as evidence for their dating. This, on the other hand, becomes problematic as it relies on circular argumentation and tautological assumptions, rendering results that commonly make sense only within the closed circuit of available coin data, while presenting little absolute chronology.[15]

---

[11] These should not be confused with the Pallavas dynasty of southern India in later centuries. However, a memory of the Pahlavas (if assumed to be inspired by the Indo-Parthians) remains in Sanskrit texts such as the Mahabharata and Puranic texts. The connection between the two is commonly assumed (e.g. Simonetta 1958), although I have decided not to utilise it in the present work to prevent confusion.

[12] The Indo-Parthian dynasty is known mostly through its coinage, since written materials are quite scarce. The principal studies of these coins are Mitchiner 1975a and Senior 2001–6. In both cases, the authors consider the Indo-Parthians to be a 'Scythian' dynasty, gaining prominence in Sistan as the result of the Saka invasions of the reign of Phraates II and Artabanus I, as mentioned by Justin, 41.2.

[13] Schipmann 1986; this is basically the prevailing supposition in the studies of Mitchiner 1975a or Senior 2001–6.

[14] Names such as Indo-Parthians, Indo-Sakas, and Indo-Scythians are modern scholarly designations for these dynasties, whose names are only known in a cursory manner from the Indian historical-legendary sources, including the great epic Mahabharata. Some modern scholars use the term Śaka for the 'Indo-Scythians' (Alram 1986: 217–44), while the Indo-Parthans are called the Pahlavas (Alram 1986: 244–5). Here, we adopt the artificial scholarly naming conventions to facilitate the understanding of the complicated political history of this region. In the following paragraphs Indo-Saka/Indo-Scythian is used as an alternative for the Śaka or the dynasties of Maues and Azes, and Indo-Parthian for the Pahlavas or the dynasty of Gondophares and his successors, including the aforementioned Farn-Sasan.

[15] See MacDowall 2007: 103–10 for a discussion of the absolute chronology. Despite his arguments, the fixing of the absolute chronology of the Indo-Parthians, as well as the Kushans, is still quite uncertain.

From the numismatic point of view, the early Indo-Parthians before the rise of Gondophares were little-known authorities who produced coins initially in the style of the Parthians (i.e. Arsacids) and then the Indo-Scythian kings such as Maues.[16] They might have been Parthian, or possibly 'Saka', satraps of Sakistan/Sistan appointed by the Arsacid ruler. This can be observed from the coins of *Cheiroukes*, who calls himself a 'satrap' of the Marsakes region, matching the eastern provinces of the Arsacid Empire, and later Sistan proper.[17] The coinage of a series of authorities whose names are given as Tanlis, Tanlis Mardates, and probably a queen named Rangodeme[18] are quite likely to be the last series issued by these 'satraps' before the establishment of the dynasty of Gondophares in Sistan and Arachosia. The early rulers of Sakistan/Sistan can thus be characterised as Arsacid governors, possibly of Saka origin, who are appointed following the defeat of the Sakas in the region by Mithridates II (Wiesehöfer 1996: 111).

Assuming an Indo-Scythian connection, we must consider the history of the Indo-Parthians through their connection to the Indo-Scythian authorities. Maues, the first Indo-Scythian issuing authority known from inscriptions and the Greek and Kharoshti legends of his coins, was possibly the clan leader who defeated the Graeco-Bactrians, probably of the dynasty of Menander, in the northern Hindu Kush (Bopearachchi 2004; Coloru 2009). Subsequently, Maues proceeded to Paropamisdae and further into Gandhara, removing Indo-Greek rulers from the region (Senior 2005; Widemann 2003). The possible route of the Saka conquest of Paropamisdae and Gandhara can only be speculated on, some arguing that it led through the Kabul Valley or further east through Kashmir or further west, from Arachosia to Sindh and eastward to Gandhara (Senior 2005; Puri 1999: 185). Either case would have consequences for the relationship between the Indo-Scythians and Indo-Parthians. Maues, the likely leader of the Saka invasion of Paropamisdae and the founder of the Indo-Scythian power in Gandhara, appears to have followed the coinage style of Indo-Greek rulers such as Apollodotus II, with both Greek and Kharoshti legends on his coins (Senior 2005). He might in fact have been unrivalled in power in his own time (Puri 1999: 187). However, it might

---

[16] Senior 2001–6: II, issue 191. For a different scheme, see Alram 1986: 246.
[17] The relationship between these authorities and the Saka invaders is here assumed only on the basis of coin evidence; Senior 2001–6: II.144, issue 190; Alram 1986: 296–7.
[18] Senior 2001–6: II, issue 196.1; Alram 1986: 296 and 290–1.

Fig. 1.3. Silver tetradrachm of Maues (© CNG 369, Lot 299).

be wise to distinguish the wave of Saka invasions spearheaded by Maues from the wave that met the Arsacids in Drangiana and Arachosia and resulted in the death of Phraates II and Artabanus I between 138 and 124 BC (Daffinà 1967).[19]

In Gandhara, *Azes* (whose name might simply mean 'commander' and thus be a title) eventually inherited the power of Maues (Senior 2005). He is known to numismatists as Azes I on the basis of a distinction made between his coins and those of another authority with the same name (Senior 2005; Alram 1986: 226–8, 234–41). While Azes I controlled Gandhara, Jammu, parts of Sindh, and northern Arachosia, he appears to have been contemporary with two other rulers in his East Iranian vicinity. The first of these is Kujula Kadphises, the founder of the Kushan power, whose career will be discussed in the next chapter and who at the time was in the process of taking control of Bactria. Historians generally assume that the other rival of Azes was Vonones (bearing a known Arsacid royal name), who ruled in Drangiana, possibly alongside his brother *Spalahora* and followed by his nephew *Spalagadama* (Puri 1999: 187; cf. Tarn 1951: 346 n.3).

So, this is the period in which *Drangiana*, the old Achaemenid and Arsacid province, slowly morphed to form the new entity of Sakistan, resulting from the Saka conquests of East Iran. The new ruler of the province, possibly under Arsacid suzerainty, carried a royal Parthian – indeed Arsacid – name, Vonones, distinguishing him from the Sakas. Numismatic evidence shows that Vonones was

---

[19] Alram 1986: 219–21 connects the two and in fact counts Vonones and Spalirises as parts of the Indo-Saka (Śaka) dynasty ruling from Gandhara to Arachosia (Alram 1986: 217–18).

Fig. 1.4. Silver tetradrachms of Vonones with (?)Spalahores (© CNG 69 Lot 834).

followed by his brother[20] *Spalahora*,[21] and his nephew, *Spalagadama*, both carrying the element *Spala-*, an East Iranian[22] word meaning 'army' in their name. This might suggest that both names originated in military titles and might have held the same value at the time.

The next ruler of Drangiana/Sakistan is an authority known initially through the coins he issues in the region, where his personal name is given as Gondophares;[23] he was the founder of the

---

[20] In this context, the *topos* of 'brother-founders' might be of interest in the characterisation of the ruling family of Sakistan. Like the founders of the Arsacid power itself, Arsaces and Tirdates, and the future founders of the Indo-Parthian dynasty, Gondophares and his brother Gad, the early rulers of Sakistan are said to be two brothers. There is, of course, a case to be made for a historical misunderstanding of names at this point if we consider a possible confusion of names and titles, resulting in the creation of a brother-founder myth. I have elsewhere (Rezakhani 2005) argued that the brother-founders of the Arsacid dynasty, Arsaces and Tirdates, are most probably later creations, resulting from a misunderstanding on the part of historian Arianus. I suggest that Arsaces is in fact the title of the founder of the Arsacid dynasty, whose personal name was Tirdates, and who in turn was succeeded by his son Artabanus I, known from the numismatic evidence as Arsaces II (Wolski 1962). Indeed, in the historical accounts of Pompeius Trogus' *Philippic History*, epitomised by Justin, there is only mention of a single founder of Arsacid rule, Arsaces, who is then succeeded by his son, Arsaces II. One might apply the same to Gondophares and Gad, as will be detailed below, further demonstrating the presence of a brother-founder pattern for many Parthian ruling families, and possibly a misunderstanding of Parthian naming conventions. Consequently, we consider that Spalahora, the 'brother' of Vonones of Sakastan, might also be just Vonones himself, carrying the *title* of Spalahora, a military rank.

[21] See Alram 1986: 220–1 for the coins of Spalirises (*Kharoshti spaliraśasa* in genitive), who in Greek also has the title of ΒΑΣΙΛΕΩΣ ΑΔΕΛΦΟΥ '(of) the brother of the king' on the obverse of his silver issues (Alram 1986: 221, type 1, nos. 945–6), so presumably a brother of Vonones, ruling in Arachosia.

[22] The component *spala-*, from Old Iranian (OIr.) *spaδa-* meaning 'army', is well known from various Iranian contexts, including Sasanian *spahbed* from OIr. *Spaδa-paiti* 'army commander'. The transformation of Old Iranian /ð/ to East Iranian /l/ is well studied; see Harmatta 1999: 416 for the possible Saka context.

[23] His name is written ΥΝΔΟΦ(Φ)ΕΡΗΣ in Greek and in Kharoshti as *gadavharasa*, in the genitive, from OIr. *winda-farna 'may he find glory': Alram 1986: 250–5; Errington and

Indo-Parthians and the greatest ruler of the dynasty. Gondophares' initial coin issues in Sakistan were silver drachms and countermarked Arsacid silver drachms bearing his name.[24] These issues were soon followed by tetradrachms minted in southern Arachosia, in the region of Kandahar. These coins show an increasing interest in the east and the gaining of a prestigious mint, as marked by the minting of the tetradrachm.[25] Some have speculated that Gondophares might have left a relative, or a lieutenant, in charge of Drangiana/Sistan itself, where an authority named Sarpadones issued coins with the title of 'King of Kings' (Alram 1986: 262–4; Errington and Curtis 2007: 65).[26] Gondophares himself moved on to northern Arachosia and the region of Kapiśa/the Kabul Valley, and then to northwestern India, where he issued coins in the style of the Indo-Greek king Hermaios, while switching the material from billon to copper (Alram 1986: 253, no. 1168). He eventually impinged upon Indo-Scythian territories in Gandhara and issued coins in the style of the Indo-Scythian Azes II in Pushkalavati (near Peshawar) and eventually in Taxila in eastern Gandhara (Alram 1986: 253, nos. 1164–6). By moving on to Jammu, Gondophares gained control over the largest expanse of territory up to that point, stretching from northern India to 'Sistan' proper (Drangiana/Arachosia) and truly deserving the title of an 'empire'.[27] The inscription *Takht-i Bahi*[28] provides further evidence for the career of Gondophares, naming him as the king in charge of Sindh (Konow 1925: 261–82) as well as the coins issued there (Alram 1986: 252–3).

Other than his coins, a source commonly used for the history of Gondophares is the so-called *Acts of Thomas*, the Apostle who is

---

Curtis 2007: 65. I cannot see a reason for the widespread suggestion that Gondophares should be treated as a title instead of a name. Despite its quite descriptive meaning, it is not any more grandiose than Artaxerxes (Old Persian (OP) *arta-xšaça* 'righteous-ruler') or many other Iranian royal names. Instead, as I shall argue below, I believe the name of his 'brother' Gad should be treated as part of his title or a mistake for his own name. On some coins, his name is actually rendered as ΓΟΝΔΟΦΑΡΟΥ (Alram 1986: 252).

[24] Alram 1986: 250, types 1, 1/1 (nos. 1158, 1159); Senior 2001–6: I.108; Errington and Curtis 2007: 64–5.

[25] Compare with the issue of tetradrachms among the Arsacids, which was considered a privilege of the mint of the capital in Ctesiphon-Seleucia in Mesopotamia. The same is also true for the issue of tetradrachms in Bactra/Balkh under the Graeco-Bactrians and almost all successor states.

[26] However, Sarpadones probably also issued coins in northwest India (Alram 1986: 263–4) on one type of which he calls himself *maharajasa gadavhara sapedanasa* '(of) the Great King Gondophares-Sarapadones' (Alram 1986: 264, type 2).

[27] See the division of the coinage types among these geographical divisions, in Alram 1986; Fröhlich 2004.

[28] Cornish 1995 provides a convenient summary of the importance of the Buddhist site of Takht-i Bahi for understanding the context of the presence of Buddhism in the Gandhara and the period of Indo-Parthian rule.

Fig. 1.5. Silver drachm of Gondophares (© CNG 66, Lot 824).

supposed to have met Gondophares while on a proselytising mission in India (Medlycott 1905: 1–17). In Thomas' Acts, the apostle meets a king called Gundaphar, mentioned as the ruler of northwestern India alongside a brother named *Gad*. The Apostle Thomas meets the king and his brother in their capital at Taxila, the capital of Gandhara under Indo-Bactrian rule, as well as in subsequent periods. Considering the presence of a later coin authority, named Gondophares-Gadana by modern numismatists, as well as the early Indo-Parthian authority Spala-gadama, there is a possibility that Gad was in fact Gondophares himself.[29] It is quite likely that Apostle Thomas, even if he really did meet the king in Gandhara, actually just met one, the *Spalagadama* Gondophares, the conqueror from Drangiana/Sistan.

The information that can be gathered from the numismatic sources about Gondophares is quite confusing, and sometimes contradictory. Upon the death of Gondophares, his empire was split among his successors whose coinage shows the extent of their rule. Sakistan and southern Arachosia were initially ruled by Gondophares-Gad(ana) who supposedly establishes the tradition of using the name Gondophares as a title.[30] The next ruler of Sakistan and Arachosia is known from other sources as Orthangnes, who is most probably in fact the same man as Gondophares-Gadana (Mitchiner 1975a: 741; Alram 1986: 256–8).[31] Abdagases, another relative who apparently

---

[29] Cf. Senior 2001–6: IV, where he argues that the authority met by Thomas must be Sases, using the dynastic name of Gondophares.

[30] See Alram 1986: 246 for a schema of Indo-Parthian rulers in various regions.

[31] The reading 'Orthagnes' (ΟΡΘΑΓΝΗΣ) is based on the legend on the obverse of the coin, while the Kharoshti inscription on the back, on coins attributed to 'Ostiran/Arachosien' by Alram 1986: 257–8, reads *guduvharasa gudanasa*, thus 'Gondophares-Gad(ana)'!

did not adopt such a convention, ruled in Gandhara and the rest of the empire (Errington and Curtis 2007: 66; Alram 1986: 248–50). In Sistan, excluding Arachosia (Alram 1999: 41), Orthagnes was succeeded by his son Hybouzanes[32] (Alram 1986: 255; 1999: 44) who also issued coins in Jammu/northwest India (Alram 1986: 556).

Considering the possibility that Spalagadama, Gondophares, and Gad are all the same person, as presented above, I would like to suggest a simplifying scheme for the order of Indo-Parthian kings. This would be that Gondophares, issuing coins in Drangiana/Sakistan as the nephew of Vonones called Spalagadama, conquered Arachosia, Gandhara, and Jammu and established the Indo-Parthian Empire. He was succeeded in Sakistan and Arachosia by Orthagnes[33] and eventually Hybouzanes. In the east, namely Gandhara and Jammu, Abdagases, the nephew of Gondophares,[34] followed him.

Eventually a ruler known as Sases (Alram 1986: 264–6), naming himself Gondophares-Sasē on his coins (Fröhlich 2004), came to be in charge of the eastern territories of Gandhara and Jammu, as well as the Sind region. On at least one of his coins, he names himself on the reverse in Kharoshti as *aspasa bhrataputrasa* or 'nephew of Aspa', supposedly referring to Aspavarma (Errington and Curtis 2007: 66), the Apracaraja satrap of Mathura and a son of Indravarma (Alram 1986: type 1203), possibly marking a dynastic shift away from the family of Gondophares. However, this might also be a reference to an unknown member of the dynasty, as Sases also names himself as *guduvharasa sasasa* '(of) Gondophares-Sases', establishing himself as part of the Gondopharan dynasty (Alram 1986: type 1206). At this point, the control of northern Arachosia and the Kapiśa region had already passed on to the Kushan founder Kujula Kadphises, as no subsequent coin issues can be found from northern Arachosia.

With the subsequent conquest of most of the empire by the Kushans, the rule of Sakistan, as an independent province never conquered by the Kushans, eventually fell into the hands of a ruler named Sanabares. This ruler might in fact have been the founder of what, from the coins of his great-grandson Farn-Sasan, appears to be a separate line of rulers. On the obverse of his coins,

---

[32] The reverse legend of Hybuzanes' coins read ΒΑΣΙΛΕΥΣ ΥΒΟΥΖΑΝΗΣ ΥΙΟΣ ΟΡΘΑΓΝΟΥ ΒΑΣΙΛΕΩΣ, namely 'King Hybouzanes son (of) Orthagnes the King' (Alram 1986: 255).

[33] Senior 2001–6: I.110. He also suggests that Orthagnes and Gondophares-Gadana should be recognised as one and the same authority (Senior 2001–6: I.112–13). On this issue, see the earlier but still highly valid arguments of van Lohuizen-de Leeuw 1949: 344ff.

[34] Abdagases has the titles of ΑΔΕΛΦΙΔΕΩΣ and *Gadapharabhrataputrasa* 'Gondophares' brother's son' on his Gandhara issues (Alram 1986: 248; Errington and Curtis 2007: 65).

Fig. 1.6. Silver drachm of Sanabares with Pahlavi legend on the obverse (© CNG 176, Lot 106).

Sanabares uses a Pahlavi legend[35] naming him 'King Sanabares', while the reverse carries a Greek legend naming him as the Great King, ΒΑΣΙΛΕΥΣ ΜΕΓΑΣ (Alram 1986: no. 1191), and on at least one series of issues from Sakistan, as 'the Great King of Kings Sanabar' *ΒΑΣΙΛΕΥΣ* ΒΑΣΙΛΕΩΝ ΜΕΓΑΣ ΣΑΝΑΒΑΡ (Alram 1986: no. 1194).[36]

In Sakistan and Arachosia, Sanabares was most probably followed by someone who uses the title of the 'Great King of Kings' and is named Pakores (an Arsacid royal name), and who returns to the use of Kharoshti script on the reverse of his coins (Alram 1986: no. 1190). Pakores also issued coins in the style of the later Kushan King Vasudeva (Alram 1999: 42–43). At the same time, the issues of Pakores seem to be overstrikes on a series of coins by Vima Takto, the second Kushan king, previously known as *Soter Megas* (the Great Saviour). This shows great parity in time and makes it necessary for us to consider the matter of dates for the Indo-Parthian rulers of Sakistan.[37]

---

[35] Perhaps it would be more prudent to use the term 'Aramaic' for the legend in question, as 'Pahlavi' can be misleading. However, the similarity of the letter shapes to the Parthian 'Pahlavi' script and the later Middle Persian Pahlavi perhaps justifies the use of the term. For a discussion of the development of the Aramaic script in an Iranian context and possible connections to the coin legends of the Indo-Parthians, see Rezakhani 2016.

[36] The coins of Sanabares appear to have been imitations of second-century Arsacid royal issues of Vologases III (AD 111/12–146/7) and his opponent Mithradates IV (AD 130–47), helping to establish a *terminus post quem* of c. AD 130 for the date of Sanabares' rule (Alram 1986: 261). As we will see further on, this works well with the evidence on Farn-Sasan, the great-grandson of Sanabares.

[37] See a full discussion of the connection between the Indo-Parthian and Kushan coins series in Alram 1999: 19–46.

THE DATE OF INDO-PARTHIAN RULE IN SAKISTAN

The absolute dating of the ruling dynasties and personages in East Iran and northwest India is a notoriously problematic aspect of the study of the history of this region.[38] For the Indo-Parthians, an obvious point of departure is the period of the reign of the founder, Gondophares himself. Based on the consideration of the dating of the Acts of Thomas, and corroboration provided by coins, scholars have assigned the dates of AD 19 to sometime after AD 40 (AD 46 for Alram) for the rule of Gondophares, and this has been the most commonly accepted date for this ruler and a basis for dating the rest of the Indo-Parthian dynasty (Alram 1999: 44).

Alternatively, a comparison with the coins of Indo-Scythian ruler Azes I[39] has allowed Senior to argue that Gondophares ruled sometime in the last few decades BC, since his coins would make him a contemporary of Azilises and Azes II, the successors of Azes I. The argument is formed on the founding of the Era of Azes by Azes I, starting at 58 BC, putting the rule of Gondophares a few decades later, around 10 BC (Senior 2001–6: I.108–9; cf. MacDowall 2007).

A thorough discussion of various calendars and eras is not within the scope of the present work. We should, however, make a provisional attempt at reaching an approximate date that would provide at least a comparative framework for the history of the Indo-Parthians, and give a context for the political history of the dynasty in Sakistan before and during the rule of Ardashir I, the Sasanian founder.

As mentioned above, Ardashir was certainly a contemporary of Farn-Sasan, the issuer of a series of coins in Sakistan that on their reverse bear the image of a fire altar quite similar to those depicted on the reverse of the coins of Ardashir. While scholars normally consider Farn-Sasan a competitor of Ardashir and a claimant to his title (Alram 2007: 234–5), I will argue further down that Farn-Sasan was in fact senior in rank to Ardashir and that it was his defeat that finally enabled the Sasanian founder to claim the title of King of

---

[38] See the next chapter for a brief discussion of the date of Kanishka, the most controversial dating era in the history of the region.
[39] For a discussion of this from a numismatic point of view, see Senior 2001–6: I.109. Cribb 1999 discusses the different eras used in East Iran and northern India. Considering their implication for the chronology of the early Kushans, Göbl's arguments contra Cribb in the same volume and based on the same primary source, the Rabatak Inscriptions, draws a completely different conclusion; Göbl 1999.

Kings and establish his dynasty. In either case, the contemporaneity of Farn-Sasan and Ardashir cannot be denied or doubted. Since we know the dates of Ardashir's career, this might be a useful way to put the reign of Farn-Sasan and his Indo-Parthian predecessors in chronological perspective, even if establishing absolute dating seems far from achievable.

Considering the early contact between Ardashir and Farn-Sasan in the former's career, an approximate date of AD 225 be assigned for the Sasanian conquest of Sakistan. At this point, Farn-Sasan could not have been a very young man and was probably in middle age, perhaps around 40, judging the state of his career and his coinage portrait. On his coins, Farn-Sasan calls himself a son of Adur-Sasan, a grandson of Tirdat, and a great-grandson of Sanabares, the previously mentioned ruler of Sakistan (Nikitin 1994). This would put two generations between Sanabares and Farn-Sasan. There is then the possibility that Farn-Sasan was an immediate or later successor of Pakores. We have previously speculated a *terminus post quem* of AD 130 for the coins of Sanabares, Farn-Sasan's great-grandfather. This would mean that either Pakores or another authority ruled before Farn-Sasan, around AD 180–210, and a third authority, perhaps an Abdagases II (on the basis of Alram 1986: 246, type 1195), ruled around AD 150–180, and directly followed Sanabares in Sakistan and Arachosia.

Sanabares usurped the throne of Sakistan from Sases or another short-lived successor of him, putting Sases in charge of Sakistan at the end of the first century AD and his birth date around AD 60 or earlier. Considering that Sases was not an immediate successor of Gondophares and came after Abdagases, Sarpadones, and Orthagnes, he should be considered two generations younger than Gondophares, whose date of birth would fall somewhere around the date of the beginning of the Christian Era at AD 1 or earlier, possibly in the last decade BC. This would then provide us with a rough, and admittedly very speculative, chronology of the rule of the Indo-Parthians in Sakistan, and in agreement with Alram's date of Gondophares' rule from AD 19 to after AD 44. In this schema, we should keep in mind that Sanabares and his successors were in charge of parts of East Iran at the same time as the last century of the Arsacid rule in Central and Western Iran.[40]

---

[40] See a discussion of the dates and their relation to the Kushan dating in Alram 1999: 37–45.

FARN-SASAN AND ARDASHIR: THE FOUNDING OF THE SASANIAN DYNASTY

Farn-Sasan, the last member of the family of Sanabares and the contemporary of Ardashir I, is not known from any narrative sources, and even his name was previously misread on his coins, the only evidence of him that we possess. For long known as *Ardamitra* on the basis of an erroneous reading of his coin inscription,[41] Farn-Sasan demonstrates a fascinating case for the eastern connections of the Sasanians and their relation to the older authority of the Indo-Parthians.

On his coins, mostly copper issues from Sakistan, Farn-Sasan introduces himself as 'Farn-Sasan, son of Adur-Sasan, grandson of Tirdat, son of the grandson of Sanabar, the King of Kings'. This inscription, perhaps rightly called the longest genealogical inscription on any coin (Nikitin 1994: 68), has many significant points for early Sasanian history, and the iconography of the coin itself reveals even more about the eastern context of the early Sasanians.

On his coin inscription, Farn-Sasan was clearly trying to connect himself to the last well-known ruling king of his dynasty, his great-grandfather Sanabares. While there is ample evidence of the coins of Sanabares, we have no coins of Tirdat or Adur-Sasan, the grandfather or father of Farn-Sasan.[42] It thus appears that, coupled with the absence of coins, Farn-Sasan's long genealogy is hinting at a need to prove his rightful claim to the throne of Sakistan. Thus we may assume that Farn-Sasan, a member of a cadet branch of the ruling house of Sakistan, was indeed an outsider to power in the region. Most probably, only gaining the throne in a moment of chaos and disintegration in Sakistan, he was obliged to stake a firmer claim to power and clearly state his connection to the only known power in the region.

But this becomes even more curious when considering the iconography of Farn-Sasan's coins. On the obverse of his coin, a profile bust of the king is shown, wearing a cap. The reverse, however,

---

[41] See Nikitin's ingenious reading of the name Farn-Sasan, instead of the problematic Ardamitra, in Nikitin 1994. Despite the widespread acclaim for this reading and its acceptance, it still remains a problem, as the reading is attempted from a perfect form of the legend assembled from several different coins and in fact starting and ending at unexpected places on the coin.

[42] One might speculate, and hope, that at least one of Alram's *Unbekanter Königs* (Alram 1986: no. 1213–16) might belong to Adur-Sasan or Tirdat, but in fact this cannot be ascertained until the discovery of more coins. We now know that Alram types 1217 and 1218 are in fact Farn-Sasan's coins.

Fig. 1.7. Copper issue of Farn-Sasan (Courtesy of the American Numismatic Society).

shows a fire altar, surrounded by an inscription (Alram 2007: 234). Fire altars were not a common iconographic representation on the coins of Sakistan and are indeed unique on the coins of Farn-Sasan. Significantly, there was another authority at the time issuing coins with a curiously similar fire altar displayed on its reverse. This was none other than Ardashir, the upstart Sasanian lord who was conquering the east and possibly pushing very seriously against Farn-Sasan's territories. The closest source of inspiration for the image of the fire altar on the coins of Ardashir is the coinage of Persis, where several authorities used a fire altar and a single attendant, iconographically very different from the Sasanian altar, on the reverse of their coins (Klose and Müseler 2008: 56ff).

Fig. 1.8. Reverse of the coin of Vahshir, king of Persis, showing a man looking right paying respect to a fire altar (© Photo courtesy of British Museum, 1894,0506.2386).

Significantly, the fire altar does not appear on the Persis issues of Ardashir himself (Klose and Müseler 2008: 78) but only starts with his imperial issues (Alram and Gyselen 2003: 105–6, type 2–3; Shenkar 2014: 179).

The problem of whether Farn-Sasan is copying the fire altar from the reverse of Ardashir's coin or vice versa can be debated, but the fact by itself shows that the two rulers were well aware of each other's existence and claims to power. The fire altar of Farn-Sasan can scarcely be interpreted as a sign of his submission to Ardashir, nor is it necessarily a copy of the latter's coins. In fact, Farn-Sasan does by no means suggest that he considers Ardashir to be a suzerain, nor does he even acknowledge the latter. Instead, as was mentioned before, Farn-Sasan is legitimising his rule by connecting himself to Sanabares. On the coins, Farn-Sasan also uses the title 'King of Kings', the quintessential title of an Achaemenid or Arsacid great king, very creatively. He puts the title at the end of the genealogical list, where it could be interpreted as referring to Sanabares, while the latter in fact scarcely used the title (Senior 2001–6: I.107; Alram 1986: no. 1194). However, considering the position of the title on the coin, it could easily be referring to Farn-Sasan himself, suggesting that he might have directly opposed Ardashir's claim to the same title.

Another issue to consider is Farn-Sasan's name and the name of his father, Adur-Sasan. It is easy to notice the element 'Sasan' in the name, obviously used as a dynastic name by the Sasanians. The name might have also occurred as the name of the previous Indo-Parthian ruler, Gondophares-Sasēs, confirming its currency in the

Fig. 1.9. Coin of Ardashir as the Sasanian King of Kings, showing on the reverse a fire altar set on a pedestal (© CNG 997, Lot 337).

East Iranian milieu. It is curious, however, that in the only primary Sasanian source that we possess where Sasan is mentioned, he is not provided with a family relationship to Ardashir or his father Pābag. In the *Ka'aba-ī Zardusht* inscription (ŠKZ) of Shapur I (241–72), the son and successor of Ardashir, Shapur gives his titles and ancestry as such:

> An, mazdēsn bay Šābuhr, šāhān šāh Ērān ud Anērān, kē čihr az yazdān, pus mazdēsn bay Ardašīr, šāhān šāh Ērān, kē čihr az yazdān, nab bay Pābag šāh, Ēranšahr xʷadāy hēm.

> I, the Mazda-worshipping Lord Shapur, King of Kings of Iran and non-Iran, who (has) the lineage of gods, son of Lord Ardashir, King of Kings of Iran, who (has) the lineage of gods, grandson of Lord Pābag the King, I am the master of the Domain of Iran (*Ēranšahr*). (ŠKZ, 1–2)[43]

Here, Sasan, the eponymous ancestor of the dynasty, is not named at all. Instead, Sasan is simply mentioned as *bay Sāsān* 'the Lord Sasan', in a later passage, without the provision of any genealogy or connection to Ardashir or Shapur. He seems to be a rather distant, possibly divine, figure, although the possibility of his connection to the Semitic god *Sesen* has already been dismissed (Schwartz 1996: 253–7). The name Sasan, on the other hand, is mentioned on the ŠKZ ten times, apart from its use to refer to Lord Sasan, the eponymous 'ancestor' of the dynasty. Among the more interesting of these are Sasan Ornekan (ŠKZ 22), who is the first person mentioned in the list of the grandees of the court of Pābag, as well as 'Sasan Suren'[44] and 'Sasan Lord of Andegan', the adopted sons of two other noble families. This is simply an indication of the popularity of the name Sasan in the third century.

In the family of Farn-Sasan, the occurrence of the name demonstrates something of a cultural continuity with early Sasanian society, if not a direct kinship connection. It has recently been postulated that the Sasanians might have had an Eastern Iranian origin, possibly related to the Indo-Parthian royal family (Olbrycht 2016). The fact is that Pābag and his sons Shapur and Ardashir appear as

---

[43] Huyse 1999; I have used my own translation of the text with a normalised transcription based on Huyse's three versions in order to allow for easier comprehension by the non-philologically inclined readers. I naturally take all responsibility for any resulting mistakes.

[44] The Suren family is generally connected to the region of Sistan/Sakastan in later literature, being considered as either its Parthian rulers, or Parthianised Sakas who were integrated into the Arsacid, and later Sasanian, nobility. The basis of the assumption is the notice in al-Tabari (I.682), who connects the Surens to the area. However, the pervasiveness of the idea in modern literature is due to Ernst Herzfeld's essay on Sakastan and the Suren: Herzfeld 1931–2.

strangers, 'foreigners' indeed, in Persis. Neither *Pābag*[45] nor *Sasan* is a name known from the Persis rulers, and even the story told by the later Islamic sources makes it clear that the family were indeed usurpers of the throne. The early coinage of Shapur and Ardashir shows a significant stylistic shift from the known coinage of Persis, including the size of the flans and the type of the script used for the legends. The type of Aramaic script used on these coins is in fact much closer to that used by Farn-Sasan on his coins, quite different from the Aramaic script used on the Persis coins (Rezakhani 2016). The coins themselves are also minted on much larger flans than the normal Persis coins, and the portrait of the kings on the obverse and that of their father, Pābag, on the reverse would argue for the lack of relationship between the two series and the possible non-Persis origins of the coinage of Shapur and Ardashir.

Our evidence might still be too inconclusive to show a descent of the early Sasanians from the Indo-Parthians, but the clearly shared components of rule between the two entities are at least indicative of the extra-Persis context of the rise of Pābag, Shapur, and Ardashir. The late Arsacid state was anything but a unified imperial state, and was probably not intended as such. Instead, it consisted of two major powers of the Arsacids in Media and Mesopotamia and the Indo-Parthians in the east, as well as minor kingships in Persis, Elymais, and other regions between Jaxartes and Euphrates.[46] While Ardashir's claim to the title of King of Kings was established after his victory over Artabanus IV, it was not in fact completed until he managed to remove the last member of the Indo-Parthian family from the throne of Sistan, a power with which he might have had early connections and affinities. This early conquest of Sistan, as well as the Sasanian dominance of Marw, was the beginning of centuries-long Sasanian involvement in the affairs of Eastern Iran, something that was only to be intensified when they pushed further east and came into contact with the power of the Kushan Empire.

---

[45] The name *Pabēs* (ΠΑΒΗΣ) occurs on the reverse of the obols of the Da Yüeh-zhi imitations of Eucratid coins; see Jongeward and Cribb 2015: type 3; p. 27.
[46] Olbrycht 2016 argues for the existence of two 'Arsacid' Empires, designating the Indo-Parthian one as the Eastern Empire. This bold suggestion would alter our view of the history of the first two centuries of the Christian Era in the Near East and could potentially provide for a different narrative of the rise of the Sasanians.

2 *The Kushans and the Sasanians*

INTRODUCTION

The Kushan Empire was the most noteworthy power that came to existence in East Iran in the pre-Islamic period. Through their conquest of Tokharistan and eventual crossing of the Hindu Kush and invasion of northern India, the Kushans established a pattern that was followed by almost all their successors, from the Kidarites to the Alkhans, Turks, and early Islamic powers. By adopting the local cultural offerings of their territories, from the Bactrian language to Buddhism, and through engendering new ideas such as their gold coinage, they for the first time unified both sides of the Hindu Kush and created a coherent empire.[1] Their influence lasted for many centuries after their demise, and their empire became a blueprint for many succeeding states that continually strove to control both north and south sides of the Hindu Kush, even down to the Ghaznavid period. The Kushan power, and their creation and dominance of East Iran, made them the greatest challenge to the Sasanians, and possibly their greatest influence as well.

THE KUSHAN EMPIRE IN EAST IRAN

In his description of the career of Ardashir I, al-Tabari mentions that after the conquest of Sistan and Khurasan up to Khwarazm, the Sasanian founder received envoys from the kings of 'the Kūshan, of

---

[1] The case of the Achaemenids within the larger context of that empire is of course significant. However, considering that the centre of the Achaemenid Empire was never in the east, the Kushan success can be considered a first attempt at establishing an empire centred in East Iran and in full control of both sides of the Hindu Kush.

Tūrān, and of Makrān' (al-Tabari I.820).² Ardashir's son, Shapur I, in his famous inscription at *Ka'aba-ī Zardušt* (ŠKZ) also claims to be the master of 'Kushanshahr, up to Pushkabur', the region of modern Peshawar in ancient Gandhara and the traditional stronghold of powers which controlled northwestern India. Most scholars now would agree that while Shapur's claim might be just an exaggeration, al-Tabari's suggestion is a case of historical anachronism and a factual impossibility.

But what was Kushanshahr and who were the Kushans, about the control of whose lands Shapur boasted and the tribute of whose king was of such importance? In the usual narratives of Iranian history, whether traditional or modern, Kushans do not feature significantly, if indeed at all. The name is nearly unknown to Islamic historians, who appear to have only a vague idea of the Kushans' identity and possibly only knew of the term as a geographical designation rather than a historic dynasty.³ In the modern period, despite an increasing interest in Kushan history, they have not been included in the modern narratives of Iranian history and appear to be partially noticed in the national histories of India, Afghanistan, and Pakistan, in none of which they play a very crucial role. Kushans are, more than anything, the plaything of modern historians, objects of curiosity for those who dig in the darker corners of history in search of lesser-known, and thus more exciting, historical entities. Their history, through the research of such enthusiasts, has emerged through their coins, their archaeological remains, the few inscriptions they left, and the paltry remains of their actions reflected in Indian, Armenian, Roman, and Chinese historical works, mostly in the context of the expansion of Buddhism. As with the Indo-Parthians, and in fact most of the political powers of Central Asia prior to the early Islamic period, the reconstruction of their history depends greatly on numismatic research. Consequently, the basic framework of their history has changed frequently, and will surely be subject to change again, on the basis of new observations made by scholars of the field. Crucial information and ingenious discoveries have also helped to improve radically our knowledge of the period of Kushan rule and particularly their sociocultural significance. The best-known of these, perhaps, is the discovery of the genealogy of the early Kushan kings, and indeed their correct names,

---

² Also see above, Chapter 1, for a brief discussion of the route of Ardashir's eastern conquests.
³ Khurradādhbih 1967: 32 considers Kushanshah to be the title of the king of *Mawara-un-nahr* (Transoxiana).

in the inscription of Rabatak (Sims-Williams and Cribb 1996; Sims-Williams 1998), which helped us to understand the context of early Kushan coinage, as well as to redraw some of our basic narrative of it. As it stands, the following will admittedly be a sketch reflecting only our current knowledge of Kushan history and will surely be invalidated, as many previous attempts were, by the discovery of new material and sources.

KUSHANSHAHR AND THE SASANIANS

The claim of control over the rule of Kushanshahr, as made by Shapur in the ŠKZ, is commonly counted an exaggeration. Most scholars, in their reconstruction of the course of events leading to the Sasanian control of the core territories of the Kushans in Bactria, the Kabul Valley, and Gandhara, would argue that this event could not have happened before the end of the third century, and thus after the date of the carving of the ŠKZ. But aside from the issue of dating the Sasanian conquest of the Kushan territory, it is important to note that Shapur claims the control of 'Kushanshahr', but does not name, or claim victory over, any Kushan rulers. In Shapur's statement, *Kushanshahr* is a territorial designation, much as it is for al-Tabari centuries later. By naming Pushkabur as the farthest he has conquered in this region, Shapur is in fact making a claim over the territory more than actual control over a foreign political power. Kushanshahr in this inscription is a Middle Persian toponym, 'the Domain of the Kushans'. It does, no doubt, get its name from the Kushans, but its control does not necessarily mean dominance over the Kushans themselves.

In fact, a few decades later, when Shapur's son Narseh ordered the carving of another inscription on the tower of Paikuli, he named the Kushan king, so the political entity, immediately following 'Caesar and the Romans', thus extending them the same dignity (Paikuli, line 41 of Parthian text).[4] One can claim that for Narseh, and perhaps also for Shapur earlier, the Kushans were separate from Kushanshahr. They were, as a matter of fact, too powerful, or had the image of being so, for the Sasanians simply to bundle them together as a marginal power ruling over a province of the Sasanian domains. The history of the early Sasanians, in many senses, is most closely connected with the Kushans as an imperial power, and the

---

[4] The line numbering of the Paikuli inscription here is based on the arrangement and translation of Humbach and Skjærvø 1978.

breaking of Kushan power was crucial for the Sasanians' claim to control over East Iran.

FROM THE YÜEH-ZHI TO THE GREAT KUSHANS

As with many other political and social entities of Central Asia and Eastern Iran, the origin of the Kushans is shrouded in mystery and complicated scholarly debates over minute details and confusing source material. The two most important matters in the history of the early Kushans are firstly their origin, and secondly their absolute dating, the latter holding an important place for the whole of Kushan history. A complete résumé of all the various arguments on these two points would require more than the pages of this chapter, and is further provided in the works of other scholars.[5] Here, we can look at the most widely accepted opinions, and possibly provide some criticism of the assumptions made by the scholars in using Chinese and other sources. On the other hand, the matter of Kushan origin is of little consequence for the purposes of the current volume, which is focused rather on the Kushan presence in East Iran. It does, however, appear necessary to present a consistent narrative for their presence in the region, and thus it requires at least some discussion of the two questions mentioned before.

The *Kushans* is the name given by historians to a dynasty that ruled Bactria, Gandhara, and large parts of northwestern India in the early centuries of the Common Era. The name is in fact what appears as part of the title of some of the earlier kings of the dynasty and on their earlier coins (Cribb 1993). Indian sources too call them the dynasty of the *Kuśana*, confirming the name. Their origin, however, is a matter of much controversy and debate.[6] Historians therefore attempt to piece together their history by matching textual – usually Chinese – sources with numismatic and scant archaeological evidence, with occasionally confusing results.[7]

The early history of the Kushans is normally given as part of a series of westward movements of a nomadic group named the *Yüeh-zhi*, presumably caused after their defeat at the hands of the

---

[5] The issue of the date has been a debate from Marshall 1914 to the modern contributions of Cribb 1999 and Falk 2001, as well as the opposing views of Göbl 1984 and 1999 or Schindel 2014. Falk's view and his dating of the beginning of Kanishka's reign to the early second century seem for now to have found most support.

[6] See, for example, Puri 1999. For an exhaustive study of the Yüehzhi, which concludes that they are certainly the Kushans, see Benjamin 2007.

[7] For a brilliant, if equally disorienting, example of this, see Cribb and Göbl's separate, and widely differing, contributions in *Coins, Art, and Chronology*, 1999.

Xiongnu, a prominent tribal confederacy mentioned in the Chinese sources and usually equated with the Huns who are mentioned in the western ones.[8] The *Yüeh-zhi* confederacy, living somewhere around the area of the Tarim basin in modern-day western China (Chinese Turkistan or Xinjiang), are said to be the same as the *Tocharoi* (Tokharians) of the Greek and Roman sources. The Chinese sources mention that there were five tribes among the confederates of the Yüeh-zhi, and one of them, named *Guishuang* in Chinese, is alleged to be the Kushans (on the basis of the adjusted pronunciation of the Chinese characters in Early Middle Chinese).[9]

This is indeed a major problem in using the sources regarding this region, as the multiplicity of sources and languages makes it quite difficult for us to ascertain the name and affiliation of various peoples and tribes. Many of these, taken essentially from Roman, but occasionally also Iranian, sources, are matched with the Chinese ones on the basis of uncertain reconstructions of Middle and Old Chinese pronunciation. The *Xiongnu* are a good example, as their relation to the Huns of the Roman sources or the Chionites of the Byzantine texts is quite impossible to establish.[10] The presence of Middle Persian *xyōn*[11] as an ethnonym also further complicates the matter (Cereti 2010). In addition, both Chinese and Roman sources tend to be quite inexact in applying tribal and regional names, commonly using already established names from older periods to describe new people dwelling in the same region.[12]

The details of the migration of the *Yüeh-zhi* and the earliest origins of the Kushans are based on Chinese accounts such as *Shǐjì* ('Records of the Grand Historian') or *Han Shu* ('Records of the Han Dynasty'). Both records, especially the more extensive account of the *Hou Han Shu*, are written considerably after the events they

---

[8] For a convenient treatment of these, see Yü 1990. Di Cosmo 2002 discusses the role of the Xiongnu in the formation of the Chinese state extensively; this is a type of discussion that is still notably missing in the context of Iranian history and its relation to 'marginal' actors.

[9] An interesting, if somewhat lacking, study of the Kushan relations with the *Yüehzhi* is Liu 2001. It does, however, like most other works of the kind, take the testimony of the Chinese sources, particularly the modern reconstruction of ancient Chinese geographical descriptions, at face value.

[10] Atwood 2012 discusses this point at length, mainly against de la Vaissière's assertive argument (de la Vaissière 2005a) that the Iranian and Chinese terms can be linked. Despite its philological drive, the article provides a good survey of the textual sources as well.

[11] The Middle Persian form is based on Avestan *xiiaona-*, used in the Avestan texts to refer to neighbouring hostile tribes. A history of the word and its possible origins is discussed in Choksy 2012.

[12] This is similar to the practice of Greek and Roman historians who use the name 'Scythian' to describe any of the tribes that originate in the northern Black Sea region, even as late as the time of the Goths. Even in the sixth century, Menander Protector uses the terms 'Median', 'Assyrian', and 'Persian' interchangeably to describe the inhabitants of the Sasanian Empire.

describe, in this case a few centuries later (Göbl 1999). These sources tell us about the movements of a tribal confederacy called the Yüeh-zhi in the Chinese sources. Evidently, the Yüeh-zhi, allies of the Han dynasty in their fight against the Xiungnu tribes, were defeated sometime between 209 and 177 BC by Maodun, the founder of the Xiongnu Empire:

> After having returned (from a campaign against the Hu), he went to the West and smote and chased the Yüeh-zhi. (*Shiji* 110.7a)[13]

Maodun, in a letter to the Han emperor claims:

> By the good fortune of Heaven, by the good quality of our officers and soldiers and by the strength of our horses, he [general Yu-Qienwang] has destroyed and exterminated the Yüeh-zhi. He has completely beheaded and killed, subdued and vanquished them. (*Shiji* 110.10b)

Of course, Maodun's claims, made to intimidate the Han emperor, should not be taken at face value and assume a total annihilation of the Yüeh-zhi tribes. However, it seems safe to conclude that, pressured by the Xiungnu, the Yüeh-zhi were compelled to leave their original homeland on the western borders of China and migrate westwards, on the way themselves displacing another people called the *Sai* (possibly the Saka?) and taking over their territory.

> At that time the Xiungnu had already defeated the Yüeh-zhi, and they had gone to the West and attacked the Sai king. The Sai king had gone to the South and migrated to a distant (region), and the Yüeh-zhi had occupied their territory. (*Han Shu*, 61.4a)

It should be at this point that Zhang Qian considers the Yüeh-zhi to be living to the north of the Oxus, in the territories formerly occupied by the Sai (Sakas):

> The Great Yüeh-zhi live some 2,000 or 3,000 li (1,000 or 1,500 kilometres) west of Dayuan, north of the Gui (Oxus) river. They are bordered to the south by Daxia (Bactria), on the west by Anxi, and on the north by Kangju.[14] They are a nation of nomads, moving from place to place with their herds, and their customs are like those of the Xiongnu. They have some 100,000 or 200,000 archer warriors. (*Shiji* 123)

---

[13] Translations of the *Shiji* are based on Watson 1961, with some amendations to update the spelling of Chinese names considering modern conventions.
[14] The matter of matching Chinese geographical names to the actual geographic settings is a very difficult task, which is a source of constant disagreement between scholars. Anxi is generally accepted to be the name for Parthia, and Kangju is a shifting term pointing to the middle Syr Darya region and later to Sogdiana in particular. See Wan 2012 for an example of these disagreements.

Evidently, a further war between the Yüeh-zhi and their former neighbours, *Wusun*, resulted in the Yüeh-zhi moving even further west (and south), into the *Daxia* (possibly Bactria):

> When the *Liejiaomi* (*Nandoumi* [sic] son)[15] had grown up, he himself asked the xan-yü (of the Xiongnu) for permission to requite the injury (inflicted upon) his father, and subsequently he went to the west and attacked and defeated the Da-Yüeh-zhi. Then the Da-Yüeh-zhi again moved westwards and migrated to the territory of Daxia. The *Liejiaomi* seized their masses and consequently remained in (the ancient Sai territory). (*Han Shu*, 61.4a)

Thus, the Yüeh-zhi were driven out of the Central Asian plains by a combined force of the Xiongnu and other tribes, entering the territory to the south of the Oxus, known as Bactria in the Graeco-Roman sources. This is where we might first encounter them in the Graeco-Roman sources as well, where Strabo mentions the *Tocharoi* as one of the 'Scythian' tribes who attacked the Graeco-Bactrian kingdom.

> But the best known of the nomads are those who took away Bactriana from the Greeks, I mean the Asii, Pasiani, Tochari, and Sacarauli, who originally came from the country on the other side of the Iaxartes River that adjoins that of the Sacae and the Sogdiani and was occupied by the Sacae. (Strabo, *Geography* 11.8.2)[16]

The attribution of the name Tocharian/Tokharian to the Yüeh-zhi provides another designation to describe the greater confederacy under discussion, although does little to clarify the situation in Transoxiana and Bactria at this time.[17]

That the name Tocharian/Tokharian was indeed used to describe the Kushans and their greater tribal context becomes clear when it is noticed that the name *Tokharistan* indeed becomes the dominant designation for Bactria following the entry of the Yüeh-zhi into the area, as described by the *Shiji*. After providing detailed information about the Yüeh-zhi and their tribal setting, as well as the circumstances of their move to Daxia (Bactria), the *Shiji* describes their sociopolitical setting thus:

---

[15] Nandoumi of the Wusun had previously been killed by the Yüeh-zhi.

[16] Strabo's translations are based on the standard readings of Jones 1928.

[17] The name, specifically speaking, is probably a misnomer for the Tocharians as the speakers of the Tocharian language, a displaced member of the kentum substratum of Indo-European languages. For modern philologists, *Tocharian* is the name commonly, and mistakenly, used for the speakers of the two dialects of a language in which several Buddhist manuscripts have been discovered (Adams 1984). The speakers of these dialects referred to themselves as *Agnean* (*ārśi*) and *Kuchaean* (*kuśiññe*) speakers (Mallory and Adams 1997: 303). Instead, the term *twyry* appears in an Old Turkic manuscript, assigning it as the language through which Buddhist texts were translated into Old Turkic (Henning 1949).

Daxia originally had no great kings or heads, but everywhere in their walled cities and settlements they had installed small heads. The people are weak and fear war, therefore when the Yüeh-zhi came migrating, they completely subdued and tamed them. Together they support the envoys of the Han.

There are five Qi-hou (yabgu)

1. the *yabgu* of Xiumiag resides in the walled city of Ho-mo, at 2,841 li' from the (headquarters of the) governor general and at 7,802 li from the Yang gate.
2. the *yabgu* of Shuang-mi resides at the walled city of Shuang-mi, at 3,741 li' from the (headquarters of the) governor-general and at 7,782 li from the Yang gate.
3. the *yabgu* of *Kuei-shuang* resides at the walled city of Hu-tsao at 5,940 li from the (headquarters of the) governor-general and at 7,982 li from the Yang gate.
4. the *yabgu* of Qi-tun at resides at the walled city of Po-mao, at 5,962 li from the (headquarters of the) governor-general and at 8,202 li from the Yang gate;
5. the *yabgu* of Kao-fuan an resides at the walled city of Kao-fuan at 6,041 li from the (headquarters of the) governor-general and at 9,293 li from the Yang gate.[18]

These five yabgu all belong to the Great Yüeh-zhi. (*Han Shu*, 96a.14b)

This is generally interpreted as a reference to the organisation of the Yüeh-zhi tribes prior to their entry into Daxia. In particular, the third *yabgu*, that of the Kuei-shuang, are matched with the tribe of the Kushans. On the other hand, Enoki appears to be distrustful of the usual interpretations of this passage, instead preferring to consider the five 'yabgu' to have been the local divisions of Daxia, not those of the *Da* (Great) *Yüeh-zhi* (Enoki 1974–5). This would mean that the distinction between the various subsections of the Da Yüeh-zhi was following an already established administrative division of Daxia/Bactria and was imposed on the tribe after their migration into their new homeland.

In Bactria, if Daxia can safely be assumed to refer to that region indeed, the Yüeh-zhi threatened the Graeco-Bactrian kingdom around the end of the second century BC. However, archaeological remains from sites such as Aï Khanoum indicate the abandonment of this site a few decades before the arrival of the Yüeh-zhi, although fortresses and constructions of the later Kushan period can be recognised from the early periods (Bernard 2008; Liu 2001). This would create difficulties for the identification of the tribes who, from the evidence of

---

[18] The Yang Gate is the main opening, near the city of Dunhuang, towards the western steppe and, in a way, the western limit of the Chinese heartland.

Strabo, overran the Graeco-Bactrian kingdom, as the latter appear to have come into conflict with the invaders before the arrival of the Yüeh-zhi.[19] By the beginning of the first century BC, the Yüeh-zhi settled in northern Bactria, where the occupation levels of cities such as Termez and Bactra/Balkh can be identified as the Kushan period.[20]

It is during this period that coins (silver tetradrachms, drachms, and their denominations) identified specifically as Kushan (κοβανον) appear, possibly from the mint of Balkh (Göbl 1984; Errington and Curtis 2007: 67). Traditionally, these coins were attributed to a ruler called Heraios/Heraus; they circulated mostly in parts of present-day Tajikistan (Staviskij 1986: 135).[21] Calling himself the 'king' (TYPANNOY, in the genitive form) and the 'Kushan', this ruler is alleged to be the first Kushan king (MacDowall 2007; Jongeward and Cribb 2015). Scholars have for long suggested that this ruler was none other than Kujula Kadphises, the first Kushan emperor, from whom we have more extensive textual and numismatic evidence (Cribb 1993). Many of the early Kushan coins, struck as imitations of Graeco-Bactrian coins of authorities such as Heliocles and Hermaios, are attributed to various Yüeh-zhi chiefs, as well as Kujula Kadphises (Alram 1986: 291–7; Jongeward and Cribb 2015: 21–37). The occurrence of other names, such as that of ΣΑΝΑΒ on some early Kushan issues, is a matter of uncertainty, since the authorities cannot be firmly recognised.[22]

The history of the Kushans after this point becomes a matter of matching numismatic and epigraphic records with the scant narrative sources available to us. The main reference to the early Kushans in the Chinese sources is the problematic account in the *Hou Han Shu* ('the History of the Later Han') that says:

> More than a hundred years later, the prince [xihou] of Guishuang, named Qiujiuque, attacked and exterminated the four other xihou. He established himself as king, and his dynasty was called that of the Guishuang King. He

---

[19] The formation of Kushan civilisation in Bactria is discussed extensively, and with reference to available archaeological material, in Staviskij 1986: 159–94.

[20] For a complete, and alternative, take on the Hellenistic period in Bactria and the arrival of the Kushans, see Posch 1995. The history of the period is treated in Coloru 2009. Of course, as mentioned in the first chapter, the fall of the Graeco-Bactrians, and the Indo-Greeks, is better attributed to the period of the Saka invasions, resulting in the establishment of the Indo-Scythian and Indo-Parthian dynasties, despite the testimony of Strabo on the Tocharoi's role in the matter.

[21] The beginning of the Kushan coinage, and its relation to the previous Graeco-Bactrian series, are still being debated. For the latest categorisation, see Jongeward and Cribb 2015: 25, 30.

[22] The case of ΣΑΝΑΒ and the possibility of its denoting an authority, such as Sanabares of the Indo-Parthian dynasty, have not yet been fully explored; see Senior 2001–6: type B1.2T. It is presently interpreted as a control mark used by the early Kushan authorities.

Fig. 2.1. Early Kushan 'Heraios' with the word KOIIANOY (*sic*, 'of Kushan') on the reverse. The 'control mark' ΣANAB is located between the horse's legs (© CNG Triton XVIII, Lot: 265).

invaded Anxi, and took the Gaofu region. He also defeated the whole of the kingdoms of Puda and Jibin. Qiujiuque was more than eighty years old when he died. His son, Yangaozhen, became king in his place. He defeated Tianzhu and installed generals to supervise and lead it. The Yüeh-zhi then became extremely rich. All the kingdoms call the Guishuang king, but the Han call them by their original name, Da Yüe-zhi. (*Hou Han Shu*, 128.9)

This might be a reference to Kujula Kadphises, the first king of the Kushans known from his coins (Bopearachchi 2009). In turn, the son, Yangaozhen, is taken to be Kujula Kadphises' son, Vima Takto, the authority for a series of coins, who was previously known as *Soter Megas*.[23] However, Robert Göbl, highlighting the problems of dealing with the Chinese sources (Göbl 1999: 154–6), has suggested in several instances that the son, Yangaozhen, should be identified not with Vima Takto, the second known Kushan king, but rather with his son Vima Kadphises, the third Kushan king.

While both arguments take advantage of much scholarly erudition, they also appear to take the statement of the Chinese source that Yangaozhen was the *son* of Qiujiuque quite literally and without further consideration. It might be useful to interpret the statement that Qiujiuque had lived for 'more than eighty' years- less as a statement of the king's actual age – a strange knowledge on the part of the Chinese – than as an attempt to fill out a gap of

---

[23] For an account of the matter of the coins of Soter Megas and their attribution to Vima Takto, see Cribb 1999: 177–205. For an opposition to many of the points of Cribb, see Göbl 1999: 151–75. The text of the Rabatak inscription can be found in Sims-Williams 2004: 53–68. Bopearachchi perhaps represents the most radical opposition to the view that Vima Takto is the same person as the issuer of the coins of Soter Megas: Bopearachchi 2008.

many years. Assuming this, we suggest that the Chinese account of Qiujiuque's career indeed encompasses not only the career of Kujula Kadphises, but also that of Vima Takto, his son, thus justifying the long time period which is filled by an account of Qiujiuque's 'more than eighty years'. Consequently, Yangozhen could be matched with Vima Kadphises – the son of Vima Takto and a grandson of Kujula – as Göbl also suggested, while preserving the arguments for matching Qiujiuque with Kujula Kadphises, based on linguistic considerations.

From the numismatic point of view, we know that Kujula Kadphises was the first authority to call himself *Kushan Kujula Kasasa/Kadphisa Kushana* '(of) Kujula Kadphises, the Kushan' (Jongeward and Cribb 2015: 30–1; Bopearachchi 2009). On the Bactrian legends, his name is written as ΚΟΖΟΥΛΟ ΚΑΔΦΙΖΥ ΚΟΡΣΝΟΥ[24] (Jongeward and Cribb 2015: 32, coins 73–5). As mentioned before, Kujula was preceded by an Indo-Greek king called Heraios who ruled in Paropamisdae and whose posthumous coins seem to outnumber those issued during his lifetime. Kujula Kadphises initially issued coins imitating Heraios' silver coins and even including him as the main authority, and only designating himself as the *yabghu* (Jongeward and Cribb 2015: 30, coins 44–69). He later even minted imitation Roman-style silver and copper issues, perhaps influenced by coins of Emperor Augustus, a fact that might help in dating the beginning of the Kushan conquests and the establishment of their empire by establishing a *terminus post quem* for the coins (Jongeward and Cribb 2015: 34–5, coins 103–12). It is safe to assume that at this early stage, Kujula Kadphises was in control of Bactria, but he probably competed with the Indo-Parthian kings such as Gondophares and his successors over the control of the Kabul Valley.[25] That Gondophares and Kujula Kadphises were contemporaries is demonstrated by the fact that both have coins overstruck on the coins of Hermaios, with the coinage of Gondophares showing slightly earlier influences (Bopearachchi 2009). Kujula's silver and copper coins in Bactria were quite abundant and were issued in five mints (Bracey 2012).

Kujula Kadphises was also the energetic early conqueror of the Kushan dynasty. Chinese sources attribute the entry of the Kushans to the southern Hindu Kush to him, alleging that he was responsible

---

[24] For the use of Greek ΡΣ to denote the sound /š/, prior to the invention of Bactrian þ, see Humbach 1966: 41.

[25] For a discussion of the Indo-Parthian kings and the relationship between their coinage and those of the Kushans, see Alram 1999 and Chapter 1 of the present work.

The Kushans and the Sasanians 57

for capturing Kapiśa[26] and Gandhara. Establishing another mint in Kapiśa (Bopearachchi 2001) along with the already existing mint of Balkh, Kujula Kadphises was also quite prolific in the issuing of silver and bronze coins, which have survived and help us in understanding the extent of his rule. According to one of the most accepted arguments for the *Era of Kanishka*, Kujula Kadphises ruled sometime in the mid-first century AD and probably died after the year AD, a date that also matches the most commonly accepted dates for the rule of Gondophares as an older contemporary of Kujula.[27]

Although some speculate that Kujula might have had another son (Bailey 1980), his successor on the throne was the king who was known for long simply as *Soter Megas* because of the most legible inscriptions on his coins. He was initially thought to be a local governor of Bactria under Kujula Kadphises and Vima Kadphises (Whitehead 1913). On the basis of his coinage, his authority is thought to extend from Transoxiana and Bactria to Kapiśa and Gandhara and even further south to northwestern India. *Soter Megas* most probably had his capital in Balkh and might have established a summer capital near Begram/Kapiśa. Unlike Kujula's coins, the coins of *Soter Megas* are found abundantly south of the Hindu Kush in the area of Kabul and Purushapura/Peshawar, suggesting that he had managed to conquer Gandhara and parts of Punjab during his rule. These coins are mostly copper tetradrachms and drachms, some with only a Greek legend on the obverse and some with an additional Kharoshti inscription in the reverse of the coins (Jongeward and Cribb 2015: 39–51).

The personal name of *Soter Megas*, however, is one of the most fascinating discoveries in the study of Kushan history, and among the most exciting findings in recent decades. As the obverse Greek legend could be easily read, but did not include a personal name, the name *Soter Megas* or 'the Nameless King' for long became the designated appellation for this authority in the numismatic literature (MacDowall 1968). However, in 1995, an inscription from the site of Rabatak in northern Afghanistan, in the historic region of Bactria/Tokharistan, was discovered and translated (Sims-Williams and Cribb 1996; Sims-Williams 2004). The inscription, erected by Kanishka, the fourth Kushan king, provides a genealogy of the king, naming his great-grandfather as Kujula Kadphises, and his

---

[26] This is the site of Begram, in Paropamisdae/Kabulistan, near present-day Kabul; see Ghirshman 1946 for a report of French archaeological excavations and Kuwayama 1991 for the dating of the Begram monuments.

[27] See above, Chapter 1, for a discussion of the date of Gondophares.

Fig. 2.2. Coin of *Soter Megas* (© CNG 324, Lot 237).

grandfather and Kujula's son as *Vima Tak[to]*. The conclusion drawn by Joe Cribb was thus that the authority known as *Soter Megas* was indeed none other than the newly discovered Vima Tak[to].[28]

The sensational discovery also prompted a reconsideration of all that was known about early Kushan history, including their coinage. Part of this reconsideration was a new look at the coinage of *Soter Megas*, and it was noticed that in fact, on the reverse of one his coins, identified by his unique *tamgha*/royal sign, a Kharoshti inscription does include the name and title of the king: *Maharajaasa Rajadirajasa Devaputrasa Vima Takha*, '(of) the Great King, King of Kings, Son of God, Vima Takha'! Additionally, another copper coin showing the same *tamgha* includes a Bactrian inscription *OOHMO TAKT*, rendering *Wim Takt*, as well.[29] This would be a further reason for suggesting that the evidence of *Hou Han Shu* quoted above (128.9) needs to be reconsidered. Considering problems in analysing the Chinese rendering of names,[30] it would make sense to consider the possibility that *Qiujiuque* was in fact a rendition of the name

---

[28] Sims-Williams and Cribb 1996: 77–97. The identification, now widely accepted by many scholars of the Kushan period, does meet with some opposition, mainly from Bopearachchi, who suggests that *Soter Megas* was in fact a separate authority, possibly a usurper of the crown of Vima Tak[to] and thus his contemporary. Bopearachchi's reasons are the fact that the *Soter Megas* series has a completely different iconography from the rest of the early Kushan series (i.e. the pre-Vima Kadphises silver and copper issues) and thus does not belong to the general Kushan series. I find the suggestion interesting, at least for the political history of the Kushans, but do not understand its necessity in the light of the facts that the pre-Vima Kadphises series of Kushan coins generally display widely varying coin types, mainly owing to the variety of influences and localities, and that the Kushan series is not really well formed prior to the rule of the third king of the dynasty. Bopearachchi 2007: 41–53.

[29] Sims-Williams and Cribb 1995: 98; 118. In contrast, see Bopearachchi 2008.

[30] See Göbl 1999: 155–6 for a discussion of Cribb's point and Göbl's answers.

Fig. 2.3. Coin of Vima Takto, with the Kharoshti legend *Maharajaasa Rajadirajasa Devaputrasa Vima Takha* on the reverse (CoinIndia MAC 2896var).

of Kujula Kadphises[31] and *Yangaozhen* was Vima Kadphises, his grandson and the son of Vima Takto, as also suggested by Göbl.[32] A last mention of King Vima Takto is via his declaration and inscription at Dasht-e Nāwūr, where his name, titles, and claim to kingship are given in full:

> The king of kings, the great salvation, Vima Taktu the Kushan, the righteous, the just, the god worthy of worship, who has gained(?) the kingship by his own will. (Sims-Williams 1996: 95–6)

Vima Kadphises (Bactrian Οοημο Καδφισο), the next Kushan king, was the successor to his father *Soter Megas*/Vima Takto. His name is known both from the coins and from the Rabatak inscription. His familial relationship to Vima Takto, his father, and his famous son, Kanishka the Great, is also well established in the same inscription. His coin designs, a departure from the Graeco-Bactrian-influenced coins of his predecessors, are also the first to feature the Bactrian alphabet and language prominently. Vima II Kadphises was also a prolific conqueror and organiser of the early Kushan state, and he established his rule in India firmly, a fact observable through the adoption of Indian cultural icons on his coins.

Perhaps the most important and lasting contribution of Vima Kadphises in administrative and economic historical terms is the introduction of a gold coin currency into the Kushan realm, carrying, in addition to Greek names and titles, a Kharoshti inscription. These coins have several interesting features which become prominent in

---

[31] As suggested by Cribb in Sims-Williams and Cribb 1996.
[32] See also Göbl 1999: pl. 1 for his convenient chart, and Bopearachchi 2008: 45–6.

Fig. 2.4. Copper tetradrachm of Vima Kadphises, minted in Kapiśa, showing the canonical standing king on the obverse and the god Oēśo/Śiva and the bull Nandi on the reverse (CNG 361, Lot 768).

the subsequent Kushan coinage, although some had already been in use from the time of Kujula Kadphises. Among these is the use of the image of Shiva and his bull Nandi on the reverse, as well as the inclusion of the Nandipada symbol (signifying Nandi) on one of the fields of the coin's reverse. On the coins of Vima Kadphises, Oēśo/Śiva is the only god who makes an appearance (Shenkar 2014: 154), although the repertoire of the gods depicted on Kushan coins grows exponentially after the establishment of the empire under the successors of Vima II.[33]

The Indian iconographic influences, as well as the increase in the use of gold as the material for the production of coins, suggest a secure access to sources of gold in India. Additionally, the need for gold coinage of higher value might also point to the control of the trade routes, including the northeast–southwestern route, which according to *The Periplus of the Erythraean Sea* was controlled by the Kushans at this time (*Periplus* 47.16.5–6). This would thus lead one to assume that access to India was secured during the time of Vima Kadphises' father, Vima Takto, allowing Vima Kadphises to exploit the riches of the new territories. The rule of Vima Kadphises also saw the opening of the doors of the Kushan realm to international contact and exchange, including the centrality of the region for the trade passing through Central Asia. It was probably the ambassadors of the Kushans who are reported among the 'Indians,

---

[33] See Staviskij 1986: 195–230 for a survey of Kushan religious monuments and iconography, and ibid.: 228 for a brief take on the coins.

Fig. 2.5. Gold issue of Vima II Kadphises, showing the Kushan tamgha behind the king's head on the obverse and the figure of Oēšo/Śiva on the reverse, flanked by the tamgha and the Buddhist Tiratana (© CNG 152, Lot 159).

Bactrians, and Hyrcanians' who went to the court of the Roman Emperor Antoninus Pius (AD 138–61).[34]

By this time, the Kushans had also fully adopted the local Bactrian language, and its cursive Greek script, as the language and script of their empire. While the original language of the Yüeh-zhi is unknown, Kushan inscriptions show their wholehearted embrace of Bactrian, an Eastern Iranian language, as their own and in fact its status as the primary means of communication.[35] The Kushan territories, however, encompassed many lands beyond Bactria and were, of necessity, quite multicultural and multilingual. This is a fact that is obvious from Kushan architecture, showing Indian, Buddhist, Iranian, and local Bactrian influences (Ball 2008: 71–80). Additionally, even on Kushan coins, we see the existence of Kharoshti script and Gandharan (an Indo-Aryan language) next to Bactrian, as well as the inclusion of Indian gods and symbols alongside those from the Iranian, Greek, and Bactrian milieus. While particular imageries have led some to speculate about the religion of the Kushans and their particular support for Buddhism, in fact the variety of religious references and the mixture of their symbolism seem to suggest their lack of adherence to, or support of, any particular religion.[36]

Kanishka, known as the Great, and undoubtedly the most famous Kushan king, succeeded his father as the Kushan King of Kings (Bactrian *þaovavo þao*), a title influenced by Indo-Parthian, Arsacid,

---

[34] Aurelius Victor, *Ep. de Caesaribus* 15.4.

[35] Line 3 of the Rabatak inscription talks about the writing of the inscription in Greek and its translation into *Aria*, which seems to refer to Bactrian; see Sims-Williams 2004.

[36] See a discussion of the role of religion in Kushan dynastic art and ideology in Bivar 2009.

and ultimately Achaemenid royal titulature. Kanishka was the first of the 'Great Kushans', and his reign was the beginning of a sort of golden age of the Kushans, in both literal and figurative ways. Kanishka was the son of Vima Kadphises and thus the great-grandson of Kujula Kadphises, the founder of the dynasty. Upon his accession to the throne, he inherited the control of the territories in Central Asia and northwestern India. In his own inscriptions, Kanishka claims that he expanded his rule to all of northern India and even as far south as Pataliputra ($\pi\alpha\lambda\alpha\beta o\tau\rho o$ in Bactrian; Rabatak inscription, line 5). Chinese chronicles talk about his battles with the Chinese general Ban Ch'ao,[37] and he seems to have controlled much of the traditional Yüeh-zhi territories in the Tarim region (Rosenfield 1967: 42), allowing him excellent access to the trade routes to both Central Asia and India. He is also known through mentions of him in Indian epic and religious sources, where he is most associated with the spread of Buddhism in Central Asia (Bivar 1983b: 190ff; Staviskij 1986: 201–15). Despite this concentration on his support of Buddhism, however, he appears to have been a ruler more akin to Constantine the Great than Theodosius the Great, in that he did not himself convert to Buddhism, rather rendering his support to the religion.[38] He is, for example, known to have supported the formation of the Third Buddhist Council in Kashmir (Bivar 1983b: 204), rather as Constantine supported the Council of Nicea.

Apart from the old centre of power in Balkh, Kanishka's most prominent capital was at Purushapura (in the Peshawar Valley, close to the earlier site of Pushkalavati, modern Charsada), to the east of Kapiśa. Other royal residences in Kapiśa/Begram and in northern India (Mathura) were well established, displaying examples of Kanishka's support for Gandharan Buddhist and Indian arts. Judging from his own Rabatak inscription, Kanishka was in comfortable control of north and northwestern India. If taken as a genuine statement, this would suggest that Kanishka's empire extended from the Oxus to the eastern reaches of the Ganges. Since Vima I Takto and Vima II Kadphises, Kanishka's grandfather and father, had already conquered northern India, possibly as far south as Mathura, the new King of Kings had the opportunity to organise his empire into

---

[37] *Hou Han Shu* LXXVII (Chavannes 1906: 237).

[38] This can also be observed through the non-Buddhist foundations of the Kushans, including monuments to Athsho, Farro, Mihr, and others, as well as the presence of a cult of Heracles, under the Kushans; Stavinskij 1986: 215–29; see Grenet 2006 for an interesting take on Iranian/Zoroastrian deities translated through the Indian iconographic tradition during the Kushan period and beyond.

Fig. 2.6. Gold reliquary casket of Kanishka, British Museum, with figures of the Buddha and of deities (© CC BY-SA 3.0; public domain; no alterations).

a coherent political unit and establish a central administration (Rosenfield 1967: 41–2). In his new capital of Purushapura, Kanishka built his famous stupa (Bivar 1983b: 204), which was visited by the Chinese traveller Faxian (Loeschner 2012b: 2–3). It was reputed to be the largest and most adorned of all Buddhist stupas[39] and it contained a casket, adorned with some of the earliest figures of the Buddha and possibly containing his relics, with a Kharoshti inscription which describes the casket as being a donation of *Maharaja Kaniśka* (Rosenfield 1967: 34–6). The period of Kanishka is also associated with the proliferation of so-called *Gandharan art*, whose greatest remains are Buddhist devotional statues, friezes, and reliefs. It was probably under Kanishka's rule as well that Buddhism first spread to the region of Paropamisdae and eventually to the north of the Hindu Kush, leaving remains in the area of Bactria and beyond.

In fact, the spread of Buddhism might also have to do with Kanishka's military campaigns in the Tarim Basin, as Chinese sources report (Bivar 1983b: 208–9; Pulleyblank 1968). These campaigns, taken to be at the easternmost extent of Kushan power, provided the Kushans with complete control of the trade routes of Central Asia and contributed to the increasing wealth of the kingdom. Kushan art, including the find of Gandharan-style frescoes in Miran, also indicates the spread of Mahayana Buddhism under Kushan protection, something that would eventually come to change the face of the region completely. It was also through this corridor of trade

---

[39] The exact attribution of the stupa of Kanishka is still a matter of dispute. See a summary and new ideas in Loeschner 2012b.

Fig. 2.7. Gold issue of Kanishka, showing the goddess Nana on the reverse (© CNG 362 Lot 247).

and communication that Buddhism in fact reached China, and it was through the same route that many Chinese Buddhist pilgrims reached India, describing on their way the magnificent cities and monuments of the Kushans (Rosenfield 1967: 37).

The wealth of Kanishka's empire also contributed to an increase in the issue of gold coinage (Rosenfield 1967: 54ff; Jongeward and Cribb 2015: 70–88). Continuing the use of a primary mint for his gold coinage, Kanishka apparently opened a second, subsidiary mint towards the end of his reign. This second mint produced half as much as the primary one (Bracey 2012: 119) but continued its operations under Kanishka's successors. The gold issues of Kanishka included a standing figure of the king himself, in the style of his father, Vima II Kadphises, with a Bactrian inscription on the obverse. The reverse of the coins, on the other hand, was devoted to many different gods, from both the Iranian and the Indian pantheons, such as Ardoxšo, Māh (the moon), Mazdooano, and even Greek divinities such as Herakles.

Certain rare coin issues of Kanishka also included an image surrounded by a Bactrian inscription *BOΔΔO* or Buddha, which has been used to argue for the growing importance of Buddhism in Kanishka's empire.

Kanishka was also the most prolific Kushan emperor in the production of inscriptions. One of his major inscriptions, found in the sanctuary of Surkh Kotal, was the initial introduction to Kushan history for modern historians. The Surkh Kotal inscriptions specified the function of the temple building itself as a religious sanctuary, as well as confirming the establishment of the Era of Kanishka as the official date-keeping calendar of the realm (Gershevitch 1979). In the Rabatak

Fig. 2.8. Silver tetradrachm of Kanishka, with the Buddha on the reverse (© CNG 314 Lot 227).

inscription, Kanishka, like Darius the Great before him, named the language in which he has composed the inscription originally, using a term similar to what Darius had used, *Aria-* (in that case used for Old Persian), which here is used to denote Bactrian (Sims-Williams 1996; 1998).[40] In the same inscription, he also recounts his conquests and demarcates his empire, claiming authority over most of India as far as Patalitputra and Ziritambo (Śri-Champa) in northern India (Sims-Williams 2004: 56). Significantly, Kanishka also clarifies his founding of an era based on the first year of his own reign, subsequently called the Era of Kanishka, which, as mentioned before, forms the most complicated aspect of Kushan history for modern scholarship.

Huvishka, either a son or a brother of Kanishka, succeeded him. Speculations about the co-existence of a king called Vasishka as the direct successor of Kanishka (see Bivar 1983b: 202–4) were earlier put forward. However, the existence of a die link between a late coin of Kanishka and that of Huvishka (Bactrian OHÞKI) proves that the latter succeeded Kanishka after he had ruled for twenty years (Bracey 2012: 120). The kinship between the two, however, cannot be ascertained, although from the previous pattern of rule, as well as Huvishka's relatively long rule (over thirty years),[41] we

---

[40] The fact that Kanishka had issued the edict initially in Greek (ιωναγγο) and then turned it into Aryan/Arian (αριαο) (Sims-Williams 1998: 81, line 3) bears further witness to the similarity with the Behistun inscription, the first versions of which were composed in Akkadian and Elamite, before being translated into Old Persian (Arian) (Schmitt 1999).

[41] This is based on the finds of Huvishka's inscriptions ranging from Wardak near Kabul to Mathura in northern India, dated between 28 and 60 of the Era of Kanishka: Stavinskij 1986: 38.

can speculate that he was a son of Kanishka. Huvishka continued to issue gold coins after his predecessor, expanding the variety of coin designs greatly and producing more gold coins than all other Kushan authorities combined (Jongeward and Cribb 2015: 89). These were mainly produced in Balkh, north of the Hindu Kush, and Purushapura/Peshawar to the south of the Hindu Kush in Gandhara, as well as smaller centres in Kashmir and Mathura (Jongeward and Cribb 2015: 89–90; Bracey 2012: 120). Importantly, his gold issues introduce a change to the obverse portrait of the king, where instead of a full standing figure, only the bust of the king above the waist is shown, wearing various crowns and always holding a small mace in his hand. The portrait can be oriented either to the left or to the right, with a variety of gods depicted on the reverse, along with Huvishka's royal *tamgha* (Jongeward and Cribb 2015: 90–3). The variety of both obverse and reverse design is much greater in his copper issues, however (Jongeward and Cribb 2015: 91–2) The large number of the issues of Huvishka's gold coins, as well as his prolific issue of copper coins, appear to suggest a prosperous empire with a profitable control of trade routes and inflow of wealth, something that is best depicted through the increase in production of art.

The archaeology of the Kushan realm has been greatly concerned with monuments and artistic pieces (Loeschner 2012) and less interested in evidence of urbanisation, rural life, or agriculture through land surveys and other archaeological methods.[42] Conjecturally, the prosperity of the Kushan realm also tells us about the increase in agricultural prosperity, probably as the result of improved access to water in an enhancement of agricultural methods (Staviskij 1986: 58–98). These are indeed the signs of true stability and prosperity in an empire of the pre-modern period, as we would expect.

Otherwise, the reign of Huvishka in general appears to have been mostly peaceful, spent in consolidating Kushan control over northern India and largely moving the centre of power to the southern capital of Mathura. This is more evident in the iconography of his coinage, which employs more Indian deities and icons, although in at least one coin series the Egyptian god Serapis (ΣΑΡΑΠΟ) is also

---

[42] For a discussion of Kushan archaeological sites and associated problems, see Staviskij 1986: 57–99, which is concerned of course only with Bactria. See also Stavinkij 1986: 101–10 for a brief discussion of urbanisation in Bactria, based on archaeological records. A series of archaeological reports by mostly Soviet archaeologists was published; however, these are mostly concerned with northern Afghanistan and Soviet Central Asia, with sporadic information for Gandhara: Gafurov et al. 1974; 1975. Kuwayama 2002 includes discussion of much updated information on Gandhara and the rest of northwestern India.

Fig. 2.9. Copper tetradrachm of Huvishka with the god *Oado* (Wind) (© CNG 323 Lot 188).

present, a unique appearance on Kushan coinage (Jongeward and Cribb 2015: 279).[43] Another significant development on the coins of Huvishka is the devaluation of the currency, causing the weight of his tetradrachms to fall quite low and leading to the issuance of many imitations and forgeries.

The successor to Huvishka was named Vasudeva I; the name might connect him to the cult of Krishna and the city of Mathura in particular (Jongward and Cribb 2015: 135).[44] Vasudeva can in fact be considered the last of the great Kushans, and he is also the last Kushan emperor to be mentioned in the Chinese sources, since his reign coincided with internal troubles in China and the withdrawal of the Chinese from Central Asia (Pulleyblank 1968: 258). Politically, Vasudeva's rule was centred more in northern India, although he continued to use one of the two primary mints of Huvishka in Balkh, while he probably had to contend with northern incursions into his territories. His coin issues follow the same style as Kanishka's, almost canonically featuring Oēšo, with Shiva and the bull, on the reverse and mostly following the weight standard of Vima Kadphises for gold and that of Huvishka for the copper issues (Jongeward and Cribb 2015: 135–7). The relatively peaceful period of Vasudeva's rule is also evidenced by the increased artistic production during it, including his monumental foundations and statues (Staviskij 1986: 242–6).

---

[43] The Kushans' interest in a variety of gods and cults can also be found, apart from the evidence of their coinage, in Kanishka's Rabatak inscription, where, apart from Nana, the gods *Umma*, *Aurmuzd* (Ahuramazda?), *Sroshard* (Srōš), *Narasa*, and *Mihir* (Mithras) are also mentioned and honoured (Sims-Williams 1998: 82, ll. 9–10). See also Grenet 2006 for the iconography.

[44] Although the Bactrian rendering of the name, βαζυδευο, might suggest a possible Iranian root as well.

The reign of Vasudeva I (c. 191–225)[45] probably coincided with the rise of the Sasanians in Western and Central Iran (c. AD 224) (Jongeward and Cribb 2015: 135). Ardashir I made early incursions into the eastern regions, including Marw and Sakistan, which would have brought him close to the Kushans. Vasudeva's successor, Kanishka II (c. 225–45),[46] was probably the Kushan emperor who lost the northern parts of the realm, namely Bactria/Tokharistan, to Shapur I (AD 240–72). As mentioned above, in his famous inscription in Naqsh-e Rostam (ŠKZ), Shapur counts the realm of the Kushans (MP *Kushan-shahr*) 'up to Purushapura' as part of his empire, indicating the loss of Kushan control in Bactria and possibly even south of the Hindu Kush. While the accuracy of this claim, particularly the claim of the control of Purushapura/Peshawar, is sometimes debated, certain coin issues (Errington and Curtis 2007: 71) and possibly the rock relief at Rag-i Bibi might be indications that Shapur I had indeed established his rule over Bactria at this period (Grenet et al. 2007).

From this point on, the Kushans lost control of Bactria/Tokharistan to a cadet branch of the Sasanian dynasty, commonly known as the Kushano-Sasanians.[47] They ruled the region of Bactria, as far as Kapiśa and Kandahar in the south, for a hundred years, until the advent of the Iranian Huns in the second half of the fourth century (Jongeward and Cribb 2015: 179–220). Nonetheless, Kanishka II may have had some successes in re-establishing his rule over parts of Gandhara and possibly Kapiśa, an event which allowed him to establish a second Era of Kanishka on the hundredth anniversary of the original one (Bivar 2009). He also prominently featured *Ardoxšo* sitting on a throne on the reverse of his coins, essentially starting what some numismatists consider a new coin series (Zeimal 1983: 223).

The fate of the Kushan emperors after Kanishka II becomes garbled and less known. Confined to northern India and increasingly subject to the Gupta emperors, the later Kushans are known from inscriptions as well as their coins, which essentially continued to be

---

[45] This is based on finds of inscriptions, including those dated to 64 (or 67) to 98 of the Era of Kanishka (Staviskij 1986: 39). However, now see Jongeward and Cribb 2015: 4, who suggest dates of AD 190–230 for Vasudeva I. Of course, despite popular acceptance, we should keep in mind that the date of the Era of Kanishka is still a speculative matter, and historical conclusions based on it, including the narrative presented here, should be treated with all due care; see Falk 2001 and, contra, Schindel 2009; 2012.

[46] Evgeny Zeimal, however, disagrees with the succession of Kanishka II to Vasudeva, suggesting that the two were contemporaneous and ruled in different parts of the Kushan Empire as successors of Huvishka. His identification of these co-ruling kings is based on observations made on their coinage: Zeimal 1983: 225f. A similar suggestion was made by Göbl 1984.

[47] See the next chapter for a discussion of Kushano-Sasanian rule.

Fig. 2.10. Gold coin of Kanishka II, in the style of Vasudeva, with Oēšo on the reverse (© CNG 347 Lot 311).

minted in the same style as those of the Great Kushans (Jongeward and Cribb 2015: 164–80; Dani 1996: 169).

Kanishka II was followed by a successor named Vasishka who is known through four inscriptions, including a Kharoshti inscription in the Indus region, which establishes the extent of his rule in that region (Lüders 1961: 125–6). His coinage, increasingly minted on small flans and devalued, continues the canonical system established under Huvishka and Vasudeva I (Jongeward and Cribb 2015: 164–7). His successor, Kanishka III, is most famous for using the title *Kaisar* (Caesar) on his coins, displaying an awareness of Roman power and probably declaring some sort of alliance with that power (Jongeward and Cribb 2015: 169). Kanishka III was probably a son of Vasishka, if we assume that the inscription dated to the year 41 mentioning a 'Kanishka son of Vasiskha' refers to him.[48] By this time, Kushan coins were becoming smaller, the flans now visibly less than the die size and thus causing some of the legends to be missing from the margins. In this way, there are sometimes only the reverse, Kharoshti inscriptions that make it possible for us to identify the authority. Thus we can only speculate that a Vasudeva II[49] might have followed Kanishka III.

---

[48] Staviskij 1986: 36; writing before the discovery of the Rabatak inscription, Staviskij considered this to be an inscription of Kanishka I. The date 41 here is to be interpreted as a 'refounding' of the Era of Kanishka under Kanishka II, as argued by Falk 2001.

[49] As mentioned, Zeimal suggests that there was only one king named Vasudeva and that he was the one who succeeded Huvishka together with Kanishka II and made the image of Shiva and Nandi on the reverse of his coins canonical: Zeimal 1983: 233. The significance of this suggestion is that it might help us in establishing the regions that came under the control of the later, or what Dani calls 'Eastern', Kushans. Vasudeva's Shiva-and-Nandi type become the model for the later Kushano-Sasanian issues (Dani 1996: 169), thus leading us to believe

Fig. 2.11. Gold issue of Vasudeva II; note the changing facial features (© CNG 334 Lot 211).

The last Kushan rulers, known mainly through their coinage, are known under the names Mahi, Shaka, and Kipunandha (Jongeward and Cribb 2015: 174–8). These rulers acted mainly as local authorities in the Taxila region, under the overall suzerainty of the Gupta emperors, while maintaining the coinage style of the Great Kushans in greatly reduced values. As far as East Iran is concerned, Kushan rule essentially ceased to exist following the death of Kanishka II, in effect being reduced to local rule in northern India, already dominated by the Gupta emperor Samudragupta (Dani 1996: 169). The later Kushan king Kipunandha probably lost his independence directly to the Huna tribes who invaded northern India in the late fourth century (Errington and Curtis 2007: 71; Cribb 2010: 112–13). In Bactria/Tokharistan, however, the Kushans were succeeded by the Sasanians, and later the dynasty of the Kushanshahs, or the Kushano-Sasanians, who adopted many of the Kushan customs, including their gold coin series.

THE LEGACY OF THE KUSHANS

The Kushan Empire was the first power that managed to rule effectively on both sides of the Hindu Kush. Following in the footsteps of the Graeco-Bactrians and Indo-Sakas, the Kushan emperors Vima Takto and Vima II Kadphises crossed the Hindu Kush to conquer Paropamisdae (the Kabul Valley), Gandhara, Kashmir, and the rest of northern India. They extended cities such as Taxila and established

that Vasudeva's region of influence was further to the north, possibly consisting mainly of the Kushan 'homeland' of Tokharistan/Bactria.

their capital in Purushapura and later Mathura, while always keeping Balkh and Tokharistan as an important part of their empire. They had indeed given their tribal name of Tokhara to the region, and created long-lasting links between Tokharistan and the areas to the south of the Hindu Kush. By adopting Bactrian as their administrative language, they also initiated the rise of this language as one of the most prominent on both sides of the Hindu Kush, a language that was used for centuries before New Persian effectively replaced it in the early Islamic period. From India, they brought Buddhism into the Paropamisdae and Tokharistan, and helped create the Gandharan art form that spread all over their empire. They created an iconography, most significantly on their coins, that became one of the most influential forms of expressing royal power in their empire and among their successor states. By creating this world stretching from the Oxus to the Ganges, the Kushans created a coherent empire and started a geopolitical reshaping of these regions. In a sense, their unification of the northern and southern Hindu Kush was, then, the predecessor to the idea of East Iran and the forerunner of the powers who followed their paths for almost a thousand years, and crossed the Hindu Kush from Tokharistan to establish their control over northern India. The Kushans are thus the first cultural and political power that ruled over East Iran in this context.

3 The Kushano-Sasanians in East Iran

INTRODUCTION

'Kushano-Sasanian' is the name given by scholars to a dynasty of rulers who followed the Kushans in the area of Tokharistan, and eventually in Kabulistan and Gandhara. Its Sasanian connection is suggested through its use of imperial Sasanian names such as Ardashir, Wahram, and Pērōz, and some Sasanian titulature such as 'Great Kushan King'. In one case, the name Pērōz is used among the Kushano-Sasanians even before a Sasanian emperor uses it, and the title of *kay* was probably used by the Kushano-Sasanians before its adoption by the Sasanians under Yazdgerd II (AD 438–57). The Kushano-Sasanians called themselves by the name *Kushanshah* and its Bactrian equivalent, showing both continuity with the Kushan dynasty and also possibly the beginning of a geographical designation of the area of their control.[1] As a dynasty, they appear to have been a Sasanian cadet branch, possibly descendants of one of the Sasanian Kings of Kings, who founded an autonomous, and perhaps independent, dynasty ruling over the former Kushan territories in Bactria/Tokharistan. The history of the Kushano-Sasanians is known less through written sources, which are quite scarce, and more through material culture.[2] What can be said, on the other hand, is that despite their modern appellation

---

[1] For Islamic geographies, 'Kushan' is the name of the region of Transoxiana or parts of it. See for example Khurradādhbih 1967: 32, where he says 'the King of Mawara un-Nahr is called the Kushan Shah'.

[2] The most significant Kushano-Sasanian site, the *Delberjin Tepe*, excavated from 1970 to 1973, has been poorly published, mainly due to the unfortunate passing of its main excavator, Irina T. Kruglikova; see Kruglikova 1976.

and the assumptions behind it, we find little ground for classifying them as governors, or 'local viceroys', of the Sasanians over the Kushan territories, alongside other such viceroys as the *Mešanšah* or the *Sakanšah*.[3] The Kushano-Sasanians, in many senses, appear too significant to have been simply Sasanian governors, and may well reflect an early Sasanian continuation of the Arsacid imperial setting, acting as an allied, but autonomous, cadet branch of the Sasanian royal house.[4]

SASANIANS IN TOKHARISTAN

The beginning of the Sasanian presence in Bactria/Tokharistan and the early foundations of a Sasanian dynasty in the region are best observed through the famous inscription of Shapur I. In the ŠKZ, Shapur declares himself an authority over several lands, including the Kushan territories:

> An, maz]dēsn bay Šābuhr, šāhān šāh Ērān ud Anērān . . . Ērānšahr x^wadāy hēm ud dārēm šahr Pārs, Pahlaw . . . Hindestān, Kušānšahr tā frāz ō Paškābur[5] ud tā ō Kāš, Sugd ud Čāčestān. (ŠKZ 1–3)[6]

> I, the Mazda-worshipping lord, Shapur, king of kings of Iran and An-Iran . . . (I) am the Master of the Domain of Iran (*Ērānšahr*) and possess the territory of Persis, Parthian . . . Hindestan, the Domain of the Kushan up to the limits of Paškabur and up to Kash, Sughd, and Chachestan.[7]

Apart from the statement by Shapur himself, perhaps our strongest suggestion for the presence of Sasanian forces in Tokharistan at the time of Shapur I is the relief at Rag-i Bibi (Grenet et al. 2007). The relief, showing a Sasanian royal hunter, identified as Shapur I himself despite the missing head, is sitting on a galloping

---

[3] These titles, used for the Sasanian governors of various provinces and often conferred on royal princes appointed to these positions, can be found in the ŠKZ (Huyse 1999: ll. 18–19) and the constant references made to Wahram III as 'Sakan-shah' in the Paikuli inscription of Narseh (Humbach and Skjærvø 1978); against this view, see Errington and Curtis 2007: 82 and Alram 1986, among many others.

[4] The best parallel to draw for this might be the situation in Arshakuni Armenia, where the local ruling family of the Arsacids, despite kinship connections with the 'imperial' Arsacids and even occasionally their subservience to the latter, nonetheless acted independently of them and indeed survived their demise. In this sense, Armenia's position as a clearly separate realm from the Arsacid Empire allowed its independent existence. A similar situation makes most sense for the relationship between the early imperial Sasanian relations with the related, but practically independent, Kushano-Sasanians.

[5] Κουσην[ων] εθνη εως εμπροσθεν Πασκιβουρων in the Greek text of the inscription.

[6] Huyse 1999: 22–4.

[7] I have here provided a simplified text, edited to reflect only the regions which have been of interest to the current discussion.

horse, with attendants surrounding him. This relief was found near *Pul-i Khumri*, in the vicinity of the major Kushan temple of Surkh Kotal in eastern Tokharistan. It is stylistically very close to contemporary Sasanian reliefs from Persis, and in fact is reminiscent of the early Sasanian hunting and battle scenes at Naqsh-i Rostam (Herrmann and Howell 1977). While it might not prove Sasanian control extended as far as Peshawar, it certainly confirms the early Sasanian activities against the Kushans.[8]

The earliest coin issues of the Kushano-Sasanians follow the gold scyphate issues of Vasudeva I (AD c. 191–225) and Kanishka II (AD c. 225–45). An early anonymous issuer, possibly the Sasanian King of Kings, probably minted these coins before the first Sasanian *Kushanshah* was appointed. This first issuing authority mentioned on the coins is a certain *Ardasharo Koshano*, who may be called Ardashir 1[9] and is given the regnal dates of AD 230–45, contemporaneous with Kanishka II, who probably ruled only in the Gandhara region (Jongeward and Cribb 2015).[10] While Kushan-style gold scyphate dinars were being produced in Balkh, as was the practice under the Kushans, both silver and copper issues of Ardashir 1 were minted in Marw and then transported to Tokharistan for circulation (Schindel 2012: 67). Marw was the most important Sasanian administrative centre in the northeast corner of the empire and the Sasanians issued coins there from the time of Ardashir I (AD 224–41), the founder of the dynasty (Alram 2007).

---

[8] Errington and Curtis 2007: 82 use the evidence of the 'Sasanian Era' of Bactria (de Blois and Sims-Williams 2006), as reflected in the Bactrian Economic Documents (Sims-Williams 2007), as another reason to support the idea that the conquest of Kushanshahr started with Ardashir I (224–41). While I agree with the brilliant work of scholars such as de Blois and Sims-Williams, and Khan, I still have difficulty in understanding why the region of Bactria would have adopted, and faithfully maintained, a calendar based on the foundation of the Sasanian power in Persis, even after the latter's departure, when the Sasanians themselves never used such a calendar and it is not mentioned in any context (as I had previously objected in Rezakhani 2010a). I believe that while the calculations are correct and reliable, there has to be a historical reason for the start date of the Bactrian Era (henceforth BE) other than the beginning of the activities of the Sasanian founder in Persis. See Schindel 2011b for a similar view.

[9] Throughout this chapter, I use the very useful convention set by Göbl of designating Kushano-Sasanian rulers by Arabic numbers, instead of the Roman numerals commonly used for rulers. This is to distinguish them from those Sasanian kings with similar names. I prefer this method to that used by Errington and Curtis (Ardashir 'I') or that by Cribb (Ardashir I), which simply ignores the issue all together.

[10] The ŠKZ names several rulers called Ardashir, some of them ruling the areas near and around the Kushan heartland of Tokharistan (*Ardashir King of Marw* and *Ardashir King of the Saka*: ŠKZ 23). No 'Ardashir King of Kushanshahr' is named, but the proliferation of the name (many others, including a Bidakhsh and his son both bearing the name, are mentioned) should prevent anyone from presuming that the first Kushano-Sasanian authority might be identified with Ardashir I Pabagan himself.

Fig. 3.1. Sasanian relief at Rag-ī Bibi in northern Afghanistan (© François Ory).

Fig. 3.2. Copper drachm of Ardashir 1, Kushanshah, minted in Marw (© CNG 319, Lot 177).

The administration of the Kushanshahr by the Kushano-Sasanians[11] should be considered within the longer trajectory of Sasanian administrative philosophy and the move towards centralisation. It would be fair to suggest that the early Sasanian administration did not move too rapidly away from the Arsacid administration, initially adopting the same set-up of a federative empire in which petty kingdoms such as those of Mesene/Meshan, Sakistan, and others continued to be ruled by local administrators, often Sasanian princes, and under the overall control of the King of Kings. The process of centralisation was in fact a gradual one that could have scarcely been established at this early point. In this general trend, Kushano-Sasanian rule in East Iran was actually quite crucial. Considering the importance of the Kushan territories, and their already well-established administrative tradition and territorial cohesion, it was more prudent for the Sasanians to create a second power, similar to the 'Eastern Arsacid' Empire of the Indo-Parthians, and to allow it to exist independently of, but amicably with, the Sasanian Empire.[12] Among other things, the fact that the Kushano-Sasanians use the titles *kwš'n MLK'n MLK* 'the Kushan King of Kings' and οαζαρκο κορανο ραο 'the Great Kushan King' (Alram 1986: 319) is an indication of this autonomy or even independence. This becomes even more noteworthy if we consider that the Kushano-Sasanians, as most historians con-

[11] Harmatta 1969: 386–8 suggested that Sasanian 'prince-governors' were installed in Bactria following the campaigns of Ardashir I in the region. Nikitin calls them governor-*shahrabs*, using the Middle Persian title, although it is nowhere attested for the Kushano-Sasanians: Nikitin 1999: 261. But there were *shahrabs* ruling, at least in Balkh: Lerner and Sims-Williams 2011: AB 1.1, 100–1.

[12] A similar argument, which considers the numismatic evidence of the Kushano-Sasanians and the Sasanians and their iconography, is made by Schindel 2015b: 148–9.

ceive them, are seen as subordinate to the Sasanian MLK'n MLK' 'yr'n ud 'nyr'n 'King of Kings of Iran and Non-Iran'. This seems to suggest that Ardashir 1 (230–45),[13] the first issuing authority of the Kushano-Sasanian realms,[14] was also their founder.

As with Kushan history, the most intense scholarly debate concerning the Kushano-Sasanians is their absolute dating. The evidence of the ŠKZ is generally assumed to be a proof for the establishment of the Kushano-Sasanian rule in the former Kushan lands, or at least the start of the Sasanian presence in the region.[15] Careful studies of the Kushano-Sasanian coin issues and their links with the imperial Sasanian and later Kushan issues have led to some relative chronologies. But because of the lack of a firm date for the beginning of the Era of Kanishka, despite the widespread use of AD 127, it has been hard to create an absolute chronology for their Kushano-Sasanian successors as well.[16] Additionally, it has been challenging to establish the number, and occasionally the order, of the Kushano-Sasanian kings. This is mainly because scholars, associating these kings with the imperial Sasanians, have opted to use the individual crowns of each coin authority to recognise them and assign them ordinal numbers. This has also occasionally resulted in mention of three kings named Ardashir, as well as three Pērōzes and several Warahrams/Wahrams.[17] However, as Cribb has already pointed out, it is probably most prudent to consider that several Sasanian emperors also issued coins with different crowns, including Shapur I, and so we should not assign each different crown type to a new king (Cribb 1990: 153, n. 2).[18] Considering this

---

[13] This seems to be the date now suggested by Jongeward and Cribb 2015: 203–4. It should be kept in mind that the dates suggested by Cribb are not accepted by all experts; see Schindel 2012, whose dating of the Kushano-Sasanian series differs dramatically from that of Cribb.

[14] See Schindel 2014 for a discussion of the links between the coins of Ardashir 1 and those of possibly contemporary late Kushan kings.

[15] See Jongeward and Cribb 2015: 181–95 for coins assigned to the Kushano-Sasanians in imitation of Vasudeva I, as well as ibid.: 202 for coins of an unidentified king dated before Ardashir 1. This would suggest that the numismatists consider a period of direct rule by the Sasanians, or perhaps the presence of a Sasanian governor-generalship in the newly conquered Bactrian territories prior to the establishment of the Kushano-Sasanian dynasty and the issuing of the Ardashir 1 coins.

[16] See Schindel 2009 and 20014 for efforts to argue for a date other than 127 on the basis of links among the Kushan, Kushano-Sasanian, and Sasanian coins. Jongeward and Cribb 2015 appear to have settled on AD 127, on the basis of Cribb's earlier extensive arguments (see Cribb 1990; 1999; 2010; among others).

[17] For example, see Dani and Litvinsky 1996: 110–11, where two Ardashirs and two Vahrans (sic) are mentioned, and in a different order.

[18] Cribb 1990: 153, n. 2 suggests that 'the question of how many kings issued the Ardashir coins should still remain unresolved', although he suggests more recently that there was only one: Jongeward and Cribb 2015: 4.

fact, we can suggest the following order for the Kushano-Sasanian coin-issuing authorities.[19]

I   Ardashir 1[20]
II Pērōz 1
III Hormizd 1
IV Hormizd 2
V   Pērōz 2
VI Warahram/Wahram

In this scheme, the coins issued directly by the Sasanian Emperor Shapur II (309–79) and circulating in Gandhara and Begram/Kapiśa region are to be considered the final issues of the Kushano-Sasanian series (Jongeward and Cribb 2015: 224–6; Schindel 2011a). In the greater scheme of Sasanian centralisation, the end of the independent rule of the Kushano-Sasanians over Bactria and Gandhara should be considered part of the imperial Sasanians' policy of moving away from Arsacid-style administration. Instead, by doing away with petty and federated kingdoms and cadet branches like the Kushano-Sasanians, the imperial Sasanian court aimed to control its entire empire from a central administration, a move that later proved quite problematic for the court.

It is worth noting that the names of the Kushano-Sasanian kings closely resembled those of the Sasanian imperial rulers. The difference, perhaps, is that the name Pērōz (MP Pērōz 'victorious') appears in the Kushano-Sasanian line earlier than among the imperial Sasanian kings, namely in the third and the fourth century – that is, over 100 years before the reign of the Sasanian King of Kings, Pērōz (AD 459–84). The name, of course, has a common meaning, and it might have been used as an epithet for the kings according to the testimony of Ammianus Marcellinus from the siege of Amida in AD 359–60:

> Persis Saporem saansaan appellantibus et pirosen, quod rex regibus imperans et bellorum victor interpretatur.

---

[19] See also Errington and Curtis 2007: 82–5. Jongeward and Cribb 2015 suggest an anonymous issuing authority before Ardashir 1 (see also Cribb 1990: 155); they additionally consider Wahram a 'puppet' of the Kidarites, for which see the following chapter on the Huns and the Kidarites.

[20] Jongeward and Cribb 2015: 197 suggest a date range of AD 230–365 for the entire Kushano-Sasanian rule. This seems problematic since it puts the conquest of Kushanshahr under Ardashir I Pabagan, which appears unlikely. Perhaps the earliest rulers, Ardashir 1 and Pērōz 1, should be placed securely in the second half of the third century to accommodate a more realistic date for the conquest of Bactria.

the Persians called Sapor 'saansaan' and 'pirosen', which being interpreted is 'king of kings' and 'victor in wars'. (Amm. Marc. *Rer. Gest.* XIX.ii.11)[21]

Here Ammianus really over-translates *pirosen* as 'victor in wars', since it only means 'victorious'. However, considering that the whole episode involved the actions of the eastern armies of the Chionites, the Gelani, and the Sagistani,[22] there is a chance that the person so hailed by the troops was not Shapur II himself, but Pērōz 2, the Kushano-Sasanian monarch who had become an ally of Shapur II in his siege of Amida, much like the leaders of the other eastern tribes.[23]

The title *kdy/kay* is another whose appearance among the Kushano-Sasanians predates its use by the imperial Sasanian line and their Kayanid identity (Shayegan 2003). It is used prominently on imperial Sasanian coins starting only with Yazdgerd II (438–57).[24] However, in the Kushano-Sasanian series, Wahram issued coins with the legend *kdy wlhl'n kwš'n MLK'* 'Kay Warahran the Kushan King'.[25] So whether we date the Kushanshah Wahram to the latter half of the fourth century (Errington and Curtis 2007: 72, table 4) or put him in the first half of the same century (Jongeward and Cribb 2015: 221), this would mean that the use of the important title *Kay* in the Kushano-Sasanian line preceded that of the imperial Sasanian use by about 100 years.[26]

The earliest unnamed Kushanshah minted copper coins in Bactria/Tokharistan which show the goddess Anahita presenting the king with a diadem.[27] These coins are inscribed only in Pahlavi and mark the authority as the king of both Marw and the Kushans (Jongeward and Cribb 2015: 202). In the ŠKZ (line 23), the king of Marw during the reign of Shapur I is called Ardashir, but the legend on these

---

[21] All quotations from Ammianus in this and the next chapter are from J. C. Rolfe's translation and Loeb edition of 1956.
[22] See Chapter 4 on the Huns and the Kidarites for a full discussion of these passages.
[23] See Errington and Curtis 2007: 86–8 for a discussion of the use of the name/title *Pērōz*, which would be contrary to my suggestion above. Jongeward and Cribb's 2015: 197 dating of Pērōz 2 to before 330 seems highly unlikely,
[24] Daryaee 2009: 24, 34; 1995. See also Shayegan 2003 for a periodisation of Sasanian history based on the use of this title.
[25] Vondrovec 2014: 30; Göbl 1967: type 5–10; Mitchiner 1975c: 157–8, with many mistakes in reading the legend. I cannot see a reason, beside the assumption that the direction of borrowing is always from the hegemonic to the peripheral power, for Vondrovec's assumption (Vondrovec 2014: 45) that the appearance of the title of *Kay* on the coins of Kushanshah Wahram is an indication that he should be dated after Yazdgerd II (AD 438–57) and that this puts the whole series after AD 438. To me, it is quite clear that the later Sasanians were borrowing many cultural elements from the east, and this is only one indication of such borrowings.
[26] See Shayegan 2003 for a survey of the importance of the introduction of this title and its effect on Sasanian royal ideology.
[27] On the representation of Anahita on Kushano-Sasanian coins, see Shenkar 2014: 75–9.

copper issues cannot yet be read, and so we cannot be sure of the identity of this early king. As such, this earliest Kushanshah issue is iconographically and linguistically purely Sasanian, with little influence from the Kushan rulers of Bactria.

The first Kushanshah known by name, Ardashir 1, also issued copper coins, perhaps from the mint in Balkh (Jongeward and Cribb 2015: 203) or from Marw, the seat of Sasanian power in the northeast. Ardashir's coins show a clearer Kushan or at least Bactrian influence, since they carry Bactrian legends as well as Pahlavi ones. The obverse Bactrian legend of the coin of Ardashir reads APΔAÞOPO KOÞANO ÞAO 'Ardashir, the Kushan Shah'[28] (Jongeward and Cribb 2015: 203, coin 2142–3) and the reverse depicts the god Mithras (Bactrian *Miiro*, also depicted on Kushan coins). The Pahlavi legend on the obverse of some coins (Jongeward and Cribb 2015: 203–4, coins 2144–53) reads *mzdysn bgy arthštr RBA kwšan MLK'* 'The Mazda-worshipping lord Ardashir the Great Kushan Shah' (see also Alram 1986: 318). The reverse in turn depicts the goddess Anahita holding a diadem and a staff. These coins, issued mainly to the north of the Hindu Kush, have also been found to the south in the Begram/Kapiśa area alongside the issues of the Kushan king Vasishka, suggesting a period of competition between the Kushano-Sasanians and the Kushans in this region.

With the next Kushanshah, Pērōz 1, the Kushano-Sasanians start to issue gold coins in the style of the Great Kushan emperors (Jongeward and Cribb 2015: 205–9). The iconography of these coins is essentially the same as those of the Kushans, with certain modifications. The kings are depicted in full frontal view, although their dress and facial hair appear to owe more to the Sasanian iconography than the Kushan ones. Control marks such as swastikas and even Brahmi legends are also copied from the Kushan issues of Vasudeva and Vasishka. The reverse shows a god very similar to the Kushan Oēšo/Śiva, including the presence of the bull Nandi, although the Bactrian legends mark it BOPZAOANΔO IAZAΔO 'the Exalted God' (later also BAΓO BOPZOOANΔO 'the Exalted Lord' on copper units; Jongeward and Cribb 2015: 208). The obverse marks Pērōz as *the Great Kushan King*, similar to the title of Ardashir 1: ΠIPΩZO

---

[28] Jongeward and Cribb 2015: 203 read the legend as 'Lord Ardashir the great, Kushan Shah', thus suggesting that the adjective 'the great' refers to 'Ardashir' and not the 'Kushan Shah'. Considering the Pahlavi equivalent of the title, as well as the presence of similar titles such as 'the Great king of Armenia' in Sasanian inscriptions (ŠKZ 18), there is no reason to doubt that 'the great', even if it can be seen on the coin, refers to the 'Kushan Shah' and not the person of Ardashir 1.

Fig. 3.3. Gold dinar of Pērōz 1, with 'the Exalted God' on the reverse (© CNG Triton XIX Lot 2148).

OOZOPKO KOÞANO ÞAYO. In addition to gold and copper issues in Tokharistan (probably from the mint of Balkh), Pērōz also issued (a?) copper coin in Gandhara for circulation there and in Begram, and probably minted in Peshawar. It is perhaps at this stage that the Kushano-Sasanians started to displace the late Kushans from Gandhara, confining them to Mathura in north India, where they were reduced to local princes.

A great shift in Kushano-Sasanian authority occurs under the rule of Hormizd 1 (275–300). While his early gold issues from Balkh similarly call him 'Hormizd, the Great Kushan King', later issues of gold dinars from the same mint switch the king's title to ΩΥΡΟΜΟΖΔΟ OOZOPKO KOÞANO ÞAONONO ÞAO 'Hormizd, the Great Kushan King of Kings' (Jongeward and Cribb 2015: 211, type 2211). This is similarly reflected in the Pahlavi legend of his copper issues from Balkh, which read *'whrmzdy kwš'n MLK'n MLK'*[29] 'Hormizd the Kushan King of Kings' (Jongeward and Cribb 2015: 213, coin 2236). This change in the title of the Kushan king, now claiming the title of the King of Kings, as used previously by the Great Kushans, is a significant change in Kushano-Sasanian ideology and self-image, and perhaps a direct confrontation with the 'imperial' Sasanian line. The suggestion that the Sasanian prince *Ormis* rebelling against his brother Wahram II, referred to by *Panegyrici Latini* 2.17, is the same as this Hormizd 1 Kushanshah (Bivar 1979: 325–7) must now be dismissed. It is, nonetheless, safe to assume that during the time of Hormizd 1, the Kushano-Sasanians reached a new

---

[29] Throughout, I have altered Jongeward and Cribb's unconventional style of Pahlavi transliteration and normalised it by the common standard of MacKenzie 1971.

level of independence from the main Sasanian line. Perhaps to this period also belongs the episode of Mani, the famous 'prophet' of Manichaeism, who was killed in AD 276 by the Sasanian Emperor Wahram II (Sundermann 2009; Klima 1962). Upon his death, generally considered a victory for the Zoroastrianising priest Kerdir (Hinz 1971; Henning 1942), the followers of Mani fled the Sasanian territories, and a large group took refuge in Transoxiana and as far east as the Tarim Basin region (Andreas and Henning 1934). These communities of Manichaeans survived for several hundred years in the region, converting many of the local tribes to their creed, including the earliest rulers of the Uighur Empire, which followed the Western Turk period. Whether the falling out between the Manichaeans and the Sasanian emperors, such as Shapur I and Hormizd I, who initially supported them (Sundermann 1990; Sims-Williams 1990b) had any effects on Kushano-Sasanian relations with the Sasanians is unknown. However, no major presence of Manichaeans has been recognised in Tokharistan, the area of Kushano-Sasanian rule.

The briefly reigning Hormizd 2 (300–3) might perhaps be the same as Hormizd 1 with a different crown. This crown, famously bearing wings, is very similar to the crown of the Sasanian King of Kings Hormizd II (302–9), the father of the famed Shapur II. Apart from the wings, the Sasanian-style fire altar on the reverse of his coins, a feature since the coins of Hormizd 1, now shows a mixture with the Kushan style of depicting the god. In this new design, the fire altar has a bust emerging from among the flames (Jongeward and Cribb 2015: 217, coins 2338–40), a design that becomes quite common among the imperial Sasanian coins, perhaps borrowed from the Kushano-Sasanian coins (ibid.: 199; Shenkar 2014: 91). These features might

Fig. 3.4. Gold scyphate dinar of Hormizd 1, Kushan King of Kings (© CNG Triton XVIII, Lot 867).

suggest a connection between the Kushano-Sasanian and imperial Sasanian lines, and possibly the succession of Kushanshah Hormizd 2 to the imperial Sasanian throne as Hormizd II.

Pērōz 2 (303–30) continued the issue of the same type of coins as those of Hormizd 1 and Hormizd 2, with gold dinars and copper drachms issued from Bactria. To the south of the Hindu Kush in Gandhara, from the time of Hormizd 1, copper drachms had been issued in the name of the local governors Kavad and Mēzē, a tradition continued by Pērōz 2 (Jongeward and Cribb 2015: 220). The Bactrian and Pahlavi legends of the coins of Pērōz 2, however, only mark him as 'the Great Kushan King' and not the 'Kushan King of Kings', thus abandoning the claim made by his predecessors. Perhaps, with the succession of Hormizd 2 to the Sasanian throne as Hormizd II, who might have indeed himself been the initiator of the claim to *King of Kings*-ship, the need for competition with the imperial line was removed, and the Kushan kings resorted to their original positions as the Kushanshahs.

Warahran (330–65) was perhaps the last Kushanshah in Bactria. Jongeward and Cribb have recently suggested that he only issued coins in Bactria/Tokharistan, while Shapur II was concurrently issuing coins in the name of the satraps Mēzē and Kavad, and later his own name, in Gandhara (Jongeward and Cribb 2015: 198). However, earlier coins assigned to Kidara[30] had earlier been speculated to belong to Warahran, with the title *Kay* Warahran (Grenet 2002b: 205). It is, however, easy to see that Warahran's grip over the Kushano-Sasanian territories on both sides of the Hindu Kush was greatly threatened, and it was not long before his realm and power fell to the incoming Kidarites and the expanding reach of Sasanian central power. The control of Gandhara by Shapur II, known through the issue of his copper denomination there, appears to be a side effect of the increased Sasanian interest in the east. Al-Tabari reports that Shapur made many cities in Sajistan (Sakistan) and Sind (Sindh), and brought to his capital a doctor from India whose knowledge was later spread throughout the Sasanian realm (al-Tabari I.845).[31]

The visual influence of the east, particularly Kushano-Sasanian ico-

---

[30] See Chapter 4 on the Huns and the Kidarites.
[31] Bosworth, in his translation of al-Tabari (1999: 65, note 179), doubts this statement, considering that Sijistan was a frontier province 'disputed with the Sakas and their epigoni' and that the Indian province of Sind was under local Brahman rulers. However, one can now dismiss Bosworth's scepticism by considering the history of the Kushano-Sasanians and the involvement of Shapur in the affairs of Gandhara and perhaps neighbouring Sind, as well as the much less 'frontier' province of Sakistan.

nography, on imperial Sasanian iconography and artistic tradition is of much interest for the history of Sasanian relations with East Iran.[32] The proliferation of the imagery of the god Mithras, particularly in the famous Shapur II relief of Taq-i Bostan (Canepa 2009: 109), has been among the most notable examples of this artistic influence.[33] The relationship, and possible influences, including those on the continuity of the Sasanian imperial line, can only be speculated about via tangential information and creative scholarly guesswork.

In its own East Iranian context, the Kushano-Sasanian period has left some archaeological evidence that has been unveiled, although sometimes poorly published, in the past few decades. Surveys and excavations show sites in Begram, Taxila, and Dalverzin Tepe that appear to be involved in long-distance trade (Dani and Litvinsly 1999: 112). Begram, a site possibly sacked by Shapur I, also includes both Buddhist and so-called Zoroastrian sites, in the form of monuments of a 'fire cult' (Dani and Litvinsky 1996: 114). The impressive site of Kara Tepe near Termez shows the continuity of Buddhist architecture (Stavisky 1984: 95–135), including an impressive mural of a Buddha, which might show Iranian influences (Stavisky 1980: 91).

Dalverzin Tepe in the Surkhan Darya region was a large urban site under the Kushans that continued to exist under the Kushano-Sasanians, although with less intensity (Dani and Litvinsky 1996: 116; Pugachenkova and Rtveldze 1978). A site in the same region known as Zar Tepe was also Kushan, but was largely neglected after the Kushan period, and many similar Kushan-period sites in the neighbouring Qobadian region continued to exist during the Kushano-Sasanian period, although all of them show signs of decline and less intense urban settlement (Dyakonov 1953). South of the Hindu Kush, the famous Tepe Maranjan Buddhist monastery site included several Kushano-Sasanian coins, namely those of Wahram (Grenet 2002b: 206; Cribb 2010: 92–3, 98–100). The famous, and well-excavated, site of Delberjin Tepe in Qobadian includes impressive Kushano-Sasanian wall-paintings and full sculptures of the Kushano-Sasanian kings, but, as menioned earlier in this chapter, it has sadly not been published properly, thus not allowing us to consider a Kushano-Sasanian site that shows signs of prosperity (Kruglikova 1976). It seems undeniable, however, that the Kushano-Sasanians developed their own particular style in art and architecture, drawn from sources

---

[32] For an extensive discussion of various aspects of this, see now Shenkar 2014: esp. ch. 3 (47–174).
[33] Azarpay 1982; Shahbazi 1985: 184–5; Carter 1981: 74–97.

other than Iran, which included India, and formed an independent identity from the Sasanians (Nikitin 1999: 261–2). However, some scholars observe certain close stylistic similarities, possibly in silverwork, between the Sasanian and Kushano-Sasanian courts, and assign some of the famous Sasanian silverwork to East Iranian masters of the Kushanshah court (Trever and Lukonin 1987: 61–73).

The presence of Kushano-Sasanian sites, as well as coin finds, on both sides of the Hindu Kush (Cribb 2010) shows that, like the Kushans before them, the Kushano-Sasanians eventually extended their influence into the Kabul Valley and further east to Gandhara. Kushanshahs Hormizd 2, Pērōz 2, and Wahram issued coins in Gandhara, probably Taxila, and established their rule in the region. But the Kushano-Sasanian period came to an end in Tokharistan sometime around the middle of the fourth century AD, and in Gandhara perhaps shortly after. This might have been the result of Hun/Chionite invasions from the steppe, forcing Shapur II to meet the invaders directly in order to protect the eastern borders of his empire (see next chapter). We know that following the issues of Wahram in Gandhara, Shapur II himself issued coins in the same region, showing a higher standard and including an all-Pahlavi legend (Cribb 1990: 178). He had previously overstruck the Kushano-Sasanian copper issues of Hormizd 2, in the name of the satraps *Mēzē* (Cribb 1990: 154) and *Kobad/Kavad* (Errington and Curtis 2007: 84). The Kushano-Sasanian coin series in Tokharistan and Gandhara continued with issues by Kidara and a certain Pērōz (previously called Pērōz 3; Cribb 1990: 154), the first Kidarite authorities.

Following the Hun/Chionite invasions and the destruction of Kushano-Sasanian rule in East Iran, Shapur II reorganised Sasanian control of what remained in the east. Instead of relying on the independent actions of local dynasts acting as marcher lords, a continuation of the Arsacid system, Shapur established direct Sasanian control over the east. The result of his treaties with the invading Huns – allowing them to join the Sasanian troops and treating them as allies – was a new system of governance in the Sasanian Empire, as well as a deeper involvement in the affairs of East Iran.

THE LEGACY OF THE KUSHANSHAHS

The Kushano-Sasanian period is one vaguely known in the history of East Iran. As a Sasanian cadet branch replacing the Kushans in Tokharistan/Bactria, they followed both Kushan and Sasanian styles in their artistic expression, particularly their coinage. However, they appear to have formed their own independent style, mostly influenced by established local artistic, architectural, and cultural elements. Their presence in the Kabul Valley area and Gandhara is a controversial matter, but depending on how we understand the coinage of Wahram, their last king, they may have followed the pattern established by the Kushans in crossing the Hindu Kush and controlling the southern slopes of the range as well. Despite their descent from the Sasanians, they display an independent character, indeed sometimes in direct challenge to the Sasanians through the use of terms such as 'Kushan King of Kings'. Furthermore, as a cadet branch, they appear to have initiated some of the ideologies of kingship that were adopted by the imperial Sasanian line later, particularly the use of the title *kay*, an Avestan title signifying kingship. It is quite likely that during the reign of Shapur II (AD 309–79), the Kushano-Sasanians acted as Sasanian marcher lords against the Hun/Chionite tribes invading East Iran. Perhaps it was because of this invasion that the imperial Sasanians, in the person of Shapur II, had to get involved in the affairs of the east in order to halt the invading Huns, thus putting an end to the rule of the Kushano-Sasanians there.

4 The Iranian Huns and the Kidarites

INTRODUCTION

The fall of the Kushano-Sasanians probably came as the result of nomadic invasions from the steppe and the imperial Sasanian response to this invasion. Characterised by the Chinese sources as an invasion of the *Xiongnu*, these nomads were called the Chionites by the Byzantine sources, possibly under the influence of Middle Persian *Xyōn*. Upon conquering Tokharistan from the Kushano-Sasanians, these Iranian Huns – as scholars call them – fought against and eventually allied themselves with the Sasanians. Their political power, taking advantage of the power vacuum left after the demise of the Kushano-Sasanians, was manifested in the foundation of the Kidarite Kingdom. Following the pattern established by the Kushans, these Kidarites also passed the Hindu Kush and conquered Gandhara. Like the Kushans, and the Kushano-Sasanians, they considered themselves to be the *kings of the Kushan* and issued coins that showed Kushan and Sasanian influences. Their century or so of power, from the late fourth to late fifth centuries, was a continuation of the order established by the Kushans.

ARRIVAL OF THE CHIONITES

The general invasion of nomadic tribes that came to overwhelm East Iran starting in the fourth century is attributed to tribal confederations originating from the Central Asian steppe. As usual, conflicting evidence about their origin, as well as their tribal designations, is given by the Chinese and non-Chinese sources. A prominent question concerns the circumstances of the invasion of

East Iran by these tribes – the Chionites, Kidarites, Alkhans, and Hephthalites. Scholarly opinion differs as whether we are to consider them part of the same wave of invasions or whether the rise of each tribe to political power should be considered a new wave of movement from the steppe to Sogdiana and Tokharistan. From Chinese sources, it appears that different waves of invaders came via the same route, crossing the Syr Darya into Transoxiana, then invading Bactria/Tokharistan, and eventually crossing the Hindu Kush into the Kabul Valley and ultimately Gandhara. This is the opinion offered by Frantz Grenet, who suggests that 'the Kidarites represent the first wave of invaders in Bactria and Northwest India (in the latter half of the 4th century). They are identified with the Chionites [i.e. *Xiongnu*]' (Grenet 2002b: 206). A much-quoted and widely accepted view, that of a single wave of invasions, states that: 'all these dynasties and ethnic groups were part of a single episode of massive migration in about 350–360' (de la Vaissière 2012: 122). This suggests a distinct wave of invasion into East Iran by the tribal confederacy called the *Xiongnu*. It was out of this single wave that all subsequent groupings known as the Kidarites, Hephthalites, and Alkhans came to existence.

Consequently, the identification of this single massive wave of invasion becomes crucial for the study of the history of this period and for making sense of all the different names used in Chinese, Iranian, Indian, Islamic, Armenian, and Roman sources to describe the invaders. The name most associated with this group, and one that has created the speculation that they are related to the Huns of Europe, is Chionites (*Chionitae*; Amm. Marc. *Rer. Gest.* XVI.ix.4). The term might be related to the Iranian term *Xyōn*, and parallel Sogdian *xwn*, which in Avestan terms was used to describe the arch-enemies of the king, *Kay* Wishtaspa, who supported Zarathushtra and spread his religion.[1] Chinese sources refer to tribal groupings of Yüeh-zhi, themselves divided into Da Yüeh-zhi ('Great Yüeh-zhi') and the Xiao (or 'Lesser') Yüeh-zhi, as well as the Xiongnu, often identified as the aggressors who put the Yüeh-zhi to flight.[2] *Wei Shu*, the source which first talks about these invading tribes, names the *Ruanruan* (Juanjuan) as the aggressors who forced the Da Yüeh-zhi

---

[1] For the occurrence of various terms connecting Chionites to Iranian and Indian renditions of the name, see Bailey 1985: 25–40; Cereti 2010 presents a comprehensive study of the Avestan term *xiiona* and related Middle Persian terms.

[2] See Maenchen-Helfen 1973 for an archaeological view of the matter of relations between the Xiungnu and the 'Huns'; see Atwood 2012 for a study of the possible linguistic connections between the two.

to move westwards and set up their capital in *Po-lo Si* (the city of Boluo) (Enoki 1998: 60).

Whether related to the *Chionite/Xyōn* or not, the *Huns*, or the *Iranian Huns* (*Iranische Hunnen*), is the name used most commonly for these invading tribes, and appears to be the preferred name used by modern historians to refer to their general grouping.[3] In time, however, a distinction between different groups seems to have emerged in the works of modern scholars, setting apart the known Hunnic groups from the later dynastic or tribal entities such as the Hephthalites and the Alkhans. In this chapter, the first wave of Hun/Chionite invasions and the rise of the dynasty of Kidara will be discussed.

CHIONITES IN EAST IRAN

The troubles caused by a general nomadic invasion of East Iran are known from the middle of the rule of Shapur II. However, since we are ill-informed about the terminal Kushano-Sasanian period in the east, it is next to impossible to date exactly, or even give the precise nature of, the Hunnic/Chionite invasion. Numismatists, following the arguments of Robert Göbl (Göbl 1967: II, 34–6), themselves based on readings from the *Tepe Maranjān* coin hoard, consider the invasions to have taken place sometime in the middle of the fourth century AD. This is close to AD 357, when Ammianus Marcellinus reports the troubles faced by the Sasanian Emperor Shapur II:

> Saporem in extremis regni limitibus suorum sanguine fuso multiplici aegre propulsare gentes infestas ... Constantius inplicatus pacem postulat precativam. Dumque AD Chionitas et Eusenos haec scripta mittuntur, in quorum confiniis agebat hiemem Sapor, tempus interstitit longum.
>
> Sapor, on the remotest frontiers of his realm, was with difficulty and with great bloodshed of his troops driving back hostile tribesmen ... Constantius, being involved in very serious wars, entreated and begged for peace, but while these communications were being sent to the Chionitae and Euseni, in whose territories Sapor was passing the winter, a long time elapsed. (Amm. Marc. *Rer. Gest.* XVI.ix. 3–4)

Shapur, then, was most involved in the affairs of the east, trying to ward off invasions from different tribes, one of which receives the designation 'Chionitae' from Ammianus, while the other, *Euseni*, remains unknown.[4] On the basis of the previous patterns of invasion,

---

[3] Robert Göbl first used the name, as *Iranische Hunnen*, in his 1967 monumental and fundamental study of the coins of these tribes.

[4] Marquart's statement that '16, 9, 4 ist sicher *Euseni* für *Cuseni* herzustellen' (Marquart 1901: 36, n. 5), assuming that it refers to the Kushans, is too speculative, although worth consid-

particularly that of the Yüeh-zhi, we can speculate that the first wave of invasion targeted the area north of the Oxus and that the invaders initially overwhelmed eastern Sogdiana and the Badakhshan Valley, east of the Iron Gates, before crossing the Oxus and moving southwest towards Termez and Balkh, into Tokharistan. This is probably also the moment when Shapur II made a peace treaty with at least some clans of these invaders:

> Datiano et Cereali consulibus cum universa per Gallias studio cautiore disponerentur formidoque praeteritorum barbaricos hebetaret excursus, rex Persarum in confiniis agens adhuc gentium extimarum, iamque cum *Chionitis* et *Gelanis* omnium acerrimis bellatoribus ...
>
> In the consulship of Datianus and Cerealis (AD 358), while all provisions in Gaul were being made with very careful endeavour, and dismay due to past losses halted the raids of the savages, the king of Persia was still encamped in the confines of the frontier tribes; and having now made a treaty of alliance with the *Chionitae* and *Gelani*, the fiercest warriors of all ... (Amm. Marc. Rer. Gest. XVII.v.1)

The nature of the treaty is not clear, and we know even less about the Gelani, whose name is mentioned here for the first time, with a rather flattering attribute.[5] However, it appears that the treaty between the Sasanian king and the eastern invaders, as well as other allied eastern forces, was quite successful. Shapur, having secured his eastern border, turned his attention to the west. Less than two years after the above-mentioned treaty, Shapur put the frontier city of Amida under siege, this time with the help of his eastern allies:

> Persae omnes murorum ambitus obsidebant. Pars, quae orientem spectabat, Chionitis evenit qua funestus nobis ceciderat adulescens ... *Meridiano* lateri sunt destinati, tractum servabant septentrionis AlbanI, occidentali portae oppositi sunt *Segestani*, acerrimi omnium bellatores
>
> The Persians beset the whole circuit of the walls. The part which faced the east fell to the lot of the Chionitae, the place where the youth so fatal to us was slain ... The Gelani[6] were assigned to the southern side, the Albani

---

ering. If *Euseni* is somehow a reference to the Kushans, we could interpret this as either signifying the Kushano-Sasanians or an early reference to the Kidarites (see Jongeward and Cribb 2015). In the former case, it shows both the independence of the Kushano-Sasanians from the *imperial* Sasanians, and their possible co-operation with the incoming Chionites against their more powerful kinsmen. In the latter case, we could see in the *Euseni* an early reference to the Kidarites, something that matches the Kidarite coin legends designating them as the Kushan-shahs. This is corroborated by the Armenian historian, Pawstos Buzand (1989: V.vii.210–11), who seems to use the word Kʻušan exclusively to refer to the Kidarites (Zeimal 1999: 122).

[5] I cannot take seriously the suggestion that the *Gelani* are the ones who gave their name to the province of *Gīlān*, the southwestern corner of the Caspian Sea (Felix 1991). The designation for the province does not really appear earlier than the ninth century AD.

[6] The Latin text's *Meridiano* could be the *Mardi* of Pliny (6.18.47) or the *Mardyeni* of Sogdiana (Ptolemy 6.12.4). Here, the translator has chosen to consider them the same as

guarded the quarter to the north, and to the western gate were opposed the Segestani,[7] the bravest warriors of all. (Amm. Marc. *Rer. Gest.* XIX.ii.3)

Here, the selection of the allies is more varied and includes not only the Chionites, but also the Albani, allies from the Caucasus, as well as the Mardians, and most interestingly the Segestani. The last are no doubt the troops from Sakistan/Sistan, the centre of former Indo-Parthian power, who had been under Sasanian rule since the time of Ardashir I. The last mention of Sakistan in the Sasanian records prior to this would have been Narseh's *Paikuli* inscription, where his opponent Wahram (III) is called 'the King of the Sakas' (Humbach and Skjærvø 1978). This passage is, then, a confirmation that until AD 360 at least, the population of Sistan were considered a distinctive group providing a separate contingent in the Sasanian army. The passage is also interesting for the fact that it clarifies the divisions of the army, and the tribes and regions they belonged to, showing that Ammianus had a clear idea of who the Chionites were among the various tribes. The involvement of the Chionites in the siege of Amida goes beyond simple extras in Shapur's war against Rome. In fact, one character, identified as the 'king of the Chionitae', becomes the focus of a rather dramatic episode during the siege:

> Ideoque cum prima lux advenisset, rex Chionitarum Grumbates fidenter suam operam navaturus tendebat AD moenia cum manu promptissima stipatorum, quem ubi venientem iam telo forte contiguum contemplator peritissimus advertisset, contorta ballista filium eius primae pubis adulescentem lateri paterno haerentem thorace cum pectore perforato perfodit proceritate et decore corporis aequalibus antestantem.
>
> And so, at the first dawn of day, Grumbates, king of the Chionitae, wishing to render courageous service to his lord, boldly advanced to the walls with a band of active attendants; but a skilful observer caught sight of him as soon as he chanced to come within range of his weapon, and discharging a ballista, pierced both cuirass and breast of Grumbates' son, a youth just come to manhood, who was riding at his father's side and was conspicuous among his companions for his height and his handsome person. (Amm. Marc. *Rer. Gest.* XIX.i.7)

The tragic death of the son of the Chionite king then indeed becomes an important motivation for the increased Chionite involvement in

---

the Gelani, probably because of the later association with the Amardi on the southwestern Caspian coast (Strabo 11.8.8) and the assumption that the Gelani are the namesakes of Gīlān. I have preserved the translator's version, but believe that the group mentioned should be associated with the Mardi/Mardyeni of Sogdiana, as mentioned by Ptolemy and Pliny.

[7] For the Segestani, the people of the Sasanian province of Sakistan/Sistan, see Chapter 1 on the Indo-Parthians.

the war. Grumbates, the king of the Chionites, after burning the body of his son and putting the ashes in a silver urn ('Post incensum corpus ossaque in argenteam urnam conlecta'; Amm. Marc. *Rer. Gest.* XIX.ii.1), set out with his men to burn the city down, to avenge the departed prince. The standstill caused by the siege came to a bloody battle, in fact, on what seems to be the initiative of Grumbates himself:

> Vixque ubi Grumbates hastam infectam sanguine ritu patrio nostrique more coniecerat fetialis, armis exercitus concrepans involat muros.
>
> And hardly had Grumbates hurled a bloodstained spear, following the usage of his country and the custom of our fetial priest, than the army with clashing weapons flew to the walls. (Amm. Marc. *Rer. Gest.* XIX.ii.6)

This episode, on the other hand, takes place in particular isolation, as we do not know anything about the origins of Grumbates, the nature of his 'kingship' over the Chionites, or the extent of the territory he controlled. Nothing more is known about this grouping of the Chionites and the rest of the 'Iranian Huns', apart from the conclusions made from the name of Grumbates and the occurrence of the same name, in the form *Gurambād* (γοραμβαδο), in the

Fig. 4.1. Victory relief of Shapur II over Julian the Apostate (© Author).

Bactrian Documents of Rōb.[8] The survival of the name would show the continued popularity of at least part of the Chionite culture in East Iran, although it does not help in clarification of the history of the Chionites in the region. In fact, there would be no reason to believe that this first wave of Chionite/Huns were different, tribally or otherwise, from the first 'Hunnic' dynasty that came to control East Iran.

THE KIDARITES

Classical sources from the Roman world tell us of the existence of a particular group of the Huns/Chionites, known under the name of Kidarites. A notice from Priscus around AD 456 talks about Yazdgerd II asking the Roman Emperor Marcian (AD 450–7) for help against 'Huns known as Kidarites' (Priscus, fr. 33, *Exc. de Leg. Rom,*; Blockley 1983: 337). These 'Huns' are most probably the same as those earlier called the *K'ušan* by Pawstos Buzand:

> Now when the war broke out between the king of the K'ušan and the King of Persia, the K'ušan army pressed the Persian forces exceedingly. It killed many of them, took many prisoners, and drove part of them to flight ... the K'ušan routed Šapuh. (Pawstos Buzand 1989: V.vii.210–11)

In fact, another Armenian historian,Ełiše, when talking about the same Yazdgerd II, mentions that he invaded 'Italakan where the king of the Kushan lived' in AD 451 (Ełiše 1982: 18). As scholars have remarked, the name 'Kushans' was commonly used to refer to the rulers of East Iran, those ruling over the former Kushan territories (Frye 1983: 146), and specifically used by the Armenians to refer to the lands of the Kidarites (Zeimal 1999: 126).

Chinese sources in turn talk about the same political entity as the Armenian Kushans, but conflate them with the usual grouping of this population under the rubric of the *Da* ('Greater') *Yüeh-zhi*. In these sources (e.g. *Bei Shi*), a specific name is also assigned to the ruler of this dynasty, namely Jiduoluo, and interpreted as the Chinese transcription of Ki-da-ra (Kuwayama 2002: 128). *The Annals of the Wei Dynasty* (*Wei Shu*) provides the following information about the Kidarites:

> The king of the Great Yüeh-zhi called Jiduoluo, brave and fiercely, eventually dispatched his troops southwards and invaded Bei Tianzhu (northern

---

[8] Sims-Williams 1997b: 13; doc. 14. See also Sims-Williams 2010: 56; 119 for a detail of the occurrences of the name in the Bactrian Documents, as well as its possible Iranian, although non-Bactrian, etymology.

India?), crossing the great mountains to subjugate the five kingdoms which were located to the north of Gandhāra. (trans. Kuwayama 2002: 124)

The same source further tells us that the king of the Xiao (Lesser) Yüeh-zhi, determined by scholars to be in the area of Gandhara, is the son of the king of the Da (Greater) Yüeh-zhi. Previous scholars have noticed the similarity between this narrative of the rise of the Kidarites/Da Yüeh-zhi and those provided in much earlier sources (i.e. *Hou Han Shu*) for the rise of the original Da Yüeh-zhi tribe. These were the tribe who, hundreds of years earlier, had migrated westwards into Transoxiana and Bactria as the result of the onslaught of the Xiong-nu tribe under the leadership of Maodun (see Chapter 2 on the Kushans). Errington and Curtis (2007 86) suggest that the *Wei Shu* is 'echoing' the *Hou Han Shu* accounts of the rise of the Yüeh-zhi when talking about the rise of the Kidarites, because of the similarity of the Kidarites to the earlier Kushans. In fact, many conclusions about the origins of the Kidarites have been based on the Chinese historical sources which provide the above account of their rise, or the account understood to refer to their rise.

It is, however, more prudent to consider the literary nature of the Chinese historical accounts and their tendency to follow patterns established by earlier historians and to repeat similar information. Here, we can identify cases of similarity between those accounts relating to the earlier Yüeh-zhi (thus the Kushans) and the later Kidarites. As mentioned before, while talking about the Yüeh-zhi and the Kushan, the *Shiji* tells us that the Xiungnu attacked and drove the Yüeh-zhi to the west (*Shiji* 110.7a). The *Han Shu* (96a–14b) then provides information that the five *yabghu*s of the Yüeh-zhi were eventually subdued by Qiujiuque, the great prince of the Guishuang (*Hou Han Shu*, 128.9).

In turn, the *Wei Shu*'s acoount of the rise of the Kidarites is remarkably similar to the composite account of these earlier sources on the rise of the Kushans, to the extent that the *Bei Shi* also uses Guishuang (Kushan?) to refer to the tribe of Jiduoluo (Kidara).[9] The presence of five as the number of the countries 'north' of Gandhara also exactly matches the description of the five *yabghu*s of the Da Yüeh-zhi as described in the *Han Shu*, and speculated by Kazuo

---

[9] Kuwayama 2002: 128 reads *Jichang* as the Chinese name of the dynasty, amended to *Guishang* (Kushan) in Errington and Curtis 2007: 85, thus much closer to the designation given by *Hou Han Shu* to the dominant *yabghu* of the Yüeh-zhi when describing the rise of the Kushans.

Enoki to be in fact divisions of Daxia (Bactria) rather than tribal divisions of the Yüeh-zhi themselves (Enoki 1974–5: 265).

It is also worth noting that according to the *Wei Shu*, the division of the Yüeh-zhi to the *Da* (Greater) and the *Xiao* (Lesser) also holds for the Kidarites. While in the earlier account of *Shiji*, the *Xiao* Yüeh-zhi is a division of the tribe remaining behind in their homeland following the migration of the Greater Yüeh-zhi to the west, in the *Wei Shu* account, they are simply those in the kingdom of Jiduoluo's son. This kingdom is said to be located in Gandhara, with its capital at *Fu-lou-sha*, or Purushapura (Zeimal 1999: 126). The conclusion from this is simply that the later Chinese sources talking about the Kidarites should be taken not as merely 'echoing' the earlier sources on the rise of the Da Yüeh-zhi and the Kushans, but also copying them wholesale, providing a narrative for the region which they simply knew as the territory of the Da Yüeh-zhi and trying to fit in details such as the 'five countries' and the 'Lesser Yüeh-zhi' known from the earlier sources.

What we can, however, conclude is that the Kidarites indeed ruled over the territory previously dominated by the Da Yüeh-zhi/Kushans, and that their embassies were received in the Chinese court as representing this territory. The Chinese even considered Balkh (Ying-chien-shi/Liu-Chien-shi; Enoki 1969: 8–10) to be the capital of the Da Yüeh-zhi, similar to the role of that city in the Kushan administration.[10] Their path of invasion, as presented above, takes them across a certain range of mountains, identified differently by various scholars. Enoki (1969: 8) posits that the *Da Shan* (Great Mountains) referred to here is the Hindu Kush and that Bei Tianzhu is the Kabul-Jalalabad region or the classical Paropamisdae. Shoshin Kuwayama (2002: 123–4), on the other hand, holds the *Da Shan* to be the Pamirs further in the east, concluding that the Kidarites (alongside the Hephthalites) came through Tokharistan and Karakorum before entering Bei Tianzhu (Northern India/Gandhara).[11]

Whichever the path might have been, and whether the Kidarites indeed acted alongside the Hephthalites or the Alkhans from the beginning, it is the numismatic evidence that can take us further from this point on. The Kidarites issued two main types of coins: a series

---

[10] Priscus says that *Balaam* was the capital of the Kidarites, a site that is also matched with Balkh (Zeimal 1999: 126). Compare this with 'the town of *Badiyan*, which probably [means] the residence of the king', given as the capital of the Yada (the Hephthalites) in the *Bei Shi* and the *Zhoushu* (de la Vaissière 2012: 125–6).

[11] See Errington and Curtis 2007: 85–6 for a refutation of this suggestion based on the numismatic evidence.

Fig. 4.2. Silver drachm in the name of Kidara, king of the Kushans (© das Antlitz des Fremden).

of gold scyphate 'dinars' and a silver coin series of drachms/dirhams, accompanied by a copper series. The gold dinar series is simply a continuation of the Kushano-Sasanian gold issues from Balkh, stylistically continuing the coin type of 'Wahram 6'[12] (Vondrovec 2014: 140–1).

The silver drachms consist of a series of imitations of Sasanian coins ranging from those of Shapur II to the coins of Yazdgerd II with corrupt legends (Errington and Curtis 2007: 85), while displaying a wider range of influences than the Sasanian series (Cribb 2010: 105). In Bactria, presumably the earliest region under their control, the Kidarites start their coin issues in the AD 370s, supplanting the Kushano-Sasanians in Bactria and Gandhara and entering Panjab as successors of Kipunadha, the last Kushan and vassal of Samudragupta (AD 335–80). The presence of Kidarite coins in Bactria is, then, an argument against Kuwayama's suggestion that the path of Kidarite invasion of Gandhara passed further east through the Pamirs and preceded their presence in Bactria (Errington and Curtis 2007: 85–6).

The Kidarite coin types with Bactrian legends declare the rulers to be the *king of the Kushan* (κοþανο þαο), a title that is paralleled on Brahmi coin types (Vondrovec 2014: 29). A type which shows the king in frontal view and wearing a crown with ram's horns, a feature known also from the coins of the Kushano-Sasanian Wahram, has a legend in Brahmi declaring the authority to be *Sa Piroysa* 'King

---

[12] The convention of assigning each new Kushano-Sasanian coin type to a different authority is a numismatic one that carries no historical affirmation, but is useful for providing some organisation to our current state of knowledge about their coinage. For an alternative view and organisation of these coins, see now Jongeward and Cribb 2015: 227–37.

Pērōz' (Vondrovec 2014: 28–9).[13] Another coin type (type 11), paralleling the issues of Sasanian kings, carries a Brahmi legend clearly stating *Kedara Kusana saha* 'Kidara the Kushan Shah' while showing a frontal bust of a beardless king with a moustache (Vondrovec 2014: 31–2). Further, type 16 carries the name of Varā Saha 'King Vara', who might be a later authority of the Kidarites (Vondrovec 2014: 33). Establishing a sequence of Kidarite rulers, however, is quite difficult, as our current state of knowledge is not advanced enough to be able to organise the coins series, and thus their authorities, chronologically.

The presence of the title of *kdy/kay*, first appearing on the imperial Sasanian coins on the coins of Yazdgerd II (AD 438–57), has led Vondrovec (2014: 30) to suggest a *terminus post quem* for the whole of the series of AD 438 to match the beginning of the rule of Yazdgerd II. However, there is no reason to assign the coins of Kushano-Sasanian Wahram to a period after AD 438, detaching it from the rest of the Kushano-Sasanian series which were issued starting in the third century, with a continuous series starting in the early fourth century.[14] Additionally, the assumption that the direction of cultural borrowing is necessarily from the Sasanians to the Kidarites is historically unreasonable and assumes a hegemony on the part of the Sasanians which in fact need not exist. In fact, borrowings from East Iran to West Iran, particularly in terms of iconography and ideology, are well known and documented.[15] It is thus not impossible to suggest that *kdy* was in fact a known title of the eastern dynasts, being borrowed and used by the Sasanians in their process of absorbing the political power of the Kushano-Sasanian and Kidarite dynasties.

The Kidarites also seem to have issued an extensive series of copper coins, showing the prominence of monetary exchange in their territories. Their copper issues were produced in the style of the Bactrian issues of the Kushano-Sasanian Wahram. Later issues imitated the crown type of the Sasanian Shapur III (AD 383–8) and carried the legend *piorozo šao* 'the Victorious King' (Göbl 1967: III, pls. 13–19). Later bronze issues have the same crown style, but carry the Kidarite

---

[13] See Errington and Curtis 2007: 86–7 for a use of Pērōz 'victorious' as a title. Cribb 2010: fig. 43 suggests that an earlier type 1B also bore the name Pērōz, which is contested by Vondrovec 2014: 28. It seems that Cribb now suggests that this Pērōz should be considered the second Kidarite king (Jongeward and Cribb 2015).
[14] See Schindel 2012: 65–73 for a discussion of the beginning of the Kushano-Sasanian coin series.
[15] Carter 1981 on the eastern origins of the Mithras iconography; and Canepa 2009: 109–11.

Fig. 4.3. Gold dinar of Kidara-Kushan in Brahmi script (© *das Antlitz des Fremden*).

tamgha and the Brahmi 'mahanade' or the image of a fire altar and the legend *Kidara* written in Brahmi (Vondrovec 2014: 29). Another series imitates the crown of Yazdgerd II and includes the legend *Kedara Kusana Sa* in the Brahmi script (Göbl 1967: II, pls. 11–14).

The discrepancy between the numismatic evidence and the written sources has caused a major point of disagreement about the earliest date of the Kidarites. As mentioned above, Roman and Chinese sources appear to suggest a fifth-century date for the start of Kidarite rule, a possibility that is supported by some numismatic evidence such as the title of *kdy* on some of the coins (Vondrovec 2014: 30). The view of the *Tepe Maranjan* hoard held by scholars such as Gobl was dismissed by Grenet (2002b) as a misreading of the coins' legend, instead assigning them to the Kushano-Sasanian (*Kay*) Wahram. Cribb, however, has argued that the reading *Kidara* on Tepe Maranjan is not the only reason to attribute them to Kidara, and has gone to some lengths to show that the 'Kidarite' coins of Tepe Maranjan indeed belong to the Kidarite series, thus supporting a late fourth-century dating of Kidara (Cribb 2010). Considering the numismatic evidence, Errington and Curtis provide a range of AD 370–457 for the rule of the Kidarites in Bactria, Kabul, and Gandhara, and possibly AD 468 for their ultimate defeat by the Sasanian King of Kings, Pērōz (Errington and Curtis 2007: 82). However, the *Bei Shi* records a Jiduoluo embassy to the Wei court in AD 477, an event that might show a residual Kidarite control in Gandhara or the region of the Xiao (Lesser) Yüeh-zhi. Embassies might, however, be the wrong way of establishing the presence of any political power, as the Chinese records mention embassies for the years 459 and 460 from the Juchang (interpreted as Kushan by

Enoki) and then 477 from *Jeduoluo*, which in this case might be referring to Gandhara (Cribb 2010: 93).

Decades of invasion and war, and the rapid succession of political authorities, left a negative effect on Tokharistan, however. Despite a lack of widespread archaeological excavations, the available surface surveys show large-scale abandonment of the region. The plain of Balkh (*Po-Ho* in Chinese) was largely deserted, with a famous quote from the Chinese pilgrim Xuanzang that 'The city, though well fortified, is thinly populated' (Beal 1884: 44). Surface surveys show almost no occupational layers in the region in the fifth century or in the seventh century (Gardin 1957: 95). In the Wakhsh region, irrigation systems were abandoned (Litvinskii and Solov'ev 1985), while in Delberjin Tepe, the site was abandoned after the middle of the fifth century (de la Vaissière 2007: 102). However, this abandonment might have meant that the population moved from the plain to the more mountainous areas to the south of Tokharistan, possibly giving rise to the prosperity of the valleys of the Hindu Kush (Rezakhani 2010c: 122–45). In the traditional major urban sites like Balkh, Termez, or the Kunduz area, the Hunnic invasions resulted in the abandonment of the settlements and depopulation. The effect, on the other hand, was completely different in Sogdiana, which appears to have experienced the most brilliant period of agricultural production and urban expansion, allowing for the spread of Sogdian colonialism and the commercial network.[16]

LATER KIDARITES

In the fifth century, the Sasanian imperial policy turned to direct opposition to the Kidarite rule. A war between Wahram V and the Kidarites (presented anachronistically as the 'Turks') resulted in the victory of the Sasanians and the establishment of a boundary tower (al-Tabari I.863–4). The influences of the coinage of Yazdgerd II might indicate a peaceful state of affairs (Vondrovec 2014: 31). However, Pērōz (AD 457–84) decided on an offensive against the Kidarites, possibly motivated by the help rendered to him by the Hephthalites when fighting for his crown against his brother Hormizd III (al-Tabari I.872). Priscus reports the name of the Kidarite king at this point as Kunkhas (κουγχας). Following his defeat by Pērōz in 467, Kunkhas fled his capital of Balaam (Balkh?) (Priscus *frg* 41, Blockley 1983: 347–9), possibly taking refuge in

---

[16] See Chapter 7 for a discussion of the Kidarite and Hephthalite periods.

Gandhara. The Kidarites thus lost their position in Bactria to the Hephthalites, or perhaps first to the Sasanians,[17] and possibly only preserved control of Gandhara, perhaps in Swat (Göbl 1967: II, 224, issue 15).

Apart from Gandhara, however, a Kidarite kingdom may have survived in Sogdiana, possibly in the area of Ustrushana. As mentioned before, a coin type, part of the normal archer type of Samarkand, and published by Zeimal (Zeimal 1996), bears the Sogdian legend *kyδr*, which is dated to the fifth century and appears to refer to Kidara. Zeimal points out that out of 200 coins in the hoard, only seven bear this inscription, showing the short period of Kidarite control of Samarkand (Zeimal 1999: 125). However, the presence of a seal, showing a Hunnic ruler with the title of Kushanshah, may possibly point to a longer period of Kidarite presence in Sogdiana:

*** βαγο ολαργο υονανο þαο οαζαρκο κοþανοþαο σαμαρκανδο αφþιιανο

Lord Ularg the King of the Huns, the Great Kushan Shah, the Afshiyan of Samarkand[18]

The Xiongnu, if we assume that they are indeed the Kidarites, had captured Samarkand in 457 and ruled there for three generations (*Wei Shu*: de la Vaissière 2005b: 107 n. 37). The seal suggests that the ruler of Samarkand was known as the Great Kushan Shah, a title used by the Kidarites on their coins. He was additionally the king of the *Huns*, showing his connection to the wave of Chionite conquests. The title of Afshiyan is a rendition of the well-known Islamic title of *Afshin*, for kings of Ustrushana (Khurradādhbih 1967: 32) is akin to other titles from the region originating from Old Iranian *xšaita-, which also renders MP *Šāh*. The seal thus shows the position of a king of the Huns, with claims to the position of Kushanshah, living in Samarkand, a situation that matches well our other evidence for the presence of the Kidarites in Sogdiana.[19]

This Kidarite dynasty sent embassies to China until 509, after which they ceased and became part of the Hephthalite embassies

---

[17] This is indeed what can be understood from the statements of al-Tabari (I.863–4) about the campaigns of Wahram V against the 'Khaghan of the Turks', here most likely meaning the Kidarites. After defeating the 'Turks', Wahram then subdues the region they control, Bactria, and delimits it by building a tower at the frontier, at the behest of the local population. The tower of course becomes important in the campaigns of Pērōz against the Hephthalites, for which see further below.

[18] This is a composite rendition of the inscription taken from the three versions of the seals. The complete discussion of the seal is available in Rahman et al. 2006: 125, 128; the three versions are presented in Lerner and Sims-Williams 2011: 181–2, with a discussion on p.e 201.

[19] See also Vondrovec 2014: 48–9 for further observations on this seal.

(Enoki 1955b: 234). However, we should not assume that the Kidarite presence in eastern Sogdiana disappeared quickly after their demise in Tokharistan. Indeed, centuries later, in the early ninth century, the local king of Ustrushana and the Abbasid general Al-Afshin bore the personal name of *Khydhar* (al-Tabari IX.11), which was sometimes written wrongly as (Arabic) *Haydar* (Dīnawarī 1888: 203) but was specified as *Khydhar* by later writers as well (Ibn Khallikhan 2007: V.123), while at least one source has the form *Kydr* (Qudama 1965: 380). The name Kydr seems to have indeed been a popular one among the people of Ustrushana, as several characters bearing it, including a certain *Kydr b. Abdullah al-Ustrushani*, are mentioned in the Islamic sources (al-Tabari IX.259; al-Yaqubi 2010: II.495). This might also be related to the *Afšun, Khuv of Khākhsar* who is mentioned on one of the documents from the Mugh Mountain as the addressee of a rather unhappy letter from AD 722 by Dewashtich, the ruler of Samarkand and the last opponent of the Muslim conquest of Sogdiana (Grenet and de la Vassiere 2002: 159–63).

A period of Kidarite co-rule in the southern Hindu Kush is also possible, judging from art historical and numismatic evidence. Evidence from a famous bowl found in Swat in Pakistan and Chilek near Samarkand (Grenet 2002b: 211–12; Kurbanov 2013: 81) shows a co-existence of the Kidarites and the Alkhans. This is further suggested by the presence of early transitional Kidarite–Alkhan coins (Vondrovec 2014: 177–9; Pfisterer 2013) which seem to preserve signs of both political settings.

Vondrovec in his division of Kidarite emissions identifies a 'Second Phase of (Kidarite) Silver' (Vondrovec 2014: 34–5) which displays a different style in size/diameter and the portraiture of a beardless king. In this phase, a coin type 19 has a king wearing the crown type of Shapur III (383–8) and carries the inscription Parozo Šao 'King Pērōz' in Bactrian. A closely related type, 18b (Vondrovec 2014: 35–6) may carry the Brahmi legend *Khigi*, the name of the first known Alkhan authority Khingila (Pfisterer 2013: ch. 3.2), and has the *cakra* symbol S3, otherwise only seen on type 66 of Alkhan coinage, which additionally bears the Brahmi legend *Khigi* and the Bactrian *alkha* (Cribb 2010: mint D). The same legend, *Alkha*, also appears on type 11 of Kidarite coins, where the name of the authority is given as *Kedara* (Vondrovec 2014: 31). Another coin series, type 39 of the Alkhans, bearing the Alkhan *tamgha* S1, carries a legend χιδαρο βαιανο 'Kidara the King', further showing a close relationship between the Kidarites and the Alkhans, possibly in the region of the Kabul Valley (Rezakhani 2015b). These coin types thus present the possibility that several coin series were issued by Alkhan and Kidarite authorities together, and further allow for a new narrative of the terminal Kidarite period and the rise of Alkhan power in eastern Tokharistan and Gandhara.[20]

CONCLUSION

The Kidarites perhaps represent the first political power of the *Iranian Huns* after their invasion of East Iran in the middle of the fourth century. Following early clashes with the Sasanians, resulting in the destruction of the Kushano-Sasanian power in Tokharistan and Gandhara, the Huns concluded a treaty with the Sasanians. This was demonstrated via the participation of the Huns, and their 'king' Grumbates, in the Sasanian siege of Amida in AD 360. After this point, the Huns, using the power vacuum left in Tokharistan, established a kingdom in that region, founded by Kidara. The Kidarites probably acted as allies of the Sasanians in East Iran, continuing the role of the Kushano-Sasanians as the independent, but allied, rulers of that region. The Kidarites then expanded on both northern and southern fronts. In Sogdiana, they established a kingdom and issued coins, and their survival is confirmed by the evidence of a seal of the Hunnish Kushanshah. To the south, they expanded into the Kabul Valley and Gandhara, perhaps in co-operation with the Alkhans, and issued coins that adopted the local Brahmi script. Their developing style of coinage, increasingly influenced by non-Sasanian elements and showing original innovations such as beardless faces, demonstrates their independence and consolidation of power.

In Tokharistan, however, they soon came into conflict with the Sasanians and the rising power of the Hephthalites. A war with Wahram V established their border with the Sasanians and created a period of peace. However, the alliance between the Sasanian Pērōz and the Hephthalites resulted in a crushing defeat in 466/7, putting an end to their presence in Tokharistan. Kidarite regional power in Gandhara, and possibly Sogdiana, survived, to be overwhelmed only later by the Alkhans in Gandhara and the Hephthalites in Sogdiana. The Kidarites may not have left as much evidence as the Hephthalites who followed them, but their legacy was nonetheless important in the development of East Iran. The Kidarites continued the pattern of crossing the Hindu Kush from Tokharistan and controlling both

---

[20] See Chapter 5 for a discussion of the Eastern Alkhans and their possible position in the events of the last quarter of the fifth century.

sides of the mountain range. They also seamlessly continued the administrative practices of the Kushan and Kushano-Sasanian period, even to the extent of marking themselves as Kushanshahs, reflecting a continuity in the region that guaranteed the transmission of established practices. Additionally, by adopting and diffusing Sasanian coin style over a wide range, they continued to spread Sasanian influence in East Iran, providing for increasing contact between the two regions. The survival of Kidarite onomastics in Sogdiana may also be an indication of their continued influence, and possible survival in the shape of local rulers of regions such as Ustrushana, even down to the Islamic period.

5 The Alkhans in the Southern Hindu Kush

INTRODUCTION

Alkhan is the name given to a dynasty of 'Hunnic' rulers of the southern Hindu Kush who followed the Kidarites in this region. This name is taken from the Bactrian legends of their coins and most likely designates a tribal or dynastic identity. These rulers, originating from the northern Hindu Kush region, initially occupied the Kabul Valley and then Gandhara, following the pattern set by the Kushans and followed by the Kidarites. Their further conquests took them eastward to Kashmir and central India, probably as far as Malwa, where they were stopped by local Indian dynasts. Their distinctive coin style distinguished them immediately from other Hunnic authorities and is the basis of the mostly numismatic convention of separating them from the Hephthalites. On the other hand, in their initial stages, they may have been closely related to both the Hephthalites and the Kidarites, indeed issuing coins with the latter. Their rule in northern India left an important memory in Hindu literature, particularly the misrule of one of their most significant kings, Mihirakula. While never really showing a strong presence in Bactria/Tokharistan, Alkhan rule in the Kabul region and Gandhara was fundamental in the formation of a coherent region in the southern Hindu Kush and is crucial in the formation of the units of Kabulestan and Zabulestan, both important regions in the history of East Iran. The Alkhans' artistic production, including their iconography, was remembered for a long time and influenced painting styles as far north as Panjikent (Marshak 2002). Despite the near-silence of historical sources about them, the Alkhans were an important political and cultural force in East Iran, and we should assign many of the historical events previously attributed to the 'Hephthalites' to them.

THE IDENTITY OF THE ALKHANS

The quest to recognise the Alkhans as a separate entity has been a long and arduous one. Traditionally, most historians have considered them part of the Hephthalites,[1] with even some numismatists taking the same view.[2] Even today, when most numismatists and many philologists accept the presence of a separate *Alkhan* identity, their association with the Hephthalites still overshadows an independent identity. Indeed, this may not be too far from the truth, considering historical realities, since there are many shared characteristics between the two groups which can be taken as evidence of their close relations. However, there is little reason to give precedence to either of these identities, including considering the Alkhans as a subgroup of the Hephthalites. The Alkhans, alternatively also written as Alkhon and Alchon (in German spelling; see Göbl 1967 throughout), are a relatively new introduction into the historiography of this region. The name is known mainly through the Bactrian legend αλχαν(v)o 'Alkhano', and its variations, on their coins (Sims-Williams 2010: 33, no. 17). A debate over its meaning has led some scholars to suggest it as a personal name, taking into account the evidence of the name of a coin authority written *Raja Lakhāna* in Brahmi and equating it with the Bactrian αλχανο (Humbach 1966: 28–31).[3] Others have suggested that the name needs to be taken as a tribal name.[4] On the coins, the inclusion of the legend αλχανο would then mean the communication of a collective tribal identity, leading to the identification of a class of Alkhan coins as 'Early Anonymous Alkhan', where the legend αλχανο identifies the coins without giving the name of a particular ruler. To this evidence, the later mention

---

[1] For example, Bivar2004, where not only the Alkhans but also the Nezak Shah and Nezak Tarkhāns are discussed in the entry on the Hephthalites. The Alkhans are also considered part of the Hephthalites in Litvinsky's entry for the UNESCO series on Central Asia: Litvinsky 1999.

[2] See Mitchiner 1975a: 162ff., where he considers Bactrian ΑΛΧΟΝΟ as a 'Hephthalite' tribal name.

[3] For coins bearing the name *Rāja Lakhāna Udayāditya*, see Vondrovec 2014: 191–2, who disagrees with the equivalence of *Alkhano* and *Lakhāna*, and further below in the same chapter.

[4] Alram 1996. Alram and Pfisterer 2010; Vondrovec 2014: ch. 3 and further; cf. Errington and Curtis 2007: 88ff., although the clear distinction they draw between the Hephthalites and other Huns, based on *Zand ī Wahman Yasn* (Cereti 1995: 98, now needs to be revised on the basis of the better reading of Cereti 2010: 64.

of a king *Alkhana* can be added. In the fifth book of the Kashmiri chronicle of kings *Rajatarangini*, a chapter dealing with the ninth and tenth centuries AD and the rule of the *Utpala* dynasty, a local ruler is mentioned so:

> the firmly rooted fortune of Alkhāna, king of Gūjara, he [Shankaravarma of the Utpala] uprooted[5] the battle in a moment, and made long grief rise [in its place]. The ruler of Gūjara gave up to him humbly the Takka-land, preserving [hereby] his own country, as if [he had saved] his own body [at the sacrifice] of a finger. (Stein 1900: V, 149–50, 205)

The story goes on to tell the tale of the competition between Shankaravarma of Kashmir and Lalliya Shahi, the Hindu-shahi ruler of Kabul, who held the position of suzerain over Alkhāna of Gūjara. While of course reflecting the events of the ninth century, this episode shows several details in the history of the region, including the connections between the regions of western Kashmir/eastern Gandhara, the city of Gūjara, and the kingdom of Kabul. Additionally, the survival of the name Alkhāna among the rulers of this region might be an indication that Alkhan was at one point considered a personal name, and perhaps was used also in this sense at a later period. This of course does not negate the suggestion that the name acted as a dynastic one at a later stage; many other instances, including the name of Arsaces, the eponymous founder of the Arsacids, as well as that of Kidara, can indicate the same process.

From a numismatic point of view, Robert Göbl was the first person to provide a separate identity for the Alkhans, or 'Alchons' as it is written in German, in his four-volume survey of 'Iranian Huns' (1967). There he labels them as the minting authority for one of his four distinguished 'Hunnic' coin series. This is the division that has been maintained in Klaus Vondrovec's (2014) update to Göbl's work based on new evidence, where the Alkhans have a different identity from the Hephthalites. The Alkhan coin series, in this sense, are all distinguished from the Hephthalite ones because of the inscriptions on the early issues, where the world αλχανο or αλχαννο or even the plural form αλχαναυο (in various Bactrian renditions) distinguishes the first series of these coins. The appearance of the so-called *tamgha* S1 on the obverse of these coins (Vondrovec 2014: types 36–41), henceforth dubbed the *Alkhan tamgha* (Vondrovec 2014: 35; Errington 2010: 149), becomes the distinguishing mark of the coin series. The next stage of the Alkhan coin issues is the

---

[5] A word is missing in Stein's translation at this point, probably 'at'. I am not able to ascertain this in the original.

The Alkhans in the Southern Hindu Kush

Fig. 5.1. Silver drachm, unknown Alkhan authority, showing the typical Alkhan bust type on the obverse (© *das Antlitz des Fremden*).

appearance of a beardless bust of the king, marking a departure from the Sasanian norms. All of these display an increasing tendency towards distinguishing themselves from the previous coin authorities, particularly the Sasanians, and possibly reflect ethnic practices and fashions.

Compared with numismatic sources, textual sources about the Alkhans are quite scarce, a fact that has contributed to the tendency to associate them with better-known 'Hunnic' entities such as the Hephthalites.[6] The Middle Persian apocalyptic text *Zand ī Wahman Yasn*, a commentary on the no longer extant *Wahman Yasn*, part of the Younger Avestan texts (Cereti 1995), includes a notice that is interpreted as reference to the Alkhans and other Hunnic tribes:

> 58) ud xwadāyīh ud pādixšāyīh ō anērān-bunīgān rasēd, čiyōn xyōn <ud> turk ud *xudur ud *tōbīd, čiyōn *hindūg ud kōfyār ud *čīnīg ud *Kābulīg ud *subdīg ud *hrōmāyīg ud *karmīr-xyōn ud spēd-xyōn, <u-šān> pad ērān dehān ī man <ohrmazd dād> *pādixšā bawēnd framān ud kāmag ī awēšān pad gēhān rawāg be bawēd 59) pādixšāyīh az awēšān dawāl-kustīgān ud tāzīgān ud hrōmāyīgān be ō awēšān rasēd

> 58) and kingship and dominion will go to those of non-Ērānian origin, such as Xyōn, the Turk, the *Xadur*,[7] the *Tōbīd*, such as Indians, the *Kōfyār*, the Chinese, the Kabulis, the *Subdīg, the Romans, the Karmir Xyōn, and

---

[6] See Errington and Curtis 2007: 90, 98, where there is an emphasis on distinguishing the Hephthalites from the Huns.
[7] This is the name previously read as *Heftal* by Bailey 1932, which is the basis of the argument of Errington and Curits 2007: 98. It was later modified by Bailey himself to the *Khazars*, but the MS does not render either of these readings; see Cereti 1995: 191–2 for further discussion. The Pahlavi form reads as *htl*, which – considering the vagueness of the Pahlavi script – can be read in many ways. I think the possibility that it reflects either *Xydr* (Kidara?; see Rezakhani 2015b) or a less likely Pahlavi rendition of Arabic *Hytal* (a mistake for Heptal 'Hephthalite') should not be completely dismissed.

the Spēd Xyōn. They will rule over these Ērānian lands that I (Ohrmazd, have created); their orders and wishes will be current in the world. 59) Authority will go from those with the leather girdle, from the Arabs and from the Romans to them.[8]

Here, the *Karmīr Xyōn* (Red Khyon; cf. Sanskrit hala-huna= 'red/ dark Huns') is speculated to refer to the Alkhans, as *Āl* indeed means 'Red' in various Turkic languages and would thus make the combination *Al-Khan* the equivalent of Middle Persian *karmīr-xyōn* (Grenet 2002b: 207 n. 5). If this possibility is entertained, we would be faced with an ethnic identity of the Alkhans as speakers of a Turkic or Altain language, an image that is not completely strange, but quite hard to maintain (de la Vaissière 2007; Enoki 1959). Furthermore, as mentioned before, the name Alkhana appears at least once as the name of a king ruling in Western Kashmir, and thus should be considered at least initially as a personal name. Consequently, the etymology of *Alkhan* as 'Red Hun' seems hardly attainable and until better suggestions are presented, attempts to find mention of the Alkhans in *Wahman Yasn* should be abandoned.

THE BEGINNING OF ALKHAN HISTORY

The history of the Alkhans can currently be put together only through the numismatic evidence and a few art historical and epigraphic sources. In this sense, the sequence of coins established by numismatists give us the most reliable 'narrative' of Alkhan history, including the order of the rule of their kings and their territorial expansion and retraction. Additionally, these coins provide the most widely available source for understanding Alkhan culture and political ideas. The iconography of the coins, including their use of *tamghas* (distinguishing 'tribal' marks; Ilyasov 2003) and various other devices, as well as their depiction of the kings, also act as the main reference point for interpreting other evidence such as the famous Swat silver bowl (Marschak 1986: 29–34). The narrative that has been presented on the basis of these coins, in its earlier form, is founded on the conceptualisation of the Alkhans within Hephthalite history, considering them the southern branch of the Hephthalites who crossed the Hindu Kush and conquered Gandhara and northern India. Below,

---

[8] Cereti 2010: 64. Carlo Cereti, following his own edition of the *Zand ī Wahman Yasn* (Cereti 1995), leaves all the ethnic names, including the known ones, in original Middle Persian in his translation. I have modified the translation, replacing the Middle Persian names with their known equivalents, while leaving the controversial ones intact. For a further discussion of this see also Cereti 2010.

we shall first present this basic history, which is the career of three authorities known from textual and numismatic sources, namely Khingila, Toramana, and Mihirakula. Subsequently, we will go back for a deeper look at numismatic evidence to present and explain our current state of knowledge about the Alkhans.

FROM KHINGILA TO MIHIRAKULA

Khingila, known in the Brahmi incriptions of his coins as Khi-gi-la and as Khingil, χιγγιλο, in the Bactrian legends, is the most famous leader of the Alkhans in modern historiography.[9] He is most likely the leader of the Alkhan campaigns in Gandhara which took over the control of the region from the Kidarites (Vondrovec 2014: 184). His name is known from the inscription on a famous copper scroll (see discussion below) as well as other palaeographic sources (Sims-Williams 2010: 148 n. 520). As most of the Alkhan coins were previously attributed to him, it has been assumed that it is his bust that is the prototype for the characteristic Alkhan coin portraits. However, in fact the elongated skull and beardless face appear to be the common artistic feature of all Alkhan and Alkhan-influenced coins (Vondrovec 2014: ch. 3). In the *Shahnameh* of Ferdowsi, he is mentioned as *Shengil*, and is considered the king of India:

> The wise minister stood up (and) said thus: Oh just and righteous king! This world has been secured from the fear of ill wishers, and suffering and hardship have left these domains; except for the famous Shengil, one of the Indians, for whom justice seems to be agony in his soul. From India to the borders of China, thieves seem to have created chaos on earth. If he gets his hands on Iran and starts doing evil, then that would need to be remedied. You are the king and Shengil is simply the caretaker of India, why would he ask for tribute from China and Sindh? Think about this and come up with a solution for this, so that a disaster does not befall. (*Shahnameh* VI.1879ff)

The rest of the story concerns a correspondence between Bahram (Wahram V) and Shengil, delivered by Bahram himself, disguised as a messenger. Upon arriving in the court of Shengil, Bahram achieves several heroic tasks, including the killing of a dragon, and then is given the daughter of Shengil as his bride. In a manner similar to that in the story of the Sasanian founder Ardashir I and his escape

---

[9] References to other kings called *Khingila* are made in various sources, such as a garnet seal with the inscription εþκιγγιλο ρωκανο χοηο 'Eshkingil the Lord of Rōkan' (Callieri 2002). However, as they could scarcely be referring to the authority under discussion, there is no point mentioning them here. Al-Yaqubi 2010: II.479 mentions a king called *Khinjil* ruling over Kabul at the time of Abbasid Al-Mahdi (AD 775–85), obviously a namesake of Khingila. For the *Khingal dynasty* of Kabul/Kapiśa, see Kuwayama 2002: 354 and Inaba 2010b.

from the court of Ardavan (Artabanus IV), Bahram and the daughter of Shengil then escape to Iran, although Shengil catches up with them. A treaty is concluded to which the 'Faghfur' (Emperor) of China, Shengil's father-in-law, is also privy, making Shengil an ally of Bahram.

This story, apart from its legendary elements, brings to our attention several points regarding the kingdom of Shengil/Khingila. One is the association of his territories with India, which in the Islamic period mainly meant the area beyond Kabul, thus Gandhara. This matches the numismatic and epigraphic data that we have for Khingila. Another point is the date of Khingila's rule according to Ferdowsi, who makes him an older contemporary of Wahram V (AD 420–38). The date proposed by numismatists for the start of the coinage of Khingila is AD 430 (Vondrovec 2014: 184), a date that matches the narrative of the *Shahnameh* well. However, considering the evidence of the Schøyeh copper scroll (Melzer 2006; see below), a king named Khingila is supposed to have been alive around AD 492/3, which makes the early date of AD 430 impossible. However, a reconsideration of the text of the copper scroll might help us reconcile the date of AD 430 for Khingila, as would a consideration of the possibility that Khingila was the name, or title, of several different kings, as was also the case for Narendrātiya-Khinkhila, mentioned as a king of Kashmir (see further below).

It was previously thought that Khingila's son was Toramana, who then continued his father's campaigns to conquer India and succeeded him in Gandhara (Göbl 1967: II.59). However, there is no evidence to suggest that Toramana was a son of Khingila, numismatic or otherwise (Vondrovec 2014: 184). In the famous Kashmiri chronicle of kings, *Rajatarangini*, Toramana is mentioned as the son of Lalliya Shahi, the founder of the Hindu-Shahi dynasty of Kabul, chronologically out of order, and possibly confusing him with a later ruler of the same name (Stein 1900: v. 233).[10]

Toramana's name indeed appears more than that of any other Alkhan ruler on the inscriptions from northern and central India. A famous one, known commonly as the Eran Stone Boar Inscription, is dated to the fifteenth year of the '*Maharajadhiraja* Shri Toramana who is governing the earth with great fame and lustre' (Biswas

---

[10] The references to the coins of Toramana and the attempt to match them with the coins of the Kashmiri king of the same name, in Stein 1900: II.319–21, should be discarded considering the numismatic evidence. However, the possibility of the presence of two or even more Toramanas has been presented and seems to be in many cases a convincing solution to the contradictory evidence of texts, inscriptions, and coins (Vondrovec 2014: 212).

Fig. 5.2. Silver drachm of Khingila, with Bactrian inscription 'Khingila, of the Alkhan' (© *das Antlitz des Fremden*).

1973: 56). Another, known as the Khwera inscription from the Salt Range, again uses the same title: '*Maharajadhiraja* Toramana Saha Jauvlah' (Biswas 1973: 57). Jauvlah was generally thought to refer to Toramana, functioning as a title of sorts,[11] but it is now more sensible to think of it as a corrupt form of the coin authority named *sāhi javūkha* on his coins (Vondrovec 2014: 204–5). Subsequently, the Khwera inscription records the construction of the monastery from the reigns of Maharajadhiraja Toramana and Saha Jauvlah/ Shahi Javukha, showing the contemporary rule of these two authorites. Toramana's title of *Maharajadhiraja* (King of Kings), harkening back to an Iranian origin, is different from the title he holds in the Schøyen copper scroll, where he is called *devaraja* (god-king) while Javukha is called *Maharaja* (great king) in the same inscription (Melzer 2006: 274; see further below).

Toramana is also mentioned in the inscription of Gwalior, where he is identified as Mihirakula's father (Fleet 1888: 161–4). In that inscription, the building of the temple for which the inscription is created is dated to the fifteenth year of the reign of Mihirakula. The dating of the Gwalior inscription, as well as the previous ones, is impossible to ascertain, since we have no idea from what era they are dated. The connection between Mihirakula and the king of Malwa, Yashodharma, who in a final inscription from Mandasor mentions his defeat of Mihirakula, is among the few ways to assign an approximate date to the reign of Mihirakula. Considering that Yashodharma also left a foundation inscription dated to the year

---

[11] Humbach 1966: 24–8, where the name of the coin authority *Javukha* is considered a variation of the well-known title *yabghu*.

589 of the Vikrama Era, comparable to AD 532, we can consider the reign of Mihirakula to have taken place in the first half of the sixth century[12] (Vondrovec 2014: 226). In book one of *Rajatarangini*, Mihirakula is mentioned as a cruel king:

> Then his son Mihirakula, a man of violent acts and resembling Kāla (Death) ruled in the land which was overrun by the hordes of Mlecchas. ... the people knew his approach by noticing the vultures, crows, and other [birds], which were flying ahead to feed on those who were being slain within his army's [reach]. (Stein 1900: I.289, 291)

Of course it must be mentioned that in this epic, the father of Mihirakula is named not Toramana, as we would expect from the Gwalior inscription, but rather 'Mukala, sometimes called Vasukula'. The Mihirakula of *Rajatarangini* is a 'phantastic character' (Stein 1900: I.78) who undertakes expeditions to Ceylon. If he is the cruel king whom the Chinese traveller Xuanzeng meets, then he appears to be a 'pro-Brahmin' and an anti-Buddhist and might have had some leanings towards the cult of Shiva (Stein 1900: II.43 n. 289). He is considered the founder of the shrine of Shiva in Srinagar, that of Mihiresvara in Halada, and the large town of Mihirapura (Stein 1900: I.306). Mihirakula is also the grandfather of another king, 'Narendrātiya who bore the second name of Khinkhila', ruling for 'thirty six years and a hundred days' (Stein 1900: I.347). This personage may be the same as the Khingila who is called the ancestor of the Kabulshahis and will be discussed further as part of Nēzak and Turkic rule over Kabul (Inaba 2010b).

In Indian sources, the defeat of Mihirakula in Malwa is the end of the 'Huna' involvement in Indian affairs. However, there is no clear indication that the rule of the Alkhans in Gandhara and further to the west actually stopped with this event. The account of the Buddhist monk Song Yun tells us about the travelling monk meeting a Huna king east of Indus around AD 520. The family of this ruler had conquered Gandhara three generations before (Chavannes 1903b: 381); according to Song Yun's description, this happened sometime around AD 460, and it matches the possible date of Alkhan entry into the centre of Kidarite rule. The *Christian Geography* of Cosmas provides a narrative highly influenced by literary conventions, saying, 'Higher up in India, that is, farther to the north are the White Huns. The one called Gollas when going to war takes with him, it is said, no fewer than 2,000 elephants and a great force of cavalry' (trans.

---

[12] Alram and Pfisterer 2010: 26 previously proposed AD 515–540; earlier, Robert Göbl had proposed AD 515-28/42 (Göbl 1967: II.54–5).

Fig. 5.3 Billon drachm issue of the Alkhan–Nēzak 'Crossover' series (© *das Antlitz des Fremden*).

McCrindle 2010: XI, 370–1). Another source, the seventh-century account of the Buddhist monk Xuanzang, mentions the defeat of a 'cruel king' by Bālāditya of Magadha/Malwa. The identification of all these characters with Mihirakula, however, is highly suspect, as his name is actually not clearly given, and assumptions are commonly made conjecturally. It is presumably following this last setback that the Alkhans retreat back to Gandhara, and possibly even further west to Kabul, as may be indicated by the coins of the 'Rückwanderende' Alkhans (Göbl 1967: I.155ff; and see below on Nēzak rule in Kabul).

NUMISMATIC EVIDENCE FOR ALKHAN HISTORY

The initial phase of Alkhan coin series appears to have had close connections with those of the Kidarites.[13] Early Alkhan coins use the same dies as the issues of Shapur II and Shapur III, from an eastern mint that has been provisionally called the 'Kabul' mint (Alram and Pfisterer 2010: 16; Schindel 2004: 282–4). These coins show the king wearing a Shapur II or III crown, with the Bactrian legend, re-engraved on an already existing die, αλχα/αλχανο, which distinguishes them as issues of the new Alkhan authorities.[14] What

---

[13] Alram and Pfisterer 2010: 15 and Vondrovec 2014: 31 both present type 11 of the Kidarite coins which includes the Brahmi legend *Alakha*, suggested to be the same as *Alkhan* (Cribb 2010: 104). Considering the presence of the name 'Kidara the King' on type 39 of the Alkhans (Rezakhani 2015b), this seems quite plausible, although we should still remember the possibility that *Alkhan* (and thus the Brahmi *Alakha* on Kidarite type 11 coins) is originally a personal name.

[14] Vondrovec 2014: 177 calls these early issues those of *the Anonymous Clan Rulers*, appearing before the independent Alkhan issues.

is worth noting here is that these coins show direct continuity from the 'Kabul' issues of the Sasanians (Vondrovec 2014: 45). They also demonstrate that the Alkhans only started issuing coins in the southern Hindu Kush, with no early coins in Tokharistan/Bactria. This is perhaps the most important characteristic of the Alkhans, setting them apart from the Hephthalites, who conversely seem to have remained solely in Tokharistan and expanded from there to the northeast and north, but never south and southeast into the Kabul region and Gandhara, as was the case with all previous invaders.

The second stage of Alkhan coins demonstrates more confidence on the part of the new dynasty and a firmer establishment in the Kabul region, and a possible penetration into Gandhara. These coins are newly created dies, still bearing the bust of the Sasanian Shapur II (and less often Shapur III), also carrying the S1 or the Alkhan *tamgha* (Ilyasov 2003: 131–57). This *tamgha* could have originated as a local sign of the Kabul mint and only later been adopted by the Alkhan authorities as their royal insignia or clan marker (Rezakhani 2015b). The reverse of the silver issues, maintaining the canonical Sasanian reverse type of two attendants standing on either side of a fire altar, confirms the connection of this coin type with their original Sasanian prototypes. The reverses of the closely related series of copper coins, however, bear only the S1 and S2 *tamgha*s, affirming the independent Alkhan issues and slowly distinguishing themselves from the Sasanian style (Vondrovec 2014: 178–9).

The next stage of the Alkhan coins shows great progress in their history. In this stage, the portrait of the king on the obverse of the coin ceases to be a copy of the Sasanian authorities and their distinguished, bearded busts. Instead, a unique bust of an authority with elongated upper part of the skull, a prominent nose, and noticeable moustache on a beardless face appears on the coin obverse (Alram and Pfisterer 2010: 18). The bust is depicted either bareheaded or wearing various diadems or crowns, as well as earrings or other decorations, each marking a stage of coin development.[15] The coins of these 'Early Anonymous Alkhans' are found in the region of Peshawar and thus might indicate a conquest of Gandhara by the Alkhans, or the circulation of their coins in this region (Vondrovec 2014: 180). Another set of coins bearing the legend þαυο ζαοβλ αλχανο *Shaho Zaobl Alkhano* ('King of Zabul Alkhan') indicates

---

[15] This stage is called 'Early Anonymous Alkhan' by Vondrovec 2014: 179–80. The stylistic development, including the evolution of the crown types and distinguishing marks such as a hoop-shaped pearl earring, is discussed in Vondrovec 2014: 169–76 in great detail.

Alkhan control of the regions to the west and southwest of Kabul, namely the area of Ghazni and the subsequent region of Zabulistan (Vondrovec 2014: 186).

The Zabul-type coins of 'King Alkhano' occasionally also bear a personal name χιγγιλο *Khingil*. The name is known too from a subsequent series of coins with the Brahmi legend *khi-gi-la*. The appearance of the name Khingila, in various Bactrian or Brahmi forms (Sims-Williams 2010: 148, no. 520), marks the beginning of a stage where we can attempt to match the numismatic sources with other evidence. The coins of Khingila cover a large set of Alkhan coins and include coins from many different stylistic levels, suggesting that they were issued in different mints and over a long period of time (Vondrovec 2014: 183). Khingila is the first Alkhan authority whose name is attested, and he is known from other sources as well, including inscriptions on a silver bowl (Sims-Williams and Tucker 2005: 589).[16] He may indeed have been the authority who issued the previous 'Early Anonymous Alkhan' coin series (Vondrovec 2014: 184). The reverse of his coins, like those of the Early Anonymous Alkhans, shows remains of the Sasanian altar and attendants, although they are hard to distinguish because of a 'blind spot' caused by a thin flan which shows the obverse bust defacing most of the reverse (Vondrovec 2014: 179–80).

ALKHAN RULERS IN GANDHARA AND NORTHWEST INDIA

Alongside other Alkhan authorities, Khingila is also mentioned in the Schøyen copper scroll:

> In the sixty-eighth year on the seventh day of the bright half of the month Karttika: On this day this caitya of the Realized One containing relics was established by the lord of the great monastery, the son of Opanda, the Talaganika-Devaputra-Shahi, ... together with [his] father Opanda, together with [his] wife, the daughter of the Sarada- Śahi ..., together with the mistress of a great monastery Arccavamana, together with [her] father Ho ... gaya, [and] with [her] mother, the queen ..., together with the spiritual friend, the religious teacher Ratnagama, together with the great Shahi Khingila, together with the god-king Toramana, together with the mistress of a great monastery Sasa, together with the great Shahi Mehama, together

---

[16] The attempt by Dani 1996: 174, based on Biswas 1973: 137, to connect the coins of the Alkhan authority Khingila with the *Narendraditya Khinkhila* mentioned in *Rajatarangini* and living possibly in the early seventh century (Stein 1900: 346–50), should be considered void, as it cannot be supported by the numismatic evidence or by other epigraphic evidence such as the Schøyen copper scroll.

with Sadavikha, together with the great king Javukha, the son of Sadavikha, during the reign of Mehama. (Melzer 2006: 274)

The text has been used extensively to draw a picture of Alkhan history, including a chronology of events and order for the Alkhan rulers (Alram and Pfisterer 2010: 20–2; Vondrovec 2008; 2014: 184–5). The inscription includes the names Khingila, Toramana, Mehama, and Javukha, all of whom are known from numismatic and palaeographic sources. This has especially led to the conclusion that the four kings were indeed contemporary and alive around the year 492/3 (Alram and Pfisterer 2010: 22). However, as the text of the inscriptions states, the inscription was simply made during the reign of Mehama, called the *Great (or Maha) Shahi Mehama*. It does not make any direct claim to be contemporary with the other authorities mentioned, including Sadavikha, the father of Javukha, who is similarly mentioned but naturally assumed to be deceased. Consequently, the suggestions that all four authorities were reigning at the same time (Alram and Pfisterer 2010: 22) sounds untenable and an insistence on it appears counterproductive. Instead, the inscription simply evokes these authorities as previous distinguished sacrificers and benefactors of the same, or similar, stupas. In that case, the mention of their names simply shows a continuity of a tradition of dedicating stupas in the region and a reference to previous benefactors.

Apart from Khingila, the other kings mentioned in the copper scroll and known from their coin issues include Toramana, previously mentioned and extensively commemorated in Indian inscriptions. Toramana's coins only include copper issues, which bear his name, Toramana, or an abbreviated form such as *Tora* or *To*

Fig. 5.4. Silver drachm of Mihirakula with a Brahmi inscription
(© *das Antlitz des Fremden*).

(Vondrovec 2014: 211). The coins of Toramana and the copper issues of his son Mihirakula show a general correspondence, including in their heavier weight standard and also overstrikes of Mihirakula on those of Toramana. Considering the later silver issues of Mihirakula, Vondrovec assigns the copper issues to the Indian phase of the rule of Toramana and Mihirakula. In turn, he speculates that the silver drachm issues might belong to the period after Mihirakula's defeat by Yashodharma of Malwa and his return to Kashmir and then Gandhara, where silver was a currency (Vondrovec 2014: 216).

Apart from Toramana, the names of Javukha and Mehama are included in the Schøyen copper scroll and are also attested on their coin issues. I will discuss the case of Mehama later, among the Alkhan kings of the east. Javukha, as the issuer of silver coin types with the Brahmi legend *ṣāhi Javūkhaḥ*, minted coins close in style to those of Khingila, and his coins were indeed previously ascribed to either Khingila or Toramana. A particular type of his coins, showing a king riding a horse, is copied from the coins of Gupta emperors Chandragupta II (375–415) and Kumaragupta (415–55), possibly showing the area of their issue or circulation (Vondrovec 2014: 190–1). Several series among the large group of anonymous coin issues, in fact the most numerous of Alkhan coins, show a period of transition for the Alkhans, called the 'Rückwanderende' Alkhans, and includes the important anonymous coin type 150,[17] as well as the Alkhan coins with a buffalo skull (Vondrovec 2014: 197–202) and the Alkhan–Nēzak 'Crossover' series. All these show the end of the career of the Alkhans in India and their ultimate confinement in Gandhara and Kabul.

ALKHAN 'KINGS OF THE EAST': THE BIRTH OF KHURASAN?

A class of Alkhan coin authorities, including the aforementioned ruler identified as Mehama, must be classified as a separate entitiy, distinguished by the area of their influence. Among these, two kings named Zabokho and Adomano include a legend on their coins that reads μιρασανο βαο or 'the King of the East' (Vondrovec 2014: 202–6). This is particularly interesting since these rulers and their coins seem to connect to a later series of coins issued by the 'Tegin of Khurasan', who appears to be the ruler of the kingdom of Kabul under Turkic suzerainty (Vondrovec 2014: 203, and later on Western Turks). In terms of the Sasanians, this issue also relates to the division

[17] This is called Tora(mana) II by Pfisterer 2013.

of the Sasanian Empire into four distinct (military) administrative divisions (Gyselen 2001), one of which takes the Middle Persian name *Xwarāsān* 'Khurasan', with the same meaning of 'the east' as a parallel to the earlier Bactrian term, μιρασανο.

Apart from the evidence of the coin, Mehama is also known from the mention of his name in the Schøyen copper scroll, given above. Although Mehama's coins do not bear the legend 'the King of the East', his area of influence, as well as the locality of the scroll, would suggest to me an 'eastern' location for his kingdom. In the scroll he is known as *Maha-shahi Mehama* and is identified as the king under whose rule the stupa relating to the copper scroll was dedicated. He may also be be the same person whose name is mentioned on a Bactrian seal, where it is written as *me ia mo* (Lerner and Sims-Williams 2011: AA 6.3–4). Most significantly, we know his name from the Bactrian Economic Documents, where a king called *Meyam* is distinguished by the title of 'Meyam, the king of the people of Kadag,[18] the governor of the famous and prosperous king of kings Peroz' (BD II: *ea* 1 and *ed* 1).

Both Mehama and Adomano appear to have issued gold scyphate dinars in the style of the earlier Kushano-Sasanian and Kidarite ones (see Vondrovec 2014: 142–5). Adomano's silver issues all include the Bactrian legend αδομανο μιρασανο þαο 'Adomano, King of the East', and show similarities to the issues of Javukha and Mehama (Vondrovec 2014: 203–4). Mehama/Meyam's silver coins carry both Bactrian and Brahmi legends, with the Bactrian one commonly shortened to μηο (Sims-Williams 2010: 86, no. 246), while the Brahmi *saha mahama* is presented in different readings (Vondrovec 2014: catalogue 310–16). The Brahmi and Bactrian issues are stylistically close, which suggests that they were issued from the same mint, but were intended for circulation in different areas (Vondrovec 2014: 188), thus suggesting Mehama's rule over two cultural regions, or at least his claim to both. Some issues of Mehama bear the Alkhan *tamgha* S1, while types 316 and 317 are stylistically close enough to certain types of Khingila, Javukha, and Raja Lakhāna to be considered the issues of the same mint.

Zabokho, the other authority with the title of 'the King of the East', issued rare silver coins that were minted over a short period of time. These include a regular Alkhan type, with the king's bust on the obverse and the fire altar (often obliterated by the 'blind spot') on

---

[18] See also 'Āzboy ī ... boxt šāhān (?) kadag-xwadāy 'Āzboy son of ... (of) King of Boxt (my translation), the Lord of Kadag' in Gyselen 2007: 288, III/47.

The Alkhans in the Southern Hindu Kush

Fig. 5.5. Silver drachms of Zabokho, naming him as 'the King of the East' (© *das Antlitz des Fremden*).

the reverse (Vondrovec 2014: 204). The second is a 'horseman type' that is the main reason to connect his coins with those of Javukha (Vondrovec 2014: 205–6). Another reason, of course, is the philological correspondence of Bactrian *Zabokho* and Brahmi *Javukha* (Humbach 1966: 27–8; Sims-Williams 2010: 60, no. 139), showing that Javukha/Zabokho were the same authority and made a claim, much like that of Meyam/Mehama, to two linguistic/cultural areas.

Two more coin authorities issued coins that show their connection to the 'east'. The first one is *Rāja Lakhāna Udayāditya*, some of whose coins also bear Bactrian *Alkhano*.[19] His coins, not bearing any resemblance to the 'Eastern Style' coins of Zabokho and Adomano, has not been included in that series by Vondrovec. However, like Pūrvāditya, another authority who minted coins in the 'Eastern Style' (Vondrovec 2014: 207), his name may be of some relevance here. In fact, both *Udayāditya*[20] and *Pūrvāditya* mean 'east', or specifically, 'the rising/place of the sun'.[21] Linguistically, this corresponds to Bactrian μιιρασανο 'the place of the sun' and the later Middle Persian *khwarāsān* 'the place of the sun'. In the name of *Rāja Lakhāna Udayāditya* in particular, if we consider Lakhāna to be a personal name, the designation *Udayāditya* can then be assumed as a reference to the 'east' and a certain territorial claim. Here we might

---

[19] For a discussion of the relation between Brahmi *Lakhāna* and Bactrian *Alkhano*, promoted by Humbach 1966: 28–31 and followed by other philologists, but rejected by numismatists, see Vondrovec 2014: 191.
[20] As mentioned also by Vondrovec 2014: 192 n. 241, who is cautious about taking the issue further.
[21] Errington and Curtis 2007: 97 also made this suggestion, before the reading of Bactrian *miirasano* 'the east' on the coins could be made with more certainty.

be able to place the coins of this authority within the issues of the 'Kings of the East' as well.

Considering this information, we should then attempt to understand the geopolitical significance of the title 'King of the East' and its claimants. First of all, we should consider that the testimony of the coins places Mehama squarely within the Alkhan coin series, and thus in the Kabul/Gandhara region. Considering that the Kushano-Sasanians and the Kidarites issued their gold scyphate dinars from the mint of Balkh, we would expect that the production of the gold coins of Mehama and Adomano should also have taken place in Balkh. However, Vondrovec is of the opinion that the radically different style of the coinage of both rulers suggests that they were produced somewhere outside Balkh and circulated somewhere south of the Hindu Kush (Vondrovec 2014: 144–5). On the other hand, the Schøyen copper scroll identifies the locality of the stupa where it was deposited as Talaganika, identified provisionally as the city of Talaqan, in eastern Tokharistan (Melzer 2006).[22] As mentioned before, Melzer initially identified this place as the city of Talaqān in eastern Tokharistan, within the Badakhshan valley. Etienne de la Vaissière, however, has challenged this identification, instead suggesting that the city should be identified as Talagang in Gandhara, presently in the northwest of Pakistan (de la Vaissière 2012). This suggestion, placing Mehama at a location more in line with the coin evidence, has gained some popularity. The evidence from the Bactrian Documents, however, seems to place *Meyam*, if he is to be securely identified as the *Mehama* of the coins and the copper scroll, back in the region of eastern Tokharistan in Kadagestan, in a place identified by Sims-Williams as the area around Talaqan indeed, to the west of Badakhshan (Sims-Williams 2008: 98–9).[23] In this case, we are faced with the possibility that an Alkhan coin authority, Mehama, has issued coins in the region to the north of the Hindu Kush, where the Hephthalite power must have held sway. Here, the strict division between the Hephthalites and the Alkhans, maintained by numismatists, might be challenged, particularly as it concerns the connections between the Alkhans and the Hephthalites and their tribal and ethnic connections.[24]

---

[22] Although it is quite unlikely that this would be the case, but we should keep in mind that another city called *Talaqan* also existed to the *west* of Balkh, between Balkh and Marw; see Khurradādhbih 1967: 26.

[23] See also Gyselen 2007: 224, I/143 for the seal of the Ostāndār of Kadagestan, as well as the discussion in Sims-Williams 2008: 96–7 on this 'provincial administrator' of Kadagestan, a Sasanian province.

[24] On this, see Chapter 6 on the Hephthalites.

The information above can thus be considered within the context of the progress of Mehama/Meyam's career. As a local ruler of Kadagestan in eastern Tokharistan, Meyam became an ally of the Sasanian King of Kings Pērōz (AD 459–84) in his struggle against the Kidarites, and he may even have been among the people who offered Pērōz help in the initial stage of his career in his fight against his brother, Hormizd III (al-Tabari I.873). Following Pērōz's defeat of the Kidarites in AD 466, Meyam was elevated to the position of the 'governor of the famous and prosperous king of kings Pērōz', as attested by the Bactrian Documents (BD II: *ea* and *ed*). However, the power vacuum that was left after the Kidarite loss of Tokharistan allowed Meyam, like the Hephthalites (see next chapter), to stake a claim to independent, or at least autonomous, power. It is not impossible to consider that the embassy of 477 identified by Enoki as the last embassy of the 'Kidarites' to the Chinese court refers to envoys sent by one of the Kidarite successor states, possibly Mehama or an equal, trying to claim the position of the Kidarites and replacing them in the Chinese court (Enoki 1955b: 236). The next stage of Mehama's career is, then, joining the Alkhan, instead of Hephthalite, confederacy, probably accessing their Kabul stronghold via the Baghlan/Pol-e Khomri passage instead of the Samangan-Bamiyan.[25] In this sense, I would suggest that the identification of Talaganika in the Schøyen copper scroll with the Talaqan of the western Badakhshan/Panj-Ab region should be maintained, as it indeed reflects a possible course of career for an 'Alkhan' ruler of this region. That Mehama controlled, or was active in, both the eastern Tokharistan region and possibly parts of the Kabul region might be further hinted at by considering his bilingual coin issues.

The careers of the other authorities in this region can also be placed in context. Both Zabokho and Adomano identify themselves as the 'Kings of the East', a designation quite vague in geographical terms. If we consider the Gandhara region as the centre of Alkhan rule, on the basis of the issues of their coins and the written sources, the 'east' would mean that rulers such as Zabokho or Adomano indeed ruled over the regions of northern Kashmir, including Srinagar. However, it is generally agreed that the crossing over to Kashmir and further east and south to northern India was done by Toramana and Mihirakula,

---

[25] Vondrovec 2014: 225 suggested this, further positing that Meyam/Mehama might be taken as the Khar of Rōb, the main locality of the Bactrian Documents. I would rather follow Sims-Williams' original suggestion that Meyam, 'the King of the People of Kadag', should be placed further east of Rōb in the valley of Kunduz-Ab (Sims-Williams 2008: 98–9, map p. 89), or even further east in Badakhshan.

whose coins do not bear any claim to the kingship of the east. Nor do these sources imply any particular division of the Alkhan territory into western and eastern regions, one that could merit the issue of particular series concerned with the eastern parts of these territories.

In fact, the strong claim to 'the east' appears more as a claim, or a desire, than an actual statement of rule, and it may have been a place that was being progressively lost to the Alkhan rulers issuing coins in the south of the Hindu Kush. To me, this indicates that the place in question is in eastern Tokharistan, somewhere the Alkhans had been active before, but had ceased to control, possibly due to its loss to the rising power of the Hephthalites in the late fifth and early sixth centuries. So the careers of Zabokho/Javukha and Adomano can also be placed within this scheme. Both authorities, probably representing the first generation of Alkhan rulers after the loss of eastern Tokharistan to the Hephthalites, saw it as politically necessary to issue coins, in Bactrian but minted south of the Hindu Kush (Vondrovec 2014: 145), in order to stake their claims to that territory, which they perhaps saw as being under threat from the rising Hephthalite power in Tokharistan. The fact that Javukha's name is mentioned at the end of the list of kings in the Schoyen copper scroll, and only after the name of his father Sādavikhā, demonstrates that in AD 492/3, he was young compared to Khingila, or indeed Mehama, who had been active since AD 466 at least. Adomano possibly belonged to a still younger generation. Both of these authorities, based in the southern part of the Hindu Kush, possibly in the Kabul area and further west in Bamiyan and Zabulistan, issued coins claiming their rule over eastern Tokharistan. Other authorities, particularly Rāja Lakhāna Udayāditya and Pūrvāditya, might represent the next generation of Alkhan kings, who continued a claim to the 'east' by issuing coins from the same mints, and in the general style of Adomano and Zabokho/Javukha, while intending the coins for the regions they actually controlled, namely Gandhara and possibly the Kabul region. Alternatively, the Udayāditya and Pūrvāditya coins may be assigned to other known Alkhan authorities, possibly Toramana or Mihirakula, issuing coins in this style from Kabul, before abandoning the region for Gandhara in the face of pressure from the Nēzak Shahs. This might then be useful for understanding the rise of the Nēzak Shahs in the early sixth century, before AD 530 (Vondrovec 2014: 457).[26] Additionally, it will be useful for understanding several coin series which show Nēzak influences and the

---

[26] See Chapter 8 on the Nezak Shahs in Kabul and Zabul.

process of the 'return' of the Alkhans in the late sixth century to their original base in Kabul (Vondrovec 2014: ch. 8).

The development of the term *Miirasano* 'the east' as an administrative designation under these Alkhan rulers is possibly the forerunner of the Sasanian administrative division of *Khurasan*, similarly meaning 'the east'. This division of the Sasanian Empire into four administrative and military zones only happens during the reign of Khosrow I Anusheruwan (AD 531–79) (Gyselen 2001). This is also after the defeat of the Hephthalites in AD 560 and the takeover of the Hephthalite territories to the south of the Oxus, including the former region of Kadagestan in eastern Tokharistan, by the Sasanians. The transformation of the term and its correspondence to a larger region is thus a development of the late Sasanian and early Islamic periods, and will be further discussed in future chapters.

CONCLUSION

The Alkhans represent the second major division of the Iranian Huns. For long grouped together with the Hephthalites, the details of their history were left unnoticed and mingled with disparate information about the Hephthalites. Thanks to clear numismatic evidence, we are now able to clarify the textual information that relates to Alkhan history. This makes it clear that the Alkhans were active in the southern Hindu Kush, initially in the Kabul region and perhaps also in Zabulistan, while later establishing their base in Gandhara. At least a group of them, represented by Toramana and Mihirakula, attempted conquering northern India, an attempt that was ultimately unsuccessful. Other contemporaries continued to claim authority in eastern Tokharistan, where they originated as Iranian Huns. In this region, they were opposed by the Hephthalites and most likely did not succeed in creating any viable power. The Alkhans were later integrated with the Nēzak rulers of Kabul, before being overwhelmed by the wave of Turkic invasions that had previously destroyed the Hephthalite power in Sogdiana and Tokharistan.

Alkhan royal ideology, as reflected in their coins, seems to include many elements taken from their Sasanian and Kidarite predecessors. They, however, introduced innovations that became influential in the artistic representations of the wider region. The depiction of their kings with artificially elongated skulls and a prominent moustache, but without a beard, was clearly based on their ethnic customs and was a departure from the Sasanian prototypes. This was so consistent that their rule over Zabulistan and Kabulistan made them representative of this region, causing the Iranian hero Rostam, a mythical king of Zabulistan, to be depicted as an Alkhan king in the frescoes on the wall of a house in Panjikent, Sogdiana.[27] For Iranians in later periods, the Alkhans and their king Khingila represented the kings of India, and their memory was preserved within the history of Sasanian dealings with the east. The Alkhans, long forgotten by historians, have thus emerged from various sources as an independent power that was determining in the history of East Iran.

---

[27] Belenitskii and Marshak 1981: 14–15; Grenet 2002b: 218–20; for a discussion of the frescoes, see Marshak 2002.

6 The Hephthalite 'Empire' and its Successors

INTRODUCTION

The fame of the Hephthalites in the history of Central Asia is quite disproportionate to what we actually know about them from historical records. The debate on whether they are to be considered a separate entity from the Alkhans, as promoted by numismatists, is among the most important issues surrounding the identity of the Hephthalites.[1] On the other hand, their reputation as the mighty enemies of the Sasanian King of Kings Pērōz and the benefactors of his son Kavad is already quite notorious – and indeed forms the basis of our familiarity with them. In contrast, we know very little about them and what they did prior to their control of Tokharistan/Bactria, and also very little about the period of their power in the region and their fate after their defeat in AD 560. The period of their ascendance in Tokharistan and Transoxiana between AD 470 and 560 – when we hear of them in the context of their interactions with the Sasanians – has been dubbed the period of the *Imperial* Hephthalites (Grenet 2002b: 209). Following their defeat at the hands of the joint Sasanian–Western Turk confederacy, their remaining 'principalities' form autonomous small authorities, which survived under Sasanian and Western Turk rule.[2]

---

[1] See Göbl 1967: 89ff and Vondrovec 2014: 405–6. For an opposing view, see Grenet 2002b. Considering all the 'Hunnic' rulers of Tokharistan, the Kabul Valley, Gandhara, and Kashmir following the disappearance of the Kidarites as 'Hephthalites' goes back to the nineteenth century. Sir Alexander Cunningham considered the Alkhan rulers to be Hephthalites, and the designation continues even to a 2010 dissertation on the Hephthalites; see Kurbanov 2013.

[2] See Grenet 2002b: 209–20 for a discussion of the possible remains of these 'principalities.' Grignaschi 1984 has some complicated, and at times fanciful, theories about the possible

HEPHTHALITES AND SASANIANS

In textual sources, the Hephthalites are first mentioned in the context of their interaction with the Sasanians. So it seems appropriate to provide a summary of this encounter before detailing what else can be said about the Hephthalites themselves outside the context of their relations with their western neighbours. Following the defeat of the Kidarites in 466, the Hephthalite confederacy appears to have set about expanding its power over the rest of Tokharistan from an eastern base, possibly in the Badakhshan region. The Hephthalite control of Tokharistan must have been complete by 260 of the *Bactrian* Era (260 + 223: AD 483),[3] since this is the time when we first hear of a *Hephthalite Tax* being imposed on the region where the Bactrian Documents were written, namely the area of Rōb and Madr in the mountainous region to the north of Bamiyan and in southern Tokharistan (Sims-Williams 1997c; 2002).

Previously, however, as a son of Yazdgerd II, Pērōz had to compete for his throne with his brother, Hormizd III (457–9). Pērōz, based in the east as governor of Sistan (Daryaee 2009: 24; al-Tabari I.872; Anonymous 1375: 278), enlisted the help of the 'men of Tokharistan' (i.e. the Hephthalites)[4] in defeating Hormizd and claimed the crown for himself in AD 459. This episode is thus the first time we hear of the Hephthalites, and their direct involvement in installing a Sasanian King of Kings must testify to their already significant presence in East Iran. The king of the Hephthalites often mentioned in connection with these events is one *Akhshunwar*,[5] about whom we have no evidence from the coinage. The name does not render any viable etymology, although the element *xšn-* might be related to Old Iranian *xšay-* root 'to rule, to govern' (prominent in the titles of various Central Asian local rulers, from the *Ikhshid* of Ferghana to the *Afshin* of Ustrushana).[6] Consequently the name may possibly be

---

relation between the fall of the Hephthalites and the rise of the Avars in the steppe, based on one of the Chinese designations for them, connecting the Hephthalites to the 'real' Avars.

[3] This is based on the now widely accepted suggestion of de Blois for the calculation of the Bactrian Era from AD 223: de Blois 2006.

[4] Bosworth (in al-Tabari 1999: 109, n. 280) suggests either the Kidarites or the Hephthalites, which seems reasonable, although imagining them as 'early' Hephthalites is possibly more consistent with the future policy of Pērōz towards the Kidarites. For a possible connection to Alkhan history, see Chapter 5 on the 'eastern Alkhans'.

[5] Al-Tabari I.874; *Khushnawaz* in the *Shahnameh* of Ferdowsi, where he is anachronistically called 'the King of the Turks'.

[6] Henning 1936: 17 suggests Sogdian *'xš'wnd'r* 'power holder', while Widengren 1952: 75 reads it as *'xš'wnw'r* 'power bearer' in Sogdian, which does not require an assumption that Arabic و 'w' is a mistake for د 'd' as Henning requires. See also Livshits 2015d: 233. The same

considered a title, belonging to one or more kings of the Hephthalites known through narrative sources.

Following his succession to power in 459, Pērōz undertook a series of campaigns against the Kidarites in Tokharistan, resulting in a crushing defeat of the latter in AD 466/7 and their disappearance from the political scene of Tokharistan.[7] This was initially followed by a stage of Sasanian power, known through Pērōz's gold dinar issues from Balkh (Vondroverc 2014: 142).[8] This must have created a vacuum in power, allowing the Hephthalites, who at this time were present in eastern Tokharistan, to expand their power in the whole region (Czegledy 1984: 215). Their capital was probably located around the present-day city of Kunduz in eastern Tokharistan, known to Al-Biruni as *War-Walīz*, a name that might be connected with the Chinese designation of the Hephthalites as *Hua* (Czegledy 1984: 216). However, the presence of the elements *war*, Middle Persian for 'shelter, enclosure' (MacKenzie 1971: 87) and *liz*, the Bactrian word for 'fortress',[9] may imply a more local meaning.

This expansion is perhaps what brought the Hephahlites into contact with Pērōz, who according to an outlandish claim by al-Tabari attacked the Hephthalites because of their 'engagement in the sin of the people of Lot (i.e. Sodomites)'![10] Pērōz's early attempts were disastrous and ended in his having to agree to a treaty and give up Talaqan to the west of Balkh to the Hephthalites.[11] A second campaign ended with the capture of Pērōz and his agreement to the payment of thirty mule packs of silver drachms in ransom, parts of which he paid through imposing a poll tax, and for the rest left his son Kavad as a hostage with the Hephthalites (Pseudo-Joshua, 10–11).[12] Procopius suggests that *Akhshunwar* compelled Pērōz to

---

root is also related to the title Xūv, given as the general title for princes in Sogdiana (Livshits 2015d) and might also be related to Šēr, given as the title of the rulers of Khuttalan and Bamiyan in Khurradādhbih 1967: 32.

[7] See above, Chapter 4.

[8] This can also be assumed from Priscus' statement that Pērōz took Balkh (Βαλααμ) from the Kidarites (Priscus, *Exc. De Leg. Gent.* 22)

[9] BDII: 227, from *diza; cf. Middle Persian *diz* 'fortress'; MacKenzie 1971: 26.

[10] Al-Tabari I.873; Bal'ami 1386: 835; see al-Tabari 1999: 110, n. 284. See also Shahbazi 1389/2010: 470, n. 518, where he dismisses the accusation.

[11] Al-Tabari I.876; -Joshua the Stylite 2000: 9; Bal'ami 1386, 838, who considers this to be the occasion during which the boundary tower (see below) was built. There are two Talaqans in the region of Bactria/Tokharistan: one is the more famous city of Talaqan in the district of Panj-Āb in western Badakhshan, while the less famous one is the Talaqan located to the north-west of Balkh and west of Tirmidh; Anonymous 1375: 279, and also Shahbazi 1389/2010: 464, n. 507; contra Nöldeke (Nöldeke and al-Tabari 1879: 116, n. 1), who mistakes it for the more easterly city.

[12] Priscus implies that Pērōz asked Leo I (457–74) for assistance, but was refused (Blockley 1983: 344).

prostrate himself before him, a humiliating task that he undertook, advised by his Magi, by pretending to prostrate himself before the Hephthalite king, while in fact worshipping the sun or the sun god Mithras (Procopius, *Wars* I.iii.17–19). Procopius seems to suggest that the war tactic of the Hephthalites was to appear to be retreating, while in fact laying various forms of ambush for the advancing army (Procopius, *Wars* I.iii.13–17, I.iv.5–10).

On his last campaign against the Hephthalites, Pērōz approached them with a large army. Dīnawarī (1888: 88) relates that Pērōz destroyed the tower built by Wahram V as the boundary between the Sasanian territories and the land of the 'Turks', here standing for the Hephthalites. The story is repeated in al-Tabari with more details. Apparently, upon reaching the boundary tower of Wahram V, Pērōz used the trick of binding 'fifty elephants plus three hundred men linked together' to the tower, dragging it in front of his army while he marched behind the moving tower, pretending not to have violated the peace treaty of his grandfather (al-Tabari I.878–9). The last battle seems to have been a disaster, told by many authorities in the same way. Akhshunwar, not wanting to engage directly with Pērōz, dug a large trench across the battlefield while still within his own country (Procopius *Wars* I.iv.7) and covered it with shrubbery and loose wood to conceal it. When Pērōz and his men, including 'thirty of his sons' (Procopius, *Wars* I.iv.2), attacked the retreating Hephthalite army, they fell into the trench and perished in the trap; their bodies were never recovered (al-Tabari I.879). Pseudo-Joshua, in his regular spiteful way, suggests that Pērōz might have escaped the trench, but no one knows what happened to him and whether he died of hunger in a cleft in the mountain or was devoured by wild animals in a forest (pseudo-Joshua 2000: 11).

SUKHRA AND THE RESTORATION OF SASANIAN RULE

The defeat of Pērōz allowed for complete Hephthalite control of the eastern regions, and probably brought into their possession the control of the itinerant royal Sasanian mint of *BBA* (Schindel 2004: I, 154–5) which also continued to produce coins with the mintmark AS (Asurestan in Mesopotamia) (Vondrovec 2014: 400). It seems certain that Akhshunwar captured Pērōz's entourage, including his daughter 'Pērōzduxt' and his Mobeds, the priestly entourage (al-Tabari I.879). Pērōzduxt subsequently became a lady of the Hephthalite court and gave birth to a daughter who later married her uncle Kavad (Pseudo-Joshua, 15–16). The royal treasury, and the Mobeds, however, were set free by the heroic efforts of one 'Sukhra, who had the rank of Qārīn'[13] and was the ruler of Sajistan (i.e. Sistan), despite being originally from the district of Ardashir-Khurra in Fars/Persis (al-Tabari I.877). The episode of the involvement of Sukhra in Sasanian political affairs is quite fascinating, since it shows a fundamental shift in them, as well as bearing a curious resemblance to some famous Persian epic stories.

According to al-Tabari, as well as other Muslim historians such as Dīnawarī, Sukhra became an important and instrumental member of the Sasanian administrative aristocracy and effectively a king-maker. He is essential in elevating Walash (AD 484–8), Pērōz's brother and immediate successor, to power (al-Tabari I.883), and by switching sides to that of Kavad, allows the latter also to succeed to the throne (al-Tabari I.885). His son *Zarmihr* is essential too in allowing Kavad to escape his captivity (al-Tabari I.886–7), and the family of Sukhra preserved their primacy until the rise of *Shahpur-e Razi* ('Shahpur from Rayy'),[14] who seems to have destroyed their power with the support of Kavad himself (al-Tabari I.885).[15] The narrative of the rise of Sukhra additonally includes an episode of his heroic deeds, which is worth considering.

In al-Tabari's description of the aftermath of the death of Pērōz and the capture of his entourage and their recovery by Sukhra, the hero's actions are described as follows:

> Akhshunwar dispatched a mighty army against Sūkhrā. When the two sides met, Sūkhrā rode out against them, and found them eager to battle. It is said that he shot an arrow at a man who had ridden out to attack him; the arrow struck the latter's horse between the eyes and became almost totally sunk in his head. The horse fell down dead, and Sūkhrā was able to capture its rider. Sūkhrā spared his life, and instructed him to go back to his master and inform him about what he had seen. (al-Tabari I.877)

The story continues with a frightened Akhshunwar who then restores to Sukhra the treasury of the perished Pērōz and all of his entourage, including his daughter. The narrative, as can easily be observed, is

---

[13] This is a mistake by al-Tabari, assuming that the clan name of Karin was in fact an administrative rank of the Sasanians.

[14] This would conceivably make Shapur a member of the Mihranid family, one of the supposed Seven Great Families of the Sasanian Empire; for the administrative role of these in general see Lukonin 1983. An extensive study of the Seven Great Families is now Pourshariati 2008: 70ff. (on the Mihranids). Wahram Čobin (for whom see Chapter 8 on the Western Turk period) was specified as a Mihranid as well.

[15] For a discussion of the placement of this event within the reign of Kavad, see Schindel 2013.

Fig. 6.1. Silver drachm, Hephthalite, imitating the coins of Sasanian Pērōz (© *das Antlitz des Fremden*).

highly elaborate and in line with the familiar epic tales of heroes. The shot later becomes one of the three legendary shots (al-Tabari I.993) which had been instrumental in thwarting disasters. However, the acts of Sukhra – his one-man defeat of the enemy, his restoration of goods, and his instrumentality in restoring Sasanian power – are curiously similar to the stories of Rostam, the great hero of *Shahnameh*, who is also intimately associated with Sistan, where Sukhra is the governor. The name Sukhra is the Middle Persian form of Sohrāb, a name associated with the family of Rostam, who has a famous son of the same name. Considering the universal prominence of Sukhra in the Islamic historical narratives, we might postulate that these sources transmitted a narrative close to the family of Sukhra.

KAVAD AND THE HEPHTHALITES

During Kavad's stay in the Hephthalite court as a hostage, his uncle Walash, mistakenly considered a son of Peroz by al-Tabari (I.883), was raised to a position of power. Walash named himself *hukay* (Pahlavi hw-kdy) 'Good *Kay* (prince)' on his coins (Schindel 2004: 421–2), a title which is clearly following in the tradition of his father Yazdgerd II and his elder brother, Pērōz, who use the Avestan title *Kay* on their coins, replacing the established title *Šāhānšāh* (MLK'n MLK') 'King of Kings'.[16] Walash's addition of the prefix *hu-* 'Good' signifies his claim to have been the righteous, and legitimate, ruler, as opposed

---

[16] The title *kay* ushers in a new era of royal identity for the Sasanians; see Shayegan 2003. The designation, however, had already appeared much earlier on the coinage of the Kushanshahn Wahram, who on his silver issues uses *kdy* as his title; Grenet 2002b: 205; and Chapter 4 above.

to his nephew Kavad who enjoyed the support of the Hephthalites, the same power that had defeated and killed his father. Ultimately, though, a combined force of Kavad and the Hephthalites proved to be superior to that of Walash, and in 488 replaced *hukay* Walash with *Kay* Kavad I, for what came to be known by the historians as his 'first rule' (Daryaee 2009: 26–7; Schindel 2004: 436–49).

Indeed, events between 488 and 492 have significant consequences for Sasanian history, and in many senses the history of Central Asia as well. Traditionally, historians of this period, mainly the Muslim historians of the tenth and eleventh centuries, associated this period with the rise of a religious reformer, or heretic, named Mazdak, and his success in seducing Kavad to his cause (Daryaee 2009: 26–7; Yarshater 1983: 991–1024). Mazdak's heretical beliefs are said to have consisted of a call to share all wealth and to share 'wives' communally between people of different classes of society (Daryaee 2009: 86–91). Muslim historians and heresiographers considered this to be an attempt to sully the blood of the elite and to humiliate them, essentially hinting at Kavad's compliance, and even willingness, in achieving such means in order to control his over-powerful nobles. The nobility, alongside Zoroastrian clerics, rose in rebellion against such indignity and removed Kavad from the throne, imprisoning him in a notorious prison and replacing him on the throne with a brother, Jamasp (492–6) (Daryaee 2009: 27). Kavad, however, managed to escape the prison with the help of his wife and a noble retainer, Zarmihr, son of the aforementioned Sukhra, taking refuge with his former captors, the Hephthalites, and taking his throne back in AD 499 (Daryaee 2009: 27). Thereafter, he continues as a successful ruler until AD 531. Towards the end of Kavad's life, however, the Mazdakite menace seems to have appeared again, requiring the intervention of his famously righteous son, Khosrow I Anusheruwan (531–79), who then removed his old father from the throne and by massacring Mazdak and his followers, ushered in a new era of Zoroastrian rule (Daryaee 2009: 28).

This convenient, and highly symbolic, narrative has been studied, and dismissed, by many historians.[17] Details such as the absence of the name Mazdak in all contemporary sources (Joshua the Stylite, Malalas, or Procopius) have been used to demonstrate that the character of a reformer-priest like *Mazdak* was a later

---

[17] See Gaube 1982, who completely denies the existence of Mazdak. Crone 1991, in a more nuanced update of Gaube's views, suggests a sensible clarification of the chronology, dissociating Kavad's first removal from power from the Mazdakite movement at the end of his reign.

creation.[18] Many detailed studies of Zoroastrian and Muslim accusations about the Mazdakites are used to show too that the Mazdakite heresy was in fact an attempt at social reform (Christensen 1925), which most likely included Kavad's own ideas for changing the structure of Sasanian power after the serious setbacks of the reign of Pērōz (Crone 1991). The role of the so-called Mazdakite movement in creating a Zoroastrian response and thus helping to create an 'orthodox' reading of the Zoroastrian scripture is also of interest and worth consideration (Rezakhani 2015a). What might be the most significant contribution for historical purposes, however, is the admirable effort at separating the events of Kavad's long reign, providing an understanding of the differences in Kavad's first and second reigns, and highlighting the fact that Kavad's first removal owed more to the political environment of his establishment on the throne by the Hephthalites than to any religious heresy.[19]

The fact is that the first period of Kavad's reign, placed about a half century before his removal from the throne by Khosrow I and the latter's supposed massacre of the Mazdakites, most likely came to an end for reasons other than religious or social reform. Kavad was removed by force and took refuge with the Hephthalites, only gaining his throne back with their financial and military support. However, in the process of taking his throne back, Kavad is never said to have made a promise to give up his 'heretical' beliefs, nor did a supposed Zoroastrian clerical establishment impose conditions for his restoration (Rezakhani 2015a: 10–12). In fact, both his removal from the throne and his restoration are purely political, and mainly militaristic, depending on the support offered by the Hephthlites. The religious reason for this restoration is thus added at a later period in order to justify Kavad's original removal, most likely as the result of an internal coup by the anti-Hephthalite nobility. His restoration then needs to be considered in the context of his relations with, or indeed dependence on, Hephthalite backing and support.

We know that Kavad's first rule was itself the result of a clear Hephthalite intervention (Joshua2000, 23) and was only achieved via the removal of Walash from the throne, with the remarkable

---

[18] Gaube 1982; with modifications by Crone 1991; the issue is now fully treated by Crone in her 2012 study.
[19] Crone 1991, where she argues that the events leading to Kavad's removal in AD 496 are to be set apart from the Mazdakite revolt of the later period of his rule. Her argument is that the first period of Kavad's rule is signified by Kavad's own reforms, and possible heretical beliefs, which result in his removal, while the episode relating to Mazdak is a later and separate occurrence. Although a direct connection with Kavad's position as a Hephthalite appointee is not made, the implications are clear.

persistence of Sukhra in power even following the removal of his protégé (al-Tabari I.888).[20] The opposition to Kavad's succession certainly did not disappear after his ascent to the throne, most likely dividing the nobility. If we consider the testimonies of al-Tabari and Dīnawarī on the issue, the family of Sukhra at least appear to have taken Kavad's side on the issue, helping him to escape from prison following his removal. Others, however, opposed Kavad and his Hephthalite backers and, in a palace coup, removed the king in favour of a more accepted successor, his younger brother Jamasp (Daryaee 2009: 27). The involvement of Zarmihr, the son of Sukhra, is also significant in the future rule of Khosrow I, as the episode of the conception of Khosrow by a peasant girl in the midst of the 'Mazdakite conteroversy' through the help and intervention of Sukhra (al-Tabari I.887; Schindel 2013)[21] had obvious consequences for legitimizng the future monarch. As a result, Khosrow, being set apart from his brothers who might have been considered illegitimate because of Mazdakite sexual communalism, was presented as the only possible heir to Kavad.[22] After a few years at the Hephthalite court, possibly witnessing the gradual rise of the Hephthalites to a position above their former masters, the Kidarites, Kavad then managed to take his throne back and remove Jamasp.

After this episode, we do not hear anything about the state of Sasanian interactions with the Hephthalites.[23] They seem to have shifted most of their attention to the west for the remainder of Kavad's reign. It is during the reign of Khosrow I Anusheruwan (AD 531–79) that this Sasanian monarch – most beloved by the Muslim historians – managed to recover 'Sind, Bust, Al-Rukkhaj, Zābulistān, Tukhāristān, Dardistān, and Kābulistān' (al-Tabari I.894; Ibn Balkhi 1385: 94). Al-Tabari puts these events before the tale of the joint

---

[20] Procopius, *Wars* I.6.18 tells us that Walash was removed by the nobility and was blinded, although Procopius confuses Walash with Jamasp, his nephew and the brother of Kavad I, who was installed after the removal of Kavad himself in AD 496.

[21] Dīnawarī has a more detailed version of this story in which the girl is also related to Sukhra himself, further establishing the connection of the Sukhra family to power; Dīnawarī 1888: 65–6.

[22] The name of the girl is given as Niwandukht (Dīnawarī 1888: 67). Of course the mother of Khosrow I is most likely the daughter of a nobleman of the Ispahbedh family (Ibn Balkhi 1385: 85).

[23] The Sasanians, and most likely the person of Kavad himself, did leave a rather strong impression in the Hephthalite-dominated Tokharistan, though. The name of the district of Qubadian, known from Islamic sources where it is considered part of Balkh (*Mu'jam ul Buldan*, *Muntahi ul 'Irab*) and still existing to the east of Termez, should be assigned to the presence of Kavad (Arabic *Qubad*). He may have lived in the region while under Hephthalite protection, as the area is reasonably near Balkh, or he may have founded its capital city of the same name.

attack of the Sasanians and the Turkish Khagan Sinjibū against the Hephthalites (al-Tabari I.896), at last taking revenge for his grandfather, Pērōz (Ibn Balkhi 1385: 94). This event thus breaks the Hephthalite 'Empire', and causes their 'fading' from historical records (Sims-Williams 2008: 96–7).

HEPHTHALITES IN TOKHARISTAN

Outside the narrative of Sasanian history, the Hephthalites are known through ambiguous notices in Chinese and Byzantine sources, as well as numismatic evidence. Apart from the coins, which allow us to understand at least the extent, or limits of the extent, of their power, the other narratives are often confusing and contradictory, and very much open to interpretation.

The name Hephthalite is mentioned in the work of the Byzantine historian Procopius, who calls them Ἐφταλιται, while Pseudo-Joshua, who lived close to the period of Sasanian engagement with them, always calls them Huns or Chionites. A seal bearing the legend ηβοδαλο ββγο 'Yabghu/governor of the Hephthal' shows the local, Bactrian form of their name, ēbodāl, which is commonly abbreviated to ηβ on their coins (Vondrovec 2014: 404). In Armenian sources, they are known as Hep't'al, and in Middle Persian sources as ēftāl (Litvinsky 1999: 138). In Arabic and Classical Persian histories, they are often mentioned as *Hayātila* (sg. Hytāl), most likely a spelling mistake for *hbtāl/hptāl* (al-Tabari I.872–3; Bal'ami, 835). In Chinese sources, they are known as *I-ta* or *Yida* (Kuwayama 2002: 130; Enoki 1959: 7), which might have been pronounced *iepdal* (Vondrovec 2014: 406, quoting de la Vaissière), and their king was known as Yen-tai-i-li-t'o, possibly pronounced *Yeptalitha* (Enoki 1959: 7) and thus in fact their clan/dynastic name. Song-Yun, the famous Chinese traveller who visited the Hephthalites on the banks of the Oxus in AD 519, calls them *I-t'ein* (Enoki 1959: 7). Other scholars also explore the idea of the association of the Chinese term *Hua* with the Hephthalites, and its possible connection with the terms Uar/Avar (Grignaschi 1984). The matter of the 'ethnicity' or 'nationality' of the Hephthalites has been rather well discussed on the basis of the Chinese sources,[24] with a recent update and more convincing argument (de la Vaissière 2007). This suggests that the Chinese sources, more than remarking on the 'nationality' of the Hephthalites, show a chronological fact of the migrations of the 'Hunnic' tribes from

---

[24] Most influentially by Enoki 1959, with further remarks in Enoki 1970.

the Altai region to Tokharistan and further south (de la Vaissière 2007: 120). The suggestion that the Hephthalites were originally of Turkic origin and only later adopted Bactrian as their administrative, and possibly native, language (de la Vaissière 2007: 122) seems to be most prominent at present.[25]

Other sources on the history of the Hephthalites include a reference to a *yabghu* of Hephthal (ηβοδαλο ββγο) on a seal that shows the frontal bust of a king with an elaborate headdress and a beardless face (Lerner and Sims-Williams 2011: AA 7 (Hc007)). The title *yabghu*, used here for a Hephthalite ruler, is also known from the Bactrian Documents (e.g. BD II: *Ja* 1–2). The title was known at least from the Kushan period, when it was used as that of the early Kushan kings (Sims-Williams 2002: 229). It probably comes from an Early Middle Chinese form meaning 'allied prince' (Humbach 1966: 24–8) and lasted well into the period of Turkic dominance in East Iran (Sims-Williams 2002: 235; 2010: 61). The Hephthalites are also mentioned as the ones imposing a tax on the region of Rōb, where the Bactrian Documents have been localised, identified as 'the Hephthalite tax' (BD I: *li* and *j*).

Contemporary sources from Byzantium commonly consider the Hephthalites to be a type of Hun, and Pseudo-Joshua actually calls them Turks. A famous quotation from Procopius, equating the terms White Huns and Hephthalites, has given rise to much speculation.

> At a later time the Persian King Pērōzes became involved in a war concerning boundaries with the nation of the Ephthalitae Huns, who are called White Huns, gathered an imposing army, and marched against them. The Ephthalitae are of the stock of the Huns in fact as well as in name; however they do not mingle with any of the Huns known to us, for they occupy a land neither adjoining nor even very near to them; but their territory lies immediately to the north of Persia; indeed their city, called Gorgo, is located over against the Persian frontier, and is consequently the centre of frequent contests concerning boundary lines between the two peoples. For they are not nomads like the other Hunnic peoples, but for a long period have been established in a goodly land. As a result of this they have never made any incursion into the Roman territory except in company with the Median army. They are the only ones among the Huns who have white bodies and countenances which are not ugly. It is also true that their manner of living is unlike that of their kinsmen, nor do they live a savage life as they do; but they are ruled by one king, and since they possess a lawful constitution, they observe right and justice in their dealings both with one another and

---

[25] However, see Sims-Williams 2002: 234, who criticised the assumption of their Turkic background on the basis of the statement of Al-Khwarizmi that the Khalach people are descendants of the Hephthalites, and who associated the presence of Turkish terminology with the period after the destruction of the Hephthalite 'Empire' by the Sasanian/Turkic alliance.

with their neighbours, in no degree less than the Romans and the Persians. Moreover, the wealthy citizens are in the habit of attaching to themselves friends to the number of twenty or more, as the case may be, and these become permanently their banquet-companions, and have a share in all their property, enjoying some kind of a common right in this matter. Then, when the man who has gathered such a company together comes to die, it is the custom that all these men be borne alive into the tomb with him. (Procopius, *Wars* I.iii.1–7)

This description is commonly used to establish some basic characteristics of Hephthalite society and suggest a different origin for them from the rest of the 'Huns'. But the use of the term 'White Huns' (λευκοὺς οὔννων) has prompted scholars to connect the term with their mention in other sources. Among these is the Middle Persian apocalyptic text *Zand ī Wahman Yasn* 4.58–9, where the *Spēd Xyōn* (White Khion) is set apart from *Karmīr Xyōn* (Red Khion) and those simply called *Xyōn* (Cereti 2010: 64–5).[26]

What the description does suggest, however, is that for Procopius, writing from over two thousand kilometres to the west of the Hephthalite lands, the latter held different characteristics from 'any of the Huns known to us', that is, known to Procopius and his Roman audience. His further suggestion that 'they are not nomads like the other Hunnic peoples, but for a long period have been established in a goodly land' should also be understood in the context of his audience, namely people acquainted with the Huns living in the Central European steppe.[27] This, however, in no way provides a reason for us to distinguish the Hephthalites from the Huns/Xyōn who lived in their own neighbourhood, namely Central Asia and East Iran. As far as we can tell from Procopius' statement, the Hephthalites were distinguished from the European Huns in their social structure, and possibly their appearance. But at the same time, their social structure and physical appearance could have been identical to those with whom Procopius' audience would not have been familiar, namely the Karmīr and other types of Xyōns, or, for what matters to us, the Kidarites and the Alkhans.[28]

---

[26] Note that contra Bailey 1932: 945–7, Cereti 2010: 65 dismisses the idea that the word after 'Turk' can be read as 'Heftal', for palaeographic reasons. This, repeated in Errington and Curtis 2007: 95 and elsewhere, has consequences for the identification of the Hephthalites and the White Huns. See a fuller discussion of these matters in Chapter 4.

[27] See a classical study of this, however, in Altheim 1969: esp. vol. II, which specifically addresses the Hephthalites – not the rest of the Chionites – and their connections with the Central European Huns.

[28] One could also consider this a literary device, since Theophylact Simocatta V.9.10 also says: 'They say that those Indians reared in the north are born whiteskinned.' There is no need to hold that these descriptions were aiming to be accurate at all.

The king mentioned by Procopius as ruling over the Hephthalites obviously finds a marked parallel in the personage (or the position) of Akshunwar/Khushnawaz, the king of the Hephthalites in the war against Pērōz and the restoration of Kavad. This king is not known from any sources apart from the Arabic and Persian ones mentioned above. In a note on his translation of al-Tabari, Nöldeke had already connected the name *Akhshunwar* with that of the Kunkhas/Kougchas mentioned by Priscus (Blockley 1983: 348), although Kunkhas is considered the king of the defeated Kidarites by Priscus. As mentioned above, Akhshunwar is probably best interpreted as a title, akin to other central Asian titles such as *Ikhshid* and *Afshin* and based on the old Iranian root of *xšay- 'to rule'. If we considered Priscus' Kunkhas to have been derived from the same root, we might conclude that the name of Kunkhas is also simply a title used by the Kidarites. Alternatively, considering the similarity between *Khushnawāz*, the name given by Ferdowsi for the king of the Hephthalites, and the *Kunkhas* of Priscus (in fact representing *xšun-*), there might be a chance of suggesting that the name of the Hephthalite king was adapted from that of the last Kidarite ruler, of whom we similarly have no coins. It might also suggest another way of thinking about tribal identities, if we think of Kunkhas and Khushnawāz/Akhshunwar as being the same name. In this way, the demise of the Kidarites at the hands of Pērōz and the rise of the Hephthalites can be seen as a shift in power, perhaps a transfer of Kidarite power to a 'Hephthalite' ruler known to us as Akhshunwar.

COINS OF THE HEPHTHALITES

The majority of Hephthalite coins form a single continuous series following the coins of Pērōz with his third crown. Consequently, they provide a rather reliable date of AD 474 as a *terminus post quem* for the start of the coin series (Vondrovec 2014: 399) or shortly after, possibly after Pērōz's death in 484 (Alram and Pfisterer 2010: 27, 31). This is in full agreement with the historical records, including the account of Pseudo-Joshua mentioned above (Pseudo-Joshua 11) that Pērōz was compelled to pay thirty mule-loads of silver drachms to the Hephthalites as a ransom. The coins of the Hephthalites are distinguished by faithfully copying the third type of Pērōz, adding certain characteristics that distinguish them as specifically circulating in the Hephthalite region. Most important among these is the reverse legend 'ηβ' and its variations, standing for *ēbodalo* or 'Hephthalite' (Vondrovec 2014: 399; Alram and Pfister 2010: 27). Apart from this, the reverse of the coins carries a mintmark βαχλο for *Balkh*, showing that the traditional capital Bactra acted as the main minting city of the Hephthalites. The coins also carry an obverse characteristic of four 'pellets' or dots on the margins of the coin, which immediately distinguishes them from the Sasanian issues.[29] On the reverse, apart from the mintmark, the coins carry the monogram of Pērōz, MP, supposedly standing for *MLK' pylwcy* 'King Pērōz'.[30]

Variants of the Pērōz-type coins, with details including the presence of various symbols on the obverse and reverse (Alram and Pfisterer 2010: 27–33; Vondrovec 2014: 399–404), help us establish a relative chronology of the Hephthalite coin issues. The appearance of certain elements, including the prominent Sasanian star and crescent on type 1e of the Hephthalites (Alram and Pfisterer 2010: 31) that first appear on the coins of Kavad, shows the continued issue of coins in the later fifth and sixth centuries. Variants of type 287, depicting the bust of a 'Hephthalite prince' holding a cup, show influences from the later Sasanian coins, including the second reign of Kavad (Alram and Pfisterer 2010: 33). The presence of a *tamgha*, named *tamgha* S2 by Gobl (Göbl 1967; but also Ilyasov 2003: 135–41), connects Hephthalite issues with Kidarite and also the Alkhan issues from Kabul (Alram and Pfisterer 2010: 33). The *tamgha* might also be related to Hephthalite (and possibly earlier Kidarite) control of Samarkand, as it becomes prominent in the coinage of Sogdiana in the period 500–700, prior to its Islamic conquest (Alram and Pfisterer 2010: 33; Smirnova 1981).

Tamgha S2 might also provide a possible connection with 'Hephthalite' coins before their adoption of the standard Pērōz type. The coins of Tobazini, an authority issuing coins in style of Wahram IV (388–99) and later Yazdgerd I (399–420), include a type 32a which bears the *tamgha* S2, as found on the Anonymous Clan Rulers of the Hephthalites, as well as type 59a of Khingila which is inscribed entirely in Bactrian, and of course appears on the later coins of Hephthalites closely associated with Balkh (Vondrovec 2014: 389). This would put the coins of Tobazini after the period of

---

[29] Vondrovec 2014: 400, with the exception of a single coin which is missing the four dots. Alram and Pfisterer 2010: 28 point out that the four dots have a precedent in the gold scyphate issues of the Kushano-Sasanian or Kidarite *Wahram* which were issued from the same mint of Balkh, and suggest that despite the 100-year gap between the two coins 'we may view this typological similarity as not a mere coincidence'.

[30] Alram and Pfisterer 2010: 28, on the basis of Schindel 2004: I.394 and ultimately of Sarkhosh Curtis 1999. However, the suggestion is a little unusual since normally on coins and other Middle Persian documents, the word *MLKA* comes *after* the personal name of the ruler. One would have expected *pylwcy MLK'*.

The Hephthalite 'Empire' and its Successors

Fig. 6.2. Hephthalite *Tamgha* (© *das Antlitz des Fremden*)

Anonymous Clan Rulers of the Alkhans (see Chapter 5) and before the issues of Khingila and those of the Hephthalites (Vondrovec 2014: 390), while the use of *tamgha* S2 with coins inscribed exclusively in Bactrian continues to the early sixth century. Additionally, the Anonymous Alkhan Rulers type 33 was surely produced in an eastern Sasanian mint, most likely Kabul, following its capture by the Alkhans (Vondrovec 2014: 389). While no provenance is known for the coins of Tobazini, at least one coin has been found in the Termez region[31] north of Balkh on the other side of the Oxus. Considering the lack of information about the area of distribution for the coins of Tobazini, we can only assume that this one was issued in the eastern mint of 'Kabul' and was a predecessor of Khingila's type 59A and Hephthalite 287A–C coins series.

Certain types of Hephthalite, and Sasanian, coins found in the Hephthalite regions carry countermarks that are used in order to approve foreign coins for circulation within the Hephthalite sphere of influence (Vondrovec 2014: 402). One of these, countermark 97, carries an inscription which might read γηλανο χοηο (Gēlano xoēo), with the possible meaning of 'the lord of Gilano' (*sic*).[32] Other coin types also circulated in the region, including genuine Sasanian coins up to the period of Khosrow I (531–79). In fact, Sasanian and Hephthalite coins appear to have circulated widely in Central Asia and even in China, where the hoard of Ping Chen in Shanxi contains a number of Sasanian coins and at least one Hephthalite

---

[31] Vondrovec 2014: 389 quoting Vainber 1972: 133–8.
[32] Vondrovec 2014: 402; see also Humbach 1966: 68–9, who connects the *Gelano* here with the Gelani mentioned by Ammianus Marcellinus as among the adversaries of Shapur II in the east: see Chapter 4 on the Huns. Sims-Williams 2010: 137 suggests that the initial γ can also be read as τ, thus rendering *Tēlano xoēo* with uncertain meaning.

one (Alram and Pfisterer 2010: 30–2). This is in accord with the historical data provided for the period after the defeat of Pērōz in AD 474 and his death in AD 484, the result of which was the payment of a large ransom to the Hephthalites. The Hephthalites clearly used the incoming wealth to cover their trade deficit with China (Alram and Pfisterer 2010: 32). The effects of this on the rise of the Sogdian trade network will be discussed in Chapter 7. However, it is interesting to point out that in the Bactrian Documents, the switch from gold coins to silver coinage is associated with the 'good silver coins of King Kavad' (BD I: *Ss*, dated to BE 476 = AD 699/700) and no mention of the coins of Pērōz is made. Considering this, it is unusual to find relatively few Kavad coins, compared with the Pērōz coins, in Hephthalite-dominated Tokharistan. This might indicate that the coins of Pērōz were re-struck by the Hephthalites, while the coinage of Kavad, paid as tribute, continued to circulate in the region.[33]

HEPHTHALITES IN THE SIXTH CENTURY

Without a doubt, the significant setbacks experienced by the Sasanians in the last quarter of the fifth century – directly caused by the Hephthalite power – were a prime mover for the reforms undertaken by Kavad and his son Khosrow I.[34] Most significantly, the creation of four major defensive, and presumably administrative, zones in the Sasanian administration was a direct response to the inefficiency of centralised defence. The northeast and east of the Sasanian realm was entrusted to an *Ispahbed of Khwarasan* (Gyselen 2001), in fact the first time we hear of this term.

The presence of the Hephthalo-Alkhan king Meyam/Mehama is probably a good indication of the progress of Hephthalite power after their defeat of Pērōz and their prominent role in installing his son on the Sasanian throne. Initially acting as a local king, 'the king of the people of Kadag, governor of the famous (and) prosperous king of kings Pērōz' (BD I *ea* 1–2 and *ed* 1–2, dated 239 and

---

[33] Kavad himself perhaps enjoyed certain privilages during his residence in the Hephthalite court, both as a hostage for his father Pērōz before AD 484 and also as a refugee after his deposition in AD 496. Evidence for this is perhaps the name of the region of *Qobadian* (Kavadian) across the Oxus from Balkh, possibly named after him and perhaps the source of his income while in residence at the Hephthalite court. Whether any coins of Kavad can be attributed to this region is doubtful.

[34] Howard-Johnston 1995, and presenting a different view in the same volume, Rubin 1995.

252[35] BE respectively), Meyam was eventually raised to the position of *Mahāṣāhi Mehama* (Melzer 2006). The fact that the coinage of Mehama/Meyam is placed well within the Alkhan coin series (Vondrovec 2014: 187–90) should not cause a concern. It is quite possible that the east of Tokharistan was in fact more connected to the Alkhan sphere of influence than the Hephthalite one (see Chapter 5 on eastern Alkhans). The possible association of Talagan with the Talaqan of eastern Tokharistan and the independent access of eastern Bactria to the Gandhara region – the centre of Alkhan power – via the Chitral and Swat Valleys (Vondrovec 2014: 406) would make it possible that Eastern Tokharistan was independent of, and even in competition with, the Hephthalite-dominated west around Balkh.[36]

With their defeat by the joint Sasanian and West Turk armies in 560–1, the *Imperial* Hephthalite period came to an end (Grenet 2002b: 213–14). Ferdowsi, in his *Shahnameh*, treats this episode most comprehensively. In Ferdowsi's narrative, the Haytal (i.e. Heptal/Hephthal) first enter the war with the 'Faghfur of China' when they kill an envoy of the latter who was on his way to the Sasanian court with many presents to offer an alliance. The word *Faghfur*, an Arabic/Early New Persian rendition of MP *bag/y-puhr* (Bactrian βαγεποορο), means 'son of god'[37] and is the normal name for the Emperor of China in Classical New Persian texts (Dehkhoda 1930). Ferdowsi's narrative of the ensuing war and its consequences is the most comprehensive account of these events and provides us with much valuable information regarding the late Hephthalite state.

The protagonist of the Hephthalite ambush of the Chinese envoy is a Hephthalite king called Ghādfar, who is generally presented in a neutral way. The Faghfur of China, seeking revenge for the ambush, sends his *ispahbid* (general) who is called Sinjibu and holds the title of Khaghan of China, later claiming to be a son-in-law of the Chinese Faghfur. We know Sinjibu is the same as Sizibulous and Sinjibu Khan, the leader of the Western Turks (Giraud 1960). Denis Sinor has convincingly shown this Sinjibu Khan to be the same as

---

[35] Sims-Williams, on BD II: 114, points out that the date is 'less likely 242'. In either case, BE 239 (= AD 462) to BE 242 (AD 465) would put the period of Meyam's sub-ordinance to Pērōz as having been before Pērōz's defeat of the Kidarites in AD 466. The date of BE 252 (AD 475) would extend this subordinance for another ten years, but still before the final defeat and death of Pērōz at the hands of the Hephthalites in AD 484.

[36] See Kuwayama 2002: 123–4 for a discussion of various paths from the Pamirs to Kashmir and Gandhara.

[37] Most likely closely related to the Sanskrit title *devaputra*, with the same meaning; Humbach 2003: 158 n. 5.

Ištämi, the brother of Bumin Khan, the founder of the Turk Empire, who indeed was the son-in-law of the Wei Emperor (Sinor 1990). The casting of Sinjibu Khan as a mere commander of 'Chinese' armies is, of course, an exaggeration on Ferdowsi's part and perhaps a reflection of a greater desire to place the war between the two great empires of which he knew, rather than the nascent Turk Empire and the well-established Sasanians.

In any case, the forces of Sinjibu and the Hephthalites met at a location north of the Oxus called *Gol-Zarriūn*. The Battle of Gol-Zarriūn was swift and decisive and resulted in the immediate departure of Ghādfar and his followers to Sasanian territory, where they sought refuge. The Khaghan (Sinjibu) along with his advisors, and with the agreement of the nobility of the Hephthalites, then appoints a new ruler for the Hephthalites. This new ruler is a local governor of the region of Ghaghanian named Faghanish, who is said to be a direct descendant of Khushnawz/Akhshunwar, the king of the Hephthalites responsible for the defeat and death of Pērōz in AD 484.

The arrangement between the 'Chinese' (Western Turks) and the Hephthalites, including the removal of a Hepthalite king and the appointment of a new king, however, does not go well with the Sasanian king Khosrow I. The king, considering the actions of the Turks to be a threat to his sovereignty in the region, mounts a campaign against the Turks and marches towards the border in Gorgan. There, he is met by an envoy of the Turks bearing presents, and in a show of power and military might, convinces the Turks to conclude an alliance. The alliance includes the daughter of the Khaghan marrying Khosrow, thus becoming the mother of the future Ohrmizd IV (579–91), which seems historically inaccurate. But more importantly, it requires Faghanish, the new king of the Hephthalites, to go to the Sasanian court in Ctesiphon and receive the approval of Khosrow I for his rule over the Hephthalites.

This complicated episode, although unique, seems plausible in many senses. The joint action of the Sasanian and Western Turks (see Chapter 7) against the Hephthalites is mentioned by all other sources addressing this period. We can easily consider that the Turks – who were expanding westwards – made the initial attack and that the Sasanians only entered the scene when the war was well under way. The detail about the rule of Ghādfar and the coup resulting in his removal by Faghanish is justified through connecting Khosrow with the Hephthalite court. Supposedly, Kavad's sister might have been a wife of Khushnawaz, the Hephthalite king. Consequently,

Khosrow, being connected with the previous Hephthalite ruling family, is the one who gives his approval to the political coup in the Hephthalite court. Furthermore, the agreement of the nobility of the Hephthalites with Sinjibu Khan is reflective of an internal disagreement in the Hephthalite court with the policies of Ghādfar, and anticipates the subsequent submission of the Hephthalite territories to the Turks.

HEPHTHALITES AFTER THE BATTLE OF GOL-ZARRIŪN

Not much is known about the remnants of the Hephthalites, although their survival in the region seems to be indisputable and the basis of the theory that their origin was in fact local (Enoki 1959: 34–6). Al-Khwarazmi (Bosworth and Clauson 1965: 6, 8) remarks that the Khalaj Turks are the descendants of the Hephthalites. The survival of some of Hephthalite minor states in eastern Tokharistan seems to be proven by a juxtaposition of archaeological and textual sources. In about 630 (or 628; Kuwayama 1989), the Chinese traveller Xuanzang met a group of them in western Badakhshan/eastern Tokharistan and called them *Ximotolo*. Kuwayama and, following him, Grenet consider the evidence of the *Tangshu*, which located Yida in the middle course of the Surkhan River, associating them with the state of *Taihan*, and assigning the city of Huolu as their capital, to be referring to the late Hephthalites.

On the basis of the Early Middle Chinese reading of *Huolu* as *ywat-lah*, Grenet assigns the area around Pol-e Khomri, to the southwest of Baghlan and close to the Kushan site of Surkh Kotal, as the centre of late Hephthalite power. Grenet equates Huolu with *Ghur*, a name surviving in the name of *Qale-ye Ghuri* in the same region (Grenet 2002b: 215). We should, however, notice that Qale-ye Ghuri is most likely associated with the Ghurid dynasty of the twelfth to thirteenth centuries (Bosworth 1968) who at times also controlled areas in eastern Tokharistan. Furthermore, the association of the state of *Taihan* with the Nēzak *Tarkhāns* of the early Islamic sources causes some problems with the identification of the Pol-e Khomri region, as in al-Tabari's account of the wars of Qutaiba with the Nēzak Tarkhān, the latter is located in western Tokharistan near Bāghdīs and south towards Bamiyan (al-Tabari II.1218–27). In fact, Grenet himself choses the location of *Kafir Qalai* near Barfak, on the road from Samangan to Bamiyan, as the location of the Nēzak Tarkhān's final defeat by Qutaiba, through which the former was probably heading for Kabul (Grenet 2002b: 217). This would be quite to the west of Pol-e Khomri, whose access to Kabul does not pass through Bamiyan but rather goes south straight through Andarab and Bagram via the Panjshir Valley.[38]

Whether in fact continuing as a political entity or not, the Hephthalites as either a past memory or a contemporary reality survived in the Islamic sources. The encounter of Qutaiba ibn Muslim with the Nēzak Tarkhān (al-Tabari II.1218–27) is a well-known episode where the Nēzak is called a Hephthalite (Arabic *Haytal*), and even centuries later, the memory of the Hephthalites, sometimes confused with their Western Turk successors, survived in the accounts of Al-Biruni, Ferdowsi, and al-Khawarazmi. More importantly, it is under Hephthalite rule over Sogdiana that this region is reorganised as a set of city states whose merchant classes appear to have held the most power. The interactions between the Bactrian and Sogdian cultures under the Hephthalites allowed for an exchange of commercial skills gained by the Bactrians through their centuries-long position on the road from India to the north and west. The Hephthalite period brought Indian influences, including Buddhism and Indian art, to Transoxiana and created a zone of cultural and social interaction which allowed for Indian, Chinese, Iranian, and local Bactrian and Sogdian cultures to mix. This is in many senses the beginning of the rise of Transoxiana and East Iran as a pivotal part of world history in the following centuries under Islamic culture.

As an immediate aftermath, the Battle of Gol-Zarriūn and the new political reality of the Hephthalite territories brought Sasanians into direct contact, and control of, the regions to the south of the Oxus, most importantly the region of Tokharistan. The emergence of the Nēzak Shahs of Kabul and Zabul, from local authories after the fall of Pērōz to prominent power in the south of the Hindu Kush, as well as the increasing interactions between the area of Balkh and the western regions, shows a growing gravitational pull towards the Sasanian world. The Nēzak, ruling in the centres of Kidarite and Alkhan influence, used Middle Persian Pahlavi script to write their coin legends, and their attention seems to have been attracted more to the west and the control of Zabulistan and Sistan to the east of the Sasanian domains. The Nēzak Tarkhāns of Tokharistan too appear to have been concerned with the affairs

---

[38] On this, see also the testimony of Xuanzang when the Turkish chief, Tardu-Shad, offers him an escort to the Kapiśi region via the very same route (Kuwayama 2000: 41).

of the Sasanian world, including their involvement in the murder of Yazdgerd III in AD 651. We will consider the situation in Tokharistan, Kabulistan, and Zabulistan in the 'Turkic period' in the following chapter.

At the same time, the Sasanians themselves became more involved with the East Iranian world. Some of the cultural influences of Sasanian interactions with both Tokharistan and the southern Hindu Kush can be seen in early Islamic and Classical New Persian texts. Burōy-ī Tabīb (Burzōy the Physician) is a prominent composite character of many early Islamic histories whose travels to 'India' allowed him to bring copies of Indian books to Sasanian Iran and translate them. Among these was a copy of the *Pancha Tantra*, translated into Middle Persian by Burzōy and later into Arabic by the famous translator of the Abbasid court, Ibn Muqaffa. The text, *Kalila wa Dimnah*, is among the fundamental books of medieval Islamic culture and was widely read and referenced (de Blois 1990). To the same period should be assigned the increasing interest of the Sasanians in East Iranian epic, including the tales of the hero Rostam, who displays clear East Iranian characteristics (Grenet 2002b: 218–20). Frescoes depicting episodes of the Rostam cycle and related cycles can be found in Sogdian art (Marshak 2002; Shenkar 2014) and show common East Iranian artistic influences. The encounter with East Iran, both north and south of the Hindu Kush, was to have a deep effect on Sasanian ideologies and culture, something that needs to be studied in much more detail.

THE HEPHTHALITES AND THEIR LEGACY

The Hephthalites are perhaps the best known of all 'Iranian Huns' and the ones whose name has been used as an umbrella term for other political entities of the Huns/Chionites. Little, however, is known about them through contemporary sources, except the evidence of their coins, which marks them clearly as a separate political entity, centred on Tokharistan. Understanding their position within the Iranian Huns' group on the basis of their coinage, then, allows us to study the scarce textual sources that address their history. These sources show an organised state headed by a military aristocracy and strong king who then proceed to defeat the Sasanian King of Kings Pērōz and kill him. The influence of the Hephthalites over Sasanian affairs is in fact the prime motivation behind the important and urgent Sasanian reforms of the sixth century, which arguably created a completely new, and more centralised, administration.

Their control over Tokharistan and Sogdiana, and unification of these two regions, also further engendered the emergence of this area as a politically coherent unit. Despite their own demise in AD 560, the legacy of the Hephthalites largely defined the Western Turk period, and their creation of the Tokharistan and Sogdiana political unit made the nucleus of the late Sasanian and Early Islamic province of *Khurasan*.

7 Sogdiana in the Kidarite and Hephthalite Periods

INTRODUCTION

Compared to Bactria/Tokharistan, Sogdiana appears to have been less urbanised, with a less sophisticated system of irrigation and agriculture and underdeveloped commercial networks. While we have evidence of the existence of Sogdian traders in the fourth century,[1] archaeological excavations show little sign of urbanisation or centralised state structure in the region. The economy of Sogdiana was based on agriculture in the valleys of the Oxus and its tributaries, most importantly the Zarafshan or Sughd.[2] Minor kings, known at least from the time of Alexander, ruled over the area, although it seems with minimal influence. A monetary system based on low-value token coins, borrowed from the Graeco-Bactrians, also existed, which must have facilitated internal trade in the Sogdian core territories. However, starting in the fourth and fifth centuries, Sogdiana was invaded by the steppe people, and thus entered into the affairs of the larger region. It appears that in the Kidarite and Hephthalite periods, it came under the influence of powers in Bactria/Tokharistan, and thus embarked on the course of world history as we know it. Merchant networks, a city-state system, and the benefits of access to India and China launched Sogdians on a path of growth. The most important result of this was the emergence of the famous Sogdian merchant network, which controlled trade in most of Asia, from Korea to India and the Pontic Steppe until the tenth century AD. In

---

[1] For Sogdian 'Ancient Letters' see de la Vaissière 2007: 43–70, including an analysis of their contents for understanding of the pre-fifth-century Sogdian trade network.

[2] However, see Frye 1998 for the idea that the Zarafshan might never have really reached the Oxus.

the early Islamic period too, Sogdians came to be influential in both the political and the economic life of the caliphate, and, of course, it was in Sogdiana that the Samanids and other medieval powers came to establish themselves.[3] Consequently, a brief examination of the history of Sogdiana and its initial proliferation in the Kidarite and Hephthalite periods is warranted.

SOGDIANA IN THE FIFTH CENTURY AD

Specifically speaking, Sogdiana, from the local term *Sughd*, is the name most often applied to the valley of the lower Zarafshan, around the cities of Samarkand – occasionally called *Sughd* in the absolute sense – and Bukhara (Marshak and Negmatov 1999: 237–8). In *Tarikh-e Bokhara* – a tenth-century local history now available in a twelfth-century Persian translation – there is a mention of the origins of the Sughd region and the Bukhara oasis which implies that *Sughd* proper was originally a location between Samarkand and Bukhara (Al-Narshakhi 1387: 9). Eventually, however, the name came to be applied to a larger region, extending from Bukhara in the west to Khujand and even Ferghana in the east. However, for most of their histories, regions such as Ferghana and Ustrushana kept their own separate identity, in addition to their Sogdian ones (Marshak and Negmatov 1999: 262). All of these regions, located on the right bank of the Oxus, were considered the buffer zone to the steppe and were prone to invasion by the steppe nomads.

Sometime in the fourth or early fifth century[4] a nomadic group who were called *xwn* in the local sources invaded Sogdiana. Whether these are the same as the 'Hunnic' invaders of Bactria is not certain, although in the Chinese sources they appear to be associated with the same Xiongnu/Yueh-zhi movements that resulted in the invasion of Bactria during the period of Shapur II.[5] Politically, the invaders might have helped to solve a political crisis in the region, allowing for freedom of action on the part of the local aristocracy. The story of the formation of Bukhara as reflected in its local history might be symbolic of these changes. *Tarikh-e Bokhara* says that following the formation of the Bokhara (Bukhara) oasis as a result of the silting

---

[3] We will discuss the later history of Sogdiana under the Turkic rule in Chapter 7.
[4] See de la Vaissière 2007: 97–100 for problems associated with the chronology of these events.
[5] See Chapter 4; also de la Vaissière 2007: 97–100, who discusses the issue on the basis of the same Chinese sources (*Wei Shu* and *Tongdien*) used for the Bactrian invasions. See Marshak and Negmatov 1999: 239–40 for a different opinion.

up of the River Māsef – presumably the Zarafshan[6] – 'people moved over from Turkestan' and populated the region.[7] Subsequently, they chose a ruler named Abruī who established his capital in *Baikant* (i.e. Paikent)[8] and the fortress of *Dabusiye* (Al-Narshakhi 1387: 8). However, Abruī's rule was hard on the 'Dihqans and the Wealthy people', who left the city for Turkistan and established a city named *Jamukat*[9] near Taraz (Al-Narshakhi 1387: 9). Taraz is considered as part of Asbijab (al-Muqaddasi 1967: II.383) and is to the north of Chach (Taskhkent), thus making it clear that for the author of *Tarikh-e Bokhara*, the region beyond Syr Darya/Jaxartes was considered as Turkistan (Bartol'd 1928: ch. 1). The exiled Dihqans and the merchants of Bukhara, now residing in Jamukat, petitioned the Turkic Khaghan, called Qara-churin and nicknamed *Biaghu*,[10] to rid Paikent of Abruī. The Khaqan then sent his son, *Shīr-e Keshvar*,[11] to remove Abruī. Having achieved the task, the Turkish prince then became the ruler of the Bukhara oasis and the founder of the city of Bukhara itself, which appears to have replaced the old capital of Paikent.[12] The interesting detail is that upon the removal of Abruī, the old grandees of Bukhara returned from Jamukat and became the elites of the new city. The writer of this excerpt in *Tarikh-e Bokhara* even goes as far as saying that the people who stayed behind under Abruī's regime were the poor who could not afford to leave, and they became the servants of the returning aristocracy, made up of merchants, when they came back to Bukhara (Al-Narshakhi 1387: 10). The story as a whole seems to be symbolic of the fifth-century conquests of Sogdiana, and the Khaqan of the Turks most likely refers to a *Xwn* leader. Archaeological data regarding the introduction of a new ceramic type from beyond the Syr Darya in Sogdiana also appears to corroborate this information (de la Vaissière 2007:

---

[6] See Al-Narshakhi 1387: 149–52 on the names of the Zarafshan, and Lo Muzio 2009: 47 on the formation of Bukhara's position in its marshlands.

[7] For archaeological excavations in the Bukhara oasis, see Lo Muzio 2009.

[8] From both the evidence of *Tarikh-e Bokhara* and archaeological excavations and surveys, Paikent seems to be older than Bukhara and the site of its old capital, continuing its importance through late antiquity and in the early Islamic period as well; see Lo Muzio 2009: 49–50 for a short survey.

[9] Al-Narshakhi 1387: 156–7, where he specifies that this is to be read as Jamukat instead of Hamukat as in the manuscript.

[10] Frye 1954: 27 correctly suggests that this is a new Persian translation of the well-known Turkic title Yabghu, which in fact historically goes back to the Kushan period (Sims-Williams 2002: 229). See also Sims-Williams and de la Vaissière 2007.

[11] Possibly a Persian translation of Turkish *Il-Arsalan* 'Lion of the Land'; Al-Narshakhi 1387: 158.

[12] Archaeologically, the city of Bukhara itself dates to the third to fourth centuries (Lo Muzio 2009: 45).

100, quoting Burjakov 1991: 198–9). Bukhara itself generally seems to belong to the middle Syr Darya cultural region, as is evident from the ceramic finds in the region (Lo Muzio 2009: 45). People moving from beyond the Syr Darya then repopulated the Bukhara oasis in the third to fourth centuries, adopting the local Sogdian language and customs.

This resulted in intense building activities, including the foundation of the city of Panjikent, 60 kilometres to the east of Samarkand (Marshak and Negmatov 1999: 239). In the same period, Samarkand was greatly extended and the population increased markedly, with a proliferation of settlement sites in the Zarafshan Valley (de la Vaissière 2007: 103–4). Sites in the Bukhara oasis were expanded (Lo Muzio 2009: 47), and the great palace of Varakhsha (Shishkin 1963)[13] was constructed near Bukhara. The site of Afrasiab near Samarkand, in decline since the first century AD, started its expansion and became the capital of Sogdiana, with impressive building activities, new artisan quarters (Pugachenkova and Rtveladze 1984), and impressive murals (although they date to the 600s: Compareti 2008). Bukhara was protected from the nomadic invasions by the construction of an impressive wall (de la Vaissière 2005b: 105) and Samarkand was given a new citadel (de la Vaissière 2005b: 106). The fifth century, in short, provided Sogdiana with its initial start as an urban centre and major player in the affairs of Central Asia (Lo Muzio 2009: 46).

While the identity of the invaders of Sogdiana is not known, and the local term *xwn* is as vague as all other terms associated with the Huns, we know of the presence of the Kidarites in Sogdiana through the existence of coins.[14] The coins of an authority found in the vicinity of Samarkand and inscribed with the legend *kδyr* indicated the Kidarite invasion of this region sometime in the fifth century (Zeimal 1999). The *Wei Shu* and *Tongdien* provide evidence that in AD 457, the third king of a Xiongnu dynasty of Samarkand, his ancestors having invaded and killed the local king, sent embassies to

---

[13] Shishkin 1963 dates the palace to the sixth century. However, see Naymark 2003b, who associates it with the seventh century. The mural paintings of Varakhsha are among the most significant examples of Sogdian art, akin to those of Afrasiab and Panjikent.

[14] De la Vaissière 2007: 108 states that 'these Xiongu can only be the Kidarites', using the textual evidence for the date of AD 420 or later for the date of the Kidarite invasion of Bactria. Against this, see Cribb 2010 and others. I see no reason to connect the two, since the Kidarite invasion of Sogdiana took place from Tokharistan. This would make the chronology independent of the Xiongnu/Hunnic/Kidarite invasion of Tokharistan itself and would require a whole new chronological scheme, in which I do not see the numismatic vs. textual evidence discussion to be very useful.

the Chinese court (de la Vaissière 2007: 107). This would accord well with the numismatic evidence of the rule of the Kidarites, although it also suggests that the Sogdian Kidarite dynasty operated separately from the Bactrian one.

The textual evidence for the conquest of Sogdiana by the 'Huns' is not, however, much reflected in the Bukhara region, where archaeology suggests a continuation of local dynasties (Lo Muzio 2009: 46). The fourth century, nonetheless, did bring a new type of coinage to the already established monetary system of Bukhara. The long-lasting imitation types of Graeco-Bactrian Euthydemus were replaced by new silver and copper issues showing the profile bust of a male wearing a diadem, demonstrating a clear Sasanian influence (Zeimal 1978: 210). This shows possible Sasanian or Kidarite influences originating from Bactria/Tokharistan in Sogdiana, and the start of the process of integrating Sogdiana into the greater Central Asian/East Iranian world.[15] In the same period, the wall surrounding Bukhara (Kanpirak) was built, possibly as part of a larger defensive system extending all the way east to Ferghana (Shishkina 1994: 92–3).

The defeat of the Kidarites in Tokharistan by the Sasanian King of Kings Pērōz in AD 467 may have left the Kidarites in Sogdiana intact.[16] The continued prosperity of Sogdiana, including its transformation into an area of agricultural wealth, is indicative of political stability in the region, something that Tokharistan was lacking at the time (de la Vaissière 2007: 106, 109). However, we cannot be sure of the local political situation, or the relation between various local dynasties, in Sogdiana (Lo Muzio 2009: 46).

The period of Kidarite rule over Sogdiana, and the prosperity it brought, helped the foundation and growth of several urban sites and the expansion of the Sogdian network. Apart from Bukhara and Samarkand, the city of Panjikent was founded and grew until the seventh century. Much like Bukhara and Samarkand, Panjikent also had its own monetary system, usually small bronze issues, with busts of rulers copied from Sasanian issues and including Sogdian cursive inscriptions (Smirnova 1963; 1981). In fact, the normal political state of affairs in Sogdiana at this time was defined by independent city states ruled by weak local rulers and dominated by strong merchants. These merchant cities often kept their independence by

---

[15] For a similar argument, see Grenet 1994: 371ff.
[16] Despite the presence of the coinage of Kidara in Samarkand, there is no sign of Sogdiana being dependent on the dynasty of the Kidarites in Tokharistan or the 'splitting' of the Kidarites into two groups of Sogdian and Gandharan ones following the Hephthalite expansion (de la Vaissière 2007: 108).

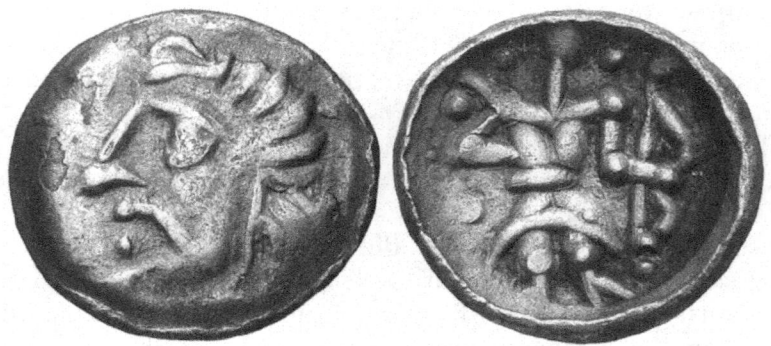

Fig. 7.1. Silver obol of anonymous local authority in Samarkand, possibly under Kidarite rule (© CNG 360, Lot 233).

acting as agents of various foreign powers, which in fact were played off against each other to keep the local political units independent. Sogdian merchants for generations carried titles bestowed on them by the Chinese court (Livshits 2015a) while other regional powers such as the Kidarites or the Hephthalites attempted to control their activities.

SOGDIANA UNDER THE HEPHTHALITES IN THE SIXTH CENTURY

On the basis of the ceasing of Sogdian and the start of Hephthalite embassies to China, some have suggested AD 509 as the date of the conquest of Sogdiana by the Hephthalites and the end of Kidarite rule (de la Vaissière 2007: 110). Apart from the destruction and rebuilding of the walls of Panjikent, there is little reason to believe that a violent takeover of Sogdiana took place at this time (Marshak and Raspopova 1990: 182; de la Vaissière 2007: 111). In Bukhara in Western Sogdiana, however, a new type of coin and coin authority seem to have come into existence under the Hephthalites; the coins are in the style of the Sasanian Wahram V, with a corrupt Pahlavi legend (Zeimal 1999 193–4). This type of coin later developed into those of the Bukhar-Khudat type that proliferated in the early Islamic period. Later types bear a Sogdian inscription that possibly reads *pwx'r xwβ k'n'* 'the Lord of Bukhara, Kānā' (Zeimal 1994: 246–7). This would accord well with the testimony of *Tarikh-e Bokhara* that the first Kānā, a textile merchant who was the Bukhar-Khudat (i.e. the title of the ruler of Bukhara: Khurradādhbih 1967: 32), was the first to put his name on the coins (Al-Narshakhi 1387: 49–50)

During this period, the continued prosperity of Sogdian city states resulted in the settlement of new sites such as Chach (modern Tashkent) to the north of Syr Darya by Sogdians. In this area, the immigrating Sogdian merchants dominated the urban setting and created a 'Sogdianised' class, as evidenced by coins and inscriptions from the region (de la Vaissière 2007: 112–13; Livshits 2015c). A much larger pattern of migration and settlement took place in Semirech'e, where Sogdians established many colonies and completely Sogdianised this part of the steppe until the tenth century (de la Vaissière 2007: 114–16), when Turkish replaced the Sogdian language (Livshits 2015d).

All this was perhaps made possible by the silver coinage arriving in Sogdiana through the Hephthalites, who in turn had acquired it from the Sasanians following their defeat of the latter (de la Vaissière 2007: 111). The already established Sogdian network, strengthened by local prosperity during the Kidarite period, found the opportunity, through the entry of Hephthalite silver, to penetrate the Chinese market, as might be further understood from the issue of Chinese coins with a square hole in the middle all over Sogdiana (Zejmal' 1999: 195).[17]

The entry of the Hephthalites into Sogdiana, and the increasing importance of Sogdiana as an agriculturally wealthy area, also caused a reorientation of the peripheral areas towards Sogdiana. Inscriptions from Afrasiab show the presence of an ambassador from Changhanian at the court of King Avarkhuman of Samarkand (Livshits 2015b: 237–41). Considering the normal position of Changhaniyan within Tokharistan (Bosworth 1990), this shows the decline in importance of Tokharistan and the rise of Sogdiana as the new political and economic power. Other regions, such as Ustrushana and Ferghana, similarly gravitated towards Sogdiana, rendering almost all of Transoxiana to the borders of the steppe as the greater Sogdian territories. Through rapid urbanisation, agricultural prosperity, colonisation, and successful commercial activities, in addition to the incoming 'Hephthalite' (ultimately Sasanian) silver, Sogdiana became the most significant part of Central Asia in the sixth to tenth centuries AD. It certainly surpassed its former rival, Tokharistan/Bactria, in wealth and commerce, although Tokharistan was still the scene of much political engagement between the Sasanians and the powers of the east.

---

[17] For a general understanding of the role of silver in the Chinese economy, despite the widespread use of token copper coinage, see von Glahn 1996.

BUDDHISM IN KIDARITE AND HEPHTHALITE SOGDIANA?

The period of Kidarite and Hephthalite rule in Sogdiana is often speculated to be the period of the rise of Buddhism in the region (Frye 1990). This is partly based on speculations on the name of Bukhara and its relation to Sanskrit *vihara* 'Buddhist temple' (Tremblay 2004: 124). However, as has been suggested before (Lo Muzio 2009: 48), there is no evidence of extensive Buddhist structures in Bukhara; the Chinese pilgrim Xuanzeng, on his visit there, mentions neither Buddhist monasteries nor any tradition relating the name of Bukhara to a Buddhist origin (Lo Muzio 2009: 48); and Buddhism appears to have been a failure in Sogdiana (Tremblay 2007: 89). The mention by several Islamic-period sources, including *Tarikh-e Bokhara*, of the presence of *Bot-Khanas* 'Buddhist temples, idol houses' has given rise to the conclusion by scholars that Buddhism was common in the region.[18] Despite the presence of Sogdian Buddhists in China (Compareti 2008: 6), the general attitude of Sogdian rulers, such as the rulers of Samarkand, seems to have been hostile towards Buddhism. Any influence of Buddhism on the region appears to have originated from the Tokharistan region, and perhaps with the further leaning of Buddhist peripheral regions of Tokharistan such as Chaghanian (Bosworth 1990) towards Sogdiana, the religion was introduced to a small group of native Sogdians. The local religion, however, appears to have been mostly a Sogdian type of Zoroastrianism, flavoured with local customs.[19]

Interesting evidence for the presence of Buddhism in Sogdiana can be found in the later Islamic sources (Bulliet 1976). This may include a notice among the records of the trial of the ninth-century Abbasid general Khaydhar al-Afshin, who was executed by the Abbasid Caliph al-Mu'tasim in AD 841. Among his charges was that he had lashed two Sogdian men who had destroyed a local *Butkada* (Arabic *'Bait kana fihi al-Asnam*) in Ustrushana, building a mosque. Afshin's answer was that his ancestors, as the local Afshins

---

[18] See the discussion in Compareti 2008: 4–6 about this issue. I would tend to agree with Bausani 1968, as referenced by Compareti, that the term *Bot/But* in Persian is ambiguous. In fact, in Classical Persian usage, the terms *But* and *Butkhana* are used in general to refer to idols and places of idol worship, quite apart from the origins of the term in the name of *Buddha* (Bailey 1932: 279–83), and as such, interpreting all references to them as evidence of the presence of Buddhism is highly misleading and counterproductive.

[19] See Compareti 2008 for a general discussion of the presence of Buddhism and other religions in Sogdiana, with reference to the artistic and archaeological remains. See also Grenet 2007 about the religions of the Sogdian trade network.

of Ustrushana, had of old an agreement with the king of Sogdiana – who was also present during the trial proceedings – that they would leave the faith of each other's peoples alone, not interfering in each other's religious practices. So, when the Sogdians, supported by their king, destroyed the 'idol temple' of the Ustrushanans and threw out its idols, Afshin had them punished for breaking the agreement (al-Athīr 1863: VI.62).

Considering the hostility demonstrated by the Sogdians towards Buddhism – for example in the case of the inscription of the Chaganian ambassador in Afrasiab, where he declares that he has no interest in preaching his local (Buddhist) faith in Samarkand (Compareti 2008: 20) – we might also be able to interpret the episode of al-Afshin's trial. Here, Al-Afshin, the hereditary ruler of the eastern province of Ustrushana, declares that he has defended the faith of its people against the aggression of the Sogdians, with whom they appear to have had an agreement not to interfere in religious matters. Despite the vagueness of the term referring to the temple (see above, n. 19), it is quite possible that Ustrushana had a sizeable Buddhist population[20] and was pressured by its larger western neighbour, Sogdiana, to abandon its practices, resulting in a need to conclude an agreement regarding religious practices. In this context, the Ustrushanan position in the relationship with the Buddhist Chinese dynasties can also be contextualised and considered.

CONCLUSION

Sogdiana emerged under Kidarite and Hephthalite rule as an integral part of the Eurasian world. Through rapid agricultural growth and the construction of irrigation systems, as well as stunning rates of urbanisation, Sogdian society was transformed from a periphery of Bactria/Tokharistan to a centre in its own right. Located on the 'buffer zone' of the Eurasian steppe, it created close ties to the region to its north and northeast and colonised regions beyond the Syr Darya such as Chach and Semirech'e. In this way, Sogdians entered the Chinese sphere and extended their trade network into the heart of China itself.

At home, a local aristocracy of merchants dominated the political scene, resulting in a loose federation of cities ruled by local dynasties.

---

[20] On archaeological evidence of the religious environment of Ustrushana, including a possible local type of 'Zoroastrianism' which included worship of idols, see Marshak and Negmatov 1999: 268–74. For the larger Sogdian extent of this local Zoroastrianism, see the summary of discussions in Compareti 2008: 8–11.

Some of these may have been of Kidarite, and later Hephthalite, stock, although that would be impossible to tell from their remains. An increasing Sasanian influence, particularly evident through the adoption of a new monetary system, also demonstrates a closer connection with the Sasanian Empire, either directly or through the Kidarites. The foundation of cities such as Panjikent, as well as the expansion of Bukhara and Samarkand, meant that the Sogdians were also gaining much prominence in their own region, apart from their influence in the larger Eurasian context. It was this stage of the development of Sogdiana which preceded the takeover of the region by the nascent Western Turk Empire, an event that truly launched Sogdians as the single most dominant cultural group in most of the Eurasian world.

8 The Nēzak and Turk Periods

INTRODUCTION

The sixth century proved to be transformative for all the political and social groups involved in the history of East Iran. The Hephthalite defeat of Sasanian Iran in the late fifth century and the loss of the eastern territories forced the Sasanians to undergo a major restructuring of their empire. This was reflected in historical sources as the reforms of Khosrow I and the rebellion of Mazdak, in fact betraying political, social, and religious changes. This successful restructuring, including the creation of autonomous military zones, rejuvenated the Sasanians, and in AD 560 allowed them to crush the Hephthalites with the help of the Western Turk Empire. The power vaccum left in the southern Hindu Kush after the deafeat of Pērōz in AD 484 had allowed for the rise of an independent dynasty in Kabulistan and Zabulistan, known as the Nēzak.[1] The Nēzak Shahs, despite never being as hegemonic as the Kidarites, Alkhans, or Hephthalites, in fact at one point dividing their territories between the two branches of Kabul and Zabul, did manage to create local cohesion and establish an influential coin style. This local cohesion was highly useful in creating a resistance to the Muslim invasions of the mid-seventh century, with widespread political and culture repercussions, including a pivotal role in forming early Islamic Persianate culture.

The Western Turk, however, having left Tokharistan in the hands of a *Yabghu of Tokharistan*, benefitted greatly from the integration of the robust Sogdian society into their ranks. While the Turk–Sogdian

---

[1] See Vondrovec 2014: 453–7 for a discussion of the chronological range of the Nezak coinage and its continuation in the Later Nezak and Turk periods.

milieu created the golden age of Sogdiana, in Tokharistan, traditionally among the stronger and more sophisticated of the societies of East Iran, experienced a period of economic decay, demonstrated in a demographic decline and the abandonment of urban sites. This was indeed a continuation of the situation from the Kidarite and the Hephthalite periods, where archaeological records show the decline of the population in traditional urban settings. Tokharistan, however, did not leave the historical scene, as new research and findings show. Local political actors, such as the Nēzak Tarkhāns of western Tokharistan or the post-Hephthalite entities of the Badakhshan region, continued to thrive, and they too later played an important role in the events leading to the fall of the Sasanian Empire and the rise of the Islamic one. The population, leaving established urban sites such as Balkh and Termez, probably settled in other regions, namely the foothills of the Hindu Kush, and took up horticultural activities instead of the traditional agriculture of the Oxus plain. This might be called, in fact, the most significant social and economic shift during the period of late antiquity in this region, and the emergence of Tokharistan, alongside Sogdiana, in a new regional setting. The Western Turk period, then, was the final stage of the transformation of East Iran, the inheritance of the Kushans, into the new concept of the Greater Khurasan, the prime geopolitical actor of the early Islamic period.

THE NĒZAK SHAHS OF KABUL

The local rulers of the region of Kabul and the neighbouring region of Zabul (*Zawul*; *Zawulestan*) had already emerged as autonomous powers in the second half of the fifth century (Vondrovec 2010). Known from their distinctive, and highly innovative coinage, the *Nēzak Shah* dynasty is classified by Göbl as one of the four major groupings of the Iranian Huns, largely on the basis of numismatic considerations. The dynasty, if indeed the issuing authorities of the Nēzak coins series can be grouped together as such, dominated the region of Kabul and beyond until the seventh century, when their waning power was replaced by a Turkic dynasty of Kabul Shahs, although their Zabuli branch may have survived for over a century, if we consider the Rutbil mentioned in the Islamic sources to have been a Nēzak authority of Zabul. The relation between the Nēzak Shahs of Kabul and Zabul and the Nēzak Tarkhāns of Tokharistan, known from the Islamic sources (Inaba 2010b: 191), provides historians with many prompts for speculation and has been largely undetermined in the discussion of their connections. It might, after all, be best to consider the Nēzak *Shahs* and the Nēzak *Tarkhāns* as two different entities, as their area of influence appears to have been sufficiently separated to justify such treatment.

The Nēzak dynasty, so called from the name *Nēzak Shah* read on an extensive series of silver and copper coins mostly from the region of Zabul and Kapiśa/Kabul, is known mainly through its coinage (Vondrovec 2014: 450; Göbl 1967: I). In textual sources, little reference is made to the Nēzak Shahs of Kabul, except in Chinese sources, where the word *Nisai* or sometimes *Nishu* is used to refer to them, despite the possible 'Hephthalite' origins of the terms (Inaba 2010b: 199). Their coins, long known as the most elaborately designed of the 'Iranian Huns'' emissions, carry a legend that reads *nycky MLK* 'nēzak šāh'[2] in Pahlavi script. The title might be related to Middle Persian *nēzag* 'spear' (Grenet 2002a), while it might also be a title used for tribal leaders of the Western Turks.[3] The fact that they use neither Bactrian nor Brahmi for the legends of their coins could be, more than anything, a political statement separating them from the sphere of influence of their immediate neighbours, and says very little about their actual ethnic identity. It might, on the other hand, say something about the political status of the Persian language as a political language in the east, or be a sign of increasing Sasanian influence and prestige in the areas dominated by the Hunnic overlords.[4] Indeed, Middle Persian appears to have been the most commonly used language in the areas of Zabulistan and Kabulistan during this period (Gyselen 2010: 235–7).

The most famous Chinese reference to the Nēzak Shahs is the account in the *Sui Shu*, which says that the king of Kabul wore a crown topped by a bull's head,[5] a detail that has been interpreted as referring to the buffalo skull appearing on top of the crown of the Nēzak Shahs on their coinage (Göbl 1967: 135). This has basically

---

[2] This coin legend was for many years, famously, misread from degenerate samples as *Napki Malka*, and the whole series was known under the same sobriquet and is sometimes still marked so in catalogues (Mitchiner 1975a). Janos Harmatta and Richard Frye both suggested the correct reading of *nycky MLK*, in independent efforts: Frye 1974; Harmatta 1969.

[3] Inaba 2010a provides a survey of the references in the Chinese sources, which complete, and sometimes correct, the sources used by Kuwayama 2000.

[4] See Sims-Williams 2008: 96 for some aspects of this increased Sasanian presence in the east. Gyselen suggests that the Pahlavi used on the coins of Zabulistan is merely a transcription of Bactrian and does not reflect official Sasanian Pahlavi (Gyselen 2010: 224).

[5] For a discussion of this and the alternative instances of 'fish head' see Kuwayama 2000: 36–7, 45–52, where he goes to great lengths to reidentify the Nezak Shah coins as those belonging to the Khingal dynasty and not that of the Hephthalites.

meant that the Chinese references to *Nisai* are taken as narratives of the Nēzak Shahs.

The Nēzak coinage, the major source for understanding their history, forms a completely independent series of coins. Although influenced by predecessors like the Alkhan or the Sasanian coins, their obverses show completely new imagery and innovations such as the addition of the famous bull (or buffalo) head to the very top of the crown. Previously, it was thought that the Nēzak coins start as the result of the Hephthalite defeat against the Western Turk/Iranian forces in AD 560. However, research shows that the Nēzak coins initially started in the late fifth century, thus shortly after the start of the Hephthalite series and long before AD 560 (Vondrovec 2014: 453). This group, called *Imperial* Nēzak by Vondrovec (analogous to the *Imperial* Hephthalite series), continues uninterrupted for many years, and their basic design is used in the coinage of East Iran and Central Asia for many centuries. The basic types of Nēzak have been divided to two groups of -ā and -š by numismatists on the basis of the appearance of the last letter of the Pahlavi legend *nycky MLKA*. A consideration of this basic division would allow us to propose some possibilities for the later history of East Iran.

In dividing the -ā and -š groups of the Nēzak coins, Vondrovec arbitrarily assigns them to the mints of 'Kabul' and 'Ghazni' (thus Kabulistan and Zabulistan) respectively.[6] He also speculated that the -š series might have ceased to exist earlier -and have been replaced by the AlkhanNēzak 'Crossover' series.[7] However, he suggests that the Later Nēzak series, a more widely issued series supposedly under Turkic suzerainty but showing the regular Nēzak iconography and legends, is a direct continuation of the type 198 coins or the -ā series (Vondrovec 2014: 516).

The Alkhan–Nēzak 'Crossover' series shows the basic Nēzak iconography, with the addition of Alkhan characteristics and gradual degradation of the Pahlavi legend *nycky MLK'* (Vondrovec 2014: 481). This series is stylistically a continuation of the Nēzak -š type and replaces the latter. Vondrovec then assigns the Alkhan–Nēzak 'Crossover' series to Göbl's *Returning Alkhans* group, mentioned above (1967: II.70–2). These are supposedly a series of Alkhans returning to the Kabul region after their defeat in Kashmir and

---

[6] Vondrovec 2014: 451, and also Vondrovec 2008.

[7] Although the -š type might also have survived directly in the coin series of another authority who called himself Sero and whose coins are simply a continuation of that type (Vondrovec 2014: 521).

Fig. 8.1. Silver drachm, early (late fifth-/early sixth-century) Nēzak, possibly from 'Ghazni'(?), with the Pahlavi inscription *Nēzak Shah* (© *das Antlitz des Fremden*).

Gandhara and either usurping the *Imperial* Nēzak power or integrating with them through marriage and alliance.[8]

Considering the possible connection between the Nēzak -š series and the Alkhan–Nēzak 'Crossover' series, it is interesting that Vondrovec choses to locate the mint of the -š series in Ghazni[9] and the -ā series in Kabul. It would make more sense to consider the longer-lasting -ā series, transitioning smoothly from the Imperial Nēzak to the Later Nēzak issues (Vondrovec 2014: 517) and showing a parallel copper half drachm as well, to have been issued further to the west and south of Kabul, in Zabulistan. This would make better sense if we take the suggestion of the 'Returning Alkhans' at all seriously and consider that at least part of the Nēzak court moved to Zabulistan, fleeing the Alkhans.[10] In fact, despite the fact that the Later Alkhans are speculated to have been issued after the AD 560 defeat of the Hephthalites, Vondrovec (2014: 517) himself admits that it is possible that 'theoretically, Late Nēzak and Alkhan-Nēzak Crossover series be struck simultaneously, although in different mints'. So, as arbitrary as it may be, we might assign the Alkhan -ā series, to the Ghazni/Zabulistan region, and the -š series to Kabul, a division that will later make sense, as we shall see.

---

[8] Vondrovec 2014: 483; see a discussion of these, called the dynasty of Khingal, further below. The whole idea might be quite unnecessary, since there are many reasons to believe that the Nēzak were part of the Alkhan tribes themselves. See also Chapter 5.

[9] Most likely simply following Göbl 1967: II.50, who located it in Zabulistan for the sake of convenience, but did not insist on this geographical identification.

[10] See also Kuwayama 2000: 25–36 for discussion of a possible Kabul–Zabul cultural and political confrontation that might reflect this.

Fig. 8.2. Billon drachm issue of the Alkhan–Nēzak 'Crossover' series with a pseudo-Pahlavi inscription (© *das Antlitz des Fremden*).

THE DYNASTY OF KHINGAL?

In a long and influential article, Shoshin Kuwayama, one of the most important authorities on the history of the Hindu Kush in the early medieval period, argued for the independent character of the Nēzak from both the Hephthalites and the Turks (Kuwayama 1999). Considering all the evidence and primary arguments for the ethnic connection of the Nēzak to either of the other two well-known entities, Kuwayama claimed that the Nēzak should be considered a local, and most likely Indian *Kshatriya*,[11] dynasty with local origins in the area of Kabul.[12] To justify their rise, he presented a series of impressive and complicated discussions about the belief system of the regions of Zabul and Kabul, strongly arguing for the non-Hephthalite character of the Nēzak Shahs (Kuwayama 2000: 37–41). He further insisted that the Turks, by following a policy of not crossing the Hindu Kush (Kuwayama 1999: 40) and not invading Gandhara, unlike the Kidarites and the Hephthalites, essentially left a power vacuum across the Hindu Kush. This power vacuum (Kuwayama 1999: 40) then allowed a later dynasty of the Nēzak Shahs (whom Kuwayama calls the *Khingal Dynasty*; 1999: 41–2) to replace the early rulers of Kapisi and subdue the regions of Kabul

---

[11] This is based on the reading of the word *Chali* in Tang-period sources, which is normally used to refer to the *kṣatriya*. An alternative present in some other Tang-period and other sources, namely *Suli* meaning 'Sogdian', is rejected by Kuwayama: '[it] does not seem of historical reality'; Kuwayama 2000: 42–3.

[12] See Inaba 2010a: 192 for a discussion of the Chinese reference to Heibishi and its equivalence with Kapiśa, the kingdom preceding that of Kabul: Kuwayama 2000: 29–32.

and Zabul, lying between the bases of Turkish power in Tokharistan and of Hephthalite power in Gandhara. In order to keep his argument consistent, however, Kuwayama then needed to justify the presence of various Turkic elements in the Kabul region, including the presence of Turkish titles in the official Chinese records, which necessitates another elaborate argument in favour of a theory of a later usurpation of the crown of Jibin/Kabul from the Khingila dynasty (Kuwayama 2000: 54–6).

Most of these arguments are based upon two major suppositions. The first was that the Nēzak power only came into existence as the result of the defeat of the Hephthalites by the collaborative actions of the Sasanian Empire and the Western Turks in AD 560. The second is the old and extremely pervasive idea that the 'Hunnic' rulers of Gandhara who replaced the Kidarites were 'Hephthalites'. The first part of this supposition is now discredited through the latest research into Nēzak coinage, as mentioned above, showing that the series started long before the Hephthalite defeat in AD 560. The second part too is now decisively dismissed by the numismatic evidence – and detailed in a Chapter 7 of the present work – as we now know that the *Alkhans*, and not the *Hephthalites*, were responsible for the invasion of Gandhara, Kashmir, and the rest of northern India after their defeat of the Kidarites. As such, there need not be any reason for the rise of the Nēzak, even if we fully attribute it to the 'Turkic period' (Inaba 2010a: 200), to have been affected by the defeat of the Hephthalites in Tokharistan. This essentially means that Kuwayama's theory of a 'power vacuum' is correct, except that the vacuum is caused not by a Turkish policy of not crossing the Hindu Kush, but rather by a Hephthalite one. The Hephthalites, by concentrating their efforts in Tokharistan and Transoxiana, left Kabul and Zabul alone, as Kuwayama so vehemently argues, and the Alkhans, after initially issuing coins in Kabul, eventually attempted to cross into Gandhara, thus leaving the Nēzak Shahs in charge. It is suggested by Vondrovec (2014: 515) that the Alkhan–Nēzak 'Crossover' series can be assigned to the dynasty of the Khingal, a possibility that would strengthen the idea that a branch of the Imperial Nēzak survived in Zabulistan, continuing the issue of the Late Nēzak series. At the same time, the increased Sasanian presence in East Iran, after their success in AD 560 and before their defeat by the Turks in 590, may also be a further sign of the influence of Sasanian cultural elements, including the proliferation of Pahlavi legends on coins, in the Zabulistan region.

The Nēzak Shahs (whether the Khingal dynasty or the Returning Alkhans) survived independently until at least 661, when a king called Hejiezhi,[13] claiming to be the twelfth king of a dynasty to reign over Jibin or Kabul, ruled in the region, according to the *Tang Shu* (Kuwayama 2000: 41). The Nēzak branch ruling over Zabulistan probably also survived to the same period, issuing coins of the -ā series as the Late Nēzak before these were replaced by new series under the Turkic rule.[14]

KABULISTAN AND ZABULISTAN UNDER THE WESTERN TURK

Providing a complete survey of the period of Turkic rule in East Iran, starting with the victory of the Western Turks in AD 560 over the Hephthalites and continuing into the early Islamic period, requires a volume separate from the present. What follows, thus, is a summary of the related information based on textual and numismatic sources, with a particular emphasis on the East Iranian regions.

Following the establishment of their power in Tokharistan, with their capital north of the Oxus, the Turks established the position of the Yabghu of Turkistan, who appears to have been the supreme governor of Turkic domains south of the Oxus, as his authority was acknowledged south of the Hindu-Kush in Kabul and Zabul as well (Kuwayama 1989: 139). In this region, we probably first hear of them through a mention of the Ser of the Turks in the Bactrian Documents (BD S) which was written in BE 470 (AD 693). A series of coins, with the title of Sero appearing alongside the Pahlavi *nycky MLKA*, further strengthens this identification, continuing the issues of the Nēzak -š series, which we assigned to the Kabul region (Vondrovec 2014: 521).[15]

At the same time, we know of the existence of this branch from the evidence of the Chinese sources that the king of Zabulistan is a nephew of the king of Kabul (Kuwayama 2000: 56). The Chinese envoy Xuanzang who visited the region in AD 640 also reports that the new ruler of Kabul was a Khalaj Turk and that the family has a branch in Zabul (Inaba 2010a: 445), while Bamiyan has an independent ruler (Kuwayama 2005). Huichao, a Korean monk, also reports that the area of Uddyana (modern Swat) was under the

---

[13] This is reconstructed to *Ghar-ilchi* by Kuwayama 2000: 41.

[14] Vondrovec 2014: 516 gives a date of AD 580–600 for the end of the Late Nēzak, but also mentions that other scholars (Pfisterer 2013) consider that the series continued to be issued after an interruption by type 150.

[15] Other Bactrian Documents mentioning the title of Ser are BD W (BE 525) and BD Y (BE 549), the latter giving the Ser the additional title of Lord: βαγο σερο (NSW 2000).

Fig. 8.3. Billon drachms of the Turk Shahis of Zawulistan, with the Bactrian inscription 'Sero' (© *das Antlitz des Fremden*).

control of the king of Jibin or Kabul (Inaba 2010a: 446), supposedly belonging to the new, incoming, Turkic ruling family.

A Bactrian Document (BD *T*) from this period brings interesting information about the area to our attention. In it, dated to BE 476 (AD 701), a princess identified as 'Bag-aziyas, the Great Turkish Princess, the Queen of Qutlugh Tapaghligh Bilga Sävüg, the Princess of the Khalach, the Lady of Kadagestan'[16] offers alms to the local god of the region of Rōb, known as Kamird, for the health of (her) child. Inaba, arguing for the Khalaj identity of the kings of Kabul, takes this document as a proof that the Khalaj princess is from Kabul and has been offered to the (Hephthalite) king of Kadagestan, thus becoming the lady of that region. The identification of *Kadagestan* as a Hephthalite stronghold is based on Grenet's suggestion of the survival of Hephthalite minor states in this region,[17] and is in contradction with Kuwayama's idea that the area was in fact a Turkic stronghold.[18] It does, however, tell us a bit about the situation around Rōb itself, immediately to the north of Bamiyan, with access to both the south and north of the Hindu Kush, and on the western road that was preferred for crossing from Tokharistan to Kabul via Bamiyan

---

[16] The region of Kadagestan, first associated with Meyam in the Bactrian Documents (BD *ed*) is identified with the region immediately to the east of the kingdom of Rōb, the locality of the Bactrian Documents (see Sims-Williams 2008: 98–9). A Sasanian administrative seal identifying a *Kadakestān Ostandār* 'Provincial Administrator of Kadagistān' (Gyselen 2002: 224) has also added to our understanding of this region, although its geographical placement in the Valley of Kunduz Ab is still a matter of speculation. See Chapter 5 for a discussion of the role of Meyam within Alkhan history.

[17] Grenet 2002b: 214–18, although not referenced in Inaba 2010b.

[18] Kuwayama 2000: 41 (among other places), where he identifies the route going through the region as the one via which the Turkic ruler offered to escort Xuanzang to Kabul.

(Inaba 2010b: 450). The local god Kamird is considered to have had enough importance for a Great Turkish princess to consider him worthy of offerings, and Rōb is central enough to be in touch with regions controlled by the Khalaj and Kadagestan.

Therefore, the position of the kingdom of Rōb is quite telling for the connections created between the northern and southern parts of the Hindu Kush, something that we see reflected in the coinage of the period as well. The coins of two later authorities, known from their coin legends as Sandan and Pangul, are inscribed with the title βαγδδιγγο 'bagddingo', which is interpreted as 'of Balkh',[19] while they both carry a mint signature of Raxvad,[20] which is located in Sistan, to the southwest of Rōb and south of Zabul. The same phenomenon occurs on the coins of 'the Bactrian Yabghu', the high administrators of the Western Turks in Tokharistan, where despite the presence of a legend *ybgw bhlk'n*,[21] the mint signature of *z'wlst'n* reveals their production in the Zabulistan region.

The king of Zabul (Caojuzha)[22] is called *Rtbyl* in the Islamic sources (al-Tabari I.2706, referred to by Kuwayama 2000: 62). Kuwayama, who also correctly speculated that there was more than one person called *Rtbyl* in Zabulestan (Kuwayama 2000: 64), previously interpreted this as a personal name. This is now proven by two sources, one of which Kuwayama was evidently unaware of despite its antiquity. The first is the evidence of *Tarikh-e Sistan*, a Persian local history of Sistan written in the eleventh century, which provides an extensive account of the wars of the *Rutbil* of Sistan and Zabulistan with the Muslim conquerors of the region, including Salm b. Ziyad (Bahar 1387: 121ff.). These wars, starting with the confrontation of Rabi' al-Hārithī in AD 666, continued well into the ninth century, when the Rutbil was only defeated by Yaghub b. Laith, the founder of the Saffarid dynasty. The second source is the newly discovered Bactrian Documents, which mention the presence of a person holding the title of *hilitbēr* in the kingdom of Rōb, essentially to the north of Zabulestan; this may be a Khalaj form of a Turkish title (Sims-Williams 2002: 235). This has allowed us to understand

---

[19] De la Vaissière 2010: 214. See de Blois 2013 for a discussion of the various renditions of the name of the city of Balkh.

[20] Vondrovec 2014: 526; 535–6 for Sandan and 545–7 for Pangul; see also Inaba 2015.

[21] See Vondrovec 2014: 527 for a discussion of the translation of this term as either 'Yabghu of the Bactrians' or 'Yabghu of Balkh'. The first translation is of course more philologically sound.

[22] See Kuwayama 2000: 29–32 for an intense discussion of the various Chinese terms referring to Kabul and Zabul and an insistence that Cao is not the shortened version of Caojuzha or any other term referring to Zabul, but rather an independent term referring to Kabul.

Rtbyl/Rutbil as a title, indeed a changed form of the Turkish title *ëltëber*. The Tang Kaozong Emperor had already bestowed the title, as *Qaradachi Eltäbär*, upon the ruler of Zabul in 719–20, and the ruler of Kabul is similarly called *Qaradachi Tegin* (Kuwayama 2000: 54). As a title, *ëltëber* seems to be a general one referring to the governor among the Western Turkic tribes, although it appears to be mostly a title referring to the leaders of the *Tiele* tribe (Inaba 2010a: 193). On coins, it appears as υιλιτοβηρο on a series of coins modelled after those of the Nēzak (Vondrovec 2014: 530–1).[23] It is interesting that at the same time an official of the kingdom of Rōb is also called υιλιτοβηρο 'hilitbēr' in documents N (BE 407 = AD 620/30), P (BE 446 = AD 668–70), and Q (BE 449 = AD 671/2), in the period before the mention of the Rutbil in *Tarikh-e Sistān* or al-Tabari's *History*.

At the same time that the early Muslim conquerors of Sistan and Zabulistan were struggling against the Rutbil –, and it really was a struggle lasting over 150 years – the Rutbil himself was using the kingdom of Kabul for refuge. Indeed, whenever the Rutbil is pressed or forced in to an alliance, he leaves for further north and east to upper Zabulistan and Kabulistan; he seems to have a huge reserve of money and soldiers either to buy off or to fend off the Muslims, and the source of this appears to lie in Kabul. Indeed, as early as the middle of the AD 650s, a king of Kabul is said to have confronted Muhallab b. Abi-Sifra in a heroic battle and agreed to peaceful coexistence (Bahar 1387: 117–18). According to Kuwayama's dating of the kingdom of Kabul, the king at this time should be the same *Qardach-ilchi* who was on the throne until 661. The appearance of the Rutbil of Zabulistan after this point, and his reliance on Kabul as a place to regroup in order to face the Muslims, might be indicative of the arrival of the new, Turkish (or as Inaba advocates, Khalaj) rulers in Kabul. However, the *Tarikh-e Sistan* never refers to the Rutbil or the king of Kabul as a Turk, although it separately mentions that the Rutbil 'gathered an army of Turks' to face the new Muslim governor of Sistan sometime after 683 (Bahar 1387: 132).

This fits quite well with the numismatic evidence of this period. An authority identified on his coins as the Tegin (Sims-Williams 2010: no. 457) issued coins, dated to post-679, which bear the inscription σρι τογινο βα(υ)ο 'His perfection, Tegin, King'. This Tegin is

---

[23] The Bactrian legend of this type 314A, χαδολαγο ιαρνο υιλιτοβηρο *xadolago iarno hilitobēro*, is undeciphered and bears certain similarities to the Brahmi legend of the coins of the 'tegin of the Khalaj' (type 208), which reads *śri-hitivira kharalāva pārame śvara śri ṣahi tiginadeva kārita* 'His perfection iltäbār of the Khalaj, devotee of the highest divinity, the perfect (?) king, the Sahi Tegin Lord had made this (coin)' (Vondrovec 2014: 530–1).

Fig. 8.4. Buddhist stupas from Kefiriat Tepe in the Kabul Valley (© 2011 Alka Patel).

most likely the same king as Burha Tegin, named as the founder of the Turki-shahi dynasty of Kabul by Al-Biruni. He is claimed to have expelled the Arabs from Kabul in 666 and, according to Gyselen, was succeeded by Rutbil in the 680s (Gyselen 2010: 237). These coins are related to a later type, issued after year 687, with the Pahlavi inscription *tkyn' bg hwt'p hwl's'n MLKA* 'Tegin, His Majesty, Lord, King of Khurasan' but bearing a mint signature of *z'wlst'an* 'Zabulistan'. There is also a later type, dated to after 703, with the Bactrian inscription ταγινο ϙωρσανο þαυο 'Tegin, King of

Fig. 8.5. Silver drachms of *Tegin, king of Khurasan*, perhaps from Kabul? (© *das Antlitz des Fremden*).

Khurasan'. Another type (208) with the same Pahlavi legends on the reverse also has a date of 77, possibly an AH date, which would mean it was issued about AD 696. The most important aspect of these coins, of course, is that like those of Pangul and the Bactrian Yabghu, they designate the geographical setting of the authority as somewhere other than the mint city, in this case Tegin of Khurasan, with the mint of Zabulistan.

The name of Khurasan (MP *Khwarāsān*) as an administrative division is known from the early Islamic period, when it was used as the general term for the entire eastern and northeastern parts of the Sasanian Empire and beyond. In the works of Islamic geographers, Khurasan was used even to designate the regions beyond the Oxus, including Sogdiana and Ustrushana, and surely Tokharistan.[24] The inclusion of Sistan (which in later Islamic geography also includes Zabulistan) and Kabul were less common, those often being counted separately. In *Tarikh-e Sistan*, the author counts the districts (*kuras*) of Khurasan, saying that before Islam, they were counted alongside those of Sistan as part of the same taxation unit. He then goes on to define Sistan as such:

> The length of Sīstān is from the border of Khorāsān to the Sindh, and its breadth is from Kerman to Hind.[25] Now the districts of Sīstān are Isfizar and Jabal Niya, and from the Valley of Hindghanan, and Farāh, and Ūq, and Khwās, and Folad, and Fešanj, and Nozad, and Bust, and Zamindawar, and Rukkhaj, Varkaš, and RŪdbār, and Zābul, and Kābul, sixteen. (Bahar 1387: 69)

Prior to this, however, we know of the occurrence of the term Khurasan in the Sasanian administration. According to al-Tabari, Khosrow I Anusherwan divided the (military) administration of his empire, which was previously held by one *Isbahbadh* (*sic*.) into four:

> Isbahbad of the East, comprising Khurāsān and its adjoining regions; the Isbahbadh of the West, the Isbahbadh of Nīmrūz, that is, the land of Yemen; and the Isbahbadh of Azarbaijan and its adjoining regions, that is, the Khazar lands. (al-Tabari 1999: 149)

This division, reflecting administrative and military changes that started under the rule of Kavad (see Shahbazi 1389/2010: n. 653),

---

[24] Khurradādhbih 1967: 28–32 seems to consider the areas to the 'east' as Khurasan in general, even counting Sistan as part of this unit. In the modern sense, the term 'Greater Khurasan' is used for varying expanses of land, often including most of northeastern Iran, Afghanistan, and various Central Asian republics; see, for example, Rante 2015.

[25] I have translated with the original Persian 'Hind' here as opposed to 'India' in order to prevent misunderstandings. For Muslim geographers, Hind started in Gandhara, basically to the east of Kabul.

is echoed more or less in most other Islamic geographical works (Al-Yaqubi 2010: 201–2; Dīnawarī 1888: 69), as well as some Armenian sources such as Ananias of Shirak. It is interesting that in the Islamic sources, Sistan is sometimes not included in the *kust* or division of Khwarasan (the east, literally 'the rising sun').[26] However, in the Armenian geography attributed to Moses of Khorene, the *kust* of *Nīmruz* (south; MP *Nēmrōz* 'Midday') includes, among others, the region of Sistan and Kerman (Marquart 1901: 16).[27] In *Tarikh-e Sistan*, Nīmrūz is considered another name for Sistan (Bahar 1387: 64–6), and we could add that the *Maliks of Nīmrūz* in the medieval period were also based firmly in Sistan (Bosworth 1994).

On the basis of the Chinese sources, Inaba confirms the rule of a *Wusan Teqin Sa* who was in power in Kabul in the fourth quarter of the seventh century and whose name appears to be a Chinese transcription of *Khurasan Tegin Shah*. This date range fits well in the period between the start of the activities of Rutbil in Sistan and the dating of the coins of Tegin of Khurasan (Inaba 2010b: 448). Wusan Teqin Sa was in power for a long time, probably about fifty years, during which time he may have concluded a treaty with Khotan, allowing for the creation of a memory of Kabul in the Khotanese chronicles, which mention that a daughter of Phrom Gesar, named Hu-ron-ga, was married to the king of Khotan, Vijaya Sangrāma.[28]

Phrom Gesar, later to morph into the Tibetan hero Gesar (Uray and Heissig 1985), is the king of Kabul known as From Kesar[29] who, according to scholars, must have ascended the throne of Kabul shortly before 738, although he was possibly a powerful viceroy based in the eastern capital of Wayhind in Uddiyana (Inaba 2010b: 448–9). He is known as *Fulin Jisuo* in the Chinese sources (Inaba 2010a: 446–7) and issued several coin series mainly using the basic type of Khosrow II. The coins carry his name and titles in Bactrian,

---

[26] Vondrovec 2014: 537 points out the closeness of the term *Khorāsān* to the Bactrian μιροοαυο 'the rising sun' that appears on the coins of the 'Eastern Alkhan' group. Sanskrit *purvāditiya* has the same meaning and similarly appears on the same series of coins in Brahmi. However, as Vondrovec specifies, there is no stylistic connections between the Eastern Alkhan coins and those of the Tegin of Khurasan. However, the Alkhan terminology might have been influential in the naming of the Sasanian military administration, which seems to be the region to which the Tegin is referring when claiming his kingship.

[27] Shahbazi 1389/2010: n. 656 doubts this and considers the inclusion of Sistan in Nīmruz to be the convention of the Abbasid period, when Sistan was seen as the south compared to Khurasan.

[28] The Khotanese chronicle only survives in a Tibetan translation. See Inaba 2010b: 446ff for a thorough study of this.

[29] See Humbach 1966: 21–2, who first discovered that the two are related. *From Kesar*, notably, is the Bactrian rendition of Middle Persian *Hrom Kēsar* 'the Roman Caesar', known from the ŠKZ.

and sometimes Brahmi, reading φορομο κησαρο ζηορο[30] βα(γο) χοδηο 'Phromo Kēsaro the Mighty (?) the King, the Lord' (Vondrovec 2014: 553, among other inscriptions). On the obverse of one type of his coins, Phromo Kēsaro calls himself 'From Kesar, His Majesty, the Lord, who smote the Arabs', in a countermark, thus showing his successes in fights against the Arabs. Considering the mintmark *z'wl* (Zabul) on at least one type (247), we could speculate that *Phromo Kēsaro* is either the same as the Rutbil of the Islamic sources, or is the Kabulshah on whom the Rutbil, possibly a series of local rulers of Zabulistan, are relying for their continued fight against the Muslim governors of Sistan. This would also make sense considering the mention of the name of the king of Xieyu (Zabul) in Chinese sources, where he is called Tegin instead of the Iltäbär (Inaba 2010b: 452). The fact that the Chinese sources appear to have more mention of Zabul than Kabul while talking about the embassies from this region might also tell us about the importance of Zabul. Indeed, in its rebellion against Tibet in 710, Kashmir asked for the help of Xieyu (Zabul) (Inaba 2010b: 451), which, along with the use of the name Tegin, could only mean that Zabul and Kabul were considered one and the same at this time.[31] This would accord very well with the geographical description of Sistan given in *Tarikh-e Sistan*, which includes both Zabulistan and Kabulistan in the greater entity of Sistan or Nīmrūz, a possible source for the Chinese designation *Xieyu*. A king called Bo Fuzhan, son of *Phromo Kēsaro*, succeeded him and was confirmed as the ruler of Jibin and Uddiyana in 745. Kuwayama, from the study of a marble statue of Ganesha in Gardez, suggested that Bo Fuzhan might have been the same as śri ṣahi Khimgāla, the dedicator of the statue, who was a king of Kabul (Inaba 2010b: 446).

Between the period of the reign of Khurasan Tegin Shah and Phrom Kesar, a series of coins showing affinities with the coins of Tegin were issued in the Zabulistan region. These were originally assigned to Phromo Kēsaro by Göbl (1967), but have more recently been studied

---

[30] This, transcribed *zēoro*, has been translated tentatively by Sims-Williams 2001 as *Zāwariya 'mighty.' Additionally, the legend ζηβαρο *Zēwaro* on type 327 of Phromo Kēsaro is considered a mistake for κησαρο *Kēsaro* by Vondrovec, alleging a mistake in the writing of a *k* that is z-shaped, a suggestion I cannot quite understand (Vondrovec 2014: 554 and note 777). I would like to posit the possibility that this is the well-known name Zawāra, known from the *Shahnameh* as the brother of the hero Rostam, and thus well placed in the cultural vicinity of Zabulistan. This would mean that the authority known from his coins as Phromo Kēsaro might have held the personal name of *Zawāra* and an additional title of *Spur*, connecting him to Spur Mardān Shah (see below).

[31] However, see Inaba 2010b: 452, who considers this a sign of the submission of Zabul to Kabul, as mentioned in *Xin Tangshu*.

Fig. 8.6. Silver drachm of Phrom Kesar, declaring his victory over the Arabs in a Bactrian inscription (© *das Antlitz des Fremden*).

by Gyselen and Vondrovec, showing different authorities involved in their production. Among these, three authorities issue closely related coins. An authority named *Spur Martan Shah*[32] (Vondrovec 2014: 549–50) issued coins based on types of Khosrow II, but with a purely inscriptional reverse, written in Pahlavi. His coins, as such, are closest to the early Islamic 'Umayyad' types (Gyselen 2010: 238).

Another authority known as Pangul (πανογολο χοαδο βαγο 'Pangul, the Lord, King'; Humbach 1996) issued silver and copper coins in Zabul and in Raxvad (al-Rukkhaj) with Bactrian and Pahlavi inscriptions (Gyselen 2010: 239; Vondrovec 2014: 545). The coins of Pangul carry several other legends that might help us identify him and place him in a historical context. The reverse of the same coin (type 245) includes the titles *Tudun* and *Tarkhān*, as well as a military title. Both the first two are known Turkic titles, with Tarkhān being a famous title belonging to a dynasty of Nēzak Tarkhāns known from the Islamic sources. One of the Nēzak Tarkhāns was a ruler of a region in the Surkhab Valley in Tokharistan,[33] who, along

---

[32] This name, *spwl mrt'n MLK'*, which is better read as Spur Mardān Šāh, has a fully Middle Persian character. Depending on how one reads it, it can be translated as 'King of Perfect Men' or 'The Perfect King of Men' or simply 'the Perfect Mardān-shah', (MacKenzie 1971: 76). In that last case it would mean that 'Mardan-shah' should be regarded as a personal name, as known from other sources and characters, including a son of Khosrow II and his famous wife Shirin (Justi 1895: 196). I thank Yusef Saadat for mentioning this idea.

[33] This should stand as a correction to Vondrovec 2014: 546, who puts the place of the rebellion in 'the Surkhab valley of Sogd', possibly mixing it up with the Surkhan Darya of Transoxiana, and considers the campaign part of Qutaiba's campaign in conquest of 'Bukhara, Samarkand and Ferghana'. The core of Nēzak Tarkhān's territories were probably in the same area, in the Surkh Ab Valley region, where he was finally caught and killed, although the initial phase of rebellion was in the Herat region, including the city of Bādghīs (Grenet 2002: 216).

Fig. 8.7. Copper drachms of Pangul with Pahlavi and Bactrian inscriptions, from the Rakhvat/Al-Rukkhaj mint in Sistan (© *das Antlitz des Fremden*).

with the ruler of Marw, participated in the defeat and assassination of Yazdgerd III in 651. A descendant of this Tarkhān, again called the Nēzak Tarkhān, was the leader of a rebellion against the Muslim rulers of the region. In his rebellion, he had the support of the rulers of Kabul (Inaba 2010b: 450), while being opposed, and betrayed, by the ruler of Rōb (al-Tabari I.1218–27). Scholars appear to be quite frustrated and unsettled by the fact that many of the coins of Pangul, as well as those of the Bactrian *Yabghu*, appear to bear references to their issue in *Zabul*, to the south of the Hindu Kush, while making a claim to rule over Tokharistan, on the north. While in the case of the Yabghu, the case might be a matter of extended authority, it appears hard to accept the rule of a minor authority such as Pangul over such an extended region. As such, Vondrovec suggests that we consider Pangul a ruler over Zabulistan while considering his claim to Tokharistan (via the use of the epithet 'of Balkh') a pretension (Vondrovec 2014: 548). Put in a historical context, however, there is little reason to be confused or frustrated by the situation. The period of Pangul's coin issues, the last quarter of the seventh and first decades of the eighth century, was the period of local resistance in Sogdiana, Tokharistan, Sistan, and Kabulistan against the new Muslim rule. The ruler of Kabul had managed to drive the Arab armies out of Kabul in 666, and the Rutbils were to fight against total Muslim control of Sistan and Zabulistan for another 100 years and more. More importantly, as mentioned before, the Nēzak Tarkhān was the leader of a major rebellion against the Muslims which was only put down by the very able Arab general Qutaiba b. Muslim in AD 710. The resistance in Sogdiana continued for about two more decades, with Ghurak of Samarkand and Dewaštič of Panjekant blocking

Muslim advancement until the end of the 720s.³⁴ So it is only natural for Pangul, whose coins, unlike those of the local rulers of Gozgan (see below), do not show any influence from the Arab–Sasanian coin designs, to have been an itinerant leader with claims over various territories he controlled on various occasions. Furthermore, considering the title of Tarkhān, there is a possibility that we can associate Pangul with the Nēzak Tarkhān who rebelled against Qutaiba and fled his onslaught, finally being cornered and killed in what Grenet speculated to be the *Kafir Kala* of Barfak in the Hindu Kush just to the north of Bamiyan (Grenet 2002a: 2016).

On some coin types, the mint is mentioned as either Zabul or Zabulistan, while a few bear the designation of Khurasan, similar to the case of the Tegin of Khurasan. A connection with the coins of Pangul also exists on type 328, whose figure wears the same lion-topped crown as Pangul, while the title *Spur* creates a connection with some issues of Phromo Kēsaro that bear the same title (Vondrovec 2014: 550). Types 212–16 of Spur Mardān Šāh include a longer legend that has been read as *PWN ŠM Y yzdt' spwl bg hwt'p whm'n'c mrt'n MLK'* 'pad nām ī yazad,³⁵ spur bay xudai Wahmānāz Mardān Šāh'³⁶ meaning 'in the name of God, Spur, the lord, the master, Wahmānāz, Mardān Shah'. Vondrovec also points out that the title of Spur occurs on the coins of Phromo Kēsaro, leading us to believe that this is indeed a title (Vondrovec 2014: 515; Gyselen 2010: 238–9). As such, I suggest that the name Wahmānāz, probably a personal name, as remarked by Vondrovec as well, is to be considered the personal name of the authority whose coins use the honorific of Spur Mardān Šah, although at present I do not have a better suggestion for a more convincing reading of the name Wahmānāz.

All these issues, including those of the Tegin, include the image of the mythical bird Senmurv/Sīmurgh on their obverse or reverse sides. While it is tempting to assign some of these coins to the region of Bactria (Vondrovec 2014: 548), the presence of Zabul on these coins alongside the Senmurv/Sīmurgh may be of some significance. In the Iranian legends concerning the ruling house of Sistan and

---

³⁴ For a detailed account of this, see Grenet and de la Vaissière 2002.

³⁵ The formula is a copy of the Islamic formula of Bismillah. On the occurrence of the name of god in the singular, as opposed to the more common Middle Persian plural *yazdān*, see now Weber 2014.

³⁶ Vondrovec 2014: 514–15, where he does not present a transcription. I have thus rendered my own transcription in which I have used the more conventional form of Mardān Shah instead of the Martan Shah form preferred by the numismatists.

Zabulistan, to which the hero Rostam also belongs, the Senmurv/ Sīmurgh is of great significance. As the foster-mother of Dastān-e Zāl, Rostam's father, she is the guardian angel and protector of the House of Zabuli and helps him several times in dire situations. This probably preserves a sort of memory from the earlier period that associated the Senmurv/Sīmurgh with Zabulistan. Consequently, the appearance of the same mythical bird on the seventh- and eighth-century coins which also occasionally bear the mint signature of Zabul seems, logically, evidence for the argument that the coins were actually produced by the rulers of Zabul, and that their use of titles such as Tarkhān[37] and of Bactrian was simply an attempt to make a claim to greater authority.

---

[37] Vondrovec 2014: 544–52 presents a discussion of various titles and appellations that appear on the coinage of Zabulistan, including their possible interrelations.

9 Tokharistan and Sogdiana in the Late Sasanian Period

INTRODUCTION

Following the division of the territories of the Hephthalites between the Turks and the Sasanians, the region to the south of the Oxus, Tokharistan, seems to have fallen to the Sasanians (Harmatta 1999: 359–60). However, this does not seem to be a period of prosperity in this area. Xuanzang describes Balkh, the ancient capital of the region, as follows: 'This city, though well [strongly] fortified, is thinly populated' (quoted in Litvinsky 1999: 152), although it did possess the important Buddhist monastery of Nau-bihar (Litvinsky and Safi 1999: 182). Bactria, 'the Land of a Thousand Cities' (Leriche 2007), was in decline, and lost most of its importance to Kapiśa/Gandhara (Harmatta 1999: 362), and probably to Sogdiana (see de la Vaissière 2005b: 199ff.). Archaeological excavations barely show a town in the Termez regions between the fifth and seventh centuries, and Chaghanian, the important Hephthalite territory, could boast only a very limited area (Litvinsky 1999: 152–3).

Sasanian control of the former Hephthalite imperial domains appears to have lasted only a few decades following the Battle of Gol-Zarriūn and the destruction of the Hephthalite Empire in AD 560. The most widely discovered coins in the region are the issues of Hormizd IV (579–90) and Wahram VI (591–2). Coins of year 11 of Hormizd IV – that is, his final year – appear to have been the most imitated. Hormizd himself issued coins in Khulm (mint signature *hlm*), as well as in Samarkand (*sml*) in his years 3–5 (AD 582–4) and in Čāč/Šāš (č'č) in his year 6, AD 585 (Vondrovec 2014: 525). This must have been the northernmost extent of Sasanian power, extending beyond the Syr Darya/Jaxartes.

Tokharistan and Sogdiana in the Late Sasanian Period

Fig. 9.1. Countermarked silver drachm of Sasanian Hormizd IV, year 11 (AD 588–9), minted in *BHL* (Balkh) (© *das Antlitz des Fremden*).

Among all the Sasanian rulers, it is Wahram VI whose associations and physical presence in this region and in the context of his relations with the Western Turks we know best. The Samanid historian and vizier Abu-Ali Balʻami presents a complete résumé of the career of Wahram VI in his partial translation of al-Tabari's universal history (Balʻami 1386: 938–49). Wahram, known as Wahram Čōbīn (sometimes Šubin, 'Wooden'), was the commander chosen by Hormizd IV for his campaign against the Turks. Apparently, Sābē Khān,[1] Hormizd's uncle and the son of the previous Khagan, attacked the Sasanian troops in Balkh, setting them to flight, and conquering Balkh, Talaqan (the one to the west of Balkh), Hari (Herat), and Bādghīs. At the same time, attacks by the Romans, Arabs, and Khazars were also reported. So Hormizd, attempting to set affairs back in order, chose Wahram Čōbīn 'of the family of Gurgin son of Mīlād' as the general of his armies against the Turks. Before these wars, the Sasanian troops were in possession of the area of western Tokharistan and were mainly stationed in Balkh, the centre of the former Hephthalite imperial power. The entrance of the Turks into this region was thus a breach of an agreement concluded between Khosrow I and the Khaghan (Sinjibu) that had set the Oxus as a boundary between the empires.

The description of the battle itself is in line with the literary *topoi* of Persian literature and includes the death of Sābē Khān at the hand of Wahram himself. The Turkish army was decisively defeated and Wahram entered the city of Balkh triumphantly, managing to

---

[1] *Šābeh* in Ibn Balkhi 1385: 98 and as well as in Anonymous 1375: 352.

control the Turkish treasury and capturing the golden throne of the Khan. An insurgent attack by Birmudha,[2] son of Sābē, was also thwarted, with the new Khan being captured and sent to Ctesiphon. Hormizd then hosted his cousin honourably for forty days and afterwards sent him back to Wahram with the instruction that he should be sent back to 'Turkistan' – presumably meaning Transoxiana at this point. Although this is not mentioned in Bal'ami, we should probably assign the year 3–5 coins of Hormizd in Samrkand and his year 6 coins from Čāč to this period.

A misunderstanding about Wahram's honesty in sending the war booty to Hormizd caused a rift between the king and his now powerful and popular general. A botched war and a series of intrigues resulted in the removal of Hormizd from the throne (al-Tabari I.993) in a court conspiracy, and the succession of his son, Khosrow II Aparwēz. This time Wahram, posing as the avenger of Hormizd IV, attacked Khosrow II and expelled him from the empire with the support of his eastern troops. Wahram then declared himself king, becoming the first monarch of the period who did not belong to the Sasanian family.[3] The episode of Khosrow's flight to Byzantium and his restoration with the help of the Byzantines is quite famous and much written about (Daryaee 2009: 32; al-Tabari 1999: 311 n. 728). Bal'ami, as well as other historians, tells us that Wahram fled to the court of the Turk Khaghan,[4] presumably the same Birmudha, son of Sābē and cousin of Hormizd IV. It must have been around this period that Wahram had issued his year 2 coins in Balkh, corresponding to AD 590–1 (Vondrovec 2014: 525). In the Turkish court, Wahram reached a high level of popularity after intervening on behalf of the Khaghan in a conspiracy against the latter by his brother Byghu (possibly an erroneous rendition of *yabghu*). Wahram himself was, however, murdered in a conspiracy initiated by Khosrow II and at the hand of a messenger of the latter.[5]

The battle between the Turks and the Sasanians over Tokharistan and the initial defeat of the Turks by Wahram Čōbīn tells us much

---

[2] Ibn Balkhi 1385: 98 has this as *Birmudeh*.
[3] For a discussion of this, see Shahbazi 1988. The possible repercussions of this event for Sasanian royal ideology and administration are considered by Christensen 1907, and more recently by Pourshariati 2008: 126–9.
[4] Al-Tabari I.1000. The whole episode is discussed extensively by Kolesnikov 1978: 121–55.
[5] Bal'ami 1386: 948; Dīnawarī 1888: 98–100 involved Wahram's own sister, Korduyē, a secret lover of Khosrow II. As Bosworth mentions, all major narratives of the events involve a woman, most commonly the Khaghan's wife: al-Tabari 1999: 316, n. 740.

about the early history of Tokharistan and Sogdiana during the early decades after the defeat of the Hephthalites. The absence of subsequent Sasanian coin issues from the region suggests that following this initial setback, the Turks managed to gain control of western Tokharistan and establish their power on both sides of the Oxus and, as mentioned before, possibly as far south and east as Zabulistan and Kabulistan. While the capital of the Western Turks was in Transoxiana, the appointment of a *Yabghu* of Tokharistan[6] as the supreme commander of Western Turk possessions south of the Oxus makes perfect sense. The coins of the *Yabghu* show a stylistic mix of various Sasanian authorities from Khosrow I to Kawad II, and possibly even Ardashir III,[7] while their crowns are most influenced by the Nēzak issues, with even some remainder of the *nycky MLKA* legend on the obverse.[8] The yabghu himself was continuing an office that was attested from the Bactrian Documents as the *Yabghu* of the Hephthal (BD 2: *jb1–2*) and enjoyed a long history in the region, at least from the Kushan period.

As mentioned before, Tokharistan was in a period of decline, with archaeological evidence showing a decrease in urbanisation and limited agricultural activities. However, newer research and a consideration of the sources can help us in modifying this bleak picture. Numismatic evidence, as well as documentary sources such as the archive of Rōb, reveal a region separated into different zones of influence, with various political entities replacing the Hephthalite Empire (see Grenet 2002b: 214–18). Agriculture, while largely reduced from its traditional forms, may have been revived in different forms of horticulture and viticulture, allowing for a more commercial approach (Rezakhani 2010c).

The presence of coins from Gozgan in the west of Tokharistan provides us with a rare glimpse into the period of Turkish control in Tokharistan. The coins, including the geographical designation of Gozgan, also have the mint names *Amber* (modern Sar-e Pol),

---

[6] Xuanzang met the Tokhara Yabghu in AD 629, and the position is still attested until AD 729 (Kuwayama 1989: 132–9).

[7] Vondrovec 2014: 528 suggests that the bust of the king, always depicted as beardless on the Yabghu coins, might have been influenced by those of Ardashir III (628–30). Apart from the fact that the date is late, we should notice that Ardashir's beardless features were an obvious reflection of his young age. However, in the case of the Yabghu, there is a possibility that the beardless portrait reflects the ethnic reality of the Turkic yabghu, much in the same way that the mature coin types of the Kidarites and the Alkhans show beardless kings with moustaches, a clear indication of the fashion of the time.

[8] See Vondrovec 2014: 527–30 for a discussion of different stylistic issues.

Fig. 9.2. Relief showing a fantastic creature; mural from Panjikent at the State Hermitage Museum (© Author).

hwr' (Khurasan?), and *mlw* (Marw).[9] The coins are obviously issued after the Arab–Sasanian series, and thus belong to sometime after AD 642, as they carry the standard Muslim invocation of Bismillah ('in the Name of god'). Two authorities are identified on the coins, one known as Kuramzad and the other as Zhulad of Gozgan.[10] Another authority named Besut, who issued coins of unique design, may also be the same as *pycwtt*, the father of a king of Panjikent in the early 700s (Vondrovec 2014: 534–5), showing the extent of the presence of Gozgan local rulers on both sides of the Oxus. Yet another authority with a relatively extensive series of coins, named Sandan, produced coins on which he calls himself βαγδδιγγo καγανo 'Khagan of Balkh' in Bactrian and *vakhudevah* 'Lord of the Oxus' in Brahmi. His coins, showing certain connections to the coins of the Tegin of Khurasan, as well as those of Pangul and the Spur Mardān Shāh, are among the coinage of East Iran in the terminal Western Turk period and the beginning of the Islamic period.

The Western Turk period was of particular importance in Sogdiana and for the Sogdians. The Turks destroyed local dynasties such as that of Paikand, but the integration of the Sogdians into the Turk state allowed for an expansion of Sogdian culture and commercial activities. The Sogdians started to colonise regions further to

---

[9] Vondrovec 2014: 532. I am sceptical about the identification of *hwr'* as Khurasan. This seems too vague a term to refer to an actual mint city, and *hwr'* should probably be sought elsewhere, in the vicinity of Sar-e Pol.

[10] Vondrovec 2014: 531–2. The name Zhulad, attested also as ζονολαδο, means 'given by Zun' or Zhun, the well-known Bactrian god (see Inaba 2005). The name is attested extensively in several Bactrian documents, designating among others, a *Khār* of Rōb; see Sims-Williams 2010: 65, no. 160.

the east, including Semirechye, thus setting up their expansion into China (Marshak and Negmatov 1999: 242). However, it seems clear that the Sogdian penetration of the steppe and commercial contacts with the steppe dwellers, including the Turk, goes back to the fifth century and predates the Turk conquest of Sogdiana (de la Vaissière 2005b: 206). The rise of the Turco-Sogdian 'milieu' was an important part of the formation of the Sogdian trade network, and the main sustenance of the Turk Empire.[11] The western extension of the network allowed trade with Sasanian Iran, where the silk received as tribute from the Tang, due to Turk military successes, was traded with the Sasanians, who greatly valued the textile. This also allowed for the opening of the Khurasan Road, creating an integration of the Sogdian network into a Sasanian one (de la Vaissière 2005b: 226ff). While Sogdians became the high administrators of the Turk state, the Sogdian language became the main language of the empire and expanded well eastwards to China, and lent its script to the Old Turkic and many subsequent Turkic and Mongolian languages (de la Vaissière 2005b: 202). In turn, the Turkic nobility became part of Sogdian society, with marriages between the families of the kings of Samarkand and that of the Turk Khaghan. Panjikent indeed had a Turkic ruler at the beginning of the seventh century (Marshak and Negmatov 1999: 242–3).

The Western Turk Empire in fact started to disintegrate rather quickly after gaining its initial quick successes. It began to lose power in the middle of the seventh century, and by AD 682, it had ceased to exist (Stark 2008; Sinor 1990). Even before that, the Tang Empire of China had started to establish a protectorate in Central Asia, known as the protectorate of *Anxi* (Kuwayama 1989: 134). Despite a restoration of the Turk power at the beginning of the eighth century (Klyashtorny 1999), the Tang held nominal power in the region until AD 751. In the 710s, Qutaiba, the governor of Khurasan, confirmed the Turkic ruler of Samarkand, Ghurak, in his position.[12] Family feuds, however, drove his sons to the court of Dewashtich, the ruler of Panjikent. The latter had a famous 'last stand' against the Muslims in 722 in his mountain fortress of Mugh, the details of which are known from the very vivid Mount

---

[11] See de la Vaissière 2005b: 215 for a detailed study of the expansion of the Sogdian network, including its involvement in the trade in silk and horses, and the importance of the Turk–Sogdian alliance.

[12] On Ghurak, or Ughrak, and the sequence of events before and after his removal from the throne of Samarkand by the Muslims, see Naymark 2013.

Mugh Documents.[13] The defeat of Dewashtich marked the beginning of the formal accession of Transoxiana to the Islamic Empire, and soon resulted in increasing Muslim control of the eastern regions as well (Grenet and de la Vaissière 2002). This started, among other things, the breakup of the Sogdian commercial network, and ultimately an integration of the Sogdians into the Islamic empire (de la Vaissière 2005b: 264–76). An important disagreement over the installation of the king of Ferghana caused a major rebellion in the region, causing the young Abbasid Empire (founded in 751) to react. Considering the closeness of the Syr Darya and Ferghana region to Khurasan – indeed, it was possibly considered part of that greater entity by Muslims – it was no wonder that the Abbasids reacted violently to Tang attempts at exerting power in the region. Transoxiana was indeed the place where the Abbasid revolution started from, and from where most early Abbasid soldiers and commanders, including Abu Muslim himself, hailed (de la Vaissière 2007). So, in the famous *Battle of Talas* on the Syr Darya, the Muslim forces of the Abbasid Caliphate defeated the Tang in 751, ending their power in the west. The security of the Abbasid eastern territories was achieved, and, Greater Khurasan finally established its eastern boundaries.

SASANIAN DESCENDANTS IN THE EAST

An important aspect of the late Sasanian relations with East Iran has to do with the final episodes of Sasanian imperial history. In taking refuge in the east, and trying to survive against the Arab conquests by relying in the support of East Iran, the Sasanians made a final statement about the political geography of Central and West Asia on the eve of Islam.

The defeat of the Sasanian armies in the Battle of Qadisiyya (AD 636) and the fall of Ctesiphon (AD 637) are hailed as the nails in the coffin of the dynasty by the later sources (Donner 1981: ch. IV, 157ff.; Hoyland 2014: 49–53, 82–7). Despite the importance of these defeats for the collapse of Sasanian control in Mesopotamia/Asuristan, we should not presume a full collapse of the dynasty immediately following these events.[14] Yazdgerd III, who according

---

[13] For these, see now the very welcome English publication of the Livshits edition of the documents: Livshits 2015e.

[14] This, however, appears to be the dominant view of historians who approach the events mainly from the point of view of the Islamic sources; see Hoyland 2014: 52 and Crone 2012: 1–3, who considers the fall of Ctesiphon as a complete collapse of Sasanian defences.

to al-Tabari was originally from Istakhr in Fars/Persis (Daryaee 2009: 37), regrouped in Istakhr and organised an army to confront the Arabs at Nihawand (AD 642) at what is considered the most important Arab-Islamic gain in Iran (Hoyland 2014: 84–5). The fact that Yazdgerd III took refuge, and was able to gather a sizeable army to face the Muslim armies, in Nihawand, despite its ultimate lack of success, still shows Sasanian control of the Iranian Plateau and the recognition of their authority in this region following their loss of Asuristan.

However, the defeat of Nihawand obviously greatly damaged Yazdgerd's authority, and the fact that his important commander, Khurrazad, joined with the Muslim armies destroyed his chances of regaining authority in the west and central parts of the plateau (Hoyland 2014: 86). It was under these circumstances that Yazdgerd fled to the northwest and the area of Neishabur/Abarshahr, attempting to use the support of the local powers of Khurasan in further fighting the Muslim armies. His campaign there was unsuccessful and he was eventually killed (AD 651), most likely at the behest of the local ruler of Bādghīs – Mahuy-ī Sūrī, according to the *Shahnameh* – in Marw (Daryaee 2009: 37; Ferdowsi 2008: VIII.265–8). Considering the circumstances, this local ruler could be a local Hephthalite commander (Grenet 2002b: 208ff).

Yazdgerd had previously (in AD 638) sent an embassy to the Tang court, asking for reinforcements to defeat the Arabs, help that seems not have been forthcoming, despite the embassy reaching the Tang court in AD 639 (Shinji 1981: 44). Following his death, his son Pērōz took refuge with the Tang in 661 (Shinji 1981: 45) and perhaps managed to set himself up briefly as a Chinese vassal in Zaranj in Sistan (Jiang 2012: 41; Shinji 1981: 45; Harmatta 1971: 373–4). This would mean that at this point, Pērōz was taking advantage of the weakened Western Turk control south of the Hindu Kush to claim the kingship of a greatly reduced 'Persian Empire' (Chinese *Po-su*). This could explain a lack of local coinage at this time, as the local Nēzak coins were more limited to the Kabul region, whence Islamic sources report rebellious activities (Dīnawarī 1888: 163). Pērōz was eventually defeated and had to withdraw to the Tang territories, where he was awarded a grand title and died around 679 (Daryaee 2009: 38). He built either a fire temple or a Buddhist shrine whose remains still stand and bear an inscription identifying him as the founder (Compareti 2003: 260).

Narseh (Ni-li-shih in Chinese), the son of Pērōz, continued his father's struggle and was similarly appointed as a Chinese general in the west. He resided for several years in Tokharistan (Crone 2012: 5) and again returned to China to retire with his father's title (Compareti 2003: 209). Wahram (Aluohan in Chinese), the second son of Yazdgerd III, appears to have had further success in Sistan, where he also attempted to restore himself to the position of king, but was ultimately defeated too. His memory and the promise of his return, however, may have been preserved in the Zoroastrian apocalyptic literature in the character of *Shah Bahram Varjāvand*, one of the many Zoroastrian saviours (Daryaee 2009: 38). His son Khosrow (Juluo in Chinese) also made an attempt to restore Sasanian rule with the help of the Turks in AD 710, but was defeated, and we hear of him in AD 737 paying homage to the Tang.[15] All the Chinese activities in this time must have been related to the establishment of the *Protectorate to Pacify the West* or the *Anxi Protectorate* and its commanders. A specific Chinese Persia expeditionary force was in fact established by the Tang in order to explore the possibility of reconquering parts of Central Asia (Jiang 2012). Reflections of this, and the continued Tang policy of aiding Central Asian rebellions against the Muslims, can be seen in the Mount Mugh Documents from the time of Dewashtich and his struggle against the Arabs in the early eighth century (see above; Grenet and de la Vaissière 2002). The presence of a 'Persian' general in the vicinity of Panjikent (Mugh A–14; Grenet and de la Vaissière 2002: 167–8) might also be related to the presence of Khosrow, as mentioned above, in the region, perhaps in conjunction with the Turks and their Khaghan, mentioned in another Mugh document (Mugh V-18; Grenet and de la Vaissière 2002: 159–60). Of course, any Chinese pretence to Central Asia was put to rest in AD 751, the hundredth anniversary of Yazdgerd's death, in the Battle of Talas, which confirmed Islamic rule of East Iran/Khurasan. The proximity of this date to that of the Abbasid Revolution, the major presence of Khurasanis in the affairs of the Islamic world, provides a fitting conclusion to the present narrative.

---

[15] Daryaee 2009: 38; Compareti 2003: 210. Crone 2012: 5 considers Khosrow a grandson of Pērōz, presumably as a son of Narseh.

10 *General Conclusions and Postscript*

In world history, certain regions emerge as dominant players in regional and interregional historical events, and they either continue their ascendance or fade into the background. We are used to viewing regions in a hegemonic way, and consider hegemony to be based on inherent and long-term advantages, showing essential centralities that are based on repeating successful patterns of historical activity. World historians such as Marshall Hodgson identified five 'civilisational cores' in Eurasia. A wedge between the Chinese and the Persianate cores, Central Asia was then placed on the periphery, the 'cleavage' between two great civilisational cores of eastern and western Eurasia (Hodgson 1963: 233–4).

Central Asia, however, proves anything but peripheral in the medieval period. The western part, the regions here called East Iran, became increasingly 'central' in the history of West and South Asia, as well as the rest of Eurasia, between the eighth and fifteenth centuries. This centrality was determining enough for a renowned world historian to dedicate a brief monograph to it, despite the fact that it relied on necessarily cursory and conjectural evidence to prove its point (Frank 1992). Many other attempts, mostly focusing on the Chinese 'Inner Asia' and the 'Silk Road', try to understand the region in the context of its importance to its neighbouring civilisations, or of the theme of the Silk Road.[1] A few others focus on the

---

[1] See the various offerings of Whitfield 1999; Wood 2002; Hansen 2012. Liu 2012 was an attempt to put the Silk Road into the concept of world history, but instead of considering the area the supposed Silk Road covers, it was most concerned, like almost with the other works with a similar focus, with the relations between the east (in this case China) and the west (Rome, Byzantium, 'Europe'). The newest offering, Frankopan 2015, a more successful attempt at applying world historical methodology, pays surprisingly close attention to the

region itself, including Peter Golden's 2011 offering, part of a series concerned with regions in world history, which despite its title, does not much address the issue of Central Asia's role in world history in the theoretical sense and in any of its known conceptualisations. A special mention here has to be made of Christopher Beckwith's controversial 2012 book, trying to connect the origins of 'medieval' science, or at least philosophical methodology, to the Buddhist monasteries of Central Asia. A full review of the thesis needs much more than the present space, but one has to only mention that throughout the book, the writer really does not go into the simple matter of where the monasteries he is speaking of are located, or what their local political, cultural, economic, or social context is. His monasteries exist mostly detached from the world around them, and reveal nothing about why they might have achieved what they supposedly did.

This, in fact, is the major reason for the existence of the present book. Through reading many contributions to the history of this region, I see that less attention is paid to the actual history of the region itself than to what it means for the places that surround it. The works concerned with the Silk Road often care about the presence of Central Asian networks in other lands, commonly China. They consider the cities along the supposed Silk Road to be 'oases' existing purely to feed the 'trade network' and to supplement commerce. Historians of China see the region as frontiers of Chinese imperialism and, much like their primary sources, count them as outlying lands of undefined character and confusing groups.[2] The historians of West Asia, in turn, consider most of the region to be the extreme east, the frontiers of the Islamic world, where the *Kafirs*[3] lived even until the early twentieth century. The term *Mawara-un-Nahr/Transoxiana*, describing the region between the Amu Darya and the Syr Darya, is itself indicative of the direction from which it was bestowed (Tor 2009; and many others).

Instead, in the present monograph, I have tried to focus on the region's own history, even if simply the political history, in order to present a local context for the importance of Central Asia. This is presented as part of the concept of East Iran, which in my opinion

Iranian and Central Asian material, a welcome approach indeed. For a critique of this, see Rezakhani 2010b.

[2] See contributions from Lattimore 1950 to Di Cosmo 2002.

[3] I am using the term 'Kafir' as the common name given to the population of the *Wakhan* corridor/Nuristan by scholars and reflected in many *Kafir Kala* 'Infidel Fortresses' around northern Afghanistan.

emphasises a particular anchor to this history, and also describes a sociocultural and political reality that emerges in the period immediately following the period of our concern. This succeeding period, that of *medieval* East Iran, when the region comes to be known as Khurasan/Khurasan, is what the book in fact attempts to explain. While the importance of Central Asia in the tenth to sixteenth centuries is undeniable and well studied, the background to this importance is unknown and vaguely described. Here, a brief summary of the rise of Central Asia in the medieval period might be useful. This would serve to provide an epilogue to the monograph itself, to describe the importance of the region, and to justify further my use of the term 'East Iran' to describe the regions under discussion.

EAST IRAN IN THE MEDIEVAL PERIOD

The Abbasid Revolution of AD 750 started in 'Khurasan' or East Iran, succeeded in replacing the Umayyads with the Abbasid Caliphate, and in a sense launched the 'Classical Age of Islam'. The political powers of this region, initially in the service of the Abbasids – providing the famed *Khurasani* troops – became essential in Abbasid policies as far afield as north Africa.[4] Dynasties with origins in Sogdiana (e.g. the *Ikhshidids* of Egypt, the *Sajjids* of the Caucasus; de la Vaissière 2007 became important players in the world of Islam. Tokharistans like the Barmakids administered the Abbasid Caliphate, and other Khurasanis such as Abu Muslim and al-Afshin were main executors of its politics. The successors of these East Iranians took matters into their own hands and instead of offering their services to the Caliphate, used them to establish their own independent powers.

The Samanids of Bukhara and Samarkand formed the most successful political unit that directly opposed the power and hegemony of Baghdad. They created for themselves a distinct culture, based on local Sogdian and East Iranian ideologies and established patterns. They claimed descent from the great Sasanian general and usurper Wahram VI, and established a grand court. Their court in fact became the refuge for prestigious scholars such as Avicenna and Al-Biruni. Persian, the administrative language of the Samanid Empire, which had acted as the vehicle for the spread of Islam in

---

[4] Kennedy 1986/2004: 112–55. What follows as a brief summary can be found in most common reference books about medieval Iran and Islam. Most accessible perhaps is the *Cambridge History of Iran* series, vols III (1983) and IV (1975). Smaller, more convenient summaries, plus an updated bibliography, are provided in Daryaee 2011: chs 8–11.

East Iran and Sogdiana (Frye 1988), became the literary language of Khurasan. By patronising great Persian poets like Rudaki, the Samanid court sponsored the emergence of Classical New Persian, so much so that they are sometimes cast as the originators of a sort of nationalism. They did, in fact, most effectively support the creation of the Persianate world,[5] the dominant cultural unit of medieval Central and West Asia.

The Samanid nemesis and successor state, the Ghaznavids of Zabulistan, themselves originating from the steppe and after controlling an essential part of East Iran, invaded India. It was, in fact, an established pattern for invaders from the steppe to conquer Tokharistan, then cross the Hindu Kush to Zabulistan and Kabulistan, then go eastward to Gandhara and Kashmir, and finally south to northern India. The Kushans had established the pattern, and it was followed by almost all of their successors. Like the Samanids, the Ghaznavids too assembled a court full of poets and scholars, taking those originating mostly from Greater Khurasan under their wings. In fact, they almost forced the Samanids to give up Al-Biruni to them, an auspicious event that, although unpleasant, gave us the gem of *Mal-Al-Hind*, the famous study of India and its Brahmanic beliefs that is still the basis for understanding the history of medieval India. The Ghaznavids also took advantage of the services of Sogdians such as the *Mikalis*, who had become the greatest family of Neishapur and dominant figures of medieval Khurasan.

Almost contemporary with the Ghaznavids, the Seljuks invaded from the steppe, took over Sogdiana, conquered East Iran, and confined the Ghaznavids to Gandhara (much like the Hephthalites and the Alkhans centuries earlier), further subjugating West Asia as far as Egypt. They too continued the Samanid and Ghaznavid sponsorship of scholarship and Classical New Persian literature. Their famous vizier Nizam ul-Mulk wrote a well-known manual of politics (a *Fürstenspiegel*) in Persian, the language that was now gaining prestige because of its established history since the time of the Samanids. The Turkmen tribes who followed the Seljuks to West Asia established their dynasties in Iran, Syria, and Anatolia, mixing the local

---

[5] The *Persianate world*, a designation which is based on the concept of the Islamicate world promoted by Marshall Hodgson (Hodgson 1974), is an attempt to create a collective sense for the regions which in the later medieval and eastern period adopted New Persian as their administrative and sometimes literary language, and which stretch from the Ottoman territories in the west to Mughal India in the south and the east. The term should not be interpreted as an expression of a sort of nationalism, as its range covers the period before the emergence of modern nation-states.

culture with their already hybrid Turkic–East Iranian one, expressed mostly through the medium of Persian, and often wrapped inside Persian mythological concepts.[6]

The Ilkhanids, the Iranian Mongol dynasty who initiated a new era of patronage for writers and scholars, this time focused on Persian, followed the Seljuk successor states. This is the period when the first universal history is written in Persian, and when philosophical ideas, often from people originating from East Iran (Tūs, Balkh, Neishabur, Samarkand, Bukhara, Herat), were expressed in Persian. This is the time when Rumi and his ilk spread the civilisation of East Iran all the way to the west, and Khurasani culture seems dominant in all aspects of life in Central and West Asia.

The Timurids, perhaps the most glorious of all dynasties originating from East Iran, succeeded the Mongols. These were Turkic natives of Transoxiana who, despite initial successes in West Asia, eventually based themselves firmly in Khurasan. The capital of Tamerlane was in *Shahr-i Sabz*, south of Samarkand. His successors established themselves in Samarkand, Bukhara, Balkh, Herat, Marw, and Kabul. The artistic revival of the Timurid period determined much of the medieval and early modern artistic heritage of the three successor states that followed them: the Ottomans of Anatolia, the Safavids of Iran, and the Mughals of India. The last were even descendants of Timur, originating from Tokharistan, and taking India over from their base in Kabul. The culture of East Iran spread most successfully through these successor states, reaching as far west as Bosnia and east as Bengal. While East Iran itself might have gone back to obscurity, only becoming important in the nineteenth century as part of 'the Great Game', and perhaps today as the focus of China's increasingly active foreign policy, the effects it has had on its successors were long lasting. The culture of medieval East Iran survived and survives until today, and acts as a source of nostalgia and even nationalism for modern states ranging from Turkey to India.

THE ROOTS OF MEDIEVAL EAST IRAN

The present monograph, then, is an attempt to describe the period that preceded the medieval period summarised above. Starting with the 'ancient' kingdoms of the Kushans and the Indo-Parthians, it

[6] Even the decidedly Turkic *Qarakhanids* of the tenth and eleventh centuries expressed themselves, at least to their Khurasani audience/subjects, in terms of Iranian epic heroes, calling themselves Afrasiabids to show their connection with the great Touranian leader (Hua 2008: 341)

looked at the establishment of patterns such as the roots of conquest through the Hindu Kush to Gandhara and Kashmir, and the emergence of cultural markers such as Buddhism. The history of the Sasanians and their indirect involvement in East Iran also included their influence on the region and their adoption of East Iranian concepts such as the *Kayanid* kingship (see Chapter 3). The period of the Chionites was essential in the formation of the regions of Tokharistan, Kabulestan, and Zabulestan as their own separate entities, which continued to develop into the medieval period. In Sogdiana, the Kidarite and the Hephthalite period set the stage for the impressive rise of the area as the leading region of Eurasia in the medieval period.

The Western Turk period, the culmination of all these influences and a period when this region gained complete political independence, alongside the unity of regions from Sogdiana to Gandhara, then proved to be the most significant period described. Developments from the Kushan period to the Turkic period fit well into an understanding of late antiquity as a period of change from the ancient imperial setting to the medieval organisation of regional variations within larger unifying cultural markers.[7] The culmination of this change in the Islamic period is thus the natural outcome of a process that had started from the ascendance of the Kushans and progressed through their successors.

From a Sasanian point of view, East Iran was a cultural core that acted as both a fascinating source of ideas and one of great political nuisance. The Sasanians were greatly interested in adopting the culture of East Iran, and their encounter with the Kushans and the Indo-Parthians showed the awe in which they held these mighty predecessors. The establishment of Kushano-Sasanian power as a cadet branch of the Sasanians but a continuation of the Kushans is quite telling for Sasan views towards the East early in their history. The Kushano-Sasanians even went as far as adopting the title 'Kushan King of Kings' despite the *imperial* Sasanian claim to the position of 'King of Kings'. The arrival of the Chionites/Huns meant over 200 years of trouble for the Sasanians, but also proved to be the root of their familiarity with the region and ever-increasing interests in its cultural contributions. Perhaps the most significant aspect of this is the adoption of East Iranian cultural markers, including

---

[7] I can think of no better way to describe this than the title of Garth Fowden's 1993 book, *Empire to Commonwealth*, despite the fact that the contents focused on the development of religious ideas. Although highly applicable to this region, I would tend to understand this development more within a political context than a religious one.

the mythological and epic stories that formed the backbone of the medieval 'Persian epic' tradition. Even after their defeat of the Hephthalites in 560, the Sasanians maintained their fascination with the east. The stories relating the travels of Burzōy to 'India' and his acquisition of books that he translated, most importantly the *Kalila wa Dimna*, are a reflection of this late Sasanian interest. Politically too, their reorganisation of the imperial administration and creation of the *Khurasan* military province, possibly based on an Alkhan origin, further allowed the emergence of medieval Khurasan.

Both local developments and Sasanian administrative influence, then, resulted in the rise of Khurasan in the early Islamic period. The political unification of East Iran with the Sasanian domains, achieved through the conquests of the Muslims, provided the political means to achieve what seemed to emerge naturally from the developments of the sixth and seventh centuries. The resulting unit rose almost immediately to the height of its potential. Less than thirty years after this unity was achieved, Khurasanis succeeded in playing the main role in one of the most important events of Islamic history, namely the Abbasid Revolution. *East Iran*, through its transformation into *Khurasan*, reached its full potential and extent. The *centrality of Central Asia* really was the result of its late antique developments.

THE WAY FORWARD

As mentioned, this monograph has largely been concerned with the political history of the regions and the dynasties it concentrates on. Its narrative is based mainly on numismatic and archaeological data, as well as lesser-known texts. Needless to say, the narrative will have to change as more material becomes available, something that is obvious from the speculative tone of much of the work. However, I hope that I have provided a clear enough story i to allow for further studies of this region and for incorporation of new material and data, as well as a reconsideration of the material already available. Despite efforts to use as wide a sample of the current state of research as possible, obviously I could not cover all that is to be said for the history of East Iran, even in our current state of knowledge. I suppose that the first avenue of research to undertake, at least for myself, is greater study of the social and economic history of the region. This is particularly important, and opportune, because of the availability of the material provided in the recent publications widely referenced throughout this work.

Transoxiana has benefitted from Soviet archaeological research and from brilliant works ever since then. Sadly, Afghanistan, the focus of much of the present book, has been wrapped in turmoil for decades, depriving us of archaeological material of any substance, apart from the works of the Soviet archaeologists and a few others. Further study of archaeology, particularly surface surveys, would help us understand the larger socio-economic conditions of Tokharistan, Kabulistan, and Zabulistan. This will hopefully be significant enough to clarify forever the Hephthalite and Alkhan confusion and bring more information regarding the Nēzak Shah rule in the southern Hindu Kush, as well as Tokharistan in the Western Turk period and its relations with the Kabul and Zabul regions.

Chinese sources are utilised extensively for the region, but no easy and convenient collection of Chinese material, with appropriate commentaries, is available. Most scholars still rely on older translations of these texts, or fragments mentioned in the works of other scholars. These are commonly hard to access, confusing, and occasionally even contradictory. A collected edition of the Chinese texts relating to East Iran would help greatly in understanding the history of the region, and also allow us to put the Chinese sources themselves in context, revealing issues such as the use of literary *topoi*, as attempted in Chapter 4.

Apart from economic and social history, the cultural and religious history of East Iran also needs to be reconsidered and studied further on the basis of the available material. Much like the larger history of the region, the religious history of East Iran, and greater Central Asia in general, is studied within the context of its relations with its neighbouring civilisations. For example, the role of East Iran in the transmission of Buddhism to China, the concern of many Chinese pilgrims whose texts we use today in fact, is considered by Buddhist historians. In turn, the role of Central Asia, particularly the aforementioned Sogdian network, in transporting West Asian religious beliefs, most significantly Manichaeism and Nestorian Christianity, is well studied too. Less attention is paid to local religious practices, including local versions of the common Iranian belief system, as well as local cults. A necessary avenue of research is thus a concentration on the religious environment of East Iran itself, considering both local cults and important belief systems.

Many other fields of historical research could be mentioned here, and experts in them could point to the necessary research better than I can. Perhaps the most important work on this region will have to be the work of world historians still, as this area is highly under-theorised. The dearth of 'facts' has resulted in a stifling of ideas, as any novel idea could be dismissed because of its weak factual basis. But these facts, commonly the forte of the seemingly disparate fields of philology, archaeology, numismatics, and textual studies, need to be joined together to present a base on which ideas and theories can be constructed. The attempt of Andre Gunder Frank in theorising this region and fitting it within his context of world history was precisely an epitome of this problem: strong ideas and theories, without much awareness of the details and facts. What future research needs to provide, then, is a foundation on which theories not so sharply in contrast with facts are built.

11 *Epilogue and Excursus on the* Shahnameh

The present volume leaves the scene of East Iran around the moment that Muhammad Abdulhayy Shaban's book on the Abbasid Revolution starts, sometime in the first half of the eighth century AD. In that sense, it also hopes to be a complement, and a tribute, to that great scholar and his work. The region in which the present book ends, and whence Shaban's Abbasid Revolutionaries emerge, is called Khurasan. It is a region that is developing a coherent identity out of the ancient regions of Bactria, Arachosia, Gandhara, and Parthia, and is slowly integrating Sogdiana, its most effective centre. Khurasan eventually rose as a centre in its own right, dominating the eastern regions of the Islamic world up to the rise of the Safavids in 1501. Even after the physical uprooting of the Timurid court from its Khurasani base in Herat, the influence of East Iran continues to shine through the culture of Mughal India, the political inheritor of Tamerlane and his empire.

During the 800, or perhaps even 1,000, years of East Iranian dominance, the region also emerged as a centre of culture for most of the Iranian world. Most of what is attributed to the 'medieval' culture of Iran, invariably considered the 'Persianate world' or something similar, is owed to Khurasan and the political powers that controlled it. Even the development of 'Persian' as the lingua franca of this Persianate world is due more to East Iranian/Khurasani efforts than those of its 'homeland' of Persis, or the Mesopotamia of the Middle-Persian-speaking Sasanians. The Samanids, emerging from Bactria and taking power in Sogdiana, chose Persian, the 'Second Language of Islam' and the administrative language of Bukhara, as their official language. It was under their rule that al-Tabari's great history and his Quranic *Tafsīr* were translated into Persian. It was under their patronage that Persian literature was also allowed to develop. The legacy of Samanid patronage of Persian art and letters, in a distinctily East Iranian garb named *Khurasani*, was continued by all their successors, including the Turkic Ghaznavids and the Seljuks.

Perhaps the most poignant example of the particularly East Iranian nature of this 'Persianate culture' is the most obvious one as well. The grand epic of the *Shahnameh*, the 'Book of Kings' of Ferdowsi, written around the end of the first Christian millennium, is the much-talked-about 'birth certificate' of the Persianate culture of Samanid and post-Samanid Iran and Central Asia. This great epic work is often envisioned as reflecting the culture of 'Iran' as it is understood from its modern point of view, or from a Sasanian, 'West Iran', vantage point. Nevertheless, its very content and setting could be the original framework for the present volume.

The *Shahnameh* of Ferdowsi starts in an unknown territory, somewhere that is nowhere in the physical world of our understanding. However, it very quickly houses itself in the surroundings of mythical Iran, where the Iranian population makes its home under the rule of the legendary king Jamshid (the Indo-Iranian Yima/Yama). It is, however, under the rule of Fereidun (Avestan *Θraētaona*) that the 'division' of the world emerges. *Ērān* (Iran) becomes the territory of the Iranian kings, while *Tūrān* (often held to be beyond the Oxus) becomes the land of Iran's eternal enemies, the Turanis.

It is within the context of this eternal fight that the most prominent hero of the *Shahnameh*, Rostam, emerges. He is most closely associated with the regions of *Zabulistan* (Zawulistan) and *Sistan* (Sagistan), both of which play a prominent role in this volume from the very beginning (from the *Indo-Parthians* to the *Rutbils*). He is an essentially East Iranian hero, whose mother is the daughter of the king of Kabul and whose wife is the daughter of the king of Samangan in Bactria/Tokharistan. It is perhaps no surprise that even before Ferdowsi, Rostam first appears visually in East Iran, although surprisingly not in Zabulistan or even Tokharistan, but rather in Sogdiana, on a mural from Panjikent. Here, his image is similar to the images of the Alkhan kings, with their elongated skulls and prominent moustaches.[1]

To the people of Sogdiana, then, Rostam was a hero from beyond the Hindu Kush, ruling over the same region that the Alkhans, Nēzaks, and Rutbils ruled. But he was also there to save the Sogdians,

---

[1] This was of course previously discussed by Grenet 2002b: 218ff., who considers the coins to belong to the Hephthalites.

Fig. 11.1. Rostam on his horse; mural from Panjikent at the State Hermitage Museum (© Author).

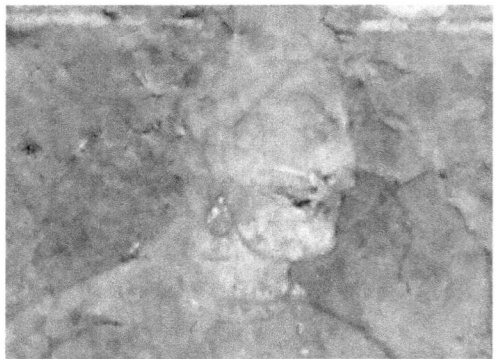

Fig. 11.2. Head of Rostam in the mural from Panjikent at the State Hermitage Museum (© Author).

Fig. 11.3. Silver drachms of Lakhana Udayaditya from Gandhara (© *das Antlitz des Fremden*).

who in fact lived beyond the Oxus, the mythical border of Iran and Turan, from the dangers that lurked further on. It is no surprise that for Ferdowsi, also living in a Sogdian-influenced region, Rostam was the hero to talk about. From the point of view of Iran today, Ferdowsi's home town of Tūs is in the extreme northeastern corner of the country. But for Ferdowsi, he lived in the centre of the world. Tūs was halfway between Bukhara, the centre of Samanid power, and Neishabur, one of their major cities. It was also close to Balkh and Marw, and not too far from Zabul and Sistan, where Rostam ruled. In this sense, centring our mental map on East Iran, we can see that Ferdowsi was not writing from a margin about marginal people and heroes, but writing from the centre of an emerging Persianate world, and about its forgotten heroes, aiming to bring them to the fore. Rostam, the quintessential Iranian hero, was then the epitome of all that East Iran had to offer, and a great part of what this Persianate world was to become.

Even in the rest of the *Shahnameh*, we can see a continuation of this trend. Beyond the mythical and heroic parts of the *Shahnameh*,[2] the Sasanians also fit within the same world. Despite their 'western' Iranian base, their stories involve a good dose of East Iranian adventures. Ardashir I is given an East Iranian background, even connecting him with India. Long episodes involving East Iran are included in the stories of kings such as Wahram V. It is no surprise that the *Shahnameh* is among the few sources that include a mention of the war between the Sasanians and the Hephthalites and the aftermath of the Battle of Gol-Zarriun.

The attention paid to East Iran in the Sasanian period is not necessarily the *Shahnameh*'s trope or bias. As has been mentioned throughout the present volume, the increasing attention of the Sasanians to their eastern territories was a consistent trend. Beyond political and military control, the Sasanian ideology was also deeply interested in appropriating an East Iranian identity, mostly through the incorporation of an Avestan geography and historiography.[3] Use of the title of *Kay*, first occurring on the coins of the Kushano-Sasanian Wahram, the adoption of an East Iranian iconography, and other outward uses of East Iranian cultural productions were further

---

[2] These are the names given by modern scholars to the parts of the *Shahnameh* dealing with the stories of the *Pishdadid* and *Kayanid* – essentially all pre-Alexandrian and pre-Sasanid – parts of the epic. It is worth remembering that for Ferdowsi, and for most of his audience until the late nineteenth century, the Pishdadis and the Kayanids, including Rostam, were as historical as Alexander and the Sasanians!

[3] For a take on this, see Cereti 2004; 2007.

evidence of this. This is even obvious in historiography, where the adoption of an Avestan history, firmly established in East Iran and Central Asia, is demonstrated through the adoption of a Kayanid ideology.[4] Even the proliferation of Avestan/Kayanid onomastics such as Kavad, Khosrow, and Kawus can be taken as a sign of this East Iranian interest of the Sasanians.

However, it can be argued that the rise of the Hephthalites deprived the Sasanians of such close connections with the east. Perhaps this was even the reason for their adoption of Kayanid historiography: to prove their 'ownership' of the east, at least in cultural terms, against its actual control by the Hephthalites. The increasing attention of the Sasanians to their western borders, demonstrated through their constant conflicts with the Eastern Roman Empire in the sixth and seventh centuries, can also be put in the context of their loss of the east.

In this sense, the narrative of the *Shahnameh*, a uniform story of the 'history of Iran' put into an Eastern Iranian framework, is the perfect metaphor for the emergence of the Persianate culture of the medieval period. The losses of the Sasanians in the east are made up for by the rise of Persianate culture, the heir of the Ērān so lamented in the *Shahnameh*, and given a convenient narrative there. Finally, Ērān conquered and dominated Turan, and made it into a centre that was to shine for many centuries.

---

[4] See Shayegan 2003 for a discussion of this period and the adoption of the ideology as a conscious Sasanian imperial strategy.

Bibliography

PRIMARY SOURCES

Primary sources that are included as part of scholarly publications and compilations as well as those known through their translators are included in the *secondary works* section.

al-Athīr, Izz ud-Din b. 1863. *Al-Kāmil Fī'l-Ta'rīkh*. Ed. C. J. Tornberg. Leiden: Brill.
Al-Baladhuri, Abu Hasan Ahmad Yahya. 1866. *Futuh Al-Buldan*. Ed. Michael J. de Goeje. Leiden: Brill.
Al-Narshakhi, Abu Bakr Mummad b. Jafar. 1387. *Tarikh-e Bokhara (History of Bokhara)*. Ed. Mohammad-Taqi Modarres Razavi. Tehran: Tous.
Ammianus Marcellinus. 1956. *Ammianus Marcellinus*. Trans. John C. Rolfe. Loeb Classical Library. Cambridge, MA: Harvard University Press.
Anonymous. 1375. *Nihayat-Ul-Irab Fi-L-Akhbar Al-Furs Wa-L-'Arab*. Ed. Muhammad-Taqi Daneshpajuh. Tehran: Anjoman-e Athat o Mafakher.
Arrian. 1976. *History of Alexander and Indica*. Trans. Peter A. Brunt. Loeb Classical Library. Cambridge, MA: Harvard University Press.
Bahar, Mohammad-Taqi, ed. 1387. *Tarikh-e Sistan (The History of Sistan, Written between 445–725 AH)*. 2nd edn. Tehran: Moein.
Bal'ami, Abu Ali, 1386. *Tarikh-e Bal'ami (History of Bal'ami)*. Ed. Mohammad-Taqi Bahar and Mohammad Parvin Gonabadi. Tehran: Hermes.
Biruni, Abu Raihan. 1910. *Al-Beruni's India*. Trans. Edward E. Sachau. London: Kegan Paul, Trench, Trubner.
Cosmas Indicopleustes. 2010. *The Christian Topography of Cosmas, an Egyptian Monk*. Trans. J. W. McCrindle. Cambridge: Cambridge University Press.
Dīnawarī, Abū Ḥanīfa Aḥmad. 1888. *Kitāb Al-Akhbār Al-Tiwāl*. Ed. Vladimir Guirgass. Leiden: Brill.
Diodorus Siculus. 1814. *The Historical Library of Diodorus the Sicilian: In Fifteen Books. To Which Are Added the Fragments of Diodorus, and*

Those Published by H. Valesius, I. Rhodomannus, and F. Ursinus. Trans. George Booth. London: W. Taylor.
Ełišē. 1982. *History of Vardan and the Armenian War.* Trans. Robert W. Thompson. Cambridge, MA: Harvard University Press.
Ferdowsi, Abolghassem. 2008. *Shahnameh.* Ed. Djalal Khaleghi-Motlagh. Winona Lake: Eisenbrauns.
Ibn A'tham al-Kufi, Ahmad. 1392. *Al-Futuh (12th Century Persian Translation of Ibn A'tham Al-Kufi).* Ed. Gholamreza Tabatabaei Majd. Trans. Muhammad b. Ahmad Mostowfi Harawi. Tehran: Elmi Farhangi.
Ibn A'tham al-Kufi, Ahmad. 1986. *Kitab Al-Futuh.* Beirut: Dar ul-Kutub al-Ilmiya.
Ibn Balkhi. 1385. *Farsnama.* Ed. Guy Le Strange and Reynold Nicholson. Tehran: Asatir.
Ibn Haukal, Abul-qasim. 1938. *Saurat Al-Ard (Opus Geographicum).* Ed. J. H. Kramers. Bibliotheca Geographorum Arabicourm. Leiden: Brill.
Ibn Khallikan, Ahmad. 1843. *Ibn Khallikan's Biographical Dictionary.* Trans. M. de Slane. London: Oriental Translation Fund of Great Britain and Ireland.
Ibn Khallikan, Ahmad. 2007. *Wafiyat Ul-'Ayah Wa-L-Anba Ul-Abna' Al-Zaman.* Ed. Ihsan 'Abbad. Beirut: Dar Sader.
Joshua the Stylite. 2000. *The Chronicle of Pseudo-Joshua the Stylite.* Trans. Frank Trombley and John W. Watt. Liverpool: Liverpool University Press.
Khorenats'i, Movses. 1978. *History of Armenians.* Trans. Robert Thompson. Cambridge: Cambridge University Press.
Khurradādhbih, Abul-qasim Ubaidullah ibn. 1967. *Kitāb Al-Masālik Wa'l-Mamālik.* Ed. M. J. De Goeje. Vol. vi. Bibliotheca Geographorum Arabicorum. Leiden: Brill.
Menander Protector. 1985. *The History of Menander the Guardsman.* Trans. Roger C. Blockley. Vol. 41. Liverpool: Francis Cairns.
al-Muqaddasi, Muhammad b. Ahmad. 1967. *Kitab Ahsan Al-Taqasim Fi Ma'rifat Al-Aqalim.* Ed. M. J. De Goeje. Leiden: .Brill.
Pawstos Buzand. 1989. *The Epic Histories Attributed to Pawstos Buzand (Buzandaran Patmut'iunwnk').* Trans. and commentary N. G. Garsoian. Cambridge, MA: Harvard University Press.
Qudama ibn Ja'far. 1965. *Kitab Al-Kharaj Wa-L-Sina'at Al Kitaba.* Ed. A. Ben Shemesh. Leiden: Brill.
Strabo. 1928. *Geography, Volume V: Books 10–12.* Trans. H. L. Jones. Loeb Classical Library 211. Cambridge, MA: Harvard University Press.
al-Tabari, Muhammad b. Jarir. 1987. *The Reunification of the 'Abbāsid Caliphate: [the Caliphate of Al-Ma'mūn]: [A.D. 812–833 – A.H. 198–213].* Trans. C. E. Bosworth. Albany: SUNY Press.
al-Tabari, Muhammad b. Jarir. 1999. *The Sāsānids, the Byzantines, the Lakhmids, and Yemen.* Trans. C. E. Bosworth. Albany: SUNY Press.
al-Tabari, Muhammad b. Jarir. 2010. *Ta'rikh Al-Rusul W'al Muluk.* Ed. Michael J. de Goeje. Leiden: Brill.

Theophylact Simocatta. 1986. *The History of Theophylact Simocatta: An English Translation with Introduction and Notes*. Trans. Michael Whitby and Mary Whitby. Oxford: Oxford University Press.

al-Yaqubi, Ahmad b. Abi-Yaqub. 2010. *Tarikh Al-Yaqubi*. Ed. Abdul-Amir Mihna. Beirut: Shirkat al-Alami li-l-Matbu'at.

SECONDARY WORKS

Adams, Douglas Q. 1984. 'The Position of Tocharian among the Other Indo-European Languages.' *Journal of the American Oriental Society* 104: 395–402.

Alram, Michael. 1986. *Nomina Propria Iranica in Nummis*. Vienna: Verlag der Österreichischen Akademie der Wissenschaften.

Alram, Michael. 1987. 'Eine Neue Drachme des Vahbarz (Oborzos) aus der Persis.' *Litterae Numismaticae Vindobonenses* 3: 147–55.

Alram, Michael. 1996. 'Alchon und Nezak zur Geschichte der Iranischen Hunnen in Mittelasien.' In *La Persia e l'Asia Centrale: Da Alessandro al X Secolo*, 517–54. Rome: Accademia Nazionale dei Lincei.

Alram, Michael. 1999. 'Indo-Parthian and Early Kushan Chronology: The Numismatic Evidence.' In *Coins, Art and Chronology: Essays on Pre-Islamic History of the Indo-Iranian Borderlands*, ed. Michael Alram and Deborah Klimburg-Salter, 19–51. Vienna: Verlag der Österreichischen Akademie der Wissenschaften.

Alram, Michael. 2003. 'Three Hunnic Bullae from Northwest India.' *Bulletin of the Asia Institute* 17: 177–84.

Alram, Michael. 2004. 'The History of the Silk Road as Reflected in Coins.' *Parthica* 6: 47–68.

Alram, Michael. 2007. 'Ardashir's Eastern Campaign and the Numismatic Evidence.' In *After Alexander: Central Asia Before Islam*, ed. Joe Cribb and Georgina Herrmann, 227–42. Proceedings of the British Academy 133. Oxford: Oxford University Press.

Alram, Michael. 2008a. 'Early Sasanian Coinage.' In *The Sasanian Era*, ed. Vesta Sarkhosh Curtis and Sarah Steward, 17–30. London: I.B. Tauris.

Alram, Michael. 2008b. 'Ein Schatzfund Hephthalitischer Drachmen aus Baktrien.' *Numismatische Zeitschrift* 116/117: 253–68.

Alram, Michael. 2009. 'Huns and Western Turks in Central Asia and Northwest India.' In *A Survey of Numismatic Research 2002–2007*, 516–19. International Association of Professional Numismatists, Special Publication 15. Glasgow.

Alram, Michael, and Rika Gyselen. 2003. *Sylloge Nummorum Sasanidarum*, 1. Vienna: Verlag der Österreichischen Akademie der Wissenschaften.

Alram, Michael, and Rika Gyselen. 2012. *Sylloge Nummorum Sasanidarum: Paris–Berlin–Wien. Band II: Ohrmazd I.–Ohrmazd II*. Vienna: Verlag der Österreichischen Akademie der Wissenschaften.

Alram, Michael, and Deborah E. Klimburg-Salter. 1999. *Coins, Art, and Chronology: Essays on the Pre-Islamic History of the Indo-Iranian Borderlands*. Vienna: Verlag der Österreichischen Akademie der Wissenschaften.

Alram, Michael, and Ciro LoMuzio. 2006. 'A New Coin Type of the Khalaj?' *Journal of Inner Asian Art and Archaeology* 1 (1): 133–9.

Alram, Michael, and Matthias Pfisterer. 2010. 'Alkhan and Hephthalite Coinage.' In *Coins, Art and Chronology II: The First Millennium C.E. in the Indo-Iranian Borderlands*, ed. Michael Alram, Deborah Klimburg-Salter, Minoru Inaba, and Matthias Pfisterer, 13–38. Vienna: Verlag der Österreichischen Akademie der Wissenschaften.

Alram, Michael, Deborah Klimburg-Salter, Minoru Inaba, and Matthias Pfisterer, eds. 2010. *Coins, Art and Chronology II: The First Millennium C.E. in the Indo-Iranian Borderlands*. Vienna: Verlag der Österreichischen Akademie der Wissenschaften.

Altheim, Franz. 1969. *Geschichte der Hunnen. Band 2: Die Hephthaliten in Iran*. Berlin: De Gruyter.

Altheim, Franz, and Ruth Stiehl. 1957. *Finanzgeschichte der Spätantike*. Frankfurt: Klostermann.

Andreas, Friedrich Carl, and Walter Bruno Henning. 1934. *Mitteliranische Manichaica aus Chinesisch-Turkestan*. Sitzungsberichte der Königlich Preussischen Akademie der Wissenschaften zu Berlin: Philosophisch-Historische Klasse 10. Berlin: De Gruyter.

Atwood, Christopher P. 2012. 'Huns and Xiongnu: New Thoughts on an Old Problem.' In *Dubitando: Studies in History and Culture in Honor of Donald Ostrowski*, ed. Brian J. Boeck, Russel E. Martin, and Daniel Rowland, 27–52. Bloomington: Slavica.

Azarnouche, Samra. 2013. *Husraw ī Kawadan ud Redag-e: Khosrow Fils de Kawad et un Page*. Paris: Association pour l'Avancement des Études Iraniennes.

Azarpay, Guitty. 1981. *Sogdian Painting: The Pictorial Epic in Oriental Art*. Berkeley: University of California Press.

Bailey, Harold W. 1932. 'Iranian Studies.' *Bulletin of the School of Oriental Studies* VI: 945–55.Bailey, Harold W. 1980. 'A Kharoṣṭhi Inscription of Senavarma, King of Oḍi.' *Journal of the Royal Asiatic Society* 112 (1): 21–9.

Bailey, Harold W. 1985. *Indo-Scythian Studies: Khotanese Texts, VII*. Cambridge; Cambridge University Press.

Ball, Warwick. 2008. *The Monuments of Afghanistan: History, Archaeology and Architecture*. London; New York: I.B. Tauris.

Bartol'd, Vasilii V. 1928. *Turkestan Down to the Mongol Invasion*. Trans. Vladimir Minorsky and Clifford Edmund Bosworth. London: Luzac.

Bausani, Alessandro. 1968. 'Religion under the Mongols.' In *The Cambridge History of Iran*, V: 538–49. Cambridge: Cambridge University Press.

Beal, Samuel. 1884. *Buddhist Records of the Western World: Translated from the Chinese of Hiuen Tsiang*. London: Trubner.

Beckwith, Christopher I. 2009. *Empires of the Silk Road: A History of Central Eurasia from the Bronze Age to the Present*. Princeton: Princeton University Press.

Beckwith, Christopher I. 2012. *Warriors of the Cloisters: The Central Asian Origins of Science in the Medieval World*. Princeton: Princeton University Press.

Belenitskii, Aleksandr M., and Boris I. Marshak. 1979. 'Вопросы хронологии живописи раннесредневекового Согда (Questions of the Chronology of Early Medieval Sogdian Paintings).' *Uspekhi Sredneaziatskoi Arkheologii* 4: 32–7.

Belenitskii, Aleksandr M., and Boris I. Marshak. 1981. 'The Paintings of Sogdiana.' In *Sogdian Painting: The Pictorial Epic in Oriental Art*, ed. Guitty Azarpay, 11–77. Berkeley; Los Angeles: University of California Press.

Benjamin, Craig. 2003. 'The Yuezhi Migration and Sogdia.' In *Ērān ud Anērān: Webfestschrift Marshak 2003* (electronic version), ed. Matteo Compareti, Paola Raffetta, and Gianroberto Scarcia. Venice: Cafoscarina.

Benjamin, Craig. 2007. *The Yuezhi: Origin, Migration and the Conquest of Northern Bactria*. Silk Roads Studies Series, XIV. Turnhout: Brepols.

Bernard, Paul. 1972. 'Campagne de Fouilles à Aï Khanoum.' *Comptes Rendus des Séances de l'Académie des Inscriptions et Belles-Lettres* 116 (4): 605–32.

Bernard, Paul. 2008. 'The Greek Colony at Ai Khanoum and Hellenism in Central Asia.' In *Afghanistan: Hidden Treasures from the National Museum, Kabul*, ed. Fredrik Hiebert and P. Cambon, 80–129. Washington, DC: National Geographic Society.

Bernard, Paul, and Henri-Paul Francfort. 1978. *Etude de Géographie Historique sur la Plaine d'Aï Kanoum(Afghanistan)*. Paris: CNRS.

Bernard, Paul, and Olivier Guillaume. 1980. 'Monnaies Inédites de la Bactriane Grecque à Aï Khanoum (Afghanistan).' *Revue Numismatique* 6 (22): 9–32.

Biriukov, B. A. 1998. 'Afrigidskii Khorezm I Sasanidskii Iran [Afrighid Khwarazm and Sasanian Iran].' In *Numizmatika Tsentral'noi Azii III*, ed. E. V. Rtveladze, 18–38. Tashkent: Akademiia Khudozhestv Respubliki Uzbekistan.

Biswas, A. K. 1973. *The Political History of the Hunas in India*. New Delhi: Munshiram Manoharlal.

Bivar, A. D. H. 1954. 'The Inscriptions of Uruzgan.' *Journal of the Royal Asiatic Society of Great Britain and Ireland* n.s. 86 (3–4): 112–18.

Bivar, A. D. H. 1963. 'The Kaniṣka Dating from Surkh Kotal.' *Bulletin of the School of Oriental and African Studies* 26 (3): 498–502.

Bivar, A. D. H. 1979. 'The Absolute Chronology of the Kushano-Sasanian Governors in Central Asia.' In *Prolegomena to the Sources on the History* of *Pre-Islamic Central Asia*, ed. János Harmatta. Budapest: Akadémiai Kiadó.

Bivar, A. D. H. 1983a. 'The Political History of Iran under the Arsacids.' In *The Cambridge History of Iran*, ed. E. Yarshater, III (1): 21–99. Cambridge: Cambridge University Press.

Bivar, A. D. H. 1983b. 'The History of Eastern Iran.' In *The Cambridge History of Iran*, ed. E. Yarshater, III (1): 181–231. Cambridge: Cambridge University Press.

Bivar, A. D. H. 2004. 'Hephthalites.' *Encyclopedia Iranica (Online)*.

Bivar, A. D. H. 2009. 'Kushan Dynasty, I: Dynastic History.' *Encyclopaedia Iranica (Online)*.

Blockley, Robert C. 1983. *The Fragmentary Classicising Historians of the Later Roman Empire*. Oxford: Francis Cairns.

Bo, Bi, and Nicholas Sims-Williams. 2010. 'Sogdian Documents from Khotan, I: Four Economic Documents.' *Journal of the American Oriental Society*, 130 (4): 497–508.

Bopearachchi, Osmund. 2001. 'Les Données Numismatiques et la Datation du Bazar de Begram.' *Topoi* 11 (1): 411–35.

Bopearachchi, Osmund. 2004. 'Indo-Greek Dynasty.' *Encyclopaedia Iranica (Online)*.

Bopearachchi, Osmund. 2007. 'Some Observations on the Chronology of the Early Kushans.' *Res Orientales* 17: 41–53.

Bopearachchi, Osmund. 2008. 'Les Premiers Souverains Kouchans: Chronologie et Iconographie Monétaire.' *Journal des Savants* 1 (1): 3–56.

Bopearachchi, Osmund. 2009. 'Kujula Kadphises.' *Encyclopaedia Iranica (Online)*.

Bosworth, C. E. 1968. *Sistan under the Arabs, from the Islamic Conquest to the Rise of the Saffarids (30–250/651–864)*. Rome: IsMEO.

Bosworth, C. E. 1969a. 'The Tahirids and Arabic Culture.' *Journal of Semitic Studies* 14 (1): 45–79.

Bosworth, C. E. 1969b. 'The Ṭāhirids and Persian Literature.' *Iran* 7: 103–6.

Bosworth, C. E. 1973. '"Ubaidallāh B. Abi Bakra and the "Army of Destruction" in Zābulistān (79/698).' *Der Islam* 50 (2): 268–83.

Bosworth, C. E. 1978. 'The Heritage of Rulership in Early Islamic Iran and the Search for Dynastic Connections with the Past.' *Iranian Studies* 11 (1–4): 7–34.

Bosworth, C. E. 1990. 'Bukhara from the Arab Invasion to the Mongols.' *Encyclopaedia Iranica (Online)*.

Bosworth, C. E. 1994. *The History of the Saffarids of Sistan and the Maliks of Nimruz (247/861 to 949/1542–3)*. Costa Mesa, CA: Mazda.

Bosworth, C. E., and Gerard Clauson. 1965. 'Al-Xwārazmī on the Peoples of Central Asia.' *Journal of the Royal Asiatic Society of Great Britain and Ireland* n.s. 97 (1): 2–12.

Bowersock, Glen W., Peter R. L. Brown, and Oleg Grabar, eds. 1999. *Late Antiquity: A Guide to the Postclassical World*. Cambridge, MA: Harvard University Press.

Bracey, Robert. 2009. 'The Coinage of Wima Kadphises.' *Gandharan Studies* 3: 25–75.

Bracey, Robert. 2011a. 'Kankali Tila and Kushan Chronology.' In *Felicitas: Essays in Numismatics, Epigraphy & History in Honour of Joe Cribb*, ed. Shailendra Bhandare and Sanjay Garg, 65–80. Mumbai: Reesha Books International.

Bracey, Robert. 2011b. 'New Histories of Central and South Asia.' In *The British Museum and the Future of UK Numismatics*, ed. Barrie Cook, 44–52. London: British Museum.

Bracey, Robert. 2012. 'The Mint Cities of the Kushan Empire.' In *The City and the Coin in the Ancient and Early Medieval World*, 117–31. BAR International Series 2402. Oxford: Archaeopress.

Brentjes, B. 1971. 'The Hoard of Hephthalite Silver Vessels Found near Samarkand.' *East and West* n.s. 21 77–8.

Brown, Peter. 1971. *The World of Late Antiquity: AD 150–750*. New York: Norton.

Brown, Peter, et al. 1997. 'The World of Late Antiquity Revisited.' *Symbolae Osloensis* 72: 5–90.

Bulliet, Richard W. 1976. 'Naw Bahār and the Survival of Iranian Buddhism.' *Iran* 14: 140–5.

Burjakov, Juri F. 1991. 'À Propos de l'Histoire de la Culture de la Région de Tachkent au Ier Millénaire avant Notre Ére et au Ier Millénaire de Notre Ére.' In *Histoire et Cultes de l'Asie Centrale Préislamique: Sources Écrites et Documents Archéologiques*, 197–204. Paris: CNRS.

Callieri, Pierfrancesco. 1994. 'Hephthalites in Margiana? New Evidence from the Buddhist Relics in Merv.' In *La Persia e l'Asia Centrale: Da Alessandro al X Secolo*, 391–400. Rome: Accademia Nazionale dei Lincei.

Callieri, Pierfrancesco. 2002. 'The Bactrian Seal of Khingila.' *Silk Road Art and Archaeology* 8: 121–41.

Canepa, Matthew P. 2009. *The Two Eyes of the Earth: Art and Ritual of Kingship between Rome and Sasanian Iran*. Berkeley; Los Angeles: University of California Press.

Carter, Martha L. 1981. 'Mithra on the Lotus: A Study of the Imagery of the Sun God in the Kushano-Sasanian Era.' *Acta Iranica* XXI: 74–98.

Carter, Martha L. 1985. 'A Numismatic Reconstruction of Kushano-Sasanian History.' *Museum Notes* 30: 213–81.

Cereti, Carlo G. 1995. *The Zand ī Wahman Yasn: A Zoroastrian Apocalypse*. Rome: Istituto Italiano per il Medio ed Estremo Oriente.

Cereti, Carlo G. 2004. 'Middle Persian Geographical Literature: The Case of *Bundahišn*.' In *Contributions à l'Histoire et la Géographie Historique de l'Empire Sassanide*, ed. Rika Gyselen, 11–36. Bures-sur-Yvette: Groupe pour l'Étude de la Civilisation du Moyen-Orient.

Cereti, Carlo G. 2007. 'Middle Persian Geographic Literature II: Chapters X and XII of the *Bundahishn*.' In *Des Indo-Grecs aux Sassanides: Données pour l'Histoire et la Géographie Historique*, ed. Rika Gyselen, 55–64. Res Orientales, XVII. Bures-sur-Yvette: Groupe pour l'Étude de la Civilisation du Moyen-Orient.

Cereti, Carlo G. 2010. 'Xiiaona- and Xyôn in Zoroastrian Texts.' In *Coins, Art, and Chronology II: The First Millennium C.E. in the Indo-Iranian Borderlands*, ed. Michael Alram and Deborah E. Klimburg-Salter, 59–72. Vienna: Verlag der Österreichischen Akademie der Wissenschaften.

Chakrabarty, Dipesh. 2009. *Provincializing Europe: Postcolonial Thought and Historical Difference*. Princeton: Princeton University Press.

Charpentier, Jarl. 1917. 'Die Ethnographische Stellung der Tocharer.' *Zeitschrift der Deutschen Morgenländischen Gesellschaft* 71: 347–88.

Chavannes, Edouard. 1903a. *Documents sur le Toukiue (Turcs) Occidentaux*. St. Petersburg: Commissionnaires de l'Académie Impériale des Sciences.

Chavannes, Edouard. 1903b. 'Voyage de Song Yun dans l'Udyāna et le Gandhāra.' *Bulletin de l'École Française d'Extrême-Orient* 3 (3): 379–441.

Chavannes, Edouard. 1904. 'Notes Additionnelles sur les Tou-Kiue (Turcs) Occidentaux.' *T'oung Pao* 5 (1): 1–110.

Chavannes, Edouard. 1906. 'Trois Généraux Chinois de la Dynastie des Han Orientaux.' *T'oung Pao* 7 (2): 210–69.

Choksy, Jamsheed. 2012. 'Xiiaona – or Hun Reconsidered.' *Acta Orientalia Academiae Scientiarum Hungaricae* 65 (1): 93–8.

Christensen, Arthur. 1907. *Romanen om Bahrâm Tschôbîn: Et Rekonstruktions-Forsøg*. Copenhagen: Tillge.

Christensen, Arthur. 1925. *Le Règne du Roi Kawādh I et le Communisme Mazdakite*. Copenhagen: Høst.

Christensen, Arthur. 1944. *L'Iran sous les Sassanides*. Copenhagen: Otto Zeller.

Christensen, Peter. 1993. *The Decline of Iranshahr: Irrigation and Environments in the History of the Middle East, 500 BC to AD 1500*. Copenhagen: Museum Tusculanum Press.

Coloru, Omar. 2009. *Da Alessandro a Menandro: Il Regno Greco di Battriana*. Studi Ellenistici 21. Pisa; Rome: Fabrizio Serra Editore.

Compareti, Matteo. 2003. 'The Last Sasanians in China.' *Eurasian Studies* 2 (2): 197–213.

Compareti, Matteo. 2006. 'The So-Called Senmurv in Iranian Art: A Reconsideration of an Old Theory.' In *Loquentes Linguis: Studi Linguistici e Orientali in Onore di Fabrizio A. Pennacchietti*, ed. P. G. Borbone, A. Mengozzi, and M. Tosco, 185–200. Wiesbaden: Otto Harrassowitz Verlag.

Compareti, Matteo. 2008. 'Traces of Buddhist Art in Sogdiana.' *Sino-Platonic Papers* 181: 1–42.

Compareti, Matteo. 2010. 'Archeology and History of Art in Pre-Islamic Iran and Central Asia.' In *Handbook of Medieval Studies*, ed. Albrecht Classen, 1: 25–38. Berlin: De Gruyter.

Cornish, Setsuko. 1995. 'A Study of Takht-I Bahi.' *Studies in Culture* 5: 109–34.

Cribb, Joe. 1981. 'Gandharan Hoards of Kushano-Sasanian and Late Kushan Coppers.' *Coin Hoards* VI: 93–108.

Cribb, Joe. 1990. 'Numismatic Evidence for Kushano-Sasanian Chronology.' *Studia Iranica* 19 (2): 151–93.

Cribb, Joe. 1993. 'The "Heraus" Coins: Their Attribution to the Kushan King Kujula Kadphises, c. AD 30–80.' In *Essays in Honour of Robert Carson and Kenneth Jenkins*, ed. Martin Price, Andrew Burnett, and Roger Bland, 107–34. London: Spink.

Cribb, Joe. 1999. 'The Early Kushan Kings: New Evidence for Chronology. Evidence from the Rabatak Inscription of Kanishka I.' In *Coins, Art, and Chronology: Essays on the Pre-Islamic History of the Indo-Iranian Borderlands*, ed. Michael Alram and Deborah E. Klimburg-Salter, 177–205. Vienna: Verlag der Österreichischen Akademie der Wissenschaften.

Cribb, Joe. 2010. 'The Kidarites, the Numismatic Evidence: With an Analytical Appendix by A. Oddy.' In *Coins, Art and Chronology II: The First Millennium C.E. in the Indo-Iranian Borderlands*, ed. Michael Alram, Deborah E. Klimburg-Salter, Minoru Inaba, and Matthias Pfisterer, 91–146. Vienna: Verlag der Österreichischen Akademie der Wissenschaften.

Crone, Patricia. 1991. 'Kavād's Heresy and Mazdak's Revolt.' *Iran* 29: 21–42.

Crone, Patricia. 2012. *The Nativist Prophets of Early Islamic Iran: Rural Revolt and Local Zoroastrianism*. Cambridge: Cambridge University Press.

Curiel, Raoul. 1954. 'Inscriptions de Surkh Kotal.' *Journal Asiatique* 242: 189–205.

Czegledy, Karoly. 1984. 'Zur Geschichte der Hephthaliten.' In *From Hecataeus to Al-Ḫuwārizmī: Bactrian, Pahlavi, Sogdian, Persian, Sanskrit, Syriac, Arabic, Chinese, Greek, and Latin Sources for the History of Pre-Islamic Central Asia*, ed. János Harmatta, 213–17. Budapest: Akadémiai Kiadó.

Daffinà, Paolo. 1967. *L'Immigrazione dei Sakā nella Drangiana*. Rome: Istituto Italiano per il Medio ed Estremo Oriente.

Dani, Ahmad Hasan. 1964. *Shaikhan Dheri Excavation, 1963 & 1964 Seasons: In Search of the Second City of Pushkalavati*. Peshawar: Department of Archaeology, University of Peshawar.

Dani, Ahmad Hasan. 1996. 'Eastern Kushans and Kidarites in Gandhara and Kashmir.' In *History of Civilizations of Central Asia*, 3: 166–80. Paris: UNESCO.

Dani, Ahmad Hasan, and F. Khan. 1974. 'Kushan Civilisation in Pakistan.' In *Tsentral Asia v Kušanskuyu Epoxu (Central Asia in the Kushan Period)*, 1.95–106. Moscow: UNESCO; Nauka.

Dani, Ahmad Hasan, and B. A. Litvinsky. 1996. 'The Kushano-Sasanian Kingdom.' In *History of Civilizations of Central Asia*, 3, ed. B. A. Litvinsky, 103–18. Paris: UNESCO.

Dani, Ahmad Hasan, Boris Anatolevitch Litvinsky, and M. H. Zimmer Zafi. 1996. 'Eastern Kushans, Kidarites in Gandhara and Kashmir, and Later Hephthalites.' In *History of Civilizations of Central Asia*, 3, ed. B. A. Litvinsky, 163–83. Paris: UNESCO.

Daryaee, Touraj. 1995. 'National History or Kayanid History: The Nature of Sasanid Zoroastrian Historiography.' *Iranian Studies* 28 (3–4): 129–41.

Daryaee, Touraj. 2003. 'The Persian Gulf in Late Antiquity.' *Journal of World History* 14 (1): 1–16.

Daryaee, Touraj. 2006. 'The Importance of Seleucid Kingship on Iranian Imperial Ideology.' *Bulletin of Ancient Iranian History* I (March).

Daryaee, Touraj. 2009. *Sasanian Persia: The Rise and Fall of an Empire*. London: I.B. Tauris.

Daryaee, Touraj. 2010. 'Ardaxšīr and the Sasanians' Rise to Power.' *Anabasis* 1: 236–55.

Daryaee, Touraj, ed. 2011. *The Oxford Handbook of Iranian History*. Oxford: Oxford University Press.

Davary, Gholam Djelani. 1982. *Baktrisch: Ein Wörterbuch auf Grund der Inschriften, Handschriften, Münzen und Siegelsteine*. Heidelberg: Groos.

De Blois, François C. 1990. *Burzoy's Voyage to India and the Origin of the Book of Kalilah Wa Dimnah*. London: Royal Asiatic Society.

De Blois, François C. 2006. 'Du Nouveau sur la Chronologie Bactrienne Post-Hellénistique: L'Ère de 223–224 Ap. J.-C.' *Comptes Rendus des Séances de l'Académie des Inscriptions et Belles-Lettres* 150 (2): 991–7.

De Blois, François C. 2013. 'Bactria, Bāxδī-, Balx.' In *Commentationes Iranicae: Vladimiro F. Aaron Livschits Nonagenario Donum Natalicium*, ed. Sergei P. Tokhtasev and Pavel Lurye, 268–71. St. Petersburg: Nestor-Historia.

De Blois, François C., and N. Sims-Williams. 2006. 'The Bactrian Calendar: New Material and New Suggestions.' In *Languages of Iran: Past and Present. Iranian Studies in Memoriam David Neil MacKenzie*, ed. Dieter Weber, 185–96. Iranica 8. Wiesbaden: Otto Harrassowitz Verlag.

Dehkan, A. 1974. 'The Relationship of the Kushan and the Parthian Empire.' In *Tsentral Asia v Kušanskuyu Epoxu (Central Asia in the Kushan Period)*, 113–17. Moscow: UNESCO; Nauka.

Dehkhoda, Ali-Akbar. 1930. *Farhang-e Farsi (Persian Dictionary)*. Tehran: University of Tehran Press.

de la Vaissière, Étienne. 1998. 'L'Inscription de Rabatak et l'Origine de l'Ère Śaka.' *Journal Asiatique* 286 (2): 571–651.
de la Vaissière, Étienne. 2003. 'Is There a "Nationality of the Hephtalites"?' *Bulletin of the Asia Institute* 17: 119–32.
de la Vaissière, Étienne. 2005a. 'Huns et Xiongnu.' *Central Asiatic Journal* 49 (1): 3–26.
de la Vaissière, Étienne. 2005b. *Sogdian Traders: A History*. Leiden; Boston: Brill.
de la Vaissière, Étienne. 2007. *Samarcande et Samarra: Élites d'Asie Centrale dans l'Empire Abbasside*. Paris; Leuven: Peeters.
de la Vaissiere, Étienne. 2010. 'De Bactres à Balkh, par le Nowbahār.' *Journal Asiatique* 298 (2): 517–33.
de la Vaissière, Étienne. 2012. 'A Note on the Schøyen Copper Scroll: Bactrian or Indian?' *Bulletin of the Asia Institute* 21: 127–30.
de la Vaissière, Étienne, and Aleksander Naymark. 2010. 'Villes et Palais du Zerafchan Face à la Conquête Arabe.' *Les Dossiers d'Archéologie*, 341: 58–61.
Di Cosmo, Nicola. 1991. 'Inner Asia in Chinese History: An Analysis of the Hsiung-Nu in the Shih Chi.' PhD dissertation, Indiana University.
Di Cosmo, Nicola. 2002. *Ancient China and Its Enemies: The Rise of Nomadic Power in East Asian History*. Cambridge: Cambridge University Press.
Dignas, Beate, and Engelbert Winter. 2007. *Rome and Persia in Late Antiquity: Neighbours and Rivals*. Cambridge: Cambridge University Press.
Dodgeon, Michael H., and Samuel N. C. Lieu. 1991. *The Roman Eastern Frontier and the Persian Wars (AD 226–363): A Documentary History*. New York: Routledge.
Dong, Ma, and Wu Hongling. 2005. 'Kuai Hu and Yeda (Hephthalite).' *Western Regions Studies* 4.
Donner, Fred M. 1981. *The Early Islamic Conquests*. Princeton: Princeton University Press.
Durkin-Meisterernst, Desmond. 2000. 'Erfand Mani die Manichäische Schrift?' In *Tudia Manichaica IV: Internationaler Kongreß zum Manichäismus, Berlin, 14.–18. Juli 1997*, ed. Ronald Emmerick, 161–78. Berlin: Akademie Verlag.
Dyakonov, M.M. 1953. *Archeologicheskeie raboti v niznem techenii reki Kafirnigana*. Materiali i Isledovania po Archeologii SSSR, 37.
Enoki, Kazuo. 1954. 'Some Remarks on the Country of Ta-Ch'in as Known to the Chinese Under the Sung.' *Asia Major* n.s. 1: 1–19.
Enoki, Kazuo. 1955a. 'Sogdiana and the Hsiung-Nu.' *Central Asiatic Journal* 1 (1): 43–62.
Enoki, Kazuo. 1955b. 'The Origin of the White Huns or Hephthalites.' *East and West* 6 (3): 231–7.
Enoki, Kazuo. 1959. 'On the Nationality of the Ephtalites.' *Memoirs of the Research Department of the Toyo Bunko* 18: 1–58.

Enoki, Kazuo. 1969. 'On the Date of the Kidarites. I.' *Memoirs of the Research Department of the Toyo Bunko* 27: 1–26.
Enoki, K. 1970. 'The Liang Chih-Kung-T'u on the Origin and Migration of the Hua or Ephthalites.' *Journal of the Oriental Society of Australia* 7 (1–2): 37–45.
Enoki, Kazuo. 1974–5. 'Hsieh, Viceroy of the Yueh-Chih: A Contribution to the Chronology of the Kushans.' In *Tsentral Asia v Kušanskuyu Epoxu (Central Asia in the Kushan Period)*, 1.265–74. Moscow: UNESCO; Nauka.
Enoki, Kazuo. 1983. 'On the Relationship Between the Shi-Chi, Bk. 123; and the Han-Shu, Bks. 61 and 96.' *Memoirs of the Research Department of the Toyo Bunko* 41: 1–31.
Enoki, Kazuo. 1998. *Studia Asiatica: the collected papers in Western languages of the late Dr. Kazuo Enoki*. Tokyo: Kyuko-shoin.
Errington, Elizabeth. 2010. 'Differences in the Patterns of Kidarite and Alkhon Coin Distribution at Begram and Kashmir Smast.' In *Coins, Art and Chronology II: The First Millennium C.E. in the Indo-Iranian Borderlands*, ed. Michael Alram, Deborah E. Klimburg-Salter, Minoru Inaba, and Matthias Pfisterer, 147–68. Vienna: Verlag der Österreichischen Akademie der Wissenschaften.
Errington, Elizabeth, and Joe Cribb. 1992. *The Crossroads of Asia: Transformation in Image and Symbol in the Art of Ancient Afghanistan and Pakistan*. Cambridge: Ancient India and Iran Trust.
Errington, Elizabeth, and Vesta Sarkhosh Curtis. 2007. *From Persepolis to the Punjab: Exploring Ancient Iran, Afghanistan and Pakistan*. London: British Museum.
Faccenna, D. 1974. 'Excavations of the Italian Archaeological Mission (IsMEO) in Pakistan: Some Problems of Gandharan Art and Architecture.' In *Tsentral Asia v Kušanskuyu Epoxu (Central Asia in the Kushan Period)*, 126–75. Moscow: UNESCO; Nauka.
Falk, Harry. 2001. 'The Yuga of Sphujiddhvaja and the Era of the Kusanas.' *Silk Road Art and Archaeology* 7: 121–36.
Felföldi, Szabolcs. 2001. 'A Prominent Hephthalite: Katulph and the Fall of the Hephthalite Empire.' *Acta Orientalia* 54 (2): 191–202.
Felix, Wolfgang. 1991. 'Chionites,. *Encyclopaedia Iranica (Online)*.
Fleet, John Faithfull, ed. 1888. *Corpus Inscriptionum Indicarum, III*. Calcutta: Office of the Superintendent of Government Printing.
Fowden, Garth. 1993. *Empire to Commonwealth: Consequences of Monotheism in Late Antiquity*. Princeton: Princeton University Press.
Francfort, Henri-Paul. 1988. 'Central Asia and Eastern Iran.' In *The Cambridge Ancient History* 4, 165–93. Cambridge: Cambridge University Press.
Frank, Andre Gunder. 1992. 'The Centrality of Central Asia.' *Studies in History* 8 (1): 43–97.

Frankopan, Peter. 2015. *The Silk Roads*. London: Bloomsbury.
Freiman, A. A., Vladimir A. Livshits, M. N. Bogoliubov, and Olga I. Smirnova. 1962–3. *Sogdiiskie Dokumenty s Gory Mug*. Moscow: Izdatel'stvo Vostochnoi Literaturi.
Fröhlich, Christine. 2004. 'Indo-Parthian Dynasty.' *Encyclopaedia Iranica (Online)*.
Frye, Richard N. 1943. 'Sughd and the Sogdians: A Comparison of Archaeological Discoveries with Arabic Sources.' *Journal of the American Oriental Society* 63 (1): 14–16.
Frye, Richard N. 1951a. 'Jamūk, Sogdian "Pearl"?' *Journal of the American Oriental Society* 71 (2): 142–5.
Frye, Richard N. 1951b. 'Tarxūn-Türxün and Central Asian History.' *Harvard Journal of Asiatic Studies* 14 (1/2): 105–29.
Frye, Richard N. 1954. *The History of Bukhara: Translated from a Persian Abridgment of the Arabic Original by Narshakhī*. Cambridge, MA: Mediaeval Acady of America.
Frye, Richard N. 1974. 'Napki Malka and the Kushano-Sasanians.' In *Near Eastern Numismatics, Iconography, Epigraphy and History: Studies in Honor of George C. Miles*, ed. Dikran K. Kouymjian, 115–22. Beirut.
Frye, Richard N. 1975. *The Golden Age of Persia: The Arabs in the East*. London: Weidenfeld and Nicolson.
Frye, Richard N. 1983. 'The Political History of Iran under the Sasanians.' In *The Cambridge History of Iran*, III (1): 116–80. Cambridge: Cambridge University Press.
Frye, Richard N. 1988. *The Golden Age of Persia: The Arabs in the East*. London: Weidenfeld and Nicolson.
Frye, Richard N. 1996. *The Heritage of Central Asia*. Princeton: Markus Wiener.
Frye, Richard N. 1998. 'Early Bukhara.' *Cahiers d'Asie Centrale*, no. 5/6: 13–18.
Frye, Richard N., and Walter B. Henning. 1957. 'Additional Notes on the Early Coinage of Transoxiana II.' *Museum Notes (American Numismatic Society)* 7: 231–38.
Fussman, Gérard. 1969. 'Une Inscription Kharoṣṭhī à Haḍḍa.' *Bulletin de l'École Française d'Extrême-Orient* 56 (1): 5–10.
Fussman, Gérard. 1974. 'Documents Épigraphiques Kouchans.' *Bulletin de l'École Française d'Extrême-Orient* 61 (1): 1–76.
Fussman, Gérard. 1980. 'Nouvelles Inscriptions Saka: Ère d'Eucratide, Ère d'Azès, Ère Vikrama, Ère de Kaniska.' *Bulletin de l'École Française d'Extrême-Orient* 67 (1): 1–44.
Fussman, Gérard. 1982. 'Documents Epigraphiques Kouchans (III): L'Inscription Kharosthi de Senavarma, Roi d'Odi: Une Nouvelle Lecture.' *Bulletin de l'École Française d'Extrême-Orient* 71 (1): 1–46.
Fussman, Gérard. 1996. 'Southern Bactria and Northern India before Islam:

A Review of Archaeological Reports.' *Journal of the American Oriental Society* 116: 243–59.

Fussman, Gérard. 1998. 'L'Inscription de Rabatak et l'Origine de l'Ère Saka.' *Journal Asiatique* 286 (2): 571–651.

Fussman, Gérard, and Marc Le Berre. 1976. *Monuments Bouddhiques de la Région de Caboul*. Vol. 22. Paris: Diffusion De Boccard.

Gafurov, B. G., G. M. Bongard-Levin, E. A. Grantovsky, L. I. Miroshnikov, and B. Y. Stavisky, eds. 1974. *Tsentral Asia v Kušanskuyu Epoxu (Central Asia in the Kushan Period)*. Vol. 1. Moscow: UNESCO; Nauka.

Gafurov, B. G., G. M. Bongard-Levin, E. A. Grantovsky, L. I. Miroshnikov, and B. Y. Stavisky, eds. 1975. *Tsentral Asia v Kušanskuyu Epoxu (Central Asia in the Kushan Period)*. Vol. 2. Moscow: UNESCO; Nauka.

Gardin, J. C. 1957. *Céramiques de Bactres*. Paris: Klincksieck.

Gaube, Heinz. 1982. 'Mazdak: Historical Realty or Invention?.' *Studia Iranica* 11: 111–22.

Gazerani, Saghi. 2016. *The Sistani Cycle of Epics and Iran's National History: On the Margins of Historiography*. Leiden: Brill.

Genito, Bruno. 1996. 'The Iranian Empires and Central Asia: An Archaeological Perspective.' In *La Persia e l'Asia Centrale: Da Alessandro al X Secolo*, 401–21. Rome: Accademia Nazionale dei Lincei.

Gentelle, Pierre. 2001. 'Irrigations Antiques en Bactriane du Nord: L'Image de Satellite, la Prospection Archelogique, les Inferences Historiques.' In *La Bactriane au Carrefour des Routes et des Civilizations de l'Asie Central*, ed. Pierre Leriche. Paris: Maisonneuve & Larose.

Gershevitch, Ilya. 1979. 'Nokonzok's Well.' *Afghan Studies* 2: 55–73.

Ghirshman, Roman. 1946. *Bégram: Recherches Archéologique et Historiques sur les Kouchans*. MDAFA 12. Cairo:L'Institut Français d'Archéologie Orientale.

Ghirshman, Roman. 1948. *Les Chionites-Hephtalites*. Cairo: L'Institut Français d'Archéologie Orientale.

Giraud, René. 1960. *L'Empire des Turcs Célestes: Les Règnes d'Elterich, Qapghan et Bilgä (680–734). Contribution à l'Histoire des Turcs d'Asie Centrale*. Paris: Librairie d'Amérique et d'Orient Adrien-Maisonneuve.

Göbl, Robert. 1962. 'Zegomonoko.' *East and West* 13: 207–12.

Göbl, Robert. 1967. *Dokumente zur Geschichte der Iranischen Hunnen in Baktrien und Indien*. Wiesbaden: Otto Harrassowitz Verlag.

Göbl, Robert. 1984. *System und Chronologie der Münzprägung des Kušānreiches*. Vienna: Verlag der Österreichischen Akademie der Wissenschaften.

Göbl, Robert. 1999. 'The Rabatak Inscription and the Date of Kanishka.' In *Coins, Art, and Chronology: Essays on the Pre-Islamic History of the Indo-Iranian Borderlands*, ed. Michael Alram and Deborah E. Klimburg-Salter, 151–75. Vienna: Verlag der Österreichischen Akademie der Wissenschaften.

Goibov, G. 1989. *Rannie Pokhody Arabov v Sredniuiu Aziiu (644–704 Gg.)* (*Early Arab Campaigns in Central Asia (644–704 CE)*). Dushanbe: Donish.

Golden, Peter B. 2006. 'Turks and Iranians: An Historical Sketch.' In *Turkic-Iranian Contact Areas: Historical and Linguistic Aspects*, ed. Lars Johanson and Christiane Bulut, 17–38. Wiesbaden: Otto Harrassowitz Verlag.

Golden, Peter B. 2011. *Central Asia in World History*. Oxford: Oxford University Press

Gorshenina, Svetlana, and Claude Rapin. 2001. *De Kaboul à Samarcande: Les Archéologues en Asie Centrale*. Paris: Gallimard.

Grabowski, Maciej. 2011. 'Ardashir's Struggle Against the Parthians: A Reinterpretation of the Firuzabad I Relief.' *Iranica Antiqua* 46: 207–33.

Greatrex, Geoffrey, and Samuel N. C. Lieu. 2005. *The Roman Eastern Frontier and the Persian Wars AD 363–628*. London; New York: Routledge.

Grenet, Frantz. 1984. *Les Pratiques Funéraires dans l'Asie Centrale Sédentaire de la Conquête Grecque à l'Islamisation*. Paris: CNRS.

Grenet, Frantz. 1993. 'Bāmiyān and the Mihr Yašt.' *Bulletin of the Asia Institute* 7: 87–94.

Grenet, Frantz. 1994. 'Crise et Sortie de Crise en Bactriane-Sogdiane aux IVe–Ve Siècles: De l'Héritage Antique à l'Adoption de Modèles Sassanides.' In *La Persia e l'Asia Centrale da Alessandro al X Secolo*, 367–90. Atti dei Convegni Lincei 127. Rome: Accademia Nazionale dei Lincei.

Grenet, Frantz. 2002a. 'Nēzak.' *Encyclopaedia Iranica (Online)*.

Grenet, Frantz. 2002b. 'Regional Interaction in Central Asia and Northwest India in the Kidarite and Hephthalite Periods.' In *Indo-Iranian Languages and Peoples: Proceedings of the British Academy 116*, 203–24. Oxford: Oxford University Press.

Grenet, Frantz. 2005a. 'Kidarites.' *Encyclopaedia Iranica (Online)*.

Grenet, Frantz. 2005b. 'The Self-Image of the Sogdians.' In *Les Sogdiens en Chine*, ed. Étienne de la Vaissière and Eric Trombert, 123–40. Paris: École Française d'Extrême-Orient.

Grenet, Frantz. 2006. 'Iranian Gods in Hindu Garb: The Zoroastrian Pantheon of the Bactrians and Sogdians, Second–Eighth Centuries.' *Bulletin of the Asia Institute* 20, 87–99.

Grenet, Frantz. 2007. Religious Diversity among Sogdian Merchants in Sixth-Century China: Zoroastrianism, Buddhism, Manichaeism, and Hinduism.' *Comparative Studies of South Asia, Africa and the Middle East* 27 (2): 463–78.

Grenet, Frantz. 2010. 'A View from Samarkand: The Chionite and the Kidarite Periods in the Archaeology of Sogdiana (Fourth to Fifth Centuries A.D.).' In *Coins, Art and Chronology II: The First Millennium C.E. in the Indo-Iranian Borderlands*, ed. Michael Alram, Deborah E.

Klimburg-Salter, Minoru Inaba, and Matthias Pfisterer, 267–81. Vienna: Verlag der Österreichischen Akademie der Wissenschaften.

Grenet, Frantz, and Samra Azarnouche. 2007. 'Where Are the Sogdian Magi?' *Bulletin of the Asia Institute* 21: 159–77.

Grenet, Frantz, and Étienne de la Vaissière. 2002. 'The Last Days of Panjikent.' *Silk Road Art and Archaeology* 8: 155–96.

Grenet, Frantz, and Zhang Guangda. 1996. 'The Last Refuge of the Sogdian Religion: Dunhuang in the Ninth and Tenth Centuries.' *Bulletin of the Asia Institute* 10: 175–86.

Grenet, Frantz, and Pénélope Riboud. 2003. 'A Reflection of the Hephtalite Empire: The Biographical Narrative in the Reliefs of the Tomb of the Sabao Wirkak (494–579).' *Bulletin of the Asia Institute* 17: 133–43.

Grenet, Frantz, and Nicholas Sims-Williams. 1987. 'The Historical Context of the Sogdian Ancient Letters.' In *Transition Periods in Iranian History: Actes du Symposium de Fribourg-en-Brisgau (22–24 Mai 1985)*, 101–22. Leuven: Peeters.

Grenet, Frantz, P. Martinez, and F. Ory. 2007. 'The Sasanian Relief at Rag-I Bibi (Northern Afghanistan).' In *After Alexander: Central Asia Before Islam*, ed. Joe Cribb and Georgina Herrmann. Proceedings of the British Academy 133. Oxford: Oxford University Press.

Grenet, Frantz, Pénélope Riboud, and Yang Junkai. 2004. 'Zoroastrian Scenes on a Newly Discovered Sogdian Tomb in Xi'an, Northern China.' *Studia Iranica* 33 (2): 273–84.

Grenet, Frantz, Nicholas Sims-Williams, and Étienne de la Vaissière. 1998. 'The Sogdian Ancient Letter V.' *Bulletin of the Asia Institute* 12: 91–104.

Grignaschi, Mario. 1984. 'La Chute de l'Empire Hephtalite dans les Sources Byzantines et Perses et le Problème des Avar.' In *From Hecataeus to Al-Ḫuwārizmī: Bactrian, Pahlavi, Sogdian, Persian, Sanskrit, Syriac, Arabic, Chinese, Greek, and Latin Sources for the History of Pre-Islamic Central Asia*, ed. János Harmatta, 219–48. Budapest: Akadémiai Kiadó.

Grousset, René. 1970. *The Empire of the Steppes: A History of Central Asia*. New Brunswick: Rutgers University Press.

Gubaev, Annagel'dy, Gennadii A. Koshelenko, and Maurizio Tosi. 1998. *The Archaeological Map of the Murghab Delta: Preliminary Reports 1990–95*. Rome.

Gulyamov, Y. G. 1974. 'Kushanskoye Tsarstbo I Drevnyaya Irrigatsiya Srednyey Asii (Irrigation in Central Asia in the Kushan Period).' In *Tsentral Asia v Kušanskuyu Epoxu (Central Asia in the Kushan Period)*, 118–22. Moscow: UNESCO; Nauka.

Gyselen, Rika. 2001. *The Four Generals of the Sasanian Empire: Some Sigillographic Evidence*. Rome: Istituto Italiano per l'Africa e l'Oriente.

Gyselen, Rika. 2002. *Nouveaux Matériaux pour la Géographie Historique de l'Empire Sassanide: Sceaux Administratifs de la Collection Ahmad Saeedi*. Cahiers de Studia Iranica 24. Leuven: Peeters.

Gyselen, Rika. 2007. *Sasanian Seals and Sealings in the A. Saeedi Collection.* Vol. 44. Leuven: Peeters.
Gyselen, Rika. 2010. '"Umayyad" Zavulistan and Arachosia: Copper Coinage and the Sasanian Monetary Heritage.' In *Coins, Art and Chronology II: The First Millennium C.E. in the Indo-Iranian Borderlands*, ed. Michael Alram, Deborah Klimburg-Salter, Minoru Inaba, and Matthias Pfisterer, 219–41. Vienna: Verlag der Österreichischen Akademie der Wissenschaften.
Hansen, Valerie. 2012. *The Silk Road: A New History.* Oxford: Oxford University Press.
Harmatta, János. 1969. 'Late Bactrian Inscriptions.' *Acta* 17: 297–432.
Harmatta, János. 1971. 'The Middle Persian–Chinese Bilingual Inscription from Hsian and the Chinese–Sasanian Relations.' In *La Persia nel Medioevo*, 363–76. Rome: Accademia Nazionale dei Lincei.
Harmatta, János. 1979. *Prolegomena to the Sources on the History of Pre-Islamic Central Asia.* Budapest: Akadémiai Kiadó.
Harmatta, János. 1980. 'Kidara and the Kidarite Huns in Kasmir.' *Acta Antiqua Acadmiae Scientiarum Hungaricae* 28 (1–4): 185–9.
Harmatta, János. 1984. *From Hecataeus to Al-Ḥuwārizmī: Bactrian, Pahlavi, Sogdian, Persian, Sanskrit, Syriac, Arabic, Chinese, Greek, and Latin Sources for the History of Pre-Islamic Central Asia.* Budapest: Akadémiai Kiadó.
Harmatta, János. 1990. *From Alexander the Great to Kül Tegin: Studies in Bactrian, Pahlavi, Sanskrit, Arabic, Aramaic, Armenian, Chinese, Türk, Greek, and Latin Sources for the History of Pre-Islamic Central Asia.* Budapest: Akadémiai Kiadó.
Harmatta, János. 1992. 'Languages and Scripts in Graeco-Bactria and the Saka Kingdoms' In *History of Civilizations of Central Asia*, 2, ed. Ahmad H. Dani and Vadim M. Masson, 397–416. Paris: UNESCO.
Harmatta, János. 1994. 'Languages and Literature in the Kushan Empire.' In *History of Civilizations of Central Asia*, 2, ed. Ahmad H. Dani and Vadim M. Masson, 417–40. Paris: UNESCO.
Harmatta, János. 1996. 'Annexation of the Hephthalite Vassal Kingdoms by the Western Türks.' *History of Humanity* 3: 475–6.
Harmatta, János. 1999. 'Alexander the Great in Central Asia.' *Acta Antiqua* 39 (1–4): 129–36.
Harmatta, János, B. A. Litvinsky, et al. 1996. 'Tokharistan and Gandhara under Western Türk Rule (650–750).' In *History of Civilizations of Central Asia*, 3, ed. B. A. Litvinsky, 367–402. Paris: UNESCO.
Henning, Walter Bruno. 1936. 'Neue Materialien zur Geschichte des Manichäismus.' *Zeitschrift der Deutschen Morgenländischen Gesellschaft* 90 (1): 1–18.
Henning, Walter Bruno. 1942. 'Mani's Last Journey.' *Bulletin of the School of Oriental and African Studies* 10 (4): 941–53.
Henning, Walter Bruno. 1949. 'The Name of the "Tokharian" Language.' *Asia Major* n.s. 1: 158–62.

Henning, Walter Bruno. 1952. 'A Farewell to the Khaġan of the Aq-Aqatärān.' *Bulletin of the School of Oriental and African Studies* 14 (3): 501–22.
Henning, Walter Bruno. 1960. 'The Bactrian Inscription.' *Bulletin of the School of Oriental and African Studies* 23 (1): 47–55.
Henning, Walter Bruno. 1965. 'Surkh-Kotal und Kaniṣka.' *Zeitschrift der Deutschen Morgenländischen Gesellschaft* 115 (1): 75–87.
Herrmann, Georgina, and R. Howell. 1977. 'Naqsh-i Rustam 5 and 8, Sasanian Reliefs Attributed to Hormuzd II and Narseh.' *Iranische Denkmäler* 8.
Herzfeld, Ernst. 1931–2. 'Sakastan' *Archäologische Mitteilungen aus Iran* IV, 1–44.
Hinz, Walther. 1971. 'Mani and Kardēr.' In *La Persia nel Medioevo*, 485–99. Rome: Accademia Nazionale dei Lincei.
Hodgson, Marshall G. S. 1963. 'The Interrelations of Societies in History.' *Comparative Studies in Society and History* 5 (2): 227–50.
Hodgson, Marshall G. S. 1974. *The Venture of Islam. Vol. 1: The Classical Age of Islam*. Chicago: University of Chicago Press.
Honigmann, Ernst, and André Maricq. 1953. *Recherches sur les 'Res Gestae Divi Saporis.'* Brussels: Palais des Académies.
Hopkirk, Peter. 2001. *Foreign Devils on the Silk Road: The Search for the Lost Cities and Treasures of Chinese Central Asia*. Oxford: Oxford University Press.
Howard-Johnston, James. 1995. 'The Two Great Powers in Late Antiquity: Comparison.' In *States, Resources and Armies*, ed. Averil Cameron, 157–226. Byzantine and Early Islamic Near East 3. Princeton: Darwin Press.
Howard-Johnston, James. 2006. *East Rome, Sasanian Persia and the End of Antiquity: Historiographical and Historical Studies*. Variorum 848. Aldershot: Ashgate.
Howard-Johnston, James. 2008. 'Byzantium and Its Neighbours.' In *The Oxford Handbook of Byzantine Studies*, ed. Robin Cormack, John F. Haldon, and Elizabeth Jeffreys, 939–56. Oxford: Oxford University Press.
Hoyland, Robert G. 2014. *In God's Path: The Arab Conquests and the Creation of an Islamic Empire*. Oxford: Oxford University Press.
Hua, Tao. 2008. 'The Muslim Qarakhanids and Their Invented Ethnic Identity.' In *Islamisation de l'Asie Centrale: Processus Locaux d'Acculturation du VIIe au XIe Siècle*, ed. Étienne de la Vaissière, 339–50. Studia Iranica 39. Paris; Leuven: Peeters.
Huff, D., Charir Pidaiev, and C. Chaydoullaev. 2001. 'Uzbek–German Archaeological Researches in the Surkhan Darya Region.' In *La Bactriane au Carrefour des Routes et des Civilizations de l'Asie Central*, ed. Pierre Leriche and Charir Pidaev, 291–333. Paris: Maisonneuve & Larose.
Hulsewé, Anthony F. P., and Michael A. N. Loewe. 1979. *China in Central Asia: The Early Stage, 125 BC–AD 23: An Annotated Translation of*

Chapters 61 and 96 of the History of the Former Han Dynasty. Vol. 14. Leiden: Brill.

Humbach, Helmut. 1966. *Baktrische Sprachdenkmäler*. Vol. 1. Wiesbaden: Otto Harrassowitz Verlag.

Humbach, Helmut. 1967. 'Two Inscriptions in Graeco-Bactrian Cursive Script from Afghanistan.' *East and West* 18: 25–6.

Humbach, Helmut. 1996. 'Pangul, a Turco-Bactrian Ruler.' *Bulletin of the Asia Institute* 10: 247–51.

Humbach, Helmut. 2003. 'The Great Surkh Kotal Inscription.' In *Religious Themes and Texts of Pre-Islamic Iran and Central Asia: Studies in Honour of Professor Gherardo Gnoli on the Occasion of His 65th Birthday on 6th December 2002*, ed. Carlo G. Cereti, Mauro Maggi, and Elio Provasi. Wiesbaden: Reichert Verlag.

Humbach, Helmut, and P. O. Skjærvø. 1978. *The Sassanian Inscription of Paikuli*. 3 parts. Wiesbaden: Dr. Ludwig Reichert Verlag.

Huntington, G. W. B. 1980. *The Periplus of the Erythraean Sea*. London: Hakluyt Society.

Huyse, Philip. 1999. *Die Dreisprachige Inschrift Šābuhrs I. an Der Ka'ba-I Zardušt (ŠKZ)*. Vol. 1. London: School of Oriental and African Studies.

Ilyasov, Jangar Ya. 2001. 'The Hephthalite Terracotta.' *Silk Road Art and Archaeology* 7: 187–200.

Ilyasov, Jangar Ya. 2003. 'On a Number of Central Asian Tamghas.' *Silk Road Art and Archaeology* 9: 131–57.

Inaba, Minoru. 2005. 'The Identity of the Turkish Rulers to the South of Hindukush from the 7th to the 9th Centuries AD.' *Zinbun* 38: 1–19.

Inaba, Minoru. 2010a. 'From Kesar the Kabulshah and Central Asia.' In *Coins, Art and Chronology II: The First Millennium C.E. in the Indo-Iranian Borderlands*, 443–55. Vienna: Verlag der Österreichischen Akademie der Wissenschaften.

Inaba, Minoru. 2010b. 'Nezak in Chinese Sources.' In *Coins, Art and Chronology II: The First Millennium C.E. in the Indo-Iranian Borderlands*, 191–202. Vienna: Verlag der Österreichischen Akademie der Wissenschaften.

Inaba, Minoru. 2010c. '泥孰攽 (Notes on Ni-Shu).' *Toho Gakuho: Journal of Oriental Studies, Kyoto* 85: 674–92.

Inaba, Minoru. 2015. 'From Caojuzha to Ghazna/Ghaznīn: Early Medieval Chinese and Muslim Descriptions of Eastern Afghanistan.' *Journal of Asian History* 49 (1–2): 97–117.

Jaafari-Dehaghi, Mahmood. 2012. 'The Rabatak Inscription.' *Journal of Teaching Language Skills* 1 (1): 1–20.

Jiang, Boqin. 2012. 'The Chinese Persia Expeditionary Force as Referenced in the Turfan Documents.' In *Chinese Scholars on Inner Asia*, ed. Xin Luo, 41–58. Bloomington: Indiana University Press.

Jongeward, David, and Joe Cribb. 2015. *Kushan, Kushano-Sasanian, and Kidarite Coins*. New York: American Numismatic Society.
Juliano, Annette L., and Judith Lerner. 2001. *Monks and Merchants: Silk Road Treasures from Northwest China, Gansu and Ningxia, 4th–7th Century*. New York: Harry N. Abrams with the Asia Society.
Justi, Ferdinand. 1895. *Iranisches Namenbuch*. Marburg: N. G. Elwert.
Kageyama, Etsuko. 2002. 'Use and Production of Silks in Sogdiana.' *Bulletin of the Society for Near Eastern Studies in Japan (Nippon Oriento Gakkai)* 45 (1): 37–55.
Kageyama, Etsuko. 2007. 'The Winged Crown and the Triple-Crescent Crown in the Sogdian Funerary Monuments from China: Their Relation to the Hephthalite Occupation of Central Asia.' *Journal of Inner Asian Art and Archaeology* 2 (1): 11–22.
Kashani-Sabet, Firoozeh. 2014. *Frontier Fictions: Shaping the Iranian Nation, 1804–1946*. Princeton: Princeton University Press.
Kennedy, Hugh. 1986/2004. *The Prophet and the Age of the Caliphates*. New York: Routledge.
Khan, Gul Rahim, and Joe Cribb. 2012. 'Coins of Kujula Kadphises from Taxila.' *Journal of Gandharan Studies* 6: 81–211.
Kim, Hyun Jin. 2016. *The Huns*. New York: Routledge.
Klíma, Otakar. 1962. *Manis Zeit und Leben*. Prague: Verlag der Tschechoslowakischen Akademie der Wissenschaften.
Klimburg-Salter, Deborah. 1989. *The Kingdom of Bāmiyān: Buddhist Art and Culture of the Hindu Kush*. Naples: Istituto Universitario Orientale, Dipartimento di Studi Asiatici.
Klose, Dietrich O. A., and Wilhelm Müseler. 2008. *Statthalter, Rebellen, Könige: Die Münzen aus Persepolis von Alexander dem Großen zu den Sasaniden*. Munich: Staatliche Münzsammlung.
Klyashtorny, S. G. 1999. 'Al-Biruni's Version of an Old Turkic Genealogical Legend: On the Semantics of Turkic Baraq.' *Turkic Languages* 2 (2): 247–52.
Kolesnikov, Aliy I. 1978. *Iran Dar Āstāne-Ye Yoreš-E Tāziyān (Persian Translation of Иран накануне арабского завоевания)*. Trans. M. R. Yahyayi. Tehran: Agah.
Konow, Stan. 1925. 'So-Called Takht-i-Bahi Inscription of the Year 103.' *Epigraphica Indica* XVIII: 261–82.
Konow, Stan. 1929. *Kharosthi Inscriptions (with the Exception of Those of Asoka)*. Vol. II/1. Corpus Inscriptionum Indicarum. Calcutta Government of India Central Publication Branch.
Kraemer, Joel L. 1992. *Humanism in the Renaissance of Islam: The Cultural Revival During the Buyid Age*. Leiden: Brill.
Kruglikova, I. T. 1976. 'Natenn'ey Rospisi Dil'berdjina.' In *Material' Sovietsko-Afganskoi Expeditsii, 1969–1973 Gg*, ed. I. T. Kruglikova, 87–110. Moscow: Nauka.

Kurbanov, Aydogdy. 2013. *The Archaeology and History of the Hephthalites*. Bonn: Verlag Dr. Rudolf Habelt.
Kuwayama, Shoshin. 1976. 'The Turki Śāhis and Relevant Brahmanical Sculptures in Afghanistan.' *East and West* 26 (1–2): 375–407.
Kuwayama, Shoshin. 1982. 'Kapisi and Gandhara According to Chinese Buddhist Sources.' *Orient* 18: 133–9.
Kuwayama, Shoshin. 1987. 'Literary Evidence for Dating the Colossi in Bàmiyàn.' *Orientalia Iosephi Tucci Memoriae Dicata* 2: 703–27.
Kuwayama, Shoshin. 1989. 'The Hephthalites in Tokhharistan and Northwest India.' *Zinbun* 24: 89–134.
Kuwayama, Shoshin. 1991. 'The Horizon of Begram III and Beyond: A Chronological Interpretation of the Evidence for Monuments in the Kāpiśī-Kabul-Ghazni Region.' *East and West* 41 (1): 79–120.
Kuwayama, Shoshin. 1998. 'Not Hephthalite but Kapisian Khingal: Identity of the Napki Coins.' In *Ex Moneta: Essays on Numismatics, History and Archaeology in Honour of Dr. David W. MacDowall*, ed. Amal K. Jha and Sanjay Garg, 2: 331–49. New Delhi: Harman.
Kuwayama, Shoshin. 2000. 'Historical Notes on Kāpiśī and Kābul in the Sixth–Eighth Centuries.' *Zinbun* 34 (1): 25–77.
Kuwayama, Shoshin. 2002. *Across the Hindukush of the First Millennium: A Collection of the Papers*. Kyoto: Institute for Research in Humanities.
Kuwayama, Shoshin. 2005. 'Chinese Records on Bamiyan: Translation and Commentary.' *East and West* 55 (1/4): 139–61.
Lattimore, Owen. 1950. *Pivot of Asia: Sinkiang and the Inner Asian Frontiers of China and Russia*. New York: Little, Brown.
Leriche, Pierre. 2007. 'Bactria, Land of a Thousand Cities.' In *After Alexander: Central Asia Before Islam*, ed. Joe Cribb and Georgina Herrmann, 121–53. Proceedings of the British Academy 133. Oxford: Oxford University Press.
Leriche, Pierre, and Sakirdzan Rasulevic Pidaev. 2007. 'Termez in Antiquity.' In *After Alexander: Central Asia Before Islam*, ed. Joe Cribb and Georgina Herrmann, 177–211. Proceedings of the British Academy 133. Oxford: Oxford University Press.
Lerner, Judith A. 1995. 'Central Asians in Sixth-Century China: A Zoroastrian Funerary Rite.' *Iranica Antiqua* 30: 179–90.
Lerner, Judith A. 2009. 'Animal Headdresses on the Sealings of the Bactrian Documents.' In *Exegisti Monumenta: Festschrift in Honour of Nicholas Sims-Williams*, ed. Werner Sunermann, Almut Hintze, and Francois de Blois, 215–26. Wiesbaden: Otto Harrassowitz Verlag.
Lerner, Judith A. 2011. 'Zoroastrian Funerary Beliefs and Practices Known from the Sino-Sogdian Tombs in China.' *Silk Road* 9: 18–25.
Lerner, Judith A. 2013. 'Some Thoughts on a Sogdian Double Portrait Seal.' In *Commentationes Iranicae, Vladimiro Aaron Livschits Nonagenario Donum Natalicium*, ed. Sergei P. Tokhtasev and Pavel Lurye, 326–34. St. Petersburg: Nestor-Historia.

Lerner, Judith A., and Nicholas Sims-Williams. 2011. *Seals, Sealings and Tokens from Bactria to Gandhara (4th to 8th Century CE)*. Vienna: Verlag der Österreichischen Akademie der Wissenschaften.

Lerner, Judith A., Ahmad Saeedi, and Nicholas Sims-Williams. 2009. 'The Bactrian Sealings in the A. Saeedi Collection (London).' In *Trésors d'Orient: Mélanges Offerts à Rika Gyselen*, ed. Philippe Gignoux, F. Jullien, and C. Jullien, 211–35. Cahiers de Studia Iranica 42. Paris: Association pour l'Avancement des Études Iraniennes.

Le Strange, Guy. 1905. *The Lands of the Eastern Caliphate: Mesopotamia, Persia, and Central Asia, from the Moslem Conquest to the Time of Timur*. Vol. 4. Cambridge: Cambridge University Press.

Litvinskii, Boris A., and V. V. Solov'ev. 1985. *Srednevekovaia kul'tura Tokharistana*. Moscow.

Litvinsky, Boris Anatolevitch. 1994. 'Cities and Urban Life in the Kushan Kingdom.' In *History of Civilizations of Central Asia*, 2 ed. Ahmad H. Dani and Vadim M. Masson. Paris: UNESCO.

Litvinsky, Boris Anatolevitch. 1999. 'The Hephthalite Empire.' In *History of Civilizations of Central Asia*, 3, ed. B. A. Litvinsky, 135–62. Paris: UNESCO.

Litvinsky, Boris Anatolevitch, and M. H. Zamir Safi. 1999. 'Later Hephthalites in Central Asia.' In *History of Civilizations of Central Asia*, 3, ed. B. A. Litvinsky, 180–7. Paris: UNESCO.

Liu, Xinru. 2001. 'Migration and Settlement of the Yuezhi-Kushan: Interaction and Interdependence of Nomadic and Sedentary Societies.' *Journal of World History* 12 (2): 261–92.

Liu, Xinru. 2012. *The Silk Roads: A Brief History with Documents*. Basingstoke: Palgrave Macmillan.

Livshits, Vladimir. 1979. 'Rulers of Panch (Sogdians and Turks).' *Narody Azii iAfriki (Moscow, 1979.4)*, 56–68.

Livshits, Vladimir. 2000. 'Sogdian Sānak, a Manichaean Bishop of the 5th–Early 6th Centuries.' *Bulletin of the Asia Institute* 14: 47–54.

Livshits, Vladimir. 2008. 'The Sogdian "Ancient Letters" (I, III).' *Iran and the Caucasus* 12 (2): 289–93.

Livshits, Vladimir. 2015a. 'A Sogdian Document from Old Samarkand.' In *Sogdian Epigraphy of Central Asia and Semirech'e*, ed. Nicholas Sims-Williams, trans. Tom Stableford. Corpus Inscriptionum Iranicarum, Part II: Inscriptions of the Seleucid and Parthian Periods and of Eastern Iran and Central Asia, Vol. III: Sogdian, 261–7. London: School of Oriental and African Studies.

Livshits, Vladimir. 2015b. 'Kesh (Shahrisabz) in Sogdian Texts and Coin Legends.' In *Sogdian Epigraphy of Central Asia and Semirech'e*, ed. Nicholas Sims-Williams, trans. Tom Stableford. Corpus Inscriptionum Iranicarum, Part II: Inscriptions of the Seleucid and Parthian Periods and of Eastern Iran and Central Asia, Vol. III: Sogdian, 203–32. London: School of Oriental and African Studies.

Livshits, Vladimir. 2015c. 'Sogdian Epigraphy of Semirech'e.' In *Sogdian Epigraphy of Central Asia and Semirech'e*, ed. Nicholas Sims-Williams, trans. Tom Stableford. Corpus Inscriptionum Iranicarum, Part II: Inscriptions of the Seleucid and Parthian Periods and of Eastern Iran and Central Asia, Vol. III: Sogdian, 269–82. London: School of Oriental and African Studies.

Livshits, Vladimir. 2015d. 'The Leader of the People of Chāch in Sogdian Inscriptions and Coin Legends.' In *Sogdian Epigraphy of Central Asia and Semirech'e*, ed. Nicholas Sims-Williams, trans. Tom Stableford. Corpus Inscriptionum Iranicarum, Part II: Inscriptions of the Seleucid and Parthian Periods and of Eastern Iran and Central Asia, Vol. III: Sogdian, 233–60. London: School of Oriental and African Studies.

Livshits, Vladimir A. 2015e. *Sogdian Epigraphy of Central Asia and Semirech'e*, ed. Nicholas Sims-Williams, trans. Tom Stableford. Corpus Inscriptionum Iranicarum, Part II: Inscriptions of the Seleucid and Parthian Periods and of Eastern Iran and Central Asia, Vol. III: Sogdian. London: School of Oriental and African Studies.

Loeschner, Hans. 2012a. 'Kanishka in Context with the Historical Buddha and Kushan Chronology.' In *Glory of the Kushans: Recent Discoveries and Interpretations*, ed. Vidula Jayasval, 137–94. New Delhi: Aryan Books International.

Loeschner, Hans. 2012b. 'The Stūpa of the Kushan Emperor Kanishka the Great, with Comments on the Azes Era and Kushan Chronology.' *Sino-Platonic Papers* 227: 1–24.

Loginov, Sergej D., and Alexandr B. Nikitin. 1993a. 'Coins of Shapur II from Merv.' *Mesopotamia* XXVIII: 247–69.

Loginov, Sergej D., and Alexandr B. Nikitin. 1993b. 'Sasanian Coins of the Late 4th–7th Centuries from Merv.' *Mesopotamia* XXVIII: 271–313.

Loginov, Sergej D., and Alexandr B. Nikitin. 1993c. 'Sasanian Coins of the Third Century from Merv.' *Mesopotamia* XXVIII: 225–46.

Lombard, M. 1975. *The Golden Age of Islam*. Amsterdam: North-Holland.

Lo Muzio, Ciro. 2009. 'An Archaeological Outline of the Bukhara Oasis.' *Journal of Inner Asian Art and Archaeology* 4 (1): 43–68.

Lüders, Heinrich. 1961. *Mathurā Inscriptions*. Göttingen: Vandenhoeck & Ruprecht.

Lukonin, Vladimir G. 1983. 'Political, Social and Administrative Institutions: Taxes and Trade.' In *The Cambridge History of Iran*, III (1): 681–746. Cambridge: Cambridge University Press.

Lurye, Pavel. 2013. 'О СЛЕДАХ МАНИХЕИЗМА В СРЕДНЕЙ АЗИИ (Traces of Manichaeism in Middle Asia).' In *СОГДИЙЦЫ,ИХ ПРЕДШЕСТВЕННИКИ,СОВРЕМЕННИКИИ НАСЛЕДНИКИ* (*Sogdians, Their Precursors, Contemporaries and Heirs; Memorial Boris I. Marshak*), 219–51. St. Petersburg: State Hermitage.

Lyonnet, Bertille. 1997. *Prospections Archéologiques en Bactriane Orientale (1974–1978)*. Vol. 2. Mémoires de la Mission Archéologique Française en Asie Centrale 8. Paris: Éditions Recherche sur les Civilisations.

MacDowall, David W. 1968. 'Soter Megas, the King of Kings, the Kushana.' *Journal of the Numismatic Society of India* 30: 28–48.

MacDowall, David W. 1974. 'Implications for Kushan Chronology of the Numismatic Context of the Nameless King.' In *Tsentral Asia v Kušanskuyu Epoxu (Central Asia in the Kushan Period)*, 246–64. Moscow: UNESCO; Nauka.

MacDowall, David W. 2002. 'The Rabatak Inscription and the Nameless Kushan King.' *Cairo to Kabul: Afghan and Islamic Studies Presented to Ralph Pinder-Wilson*, 163–9.

MacDowall, David W. 2007. 'The Eras of Demetrius, Eucratides, and Azes.' In *Des Indo-Grecs aux Sassanides: Données pour l'Histoire et la Geographie Historique*, ed. Rika Gyselen, 103–10. Res Orientales, XVII. Bures-sur-Yvette: Groupe pour l'Étude de la Civilisation du Moyen-Orient.

MacKenzie, David Neil. 1970. 'The Kartir Inscriptions.' In *W. B. Henning Memorial Volume*, ed. Mary Boyce and Ilya Gerschevitch, 109–20. London: Lund Humphries.

MacKenzie, David Neil. 1971. *A Concise Pahlavi Dictionary*. London: Oxford University Press.

Macuch, Maria. 2014. 'Ardashir's Genealogy Revisited.' *Iran Nameh: A Special Issue Honoring Jaleh Amouzgar*, ed. Parvaneh Pourshariati and Mohammad Tavakoli Targhi, 29: 80–94.

Maenchen-Helfen, Otto. 1945. 'The Yüeh-Chih Problem Re-Examined.' *Journal of the American Oriental Society* 65: 71–81.

Maenchen-Helfen, Otto. 1973. *The World of the Huns: Studies in Their History and Culture*. Berkeley; Los Angeles: University of California Press.

Malatesta, Luca Claude, Sébastien Castelltort, Simone Mantellini, Vincenzo Picotti, Irka Hajdas, Guy Simpson, Amriddin Ergashevich Berdimuradov, Maurizio Tosi, and Sean Douglas Willlett. 2012. 'Dating the Irrigation System of the Samarkand Oasis: A Geoarchaeological Study.' *Radiocarbon* 54 (1): 91–105.

Mallory, J. P., and Douglas Q. Adams. 1997. *Encyclopedia of Indo-European Culture*. Chicago; London: Fitzroy Dearborn.

Mandel'shtam, A. M. 1974. 'Proicxozhdeniye i Rannyaya Istriya Kushan v Svete Arxeologicyeckix Dann'ix (Archaeological Data on the Origin and Early History of the Kushans).' In *Tsentral Asia v Kušanskuyu Epoxu (Central Asia in the Kushan Period)*, 190–7. Moscow: UNESCO; Nauka.

Maricq, André. 1958. 'Inscription de Surkh-Kotal: Baghlān. La Grande Inscription de Kaniṣka et l'Étéo-Tokharien, l'Ancienne Langue de la Bactriane.' *Journal Asiatique* 246: 345–440.

Marquart, J. 1901. *Ērānšahr nach der Geographie des ps. Moses Xorenacci: Mit historisch-kritischen Kommentar und historischen und topographischen Excursen.* Berlin: Weidmannsche Buchhandlung.

Marschak, Boris I. 1986. *Silberschätze des Orients: Metallkunst des 3.–13.* Leipzig: E. A. Seemann.

Marshak, Boris I. 1990. 'Wall Paintings from a House with a Granary, Penjikent, 1st Quarter of the 8th Century.' *Silk Road Art and Archaeology* 1: 123–76.

Marshak, Boris I. 1992. 'The Historico-Cultural Significance of the Sogdian Calendar.' *Iran* 30: 145–54.

Marshak, Boris I. 2001. 'The Sogdians in Their Homeland.' In *Monks and Merchants: Silk Road Treasures from Northwest China, Gansu and Ningxia, 4th–7th Century*, ed. Annette L. Juliano and Judith Lerner, 231–7. New York: Harry N. Abrams with the Asia Society.

Marshak, Boris I. 2002. *Legends, Tales, and Fables in the Art of Sogdiana.* Ehsan Yarshater Lectures, SOAS 1. New York: Bibliotheca Persica.

Marshak, Boris I. 2004. '233 г. н.э. = 101 г. эры Канишки? (233 AD = 101 of the Era of Kanishka?).' In *Уходя, оставить свет … Памяти Евгения Владиславовича Зеймаля (E. V. Zejmal Memorial Volume)*, 46–9. St. Petersburg: State Hermitage.

Marshak, Boris I., and N. N. Negmatov. 1999. Sogdiana.' In *History of Civilizations of Central Asia. Vol. III*, 237–81. Paris: UNESCO.

Marshak, Boris I., and V. I. Raspopova. 1990. A Hunting Scene from Panjikent.' *Bulletin of the Asia Institute* 4: 77–94.

Marshall, John H. 1914. 'The Date of Kanishka.' *Journal of the Royal Asiatic Society of Great Britain and Ireland* (Oct.) 973–86.

Medlycott, A. E. 1905. *India and the Apostle Thomas: An Inquiry, with a Critical Analysis of the Acta Thomae.* London: David Nutt.

Meisami, Julie Scott. 2000. 'Why Write History in Persian? Historical Writing in the Samanid Period.' In *Studies in Honour of Clifford Edmund Bosworth*, ed. Carole Hillenbrand, 2: 348–74. Leiden: Brill.

Melzer, Gudrun. 2006. 'A Copper Scroll Inscription from the Time of the Alchon Huns. In Collaboration with Lore Sander.' In *Manuscripts in the Schøyen Collection: Buddhist Manuscripts*, ed. J. Braarvig. Vol. 3, 251–314. Oslo: Hermes.

Minorsky, Vladimir. 1937. *Hudud Al 'Alam: The Regions of the World: A Persian Geography, 372 A.H.–982 A.D.* Oxford: Oxford University Press.

Minorsky, Vladimir. 1953. *Studies in Caucasian History.* Cambridge: Cambridge University Press.

Mitchiner, Michael. 1975a. *Indo-Greek and Indo-Scythian Coinage.* 9 vols. London: Hawkins.

Mitchiner, Michael. 1975b. 'A Hoard of Late Kushan Gold Staters.' *East and West* 25 (1/2): 147–56.

Mitchiner, Michael. 1975c. 'Some Late Kushano-Sassanian and Early Hephthalite Silver Coins.' *East and West* 25 (1/2): 157–65.
Mitchiner, Michael. 1975d. 'Who Were Napki Malik?" *East and West* 25 (1/2): 167–74.
Mohammadi Malayeri, Mohammad. 1379/2000. *Tarikh o Farhang-e Iran dar Dowrān-e Enteqāl az Asr-e Sāsānī be Asr-e Eslāmi* (History and Culture of Iran in the Period of Transition from the Sasanian Epoch to the Islamic Epoch). Tehran: Tūs.
Morony, Michael G. 1984. *Iraq After the Muslim Conquest*. Princeton: Princeton University Press.
Mustamidy, C. 1974. 'Les Nouvelles Fouilles de Hadda.' In *Tsentral Asia v Kušanskuyu Epoxu* (Central Asia in the Kushan Period), 107–12. Moscow: UNESCO; Nauka.
Narain, Awadh Kishore. 1957. *The Indo-Greeks*. Oxford: Clarendon Press.
Naveh, Joseph, and Shaul Shaked. 2012. *Aramaic Documents from Ancient Bactria*. London: Khalili Collections.
Naymark, Aleksandr. 1995. 'O Nachale Chekanki Mednoi Monety v Bukharskom Sogde.' In *Numizmatika Tsentral'noi Azii*. Tashkent: Akademiia Khudozhestv Respubliki Uzbekistan.
Naymark, Aleksandr. 1999. 'The Size of Samanid Bukhara: A Note on Settlement Patterns in Early Islamic Mawarannahr.' In *Bukhara: The Myth and the Architecture*, ed. Attilio Petruccioli, 39–60. Cambridge, MA: Aga Khan Program for Islamic Architecture.
Naymark, Aleksandr. 2003a. 'A Note on Sogdian Coroplastics: Two Ossuary Fragments from Afrasiab.' In *Ērān ud Anērān: Webfestschrift Marshak 2003* (electronic version), ed. Matteo Compareti, Paola Raffetta, and Gianroberto Scarcia. Venice: Cafoscarina.
Naymark, Aleksandr. 2003b. 'Returning to Varakhsha.' *The Silk Road Foundation Newsletter* 1 (2): 9–22.
Naymark, Aleksandr. 2010a. 'Drachms of Bukhār Khudā Khunak.' *Journal of Inner Asian Art and Archaeology* 5 (1): 7–32.
Naymark, Aleksandr. 2010b. 'Les Villes Sogdiennes Après les Grecs.' *Dossiers d'Archéologie* 341: 44–6.
Naymark, Aleksandr. 2013. 'One More About the Coinage of Samarqand Ikhshid Ughrak.' In *Commentationes Iranicae, Vladimiro Aaron Livschits Nonagenario Donum Natalicium*, ed. Sergei P. Tokhtasev and Pavel Lurye, 343–67. St. Petersburg: Nestor-Historia.
Naymark, Aleksandr, and Luke Treadwell. 2011. 'An Arab-Sogdian Coin of AH 160: An Ikhshid in Ishtihan?' *Numismatic Chronicle* 171: 359–66.
Neelis, Jason. 2010. *Early Buddhist Transmission and Trade Networks: Mobility and Exchange Within and Beyond the Northwestern Borderlands of South Asia*. Leiden: Brill.
Nikitin, Alexander B. 1994. 'Coins of the Last Indo-Parthian King of Sakastan: A Farewell to Ardamitra.' *South Asian Studies* 10 (1): 67–9.

Nikitin, Alexander B. 1999. 'Notes on the Chronology of the Kushano-Sasanian Kingdom.' In *Coins, Art, and Chronology: Essays on the Pre-Islamic History of the Indo-Iranian Borderlands*, ed. Michael Alram and Deborah E. Klimburg-Salter, 259–63. Vienna: Verlag der Österreichischen Akademie der Wissenschaften.

Nikitin, Alexander B. 2013. 'Moneti Baxrama Čubina i Bistama i Xronologiia Sobitii v Iranye v Pervie Godi Pravlyeniia Xosrova II (Coins of Bahrām VI Čōbīn and Bistam and the Chronology of Events in Iran in the First Years of the Reign of Khosrow II).' In *Commentationes Iranicae, Vladimiro Aaron Livschits Nonagenario Donum Natalicium*, ed. Sergei P. Tokhtasev and Pavel Lurye, 166–70. St. Petersburg: Nestor-Historia.

Nikitin, Alexander, and Gunter Roth. 1995. 'A New Seventh-Century Countermark with a Sogdian Inscription.' *Numismatic Chronicle* 155: 277–9.

Nöldeke, Theodor, and Muhammad b. Jarir al-Tabari. 1879. *Geschichte der Perser und Araber zur Zeit der Sasaniden*. Leiden: Brill.

Okazaki, Takashi. 1971. 'Tentative Chronology on the Eastward Extension of Sasanian Persian Culture.' *Orient* 7: 49–57.

Olbrycht, Marek J. 2016. 'Dynastic Connections in the Arsacid Empire and the Origins of the House of Sāsān.' In *The Parthian and Early Sasanian Empires: Adaptation and Expansion*, ed. Vesta Sarkhosh Curtis, Elizabeth Pendelton, Michael Alram, and Touraj Daryaee. BIPS Archaeological Monograph Series V. Oxford: Oxbow Books.

Paiman, Zafar, and Michael Alram. 2010. 'Tepe Narenj: A Royal Monastery on the High Ground of Kabul, with a Commentary on the Coinage.' *Journal of Inner Asian Art and Archaeology* 5 (1): 33–58.

Payne, Richard. 2014. 'The Reinvention of Iran: The Sasanian Empire and the Huns.' In *The Cambridge Companion to the Age of Attila*, ed. Michael Maas, 282–99. Cambridge: Cambridge University Press.

Pelliot, Paul. 1920. 'À Propos des Comans.' *Journal Asiatique* 15: 125–85.

Petruccioli, Attilio. 1999. *Bukhara: The Myth and the Architecture*. Vol. 3. Cambridge, MA: Aga Khan Program for Islamic Architecture.

Pfisterer, Matthias. 2013. *Hunnen in Indien*. Vienna: Verlag der Österreichischen Akademie der Wissenschaften.

Posch, Walter. 1995. *Baktrien Zwischen Griechen und Kuschan: Untersuchungen zu Kulturellen und Historischen Problemen Einer Übergangsphase: Mit Einem Textritischen Exkurs zum Shiji 123*. Wiesbaden: Otto Harrassowitz Verlag.

Pourshariati, Parvaneh. 2008. *Decline and Fall of the Sasanian Empire: The Sasanian–Parthian Confederacy and the Arab Conquest of Iran*. London: I.B. Tauris.

Pugachenkoba, Galina, and E. V. Rtveladze. 1978. *Dal'verzitepe Kushanskij gorod na juge Uzbekistana*. Tashkent.

Pugachenkova, Galina Anatol'evna, and E. V. Rtveladze. 1984. 'Afrasiab.' *Encyclopaedia Iranica (Online)*.

Pulleyblank, Edwin George. 1968. 'Chinese Evidence for the Date of Kaniṣka.' In *Papers on the Date of Kanishka*, ed. Arthur L. Basham, 247–58. Leiden: Brill.

Puri, Baji N. 1974. 'The Nationality of the Kushans.' In *Tsentral Asia v Kušanskuyu Epoxu (Central Asia in the Kushan Period)*, 182–9. Moscow: UNESCO; Nauka.

Puri, Baji N. 1999. 'The Kushans.' In *History of Civilizations of Central Asia*, 2, ed. Ahmad H. Dani and Vadim M. Masson, 247–64. Paris: UNESCO.

Rahman, Aman ur, Frantz Grenet, and Nicholas Sims-Williams. 2006. 'A Hunnish Kushan-Shah.' *Journal of Inner Asian Art and Archaeology* 1 (1): 125–31.

Rante, Rocco. 2015. *Greater Khorasan: History, Geography, Archaeology and Material Culture*. Berlin; Boston: De Gruyter.

Rapin, Claude, and Muhammadjon Isamiddinov. 2013. 'Entre Sédentaires et Nomades: Les Recherches de la Mission Archéologique Franco-Ouzbèke (MAFOuz) de Sogdiane sur le Site de Koktepe.' *Cahiers d'Asie Centrale* 21/2: 113–33.

Rekavandi, Hamid Omrani, Eberhard W. Sauer, Tony Wilkinson, Ghorban Ali Abbasi, Seth Priestman, Esmail Safari Tamak, Roger Ainslie, et al. 2008. 'Sasanian Walls, Hinterland Fortresses and Abandoned Ancient Irrigated Landscape.' *Iran* 46: 151–78.

Rezakhani, Khodadad. 2005. 'Tirdād o Ardawān: Negāhi be Nasabnāme-ye Noxostīn Šāhān-e Aškāni (Tirdates and Artabanus: A Look at the Genealogy of the Early Arsacid Kings).' *Farhang* 49/50.

Rezakhani, Khodadad. 2010a. 'Balkh and the Sasanians: Economy and Society of Northern Afghanistan as Reflected in the Bactrian Economic Documents.' In *Ancient and Middle Iranian Studies: Proceedings of the 6th European Conference of Iranian Studies, Held in Vienna, 18–22 September 2007*, ed. Maria Macuch, Dieter Weber, and Desmond Durkin-Meisterernst, 191–204. Wiesbaden: Otto Harrassowitz Verlag.

Rezakhani, Khodadad. 2010b. 'The Road That Never Was: The Silk Road and Trans-Eurasian Exchange.' *Comparative Studies of South Asia, Africa and the Middle East* 30 (3): 420–33.

Rezakhani, Khodadad. 2010c. 'Empires and Microsystems: Late Antique Regional Economy in Central and West Asia, 500–750.' PhD diss., UCLA.

Rezakhani, Khodadad. 2015a. 'Mazdakism, Manichaeism and Zoroastrianism: In Search of Orthodoxy and Heterodoxy in Late Antique Iran.' *Iranian Studies* 48 (1): 55–70.

Rezakhani, Khodadad. 2015b. 'A Note on the Alkhan Coin Type 39 and Its Legend.' *DABIR* 1: 24–7.

Rezakhani, Khodadad. 2016. 'From the "Cleavage" of Central Asia to Greater Khurasan: History and Historiography of Late Antique East Iran.' *Iranian Studies* 49 (2): 205–15.

Rosenfield, John M. 1967. *The Dynastic Arts of the Kushans*. Berkeley; Los Angeles: University of California Press.
Roux, Jean-Paul. 1997. *L'Asie Centrale: Histoire et Civilisations*. Paris: Librarie Arthéme Fayard.
Rtveladze, E. V. 1987. *The Ancient Coins of Central Asia*. Tashkent: Akademiia Khudozhestv Respubliki Uzbekistan.
Rtveladze, E. V . 1997. 'Pre-Muslim Coins of Chach.' *Silk Road Art and Archaeology* 5: 307–28.
Rtveladze, E. V. 2003. 'Coins from Kish: 3rd–2nd Century BC – 8th Century AD.' In *Ērān ud Anērān: Webfestschrift Marshak 2003* (electronic version), ed. Matteo Compareti, Paola Raffetta, and Gianroberto Scarcia. Venice: Cafoscarina.
Rubin, Zeev. 1995. 'The Reforms of Khusro Anushirwan.' In *States, Resources and Armies*, ed. Averil Cameron, 227–97. Byzantine and Early Islamic Near East 3. Princeton: Darwin Press.
Samolin, William. 1956. 'A Note on Kidara and the Kidarites.' *Central Asiatic Journal* 2 (4): 295–7.
Sarianidi, Viktor Ivanovich. 1998. *Margiana and Protozoroastrism*. Athens: Kapon Editions.
Sarkhosh Curtis, Vesta. 1999. 'Some Observations on the Coins of Peroz and Kavad I.' In *Coins, Art, and Chronology: Essays on the Pre-Islamic History of the Indo-Iranian Borderlands*, ed. Michael Alram and Deborah E. Klimburg-Salter, 303–13. Vienna: Verlag der Österreichischen Akademie der Wissenschaften.
Schindel, Nikolaus. 2004. *Sylloge Nummorum Sasanidarum 3*. Vienna: Verlag der Österreichischen Akademie der Wissenschaften.
Schindel, Nikolaus. 2009. 'Ardashir 2 Kushanshah and Huvishka the Kushan: Numismatic Evidence for the Date of the Kushan King Kanishka I.' *Journal of the Oriental Numismatic Society* 198: 12–14.
Schindel, Nikolaus. 2011a. 'Die Münzstätte Sakastan unter Shapur II.' *Schweizerische Numismatische Rundschau/Revue Suisse de Numismatique* 90: 79–110.
Schindel, Nikolaus. 2011b. 'The Era of the Bactrian Documents: AReassessment.' *Gandharan Studies* 5: 1–10.
Schindel, Nikolaus. 2012. 'The Beginning of Kushano–Sasanian Coinage.' In *Sylloge Nummorum Sasanidarum: Paris–Berlin–Wien. Band II: Ohrmazd I.–Ohrmazd II.*, by Michael Alram and Rika Gyselen, 65–73. Vienna: Verlag der Österreichischen Akademie der Wissenschaften.
Schindel, Nikolaus. 2013. 'Farewell to the Coins of Ohrmazd III.' *Studia Iranica* 42 (1): 121–31.
Schindel, Nikolaus. 2014. 'Ardashir 1 Kushanshah and Vasudeva the Kushan: Numismatic Evidence for the Date of the Kushan King Kanishka I.' *Journal of the Oriental Numismatic Society* 220: 27–30.

Schindel, Nikolaus. 2015a. 'Sakastan in the Fourth and Fifth Century AD: Some Historical Remarks Based on the Numismatic Evidence.' *Electrum* 22: 227–48.

Schindel, Nikolaus. 2015b. 'Sasaniden, Kushan, Kushano-Sasaniden: Münzprägung, Propaganda und Identitäten zwischen Westiran und Ostiran.' *Haller Münz Blätter* VIII: 137–67.

Schippmann, Klaus. 1986. 'Arsacids. II: The Arsacid Dynasty.' *Encyclopaedia Iranica (Online)*.

Schlumberger, Daniel. 1953. 'Surkh Kotal: A Late Hellenistic Temple in Bactria.' *Archaeology* 6 (4): 232–8.

Schlumberger, Daniel . 1961. *The Excavations at Surkh Kotal and the Problem of Hellenism in Bactria and India: Albert Reckitt Archaeological Lecture, British Academy, 31 May 1961*. Oxford: Oxford University Press.

Schmitt, Rüdiger. 1999. *Beiträge zu Altpersischen Inschriften*. Wiesbaden: Reichert Verlag.

Schwartz, Martin. 1995. 'Sesen: A Durable East Mediterranean God in Iran.' In *Proceedings of the Third European Conference of Iranian Studies Held in Cambridge, 11th to 15th September*, 9–13.

Schwartz, Martin. 1996. '*Sasm, Sesen, St. Sisinnios, Sesengen Barpharangēs, and . . . "Semanglof".' *Bulletin of the Asia Institute* 10: 253–7.

Semenov, A. A. 1945. *Material'nye Pamiatniki Iranskoi Kul'tury v Srednei Azii*. Stalinabad (Dushanbe).

Semenov, Grigorij L. 1996. *Studien zur Sogdischen Kultur an der Seidenstrasse*. Vol. 36. Wiesbaden: Otto Harrassowitz Verlag.

Senior, Robert C. 2001–6. *Indo-Scythian Coins and History*. Lancaster, PA: Classical Numismatic Group.

Senior, Robert C. 2005. 'Indo-Scythian Dynasty.' *Encyclopaedia Iranica (Online)*.

Shaban, Muhammad Abdulhayy. 1979. *The 'Abbāsid Revolution*. Cambridge: Cambridge University Press.

Shahbazi, A. Shapur. 1389/2010. *Tarikh-e Sasanian (Sasanian History)*. Tehran: Nashr-e Daneshgahi.

Shahbazi, A. Shapur. 1985. 'Studies in Sasanian Prosopography II: The Relief of Ardašir II at Taq-i Bustan.' *Archäologische Mitteilungen ans Iran* 18: 181–5.

Shahbazi, A. Shapur. 1988. 'Bahrām VI Čōbīn. *Encyclopaedia Iranica (Online)*.

Shayegan, M. Rahim. 2003. 'Approaches to the Study of Sasanian History.' In *Paitimāna: Essays in Iranian, Indo-European, and Indian Studies in Honor of Hanns-Peter Schmidt*, ed. Siamak Adhami, 363–84. Costa Mesa, CA: Mazda.

Shayegan, M. Rahim. 2011. *Arsacids and Sasanians: Political Ideology in Post-Hellenistic and Late Antique Persia*. Cambridge: Cambridge University Press.

Shenkar, Michael. 2014. *Intangible Spirits and Graven Images: The Iconography of Deities in the Pre-Islamic Iranian World.* Leiden: Brill.

Shinji, Maeijima. 1981. 'The Zoroastrian Kingdoms in Mazandaran and the T'ang Empire.' *Acta Asiatica* 41: 29–46.

Shirinov, Timur, and Maurizio Tosi. 2001. 'Land behind Samarkand: The Archaeological Map of the Middle Zeravshan Valley: Perspectives and Geographical Repartitions.' In *Italo-Uzbek Scientific Cooperation in Archaeology and Islamic Studies: An Overview (Rome, January 30, 2001)*, ed. Samuela Pagani, 13–40. Tashkent; Rome: Istituto Italiano per l'Africa e l'Oriente; Institute of Archaeology of the Academy of Sciences of Uzbekistan – Samarkand; al-Beruni Institute of Oriental Studies of the Uzbek Academy of Sciences.

Shishkin, Vasilii. 1936. *Architectural Monuments of Bukhara.* Tashkent.

Shishkin, Vasilii. 1963. *Varakhsha.* Moscow: Izdatel'stvo Akademii Nauk.

Shishkina, G. V. 1994. 'Ancient Samarkand: Capital of Soghd.' *Bulletin of the Asia Institute* 8: 81–99.

Simonetta, Alberto M. 1958. 'A New Essay on the Indo-Greeks: The Śakas and the Pahlavas.' *East and West* 9 (3): 154–83.

Simonetta, Alberto M. 1974. 'The Indo-Parthian Coinage and Its Significance in the Chronology of the Kushans.' In *Tsentral Asia v Kušanskuyu Epoxu (Central Asia in the Kushan Period)*, 283–8. Moscow: UNESCO; Nauka.

Simonetta, Alberto M., and François Widemann. 1978. 'The Chronology of the Gondopharean Dynasty.' *East and West* 28 (1/4): 155–87.

Sims-Williams, Nicholas. 1976. 'The Sogdian Fragments of the British Library.' *Indo-Iranian Journal* 18 (1): 43–82.

Sims-Williams, Nicholas. 1983. 'Chotano-Sogdica.' *Bulletin of the School of Oriental and African Studies* 46 (1): 40–51.

Sims-Williams, Nicholas. 1989. 'The Sogdian Inscriptions of the Upper Indus: A Preliminary Report.' In *Antiquities of Northern Pakistan: Rock Inscriptions in the Indus Valley*, ed. Karl Jettmar et al., 131–7. Mainz: Verlag Philipp von Zabern.

Sims-Williams, Nicholas. 1990a. 'Chotano-Sogdica II: Aspects of the Development of Nominal Morphology in Khotanese and Sogdian.' In *Proceedings of the First European Conference of Iranian Studies*, 1: 275–96.

Sims-Williams, Nicholas. 1990b. 'The Sogdian Fragments of Leningrad II: Mani at the Court of the Shahanshah.' *Bulletin of the Asia Institute* 4: 281–8.

Sims-Williams, Nicholas. 1996. 'The Sogdian Merchants in China and India.' In *Cina e Iran da Alessandro Magno alla Dinastia Tang*, ed. A. Cadonna and L. Lanciotta, 45–67. Florence: Leo S. Olschki Editore.

Sims-Williams, Nicholas. 1997a. 'A Bactrian Deed of Manumission.' *Silk Road Art and Archaeology* 5: 191–211.

Sims-Williams, Nicholas. 1997b. 'Four Bactrian Economic Documents.' *Bulletin of the Asia Institute* 11: 3–15.

Sims-Williams, Nicholas. 1997c. 'New Light on Ancient Afghanistan: The Decipherment of Bactrian: An Inaugural Lecture Delivered on 1 February 1996.' London: School of Oriental and African Studies.

Sims-Williams, Nicholas. 1998. 'Further Notes on the Bactrian Inscription of Rabatak, with an Appendix on the Names of Kujula Kadphises and Vima Taktu in Chinese.' In *Proceedings of the Third European Conference of Iranian Studies. Part 1: Old and Middle Iranian Studies*, 79–93.

Sims-Williams, Nicholas. 1999. 'From the Kushan-Shahs to the Arabs: New Bactrian Documents Dated in the Era of the Tochi Inscriptions.' In *Coins, Art, and Chronology: Essays on the Pre-Islamic History of the Indo-Iranian Borderlands*, ed. Michael Alram and Deborah E. Klimburg-Salter, 245–58. Vienna: Verlag der Österreichischen Akademie der Wissenschaften.

Sims-Williams, Nicholas. 2001a. *Bactrian Documents from Northern Afghanistan. Vol. I: Legal and Economic Documents*. Oxford; New York: Nour Foundation in association with Azimuth Editions and Oxford University Press.

Sims-Williams, Nicholas. 2001b. 'The Sogdian Ancient Letter II.' In *Monks and Merchants: Silk Road Treasures from Northwest China, Gansu and Ningxia, 4th–7th Century*, ed. Annette L. Juliano and Judith Lerner, 147–9. New York: Harry N. Abrams with the Asia Society.

Sims-Williams, Nicholas. 2002. 'Ancient Afghanistan and Its Invaders: Linguistic Evidence from the Bactrian Documents and Inscriptions.' In *Indo-Iranian Languages and Peoples*, ed. Nicholas Sims-Williams, 225–42. Oxford: Oxford University Press.

Sims-Williams, Nicholas. 2003. 'A Bactrian Quarrel.' *Bulletin of the Asia Institute* 17: 9–15.

Sims-Williams, Nicholas. 2004. 'The Bactrian Inscription of Rabatak: A New Reading.' *Bulletin of the Asia Institute* 18: 53–68.

Sims-Williams, Nicholas. 2005. 'Toward a New Edition of Sogdian Ancient Letters: Ancient Letter 1.' In *Les Sogdiens en Chine*, ed. Étienne de la Vaissière and Eric Trombert, 181–93. Paris: École Française d'Extrême-Orient.

Sims-Williams, Nicholas. 2007. *Bactrian Documents from Northern Afghanistan. Vol. 2: Letters and Buddhist Texts*. London: Nour Foundation in association with Azimuth Editions.

Sims-Williams, Nicholas. 2008. 'The Arab-Sasanian and Arab-Hephthalite Coinage: A View from the East.' *Cahiers de Studia Iranica* 39: 115–30.

Sims-Williams, Nicholas. 2010. *Bactrian Personal Names. Iranisches Personennamenbuch*, Vol. II, Faszikel 7. Vienna: Verlag der Österreichischen Akademie der Wissenschaften.

Sims-Williams, Nicholas. 2011. 'Early New Persian in Syriac Script: Two Texts from Turfan.' *Bulletin of the School of Oriental and African Studies* 74 (3): 353–74.

Sims-Williams, Nicholas, and Joe Cribb. 1996. 'A New Bactrian Inscription of Kanishka the Great.' *Silk Road Art and Archaeology* 4: 75–142.
Sims-Williams, Nicholas, and François de Blois. 1996. 'The Bactrian Calendar.' *Bulletin of the Asia Institute* 10: 149–65.
Sims-Williams, Nicholas, and Étienne de la Vaissière. 2007. 'Jabguya i. Origin and Early History.' *Encyclopaedia Iranica (Online)*.
Sims-Williams, Nicholas, and James Hamilton. 1990. *Documents Turco-Sogdiens du IXe–Xe Siècle de Touen-Houang*. Vol. 3. Corpus Inscriptionum Iranicarum 3. London: School of Oriental and African Studies.
Sims-Williams, Nicholas, and Elizabeth Tucker. 2005. 'Avestan Huuōišta and Its Cognates.' In *Indogermanica: Festschrift Gert Klingenschmitt*, ed. Günter Schweiger, 587–604. Taimering: Schweiger.
Sims-Williams, Nicholas, Frantz Grenet, and Paul Bernard. 1991. 'Mithra the Baga.' In *Histoire et Cultes de l'Asie Centrale Préislamique*, ed. Paul Bernard and Frantz Grenet, 177–86. Paris: Editions du CNRS.
Sinor, Denis. 1990. 'The Establishment and Dissolution of the Türk Empire.' In *The Cambridge History of Early Inner Asia*, ed. Denis Sinor, I: 285–316. Cambridge: Cambridge University Press.
Smirnova, Natalia. 1992. 'Coins of Eucratides in Museum Collections.' *East and West* 42 (1): 85–102.
Smirnova, Olga I. 1963. *Katalog Monet S Gorodishcha Pendzhikent: Materialy 1949–1956 Gg*. Moscow: Izd'vo vostochnoĭ lit'ry.
Smirnova, Olga I. 1981. *Svodnyi Katalog Sogdiiskix Monet, Bronza*. Moscow: Nauka.
Stark, Sören. 2006. 'On Oq Bodun: The Western Türk Qağanate and the Ashina Clan.' *Archivum Eurasiae Medii Aevi* 15: 159–72.
Stark, Sören. 2008. 'Approaching the Periphery: Highland Ustrūshana in the Pre-Mongol Period.' In *Islamisation de l'Asie Centrale: Processus Locaux d'Acculturation du VIIe au XIe Siècle*, ed. Étienne de la Vaissière, 215–35. Studia Iranica Cahier 39. Leuven: Peeters.
Stark, Sören. 2009. 'Central and Inner Asian Parallels to a Find from Kunszentmiklós-Bábony (Kunbábony): Some Thoughts on the Early Avar Headdress.' *Ancient Civilizations from Scythia to Siberia* 15 (3): 287–305.
Staviskij, Boris Ja. 1986. *La Bactriane sous les Kushans: Problèmes d'Histoire et de Culture*. Trans. Paul Bernard, M. Burda, F. Grenet, and P. Leriche. Paris: Librarie Jean Maissonneuve.
Stavisky, Boris J. 1980. '"Buddha-Mazda" from Kara-tepe in Old Termez (Uzbekistan): A Preliminary Communication.' *Journal of the International Association of Buddhist Studies* 3 (2): 89–94.
Stavisky, Boris J. 1984. 'Kara Tepe in Old Termez: A Buddhist Religious Centre of the Kushan Period on the Bank of the Oxus.' In *From Hecataeus to Al-Ḫuwārizmī: Bactrian, Pahlavi, Sogdian, Persian, Sanskrit, Syriac,*

Arabic, Chinese, Greek, and Latin Sources for the History of Pre-Islamic Central Asia, ed. János Harmatta, 95–135. Budapest: Akadémiai Kiadó.
Stein, Mark Aurel. 1900. *Kalhana's Rajatarangini: A Chronicle of the Kings of Kasmir*. London: Archibald Constable.
Stride, Sebastian. 2007. 'Regions and Territories in Southern Central Asia: What the Surkhan Darya Province Tells Us about Bactria.' In *Proceedings of the British Academy* 133: 99–107. Oxford: Oxford University Press.
Sundermann, Werner. 1990. 'Shapur's Coronation: The Evidence of the Cologne Mani Codex Reconsidered and Compared with Other Texts.' *Bulletin of the Asia Institute* 4: 295–9.
Sundermann, Werner. 1992. *Der Sermon vom Licht-Nous: Eine Lehrschrift des Ostlichen Manichaismus: Edition der Parthischen und Soghdischen Version*. Berliner Turfantexte 17. Berlin: Turfan Vorschung.
Sundermann, Werner. 1996. 'Origin and Rise of the Chionites/Xyon/Huns.' *History of Humanity: From the Seventh Century BC to the Seventh Century AD* 3: 473.
Sundermann, Werner. 2009. 'Mani.' *Encyclopaedia Iranica (Online)*.
Tabatabaee, S. Javad. 1388/2009. *Darāmadi bar Tārīkh-e Andishe-ye Siyāsī dar Īrān (A Prolegomenna to the History of Political Thought in Iran)*. Tehran: Kavir.
Tarn, William W. 1951. *The Greeks in Bactria and India*. Cambridge: Cambridge University Press.
Thapar, B. 1974. 'The Kushan Civilisation in India: An Appraisal of the Component Elements.' In *Tsentral Asia v Kušanskuyu Epoxu (Central Asia in the Kushan Period)*, 90–4. Moscow: UNESCO; Nauka.
Thomas, F. W. 1914. 'The Date of Kanishka.' *Journal of the Royal Asiatic Society* n.s. 46 (4): 987–92.
Tor, Deborah G. 2009. 'The Islamization of Central Asia in the Sāmānid Era and the Reshaping of the Muslim World.' *Bulletin of the School of Oriental and African Studies* 72 (2): 279–99.
Tremblay, Xavier. 2001. *Pour une Histoire de la Sérinde: Le Manichéisme Parmi les Peuples et Religions d'Asie Centrale d'Après les Sources Primaires*. Vol. 28. Veröffentlichungen der Kommission für Iranistik. Vienna: Verlag der Österreichischen Akademie der Wissenschaften.
Tremblay, Xavier. 2004. 'La Toponymie de la Sogdiane et le Traitement de *xϑ et *fϑ en Iranien: Essais de Grammaire Comparée des Langues Iraniennes VII.' *Studia Iranica* 23: 113–49.
Tremblay, Xavier. 2005. 'Irano-Tocharica et Tocharo-Iranica.' *Bulletin of the School of Oriental and African Studies* 68 (3): 421–49.
Tremblay, Xavier. 2007. 'The Spread of Buddhism in Serindia: Buddhism Among Iranians, Tocharians and Turks before the 13th Century.' In *The Spread of Buddhism*, ed. Ann Heirman and Stephan Peter Bumbacher, 75–130. Leiden: Brill.
Trever, K. V. and Lukonin, V. G. 1987. *Sasanidskoe serebro Sobranie Gosudarstvennogo Ermitaza*. Moscow: Isskustvo.

Uray, Geza, and Walther Heissig. 1985. 'Vom Römischen Kaiser bis zum König Gesar von Glin.' In *Fragen der Mongolischen Heldendichtung, III*, 530–48. Wiesbaden: Otto Harrassowitz Verlag.

Vainberg, B. I. 1972. 'Nekotorye voprosyistorii Tokharistana v IV–V vv [Issues in the History of Tokharistan IV–V Century].' *Kara-Tepe* 3. Moscow: Nauka.

van Lohuizen-de Leeuw, Johanna E. 1949. *The 'Scythian' Period*. Vol. 2. Orientalia Rheno-Traiectina. Leiden: Brill.

Vondrovec, Klaus. 2008. 'Obole in der Münzprägung der Iranischen Hunnen.' *Numismatische Zeitschrift* 116: 273–304.

Vondrovec, Klaus. 2010. 'Coinage of the Nezak.' In *Coins, Art and Chronology II: The First Millennium C.E. in the Indo-Iranian Borderlands*, ed. Michael Alram, Deborah E. Klimburg-Salter, Minoru Inaba, and Matthias Pfisterer, 169–90. Vienna: Verlag der Österreichischen Akademie der Wissenschaften.

Vondrovec, Klaus. 2014. *Coinage of the Iranian Huns and Their Successors from Bactria to Gandhara: 4th to 8th Century CE*. Vienna: Verlag der Österreichischen Akademie der Wissenschaften.

von Glahn, Richard. 1996. *Fountain of Fortune: Money and Monetary Policy in China, 1000–1700*. Berkeley; Los Angeles: University of California Press.

von Mitterwallner, Gritli. 1973. 'Kamra Inscription of Vajheshka (Vāsishka).' *Indian Museum Bulletin* 7 (2): 111–17.

von Staël-Holstein, A. 1914. 'Was There a Kusana Race?' *Journal of the Royal Asiatic Society* n.s. 46 (1): 79–88.

Wallerstein, Immanuel Maurice. 2004. *World-Systems Analysis: An Introduction*. Durham, NC; London: Duke University Press.

Wan, Xiang. 2012. 'A Study on the Kidarites: Reexamination of the Documentary Sources.' *Archivum Eurasiae Medii Aevi* 19: 43–301.

Watson, Burton. 1961. *Records of the Grand Historian of China, Translated from the Shih Chi of Ssu-Ma Ch'ien*. New York; London: Columbia University Press.

Weber, Dieter. 2003. *Berliner Papyri, Pergamente und Leinenfragmente in Mittelpersischer Sprache*. Vol. 3. London: School of Oriental and African Studies on behalf of Corpus Inscriptionum Iranicarum.

Weber, Dieter. 2014. 'Arabic Activities Reflected in the Documents of the Pahlavi Archive.' In *Documents, Argenterie et Monnaies de Tradition Sassanide*, ed. Rika Gyselen, 179–89. Res Orientales XXII. Leuven: Peeters.

Whitby, Michael, and Mary Whitby. 1986. *The History of Theophylact Simocatta: An English Translation with Introduction and Notes*. Oxford: Oxford University Press.

Whitehead, R. B. 1913. 'Two Coins of Soter Megas, the Nameless King.' *Journal of the Royal Asiatic Society* 45 (3): 658–61.

Whitfield, Susan. 1999. *Life along the Silk Road*. Berkeley: University of California Press.

Whitfield, Susan, and Ursula Sims-Williams, eds. 2004. *The Silk Road: Trade, Travel, War and Faith.* Chicago: Serindia.

Widemann, François. 2003. 'Maues King of Taxila: An Indo-Greek Kingdom with a Saka King.' *East and West* 53 (1/4): 95–125.

Widengren, Geo. 1952. 'Xosrau Anošurvan, les Hephthalites et les Peuples Turcs: Etudes Préliminaires des Sources.' *Orientalia Suecana* 1: 69–94.

Wiesehöfer, Josef. 1994. *Die 'dunklen Jahrhunderte' der Persis: Untersuchungen zu Geschichte und Kultur von Fārs in Frühhellenistischer Zeit (330–140 v. Chr.).* Berlin: C. H. Beck.

Wiesehöfer, Josef. 1996. *Ancient Persia from 550 BC to 650 AD.* London: I.B. Tauris.

Wiesehöfer, Josef. 1998. *Das Partherreich und Seine Zeugnisse: The Arsacid Empire: Sources and Documentation: Beiträge des Internationalen Colloquiums, Eutin (27.–30. Juni 1996).* Stuttgart: Franz Steiner Verlag.

Wolf, Eric R. 2010. *Europe and the People without History.* Berkeley; Los Angeles: University of California Press.

Wolski, Józef. 1962. 'Arsace II et la Généalogie des Premiers Arsacides.' *Historia: Zeitschrift fur Alte Geschichte* 11 (2): 138–45.

Wood, Frances. 2002. *The Silk Road: Two Thousand Years in the Heart of Asia.* Berkeley: University of California Press.

Yakubovich, Ilya. 2002. 'Mugh 1.1. Revisited.' *Studia Iranica* 31 (2): 231–53.

Yarshater, Ehsan. 1983. 'Iranian National History.' In *The Cambridge History of Iran*, III (1): 359–477. Cambridge: Cambridge University Press.

Yü, Wing-Shih. 1990. 'The Hsiung-Nu.' In *The Cambridge History of Early Inner Asia*, ed. Denis Sinor, I: 118–49. Cambridge: Cambridge University Press.

Zarrinkoub, Abdolhossein. 1975. 'The Arab Conquest of Iran and Its Aftermath.' In *The Cambridge History of Iran*, ed Richard N. Frye, IV. Cambridge: Cambridge University Press.

Zeimal, Evgeny V. 1978. 'Politicheskaia Istoriia Drevnei Transoksiany Po Numismaticheskim Danym. (The Polical History of Ancient Transoxiana According to Numismatic Data).' In *Kul'tura Vostoka: Drevnost' I Rannee Srednevekov'e. Sbornik Statei*, ed. V. G. Lukonin, 131–50. Leningrad: Avrora.

Zeimal, Evgeny V. 1983. *Drevnie Monety Tadzihkistana.* Dushanbe.

Zeimal, Evgeny V. 1994. 'The Circulation of Coins in Central Asia during the Early Medieval Period (Fifth–Eighth Centuries AD).' *Bulletin of the Asia Institute* 8: 245–67.

Zeimal, Evgeny V. 1996. 'Münzen von der Seidenstrasse.' In *Weihrauch und Seide: Alte Kulturen an der Seidenstrasse*, ed. Wilfried Seipel, 357–80. Vienna: Kunsthistorisches Museum.

Zeimal, Evgeny V. 1999. 'The Kidarite Kingdom in Central Asia.' In *History of Civilizations of Central Asia*, 3, ed. B. A. Litvinsky, 123–37. Paris: UNESCO.

Index

Abarshahr *see* Neishapur
Abbasid Caliphate, 9–10, 182, 184, 187
Abdagases, 36–7
Abdagases II, 40
Abruī, 149
Abulsaj Dēvdād ibn Dēvband, 10
Acts of Thomas, 35–6, 39
Adomano, 117, 118, 120–2
Adur-Sasan, 40, 41, 43
Afrasiab, 150, 153, 155
Afshin (Islamic title), 100–1, 126
Al-Afshin (Khydar), 10, 155, 187
Afshiyan *see* Afshin
Afšun, Khuv of Khākhsar, 101
agriculture, 66, 145, 158, 179
Aï Khanoum, 53
Akhshunwar, 126–9, 137, 142
Albani, 90–1
Alkhana, 106–8
Alkhans, 88, 89, 101–2, 104–24, 141, 161, 163
    chronology, 110–12, 115–16
    'King of the East' titles, 117–22
    numismatic evidence, 106–9, 113–15, 116–20
    their name, 105–6, 108
Altai region, 134
Amber (mint), 179
Amida, siege of, 78–9, 90–1, 102
Ammianus Marcellinus, 78–9, 89–92
Anahita, on coinage, 79–80
Ananias of Shirak, 170
Andarab, 144
Anxi, 181
Arachosia, 27, 31–3, 35–8, 40
Ardamitra *see* Farn-Sasan
Ardasharo Koshano *see* Ardashir 1
'Ardashir', several Kushano-Sasanians named, 77–8

Ardashir 1 (Kushan king), 74, 77–8, 80
Ardashir I, 27–30, 39–45, 46, 68, 74, 197
    coinage of, 39, 42–3, 45
    conquests of, 29–30, 40
    defeat of Farn-Sasan, 39–40
Ardashir-Khurra, 129
Ardoxšo (on coins), 68
argbed, 29
Armenian sources, 93, 134
Arsacids, 27, 31, 32, 33, 40, 45
Artabanus I, 31, 33
Artabanus IV, 27, 29, 45
Asbijab, 149
Aspa *see* Aspavarma
Aspavarma, 37
Avarkhuman, 153
Avars, 134
Azes (dynasty), 31
Azes I, 33, 39
    coinage of, 33
Azes II, 39
Azilises, 39

Bactra *see* Balkh
Bactria, 33, 48, 49, 52–4, 56–7, 61, 63, 68, 70, 72–3, 78, 79–80, 83, 88, 94–6, 98, 100, 125, 147–8, 151, 176
Bactrian (language), 46, 59, 71, 72, 134, 135
    as language of Kushans, 61, 65, 71
Bactrian Documents (BD), 25, 92–3, 118, 120–1, 126, 135, 140, 164–6, 179
Badakhshan Valley, 90, 120–1, 126, 143, 158
Bādghīs, 143, 177, 183
Bag-aziyas, 165
Baghlan, 143

Bagram, 144
Bahram *see* Wahram V
Baikent *see* Paikent
Balaam, 99
Bālāditya, 113
Bal'ami, 7, 177–8
Balāsh (Walāš), 29
Balkh, 7, 29, 54, 57, 62, 67, 71, 90, 95, 99, 139, 141, 144, 158, 176, 177, 189
  mint of, 54, 57, 66–7, 74, 80–1, 96, 120, 127, 138, 166, 178
Bamiyan, 121–2, 126, 143, 164–5, 174
Barfak, 143, 174
Barmakids, 187
BBA see coinage: Sasanian
Begram, 84; *see also* Kapiśa
Bei Shi, 98
Besut (coin authority), 180
Biaghu *see* Qara-churin
Bih Ardashir, 29
Birmudha, 178
Al-Biruni, 7, 127, 144, 168, 188
Bo Fuzhan, 171
Bot-Khanas, 154
Buddhism, 46, 47, 61, 62–4, 71, 154–5
  architecture and archaeological sites, 84, 154
Bukhara, 7, 148–52, 154, 156, 187, 194
Bukhar-Khudat, 152
Bumin Khan, 142
Burha Tegin, 168
Burōy-ī Tabīb *see* Burzōy
Burzōy, 145, 191
Bust, 133
'Byghu', 178

Čāč (mint), 176, 178
Ceylon, 112
Chach *see* Čāč (mint); Tashkent
Chaghanian, 153, 154, 176
Cheiroukes, 32
Chilek, 101
Chinese sources, 23–4, 49–56, 58, 62, 63, 67, 87–9, 93–5, 98–9, 134, 148, 159, 164, 170, 171; *see also Bei Shi*; *Han Shu*; *Hou Han Shu*; *Shǐjì*; *Sui Shu*
Chionites, 50, 79, 85–6, 87–93, 100; *see also* Hephthalites
Chitral Valley, 141
Christian Geography see Cosmas

coinage
  Alkhan-Nēzak 'crossover', 160–1, 163
  Alkhanid, 105–9, 113–15, 116–19, 141, 160
  Bukhar-Khudat type, 152
  Hephthalite, 137–40, 152, 153
  Indo-Parthian, 27, 31–2
  inscriptions and legends: Aramaic, 45; Bactrian, 64, 80, 83, 101, 105, 113, 118, 138–9, 168, 170, 172, 180; Brahmi, 96–8, 101, 109, 115, 117–18, 171, 180; Greek, 32, 38, 57; Gupta motifs, 117; Indian cultural figures, 59–61, 64, 67, 80; Kharoshti, 32, 37, 38, 57–9, 61; Muslim legends, 180; Pahlavi, 38, 79–81, 83, 85, 144, 152, 159, 163, 164, 168–9, 172; Sogdian, 100, 151–2
  Kidarite, 95–8, 100–2
  Kidarite-Alkhan, 101
  Kushan, 38, 48, 49, 54–61, 64–71
  Kushano-Sasanian, 74, 77–86, 97
  of Nēzak Shahs, 159–61, 164, 183
  Sasanian, 77–8, 83, 85, 114, 126, 128
  Turkish, 179
Cosmas, 112

Dabusiye, 149
Dalverzin Tepe, 84
Darabjird, 29
Dardistān, 133
Dasht-e Nāwūr, 59
Dastān-e Zāl, 175
Daxia, 52–3, 95; *see also* Bactria
Delberjin Tepe, 84, 99
Dēwaštīch, 10, 101, 173, 181–2, 184
Dihqans, 149
Dīnawarī, 128, 129, 133
dragons, 109
Drangiana, 27, 33–7
  becoming Sakistan, 33

ēbodalo see Hephthalites
Ełiše, 93
ëltëber (title), 167
Elymais, 45
Eran Stone Bear Inscription, 110
ērānšahr, 11, 44
Euseni, 89

Index

Faghanish, 142
Faghfur, the, of China, 141
Farn-Sasan, 30, 37, 39–45
  coinage of, 37, 39, 40–3, 45
Ferdowsi *see Shahnameh*
Ferghana, 126, 148, 151, 153, 182
fire altars, on coinage, 42–3, 82, 98, 118
fire cults, 84
From Kesar *see* Gesar

Gad, 36–7
Gandhara, 31–3, 35–7, 47–9, 57, 66, 68, 70, 72, 74, 78, 81, 83, 85–6, 87–8, 94–6, 98, 100, 102, 104, 106, 108–10, 112, 113–14, 117, 120, 121, 122, 123, 141, 161, 162–3, 176, 188
Gandharan art, 63, 71
Gelani, 79, 90
Gesar, 170–1, 174
Ghādfar, 141–3
Ghaznavids, 46, 188
Ghazni, 115, 160–1
Ghur *see* Huolu
Ghurak of Samarkand, 173, 181
Ghurid dynasty, 143
Gol-Zarriūn, Battle of, 142, 144, 176, 197
Gondophares, 27, 32, 34–7, 39, 40, 56–7
  coinage of, 34–6, 56
Gondophares-Gadana, coinage of, 36
Gondophares-Sasēs, 37, 40, 43
  coinage of, 37
Gorgan, 142
Gozgan, numismatic evidence from, 174, 179–80
Graeco-Bactrians, 32, 53–4, 70, 151
Grumbates, 91–3, 102
Guishuang *see* Kūshan Empire: origins of
Gūjara, 106
Gundaphar *see* Gondophares
Gupta emperors, 68, 70
Gurambād *see* Grumbates
Gwalior inscription, 111

Halada, 112
Han Shu, 50–3, 94
Hari (Herat), 177
Haytal *see* Hephthalites
Hejiezhi, 164
Heliocles, 54

Hephthalites, 88, 89, 95, 99, 100, 102, 104–5, 107, 108, 120, 121, 123, 125–46, 152, 154, 163, 165
  defeat of, 141
  evidence, in texts and inscriptions, 134–7
  numismatic evidence, 137–40
  wars with the Sasanians, 126–8, 141
Heraios/Heraus, 54, 56
  coinage of, 56
Hermaios, 35, 54, 56
hilitbēr, 166–7
Hindu Kush, 46, 56–7, 63, 70–1, 85–6, 87–8, 95, 99, 101, 102–3, 104, 108, 114, 120, 122, 123, 144, 145, 157–8, 162, 164, 165–6, 173, 174, 183, 188
Hindu-Shahi dynasty, 106, 110
Hormizd 1 (Kushano-Sasanian king), 78, 81, 83
Hormizd 2, 78, 82–3, 85
Hormizd I (Sasanian), 82
Hormizd II (Sasanian), 82–3
Hormizd III, 99, 121, 126
Hormizd IV, 176, 177–8
Hou Han Shu, 50, 54–5, 94
Hu-ron-ga, 170
Hua *see* Hephthalites
Huichao, 164–5
hukay, 130
Huna tribes, 70
Huns, 50, 85–6, 89, 100, 150–1; *see also* Hephthalites; Huns, Iranian
Huns, Iranian, 68, 87–9, 92–3, 102, 123, 145, 158–9; *see also* Hephtahlites; Nēzak Shahs
Huolo, 143
Huvishka (Kushan king), 65–7
Hybouzanes, 37

Ikshid (title), 126
Ilkhanids, 189
Indo-Greeks, 32, 35, 70
Indo-Parthian dynasty, 27–8, 30–2, 35–7, 41, 43, 44–5, 56, 76
  chronology of, 31, 38, 39–40
Indo-Saka (Indo-Scythian), 31–2, 35, 39
Indravarma, 37
Iron Gates, 90
Ishtami *see* Sinjibu Khan
Ispahbed of Kwarasan (title), 140
Istakhr, 29, 183
Italakan, 93

Jamasp, 131, 133
Jammu, 31, 33, 35, 37
Jamukat, 149
Jauvlah, 111; see also Javukha
Javukha, 116–19, 121; see also Zabokho
Jibin, 163–5, 171
Jiduoluo see Kidara
Jūr, 29
Jurjān, 29
Jūzihr/Gozihr, 29

Ka'aba-ī Zardušt, 44, 47–8, 68, 73, 77, 79
Kabul, 98, 104, 106, 110, 112, 114, 117, 120, 121–3, 144, 158–9, 162–5, 167–71, 173, 183, 189
  Kingdom of, 106, 117, 167–8, 171
  mint of, 113–15, 122, 138–9, 160–1, 163–4
Kabul Valley, 32, 35, 37, 48, 56–7, 70, 85–6, 88, 101–2, 104; see also Kapiśa; Paropamisdae
Kabulistan, 17, 22, 72, 104, 124, 133, 157, 159, 167, 171, 173, 179, 188
Kabulshahs, 112, 158, 168, 171
Kadag, 118, 140
Kadagestan, 120–1, 123, 165–6
  princess of, 165–6
Kafır Kala, 174
Kafırs, 186
Kaisaro (Caesar), title on coins, 69
Kalila wa Dimnah see Burzōy
Kamird, 165–6
Kānā, 152
Kandahar, 35, 68
Kanishka (Kushan king), 57, 59, 61–7
  inscriptions of, 64–5
Kanishka II, 68–70, 74
Kanishka III, 69
Kanishka, Era of, 57, 64–5
Kanishka, Second Era of, 68
Kanpirak (wall around Bukhara), 151
Kapiśa, 57, 62, 68, 78, 80, 81, 159, 162, 176
Kara Tepe, 84
Karakorum, 95
Karmīr Xyōn see Alkhans
Kārnāmag, 28
Kashmir, 31, 32, 66, 70, 104, 106–8, 110, 121, 160, 163, 171, 188
  Third Buddhist Council of, 62
Kavad, 83, 85, 125, 127, 129, 130–3, 137, 138, 140, 142, 169

'first rule' of, 131–3
kay (kdy; title), 72, 79, 83, 86, 97, 130, 197
Kayanid, 79
Kerdir, 82
Kerman, 29, 170
Khaghan (Turkish title), 178, 180, 181, 184
Khaghan Sinjibū, 134, 177
Khalaj Turks, 143, 164–6
Kharoshti (inscriptions), 63, 69
Khaydhar al-Afshin, 154
Khimgāla, 171
Khingal dynasty see Nēzak Shahs
Khingila, 101, 109–10, 115–17, 118, 122, 124, 138–9
Khosrow, Sasanian successor, 184
Khosrow I Anusheruwan, 123, 131–2, 133, 140, 142–3, 157, 169, 177
Khosrow II Aparwēz, 178
Khotan, 170
Khujand, 148
Khulm, 176
Khurāsān, 8–9, 29, 46, 118, 123, 146, 158, 169–70, 174, 182, 183, 184, 187, 188–9, 191, 194
Khurasan Road, 181
Khurrazad, 183
Khushnawaz see Akshunwar
Khuzestan, 29
Khwarazm, 29, 46
Al-Khwarazmi, 143, 144
Khwera inscription, 111
Kidara, 83, 85, 89, 93, 98, 100, 102
Kidarites, 46, 83, 87–8, 93–103, 121, 150–1, 154
  archaeological evidence, 99
  chronology of, 98–103
  numismatic evidence, 95–8, 100–2, 150–1
  origins, 93–5
  'King of Kings', 39–40, 44, 45, 59, 61, 62, 76, 82, 83, 86, 111, 190
  and coinage, 35, 41, 43, 58, 81, 130
Kipunandha, 70, 96
Kobad see Kavad
Kshatriya, 162
Kujula Kadphises, 33, 37, 54–60, 62
Kunduz, 99, 127
Kunkhas (Kidarite king), 99, 137
Kuramzad (coin authority), 180
Kūshan Empire, 29–30, 33, 37, 46–9, 61–71, 84
  archaeological evidence, 66

chronology of, 54–62, 65–70
historical evidence for, 47–8
origins of, 49–54
Kushano-Sasanians, 68, 70, 72–86
  archaeological evidence, 84, 85
  art and iconography of, 84–6
  chronology of, 77–83
  fall of, 87, 89
  use of Sasanian names and titles, 72, 78
Kushanshahr, 47, 48, 68, 74, 76, 78
Kushanshahs see Kushano-Sasanians

Lakhana, 118–19, 122
Lalliya Shahi, 106, 110

Ma thura, 31, 37, 62, 66–7, 71, 81
Madr, 126
Mahi, 70
Mahuy-ī Sūrī, 183
Makrān, 29, 47
Malwa (Magadha), 104, 111, 112, 113, 117
Mandasor inscription, 111
Mani, 82
Manichaeans, 82
Maodun, 51, 94
Mardians, 90–1
Marsakes, 32
Marw, 27, 29–30, 45, 68, 74, 79–80, 173, 183
  mint of, 180
Maues, 31, 32–3
  coinage of, 32
Mazdak, Mazdakism, 131–3, 157
Media, 29, 45
Mehama, 116–22, 140–1
Menander (dynasty), 32
Mesene (Meshān), 29, 76
Mesopotamia, 45
Meyam see Mehama
Mēzē, 83, 85
Mihirakula, 104, 111–13, 117, 121, 122, 123
Mihirapura, 112
Mihiresvara, shrine of, 112
Mikalis, 188
Miran, 63
Mithras
  iconography of, 84
  on coinage, 80
Mithridates II, 32
Moses of Khorene, 170

Mugh Mountain, documents of, 24, 101, 181–2, 184
Al-Muʿtaṣim, 154

Naqsh-e Rostam, 68, 74
Narendrātiya-Khinkhila, 110, 112
Narseh, 48; see also Paikuli inscription
Narseh (son of Pērōz), 183–4
Nau-bihar, 176
Neishapur, 29, 183, 188
Nēzak Shahs, 122–3, 144, 157–64, 167
  numismatic evidence, 159–60, 163–4
Nēzak Tarkhāns, 143–4, 158–9
Nihawand, 183
Nīmrūz, 170, 171
Nizam ul-Mulk, 188
noses, prominent, on coins, 114
numismatic see coinage

Ohrmizd IV, 142
Ormis, not identical to Hormizd I, 81
Othangnes, 36–7, 40
  possibly the same as Gondophares-Gadana, 36

Pābag, 29, 44–5
Pahlavas see Indo-Parthian dynasty
Paikand (dynasty), 180
Paikent, 149
Paikuli inscription, 48, 91
Pakores, 38, 40
Pamirs (mountains), 95
Panegyrici Latini, 81
Pangul (coin authority), 166, 169, 172–4
Panjikent, 104, 124, 150–2, 156, 180, 181, 184
Panjshir Valley, 144
Paropamisdae, 32, 56, 63, 70, 71, 95; see also Kabulistan
Parthian see Arsacid
Pataliputra, 62, 65
Pawstos Buzand, 93
Periplus of the Erythraean Sea, 60
Pērōz (as a Kushano-Sasanian name), 72, 77–9
Pērōz 1 (Kushano-Sasanian king), 80–1
Pērōz 2 (Kushano-Sasanian king), 83, 85
Pērōz, the Kidarite, 85
Pērōz, Sasanian king, 99, 102, 120–1, 125–30, 132, 134, 137, 140, 145, 151, 157
Pērōz, son of Yazdgerd III, 183

Pērōzduxt, 128–9
Persian language(s), 9, 71, 159, 187–9, 194
Persis, 28–9, 45
  coinage, 42–3, 45
Peshawar, 35, 47–8, 57, 62–3, 66, 68, 71, 74, 81, 95, 114
Phraates II, 31, 33
Phrom Gesar *see* Gesar
Ping Chen, hoard of, 139
Po-lo Si (Buluo), 89
Pol-e Khomri, 143–4
Priscus (as source), 93, 99, 137
Procopius (as source), 127–8, 134, 135–7
Pseudo-Joshua, 128, 134, 135, 137
Pul-i Khumri, 74
Punjab, 57
Purushapura *see* Peshawar
Pūrvāditiya, 119, 122
Pushkabur *see* Peshawar
Pushkalavati *see* Peshawar

Qadisiyya, Battle of, 182
Qara-churin, 149
qaradachi (title), 167
Qiujiuque, 55–6, 58
Qobadian region, 84
Qutaiba ibn Muslim, 143–4, 173–4, 181

Rabatak, inscription of, 48, 57, 59, 62, 64–5
Rag-i Bibi, relief of, 68, 73
Rajatarangini, 106, 110, 112
Rangodeme, 32
Raxvad, 133, 166, 172; *see also* Arachosia
'Red Huns', 108, 136
Rōb, 165–7, 173
Rōb, Bactrian Documents of *see* Bactrian Documents
Rostam, 130, 145, 175, 195–7
  depicted as an Alkhan king, 124
Ruanruan (Juanjuan), 88
Al-Rukkhaj *see* Raxvad
Rumi, 189
Rutbil, the, 158, 166–8, 170–1, 173

Sābē Khān, 177–8
Sadavikha, 116, 122
Sagistani, 79
Sai (Saka), 51
Sajistan *see* Sistan

Saka, 31, 32, 33
Sakistan, 76, 91; *see also* Sistan
Salm ibn Ziyad, 166
Samanids, 7, 148, 187, 194
Samarkand, 100–1, 138, 148, 150–1, 153–6, 181, 187, 189
  mint of, 100, 176, 178
Samudragupta, 70, 96
Sanabares, 28, 37–8, 40–1, 43
  coinage of, 37–8, 40–1
Sandan (coin authority), 166, 180
Sar-e Pol *see* Amber
Sarapadones, 35, 40
Sasan, 28, 43–5
  Other Sasans, 44
Sasanians (*passim*)
  administrative practices and policies, 76, 78, 85, 123, 140, 157, 169–70
  army, 91
  campaigns against Hephthalites, 127–8, 134, 142, 157
  collaboration with Western Turks, 163
  Eastern influences on, 97, 145, 190
  founding of, 41
  historiography of, 14–17
  imperial policy, 99
  origins, 28–9, 44, 45
  presence of, in Bactria/Tokharistan, 73–4
  rise of, in West, 68
  survival, after Arab conquests, 182–4
  visual influence of Kushano-Sasanians on, 84
  wars with the Turks, 177, 178–9
Schøyeh copper scroll, 110, 111, 115–18, 120, 122
Scythians, 52
Segestani, 90–1
Seljuks, 188
Semirech'e, 153, 155, 181
Ser, Sero, 164
Serapis, on Kushan coinage, 66
Shah Bahram Varjāvand, 184
Shahnameh (Ferdowsi), 109–10, 130, 141, 183, 195–8
Shahr-i Sabz, 189
Shaka, 70
Shankaravarma of Kashmir, 106
Shapur I, 44–5, 47, 48, 68, 73, 77, 82, 84
  coinage of, 45
Shapur II, 79, 82–6, 89–91
Shapur-e Razi, 129

Shengil *see* Khingila
Shǐjì, 50–2
Shīr-e Keshvar, 149
Shiva, cult of, 112
'Silk Road', 185–6
silk trade, 181
Sīmurgh, on coins, 174–5
Sindh, 31, 32, 33, 35, 37, 133
Sinjibu Khan, 141–2, 143, 177
Sistan, 9, 27–32, 35–41, 45, 46, 68, 83, 91, 126, 129–30, 144, 166, 169–71, 173, 184, 195
Sizibulous *see* Sinjibu Khan
ŠKZ *see* Ka'aba-ī Zardušt
Sogdiana, 88, 90, 99, 100–2, 123–4, 138, 144, 146, 147–56, 158, 169, 173, 176, 180–2, 186, 188, 195, 197
   Sogdian language, 181
Song Yun, account of, 112, 134
Soter Megas (great saviour), 38, 55, 57–9
Spalagadama, 33–4, 36–7
Spalahora, 33–4
Spur Mardān Shah (coin authority), 172, 174
Srinagar, 112, 121
Strabo, 52, 54
stupa, 63
Sughd *see* Sogdiana
Sui Shu, 159
Sukhra, 129–30, 133
   name as MP form of Sohrāb, 130
Suristan (Mesopotamia), 29
Surkh Kotal, 74, 143
   inscriptions, 64
Surkhan Darya, 84
swastika, 80
Swat, 100, 101, 141, 164
Syr Darya, 88, 149–50, 153, 176, 182

Al-Tabari, 28–9, 46–7, 48, 83, 127, 128, 129, 130, 133–4, 143, 167, 169, 183, 194
Taihan, 143
Takht-i Bahi, 35
Talagang *see* Talaqan
Talaqan, 120–1, 127, 141, 177
Talas, Battle of, 182, 184
Tamerlane, 189
tamgha (royal sign on coins), 58, 66, 98, 106, 114, 118, 138–9
Tang Dynasty, 181–4
Tang Shu, 143, 164

Tanlis, 32
Tanlis Mandates, 32
Taq-i Bostan relief, 84
Taraz, 149
Tarikh-e Bokhara, 148–9, 152, 154
Tarikh-e Sistan, 166–7, 169–71
Tarim basin, 50, 62, 63, 82
Tarkhān, as title, 172–5
Tarkhāns, Nēzak, 143, 172–4
Tashkent, 149, 153, 155
Taxila, 35, 36, 70, 84, 85
Tegin (coin authority), 167–8
Tegin Shah of Khurasan, 117, 168–70, 174
Tepe Maranjan (Buddhist monastery), 84, 89, 98
Termez, 54, 90, 99, 139, 158, 176
Tibet, 171
Timurids, 189
Tirdat, 40, 41
Tobazini (coin authority), 138–9
Tokharistan, 46, 50, 52, 71, 72–4, 81–2, 85, 87–8, 90, 95, 99, 101, 102, 114, 120–3, 125–7, 133, 141, 143–6, 147, 151, 153, 154, 157–8, 163–6, 169, 173, 176–9, 184, 187, 188; *see also* Bactria
Tongdien (source), 150
Toramana, 110–11, 116–17, 121, 122, 123
Transoxiana, 13, 52, 57, 82, 88, 94, 125, 153, 163, 178, 182, 189
Tūrān, 29, 47, 195, 197
Turkestan, 149, 178
Turki-shahi dynasty, 168
Turks, 56, 142–3, 149, 157, 162, 164–7, 178–81, 184
   bearing gifts, 142
   Turkic language(s), 153, 181
   see also Nēzak Shahs

Udayāditiya, 119, 122
Uddyana, 164, 170; *see also* Swat
Uighur Empire, 82
Ustrushana, 100–1, 103, 126, 148, 153, 154–5, 169

Varakhsha, palace of, 150
Vasishka, 65, 69, 80
Vasudeva I (Kushan King), 38, 67–8
Vasudeva II, 69
vihara, 154
Vijaya Sangrāma, 170
Vima Kadphises, 55–7, 59–60, 62, 67

Vima II Kadphises, 59, 62, 70
Vima Takto (Kushan King), 38, 55–6, 58–60, 62, 70
Vonones, 33, 37

Wahmānāz, 174
Wahram, several Kushano-Sasanians named, 77, 79, 84, 85–6
Wahram (son of Yazdgerd III), 184
Wahram II, 81–2
Wahram III, 'King of the Sakas', 91
Wahram IV, 138
Wahram V, 99, 102, 109–10
Wahram VI, 176–8, 187
Wakhsh region, 99
Walash, 129, 130–2
War-Walīz see Kunduz
Warahram, 78
Warahran, 79, 83
Wayhind, 170
Wei Shu, 88–9, 93–5, 150
Western Turks, 177, 179, 180–1, 183
White Huns see Hephthalites
Wishtaspa, 88
Wusan Teqin Sa see Tegin Shah
Wusun, 52

Xieyu see Zabul
Ximotolo, 143
Xinjiang, 50
Xiongnu, 50–2, 87–8, 94, 100, 148, 150

Xuanzang, 112, 113, 143, 154, 164, 176
xwn, 148, 149–50
xyōn, 50, 87–9, 136

yabghu (title), 53, 56, 134, 135, 157, 164, 166, 173, 178, 179
Yaghub ibn Laith, 166
Yangaozhen, 55, 59
Yashodharma, 111, 117
Yazdgerd I, 138
Yazdgerd II, 79, 93, 97, 126
Yazdgerd III, 145, 182–3
Yida, 143
Yüeh-zhi, 49–54, 61, 62, 88–90, 93–5, 98, 148

Zabokho, 117, 118–19, 121–2; see also Javukha
Zabul, 144, 158–9, 162–4, 166–7, 171–5
  King of, 166
Zabulistan, 27, 104, 115, 122–4, 133, 144, 157, 159, 161, 163–9, 171, 174–5, 179, 188, 195; see also Arachosia
Zand ī Wahman Yasn, 107–8
Zar Tepe, 84
Zaranj, 183
Zarmihr, 129, 131, 133
Zhulad (coin authority), 180
Ziritambo (Sri-Champa) 65
Zoroastrian apocalyptic literature, 184

EU representative:
Easy Access System Europe
Mustamäe tee 50, 10621 Tallinn, Estonia
Gpsr.requests@easproject.com

www.ingramcontent.com/pod-product-compliance
Lightning Source LLC
Chambersburg PA
CBHW052048220426
43663CB00012B/2488